# PLAY *by* PLAY

Greg —
Merry Christmas!
Hope you enjoy this
"history" of sports
and broadcasting.
Best Wishes!
Bill

# PLAY *by* PLAY

## TALES FROM A SPORTS BROADCASTING INSIDER

## BILL MERCER

*Bill Mercer*

TAYLOR TRADE PUBLISHING
*Lanham • New York • Boulder • Toronto • Plymouth, UK*

Published by Taylor Trade Publishing
An imprint of The Rowman & Littlefield Publishing Group, Inc.
4501 Forbes Boulevard, Suite 200, Lanham, Maryland 20706

Estover Road, Plymouth PL6 7PY, United Kingdom

Distributed by NATIONAL BOOK NETWORK

Library of Congress Cataloging-in-Publication Data

Mercer, Bill, 1926–
    Play-by-play : tales from a sports broadcasting insider / Bill Mercer.—1st Taylor Trade pub. ed.
        p.    cm.
    Includes index.
    ISBN-13: 978-1-58979-224-1 (pbk. : alk. paper)
    ISBN-10: 1-58979-224-6 (pbk. : alk. paper)
    1. Mercer, Bill, 1926–   2. Sportscasters—United States—Biography.
I. Title.
    GV742.42.M48A3   2007
    070.4'49796092—dc22
    [B]
                                                                2006101641

∞ ™ The paper used in this publication meets the minimum requirements of American National Standard for Information Sciences—Permanence of Paper for Printed Library Materials, ANSI/NISO Z39.48-1992.

Manufactured in the United States of America.

To my current broadcast associates
and the memory of all those from the past

and

To my students

I keep six honest serving-men
(They taught me all I knew);
Their names are What and Why and When
And How and Where and Who.

—Rudyard Kipling, "The Elephant's Child" from *Just So Stories*

These [six] are the essentials of reporting. For the sports announcer they are so basic as almost to be taken for granted. Without trying to top Kipling, let me name an additional six serving-men for the radio-television sports broadcaster to call upon in his play-by-play profession. They are preparation, evaluation, concentration, curiosity, impartiality and if such can be achieved, imperturbability.

—Red Barber, from *The Broadcasters*

# Contents

Foreword      ix
  *Mike Capps*

Preface      xi

Acknowledgments      xiii

1. The Cleats I Never Wore      1

2. Romancing the Diamond      123

3. Body Slams      239

Afterword      283

Index      285

# Foreword

Tom Brokaw was right. They really were the Greatest Generation, and the business of broadcasting, especially the television news and sports industry in its infancy, proves the point. Bill Mercer's generation created from scratch, literally, what initially turned out to be a badly needed, plain, simple communications medium.

They accomplished this feat with a hodgepodge of less-than-sophisticated equipment. They did it by doing multiple jobs. News reporters filled in as sports reporters, anchors, or weather forecasters. They did it as honest, sincere information brokers who followed their own God-given instincts, pounding shoe leather and using elbow grease, covering stories from the streets where the news happened until the time their work hit the air, and then turning right around and doing the same thing the next day and the next.

It should come as no surprise that Bill Mercer broadcast Major League Baseball, the National Football League, and major college football and basketball, as well as wrestling. He accomplished the feat because he was a trained broadcaster, capable of adapting his talent to fit the need. Generations saw his work in Dallas–Ft. Worth, Chicago, and worldwide with World Class Championship Wrestling. Ah, the fine performance art of "rasslin." How could anyone not admire Bill's standing as the fourth most popular television personality in Israel during his days with World Class Championship Wrestling?

The medium this generation created through no fault of its own has since been pilloried, trivialized, and corporately overrun. The industry now is at the point where Americans have to wade through too many loud-mouthed, screaming, so-called experts, instead of true communications sources dealing in straight facts. This scourge is not what Bill's generation intended.

Bill and I still broadcast baseball in the Triple-A Pacific Coast League with the Round Rock Express, the Houston Astros top affiliate located just north of Austin. He still loves the craft, loves the play-ers, and loves being a part of the broadcast—and our fans love him. He has always been my broadcast father confessor.

It has been my honor and privilege to know Bill, to have followed his work through the years, to have admired all the wonderful broad-cast talent he has trained at the University of North Texas, and to simply call him one of my closest friends.

I hope that you will enjoy *Play-by-Play*. Its author truly represents the top of his craft. He is a communicator, broadcaster, and writer par excellence.

Mike Capps
Voice of the Round Rock Express
AAA Affiliate of the Houston Astros

# Preface

My tenure in the broadcasting business has nearly reached its fifty-eighth year. It was December 1949 when I graduated from the University of Denver and began my first radio stint as news director and announcer for KCOL in Fort Collins, Colorado. For nearly all of those more than five decades, it has been fun. For maybe three of those decades, friends and fellow professionals have suggested I write about my sports journey.

Then along came Janet Harris of Taylor Trade. Janet urged my colleague at KRLD, Bob Huffaker, to write about his reporting during the Kennedy assassination media coverage in Dallas. Bob called me, Wes Wise, and George Phenix to provide our chapters for what is now the book *When the News Went Live*.

Ms. Harris contacted me later and suggested I write a combination sports memoir and sports broadcasting history—the evolution of radio and television with various sports. I had several times briefly toyed with the idea of rewriting my master's thesis, a how-to of play-by-play sports, but never found the time. Janet suggested the public would be better served tying in the first radio broadcasts with sports and continuing that historical journey through my sports broadcasting career. I trust she is correct.

What I have learned scratching into the depths of my aging mind is that, like surviving in combat in World War II, surviving in this or any other business greatly depends on luck. It is essential to be in the right place at the right moment, and to have some one go to bat for you. A modicum of talent also helps. I set sail into the broadcast business after graduation from college without much thought about what the future might hold. That's probably true of someone starting in any business.

The person I have admired the most as I flailed around in some freaky radio stations that first year is my wife of nearly sixty years,

Ilene. Finally realizing that the current path was strewn with too many disasters, we sold Ilene's sewing machine in order to have enough money to return to my hometown, Muskogee, Oklahoma. That sewing machine money brought us to the right place at the right moment for my first sports broadcasting job, a job Ilene heard about while interviewing for a teaching position in my hometown.

Eventually, I progressed through broadcasting into teaching, which had never been even remotely on a career to-do list. Recalling all the talented young women and men who came through the University of North Texas (formerly North Texas State University) and went on to succeed in this roller coaster ride of radio and television is, I believe, my greatest achievement through broadcasting.

This is not a how-to book for broadcasting sports, but hopefully you will learn from some of the thrills and spills traipsing through my nearly sixty years of broadcasting. I sincerely hope you enjoy the book.

# Acknowledgments

As I mentioned in the preface, I owe Janet Harris, formerly of Taylor Trade, for the inspiration to write this book. It was her urging and concept that threw me into this gigantic memory jolt. I told Janet that I did not like the idea of writing a memoir just about me, and she suggested I tie in some of the history of broadcasting related to sports. That I have tried to do.

Rick Rinehart of Taylor Trade inherited this project from Janet. I appreciate the continuing support they have shown me, a first-time author.

My literary friend Bob Huffaker, he of the PhD in English and lead author of *When the News Went Live*, took my unskilled attempt at composing on the computer and put it into the proper form for the twenty-first century.

The professionals at the downtown Dallas Public Library dutifully and patiently sent me on the trail of the various publications with historical facts about broadcasting in Texas. I rampaged through film copies of the old *Dallas Times Herald*, reliving the years of local baseball and football.

I owe a debt of deep gratitude to a number of individuals and publications:

The former *Times Herald* sports reporter/columnist Frank Boggs was essential in the survey of the baseball history of the Dallas–Fort Worth Spurs.

Many of the old friends and colleagues at KRLD-AM-FM and Television delved deeply into their memories for some of the events we worked through from 1953 on.

Lamar Hunt, the late Dallas Texans owner and founder of the American Football League, and Bob Halford, his media director, provided great support and information.

Former award-winning NBC sports broadcaster Charlie Jones,

who worked with me in football and baseball in Dallas, helped lead me to some obscure history lost in the years.

My close friend with the Dallas Cowboys, Curt Mosher, went to much trouble seeking information that both of us had forgotten. However, he never found out what happened to my Super Bowl ring of 1972. It probably was trashed after I went into baseball.

The keen mind of Fred Graham, former sports information director and my partner at North Texas, put me on the right track for college sports history.

I have relied on the expertise of the former pitcher and coach Charles (Chuck) Hartenstein, who pitched those amazing 18 innings of a 26-inning game for the Spurs in 1965. Chuck lives in Austin and is my source of baseball knowledge.

My wrestling revival rested on the shoulders of many individuals and publications: Killer Karl Cox (Herb Gerwig) is a font of knowledge, as is my TV producer friend Mickey Grant; and Greg Oliver, publisher of the latest and best wrestling news today, presented some information that prevented my running a story or two that we found had been doctored by the source.

Steve Beverly, professor at Union University in Jackson, Tennessee, allowed much time for discussion of wrestling and then wrote a sound judgment on the business today.

Otis Friesen communicated several times on the early history of wrestling and radio.

So much information is available online today, and I have been helped by many sources: the Museum of TV and Radio, New York, and its research assistant, Wel Diogo; the Professional Wrestling Hall of Fame; the Professional Wrestling Online Museum; the Ring Chronicle Hall of Fame; www.wrestling-titles.com; the Dumont TV network website; and Madeline Mancini, who researched the journey of television programming across the country for me.

A special bow to the brilliant historian of professional wrestling, Michael Kenyon, who took an inordinate amount of time answering my requests.

Others contributed greatly, as in the baseball section where my fellow thespian and in-law Lee Griffin combed the Muskogee Phoenix newspapers for old Class C Giants information; Texas League President Tom Kayser, who answered questions faster than I could ask them; Mark Nasser, the Pacific Coast League broadcaster, supplied a humorous story on "modern" baseball broadcasting in the minors; and the Frisco RoughRiders broadcaster Scott Garner, who has allowed me to continue my baseball broadcasting career with him and supplied much-needed information on the history of the minor leagues. A tip of the cap to the University of Denver sports information office, which helped me with my alma mater experiences.

And of course, Mike Capps, who has been a friend and partner for more than forty years, has kept me young with the Round Rock Express Baseball broadcasts, and he came up with the original title of this book, *Bats, Balls, and Body Slams*, which was changed to protect the innocent!

And I couldn't leave out my wife, Ilene, who has labored with me for nearly sixty years and went through this book suggesting changes and better grammar.

To everyone through my life who has contributed to my career and those of late who gave me information that I needed, I am forever grateful.

# 1

# The Cleats I Never Wore

The playground at the late Longfellow Grade School in Muskogee, Oklahoma, became a hallowed field of athlete-wannabes who played tackle football at recess, after school, on weekends in the rain (preferably so we came home filthy)—with no pads, no helmets, and no football shoes. Other times, we put our teams together and played on vacant lots, some where the depression-strapped folks had staked out their milk cows to help with their food bills. Those games were sometimes dangerous, maneuvering around the cows' leavings and metal pipes where they staked out their bovines. But we never lost a player. I don't recall anyone breaking any bones, but there were plenty of sprained ankles, black eyes, and bit tongues. We discovered that it is possible to crawl across lawns for six blocks back to our homes. My classmate, Richard Goad, who went on to play high school and college football, carried the ball with his tongue stuck out; he nearly bit it off during one ferocious tackle. So when I went to West Junior High School in Muskogee for the seventh grade, the first thing to do was to go out for football—never mind that I weighed about seventy-five pounds and stood maybe five feet, and that's probably pushing it.

It was a shock to see those guys, huge guys in my estimation, in pads, knocking, tackling, blocking, and hitting each other in practice. We freshmen were not given uniforms the first day and, in my case, I never was. The coach looked at some of us and determined he would have no reason to have broken bodies, certainly not death, on his conscience. The coach diplomatically suggested we might grow and gain weight for "next season." He suggested I become a manager.

Those were the days of heavy canvas pants, heavy shirts, heavy leather helmets, heavy shoes—heavy everything. I grew muscle just lifting that stuff. I was the actual water boy on game nights; I carried a wooden traylike contraption with bottles of water. I also had to sit out during halftime rain, snow, and cold and protect the equipment left on the field.

You can learn a lot about football just listening to the coach while sitting on the bench. I also learned the dangers of the game when West played a bunch of coal miner's sons—it even might have been the coal miners themselves—down at Keota in southeastern Oklahoma. The field was sparsely covered with grass and veins of coal pushing through. When the Keota team came on the field, it was that old "the earth shook" feeling. During the annihilation of our properly dressed team of city boys, the coach sat on the bench and said to me, "Aren't you glad you aren't out there?" I must admit that I was comfortable on the bench with my water bottles.

I carried on this type of profession for a couple of years. My height, weight, and muscular growth did not occur. My best football playing was back on the hallowed grounds of Longfellow Grade School without pads, uniforms, helmets, or cleats. Everyone reaches his playing level!

My father and I were glued to the radio back in the 1930s, listening to every available football broadcast. I say "available" because, depending on the weather and unless we could move the radio around, the static killed many broadcasts coming out of the big stations in the East. After years of listening to those famous broadcasters—Graham McNamee, Ted Husing, Bill Stern, Red Barber, and others—I perceived a niche for myself. There were some obviously less-than-talented broadcasters then, as there are now, and I recall once telling my dad that I was sure I could do that. Why I thought so, I don't know, because I couldn't stand up in class and make a speech without sweating and mumbling. But, radio was my teacher and my broadcast instructor. We listened to football broadcasts every Friday and Saturday for at least thirteen years, right up to my joining the Navy in World War II.

One of the greatest football players to come out of Muskogee and Oklahoma, Jack Jacobs, lived across the alley from us. Jack was what they called a "triple threat." He could run, pass, and kick—not only punt, but drop-kick amazing yardage for extra points and field goals. The Muskogee Central High Roughers ran out of the single- and double-wing formations and Jack was the tailback. Indian Jack, he was called. He took the snap from the center, dropped back, sometimes twenty yards, and then swivel-hipped his way through the gang of tacklers. Jacobs was an awesome sight racing through the opposition, throwing passes with a football that looked like a big pie. In the time of the Great Depression, folks saved their pennies to watch Jack Jacobs play. That was part of my football education, listening to those games when the Muskogee Roughers played out of town. That, along with the major network broadcasts, was my instruction in football broadcasting.

My other talents, playing the trombone and singing, never truly developed, but a skill that served me well in the future was typing. I can't recall why I took typing. Maybe a girlfriend, of which I had few, encouraged me to go to that class with her, or more likely it was something to take instead of a harder subject. It became an important skill in the Navy. When I was on board the LCI(G)439 in the Pacific Theater, I typed the "typing-speed news" sent out on the official Armed Forces radio network. Another shipmate, Milt Schnitzlein, drew cartoons and I edited a little 439 newspaper. After the war, my typing skills earned me a job as assistant leave yeoman at Farragut Naval Base in Idaho before I was discharged. My typing skills were so successful I sent a sailor to Portland, Maine, instead of his supposed destination, Portland, Oregon. There are always mistakes made in the military.

Naturally, typing afforded me a better opportunity to write in college and my professional life. Only one thing about the typing—I learned with only one key, *g*, between my fingers. Normally people type with *g* and *h* open. Oh well. It still works.

Nineteen forty-three was high school graduation, my Navy signup, three years of duty in the South Pacific, and four campaign medals. I must give credit here where it certainly is due. Some of my friends and my children cannot believe I was one of those shy persons, as Garrison Keillor describes in his radio talks. But I certainly was. I weighed about a hundred pounds, was about 5′ 7″ in height, and wore glasses. I also had a low self-image about my academic ability. I suppose, like a lot of teenagers, I just sort of slipped through high school with little study effort. I thought I wanted to be a doctor, but found math and science way beyond me. So why push anything else? History, geography, and English were strong and pulled me through.

I memorized the eye chart in my father's office at the Veteran's Hospital where he worked so I had 20–20 eyesight in the Navy. Like that Waylon Jennings song "Pick Up the Tempo," "I learned it all in the Navy." Even today I desire a place for everything and everything in its place!

The Navy entrance exam was comparatively easy compared to high school, except for two areas: a psychiatrist and the urine sample. Stumbling through the various pokes and pressures of the physical, we then came to the psychiatrist. I had never been to one—I probably couldn't spell it then. This doctor was seated at a desk with dour expression. He asked me what I did for recreation. I told him the usual—riding bikes, going on hikes, fishing, playing games, etc. He then said, "Do you like girls?" I agreed I did. (I had kissed a few, but that was it.) "Do you like boys?" he said next. "Yessir, I have several good friends." Then, he said, "Do you like boys better than girls?" Now here I was nearly stumped. I didn't want to put down either gender, so I said that it depended on what we were doing. Not the best answer. He then asked if I went out with girls, and I replied that I did.

Then the *big* question. He said, "When was the last time you had intercourse with a girl?" Wow. I must have blushed when I blurted out that I had never done that. Never have, he quietly intoned, then said, "So you like boys better than girls." Now I was terror stricken, so I said no sir, I go with girls, and the guys and I run around together.

He looked at me, marked something on the paper, and told me to go see the doctor in the next office. In a trance of uncertainty what this had to do with Navy, I slid out in the hall where a friend of mine was looking glum. He too had the same problem.

The next doctor was one of those gentle, compassionate persons. He took my paper, smiled, and again asked if I had *such and such* with a girl. I said no. To be honest, I had little idea of such and such. Those were different times than now. We went over my relationship with the boys I knew, and that I had gone with several girls and knew about kissing, at least. He passed me.

I knew little if anything about homosexuality either, except one time in Muskogee when I went to the movie by myself early in the war, a soldier came in to the almost empty theatre and sat down beside me. I thought that was odd. It was even more odd when he put his hand on my knee. I hurriedly left the theatre, still uncertain about what might have been, but aware that this wasn't what had ever happened before. I never told anyone.

I later learned that providing a urine sample within a time limit can be difficult for everyone. On the last day of physicals, the final act was to present a sample. I hung around the "head," new term for restroom, with expectation, but nothing happened. Finally, this big Navy guy looks in and yells (few ever just spoke to you in the early days of Navy life), "You better fill that bottle or you will have wait another day and miss going to San Diego with your buddies!" I was drinking water, turned on all the faucets, flushed the johns, and finally, finally succeeded. The guys gave me a hard time over that. I had the same problem during my discharge from the Navy three years later, but borrowed a sample from my best friend. Don't let the Navy know. They might take back my honorable discharge.

Finally, we go to boot camp with all that stress, which, by the way, I loved. We were given various written tests and when I finished boot camp, I was awarded a spot in signal school. Those who didn't qualify went to sea as deckhands on various ships. I finished in the top three in signal school out of about fifty guys and developed mental and emotional confidence, along with about twenty-five pounds of muscle! The Navy opened the door to the realization I could accomplish something—after nineteen months in the Pacific and five invasions—Guam, Leyte, Luzon, Okinawa, and a small island campaign. I was a signalman on board the USS *Rixey* for the Guam campaign. The final campaigns were on the LCI(G)439 until the war ended and I came home a more confident individual.

I entered Northeastern State College in Tahlequah, thirty miles east of Muskogee, in the fall of 1946. I had two ideas—being a sports announcer or a journalist, so I enrolled in Speech 101 with Prof. James Robinson. Prof was a tall, gangling man with a large head and little hair, but he was one whale of a teacher. He taught us how to breathe, how to project vocally, how to interpret all kinds of literature—and how to speak basic English, rather than basic Oklahoman. Somewhere along the way of those Navy years, I had matured and grown confident and self-assured. Well, I thought I had.

Prof and I became close friends. I took debate from him and my debate partner and I won a state championship tourney. I became interested in theatre and won the Best Actor award for my performance as the lead of *Night Must Fall*. There was no student radio station at Northeastern, but I was given a public address microphone and cruised up and down the sidelines offering my own variety of play-by-play in a stadium that was not fan-friendly. I was master-of-ceremonies of a stage show in a downtown Tahlequah movie theatre. While romping around with all these assignments, I also wrote for the college newspaper. Prof also taught journalism and ran the paper. Those two years of development at Northeastern under Prof were the foundations of at least finding a personality and building my confidence toward a career of some kind.

One day, this beautiful girl with lovely brown, wavy hair came into class late, which she did most days, and the redhead I was kind of dating said, "There is the girl I would date if I were a guy." I did, and Ilene and I were married in September 1947. The summer of 1948, I worked on the weekly *Haskell County Tribune* in Stigler, Oklahoma, my wife's hometown. It was a fun-filled, journalistic workshop of writing, reporting, editorializing, and shooting film—about three years of education in one summer.

By happenstance, my hay fever condition, which I had been afflicted with since I was about twelve, was terrible that summer. There was no medical treatment except some high-powered Benadryl pills that would knock out the hay fever—and the person sneezing. My wife's best friend, Dorothy Dobyns, lived in Denver, Colorado, with her husband, who was attending the University of Denver. Ilene talked to Dorothy one day, when I was laid up with a cold cloth across my face, and it was suggested that we come to Denver where the air was clean and I wouldn't sneeze. I could finish my education at DU, where they had a radio and journalism department and an outstanding drama school.

I applied for admission on my GI Bill of Rights, concerned that my academic record wasn't brilliant at Northeastern State, and also concerned about taking Ilene away from Oklahoma for the first time in her twenty-two years.

I was accepted at DU and then the pain started. I was raring to go. With all that wartime travel, nineteen months overseas, I saw nothing difficult about moving to Denver. Not so for my wife's parents, especially her mother. It was a grueling month of discussion, arguments, and crying before it all fell into place and we departed for Colorado in my parent's new Studebaker.

Denver was a wonderful city with clean air, streetcars, entertainment, and those wonderful Rocky Mountains. Ilene procured a teaching position with her degree from Northeastern, and I went into the radio, journalism, and drama areas at the university. It was the beginning I had been searching for.

Denver had a little campus radio station. It was actually one of those wired-wireless kind of things wired into the dorms. But as far as I was concerned, it was CBS! They ran a variety of programs that the students produced and I ran for the sports booth. I suggested we broadcast DU home football games, something they had never done. The plan was to run a line from the visiting broadcast booth to the station. When there was no station broadcasting, we could use the booth. This was 1948 and many schools did not broadcast their road games. If there was a broadcast, we set up a table outside the booth and aired our efforts there in all kinds of weather.

One of the first problems I encountered was how to identify all those players on the field during the game. We didn't have anyone in the radio department who knew about producing a football broadcast, much less telling us about spotting boards. The first spotting board I devised consisted of some eleven hooks on wooden boards for each team. We then put the names and numbers on some paper discs, which we could hang on the hooks for the various football team positions—guard, tackle, center, etc. This looked pretty good when we set up the boards with the starting eleven of the two squads. The disaster occurred when there were substitutions and the spotter (we actually knew to have one!) began scrambling through the stacks of discs trying to find the appropriate number and place them on the boards. By the time the game was well underway, we had discs flying all over the booth.

The next step in the evolution of the spotting board was the brilliant idea of an "electronic" board. Our radio engineer, who had little to do, constructed two boards with a little light above each position—seven lights for the linemen and four for the backfield for each team. Underneath each position was a slot for the name of the player. The spotter(s) each had separate control panels to push the buttons so the lights would come on for the appropriate name of runner, receiver, or tackler, and so on. Now the spotters not only had to change names on the main boards but also on their control boxes, and then they had to identify the players and push buttons. This experiment died before the end of the first game.

It finally dawned on me that what we needed was a type of spotting board that had all of the names on it, and all the spotter had to do was point to the appropriate name and/or number. It also occurred to me that if the spotter didn't identify the player, at least I had all the names in front of me and could pick one at random—might not be the correct one, but at least the names were all there.

I don't have a copy of that first spotting board, but it was probably similar to the one I drew up and used during my professional football broadcasting career. Those days, most of the college players went both ways, offense and defense, so it was pretty easy to decide to put seven boxes across the top of the page for each of the starting end-to-end positions on the line, then two more lines of boxes beneath for the second and third teamers. Below the linemen were the four backfield players. We put the quarterback on the left and the other three backs followed, then the boxes for the second and third unit players. Within the box, you could see the player's number and name with height, weight, and year in school. My Dallas Cowboys spotting board from 1972 appears in the photospread. Eureka, it worked! Well, we did complicate it a bit by using stickpins to indicate which players were in the game, but that quickly disappeared, and my spotter just pointed at the players who were doing things. All the names of each team on separate sheets of light cardboard right there in front of this aspiring broadcaster. I would give anything to have a tape of those football broadcasts, or attempts at such, just to see what kind of picture we painted for the listener.

One of the most amusing encounters I had with visiting broadcasters happened when Denver played a prominent midwestern college. If I give the name, then someone may remember the person I am going to describe, and it may be embarrassing. Let me say the young broadcaster had been a star player on that football team. He was a nationally acclaimed player, so naturally he could broadcast football. That fallacious reasoning follows even today.

Winter in Denver comes early and we were setting up outside on a day when it was snowing. The young visiting broadcaster introduced himself and found that I was the "practicing" play-by-play announcer. He took me aside and asked me how I approached broadcasting a game. Being an expert of several games, I passed on my best reasoning about knowing the players, following the play, calling the yard lines, and lifting the excitement when there was a big play. That's about it.

The visiting broadcast booth was concrete and quite thick to keep the cold out. During the course of the game, sitting outside that thick booth with the windows closed, we could hear our "professional" broadcaster yelling his lungs out. If you aren't sure what to do, talk fast and loud. My advice was too limited to do him any good.

Football was so successful, we took on basketball. For some reason, we couldn't have a line into the field house, so we had to record the games on a wire recorder. You may never have heard of a "wire" recorder, but it existed. As its name implies, the recording part was a role of very fine, thin wire running from one side across the recording head to the pickup reel, just like tape recorders would operate when they came along.

Wire recorders were okay, but some precautions were needed. Don't jostle it too much or the wire might jump the track. Be very careful rewinding the wire; a kink in it could prove a problem. And at no time pull the power cord when rewinding. My fellow student did that one night and we had this little temple of wire that poofed up when the pickup reel stopped and the main reel kept running. It took only about two hours of careful straightening to put the wire back on the reel.

The University of Denver did not have very good football teams, and not too long after I graduated, DU dropped the program. The Denver basketball team had an All American in Vince Boryla, who in the 1948 to 1949 season was the fourth leading scorer in the nation. Vince was a high school All American in Indiana and added another All American trophy when he played his first two years at Notre Dame. He left the Fighting Irish to play on the Olympic team in 1948. Boryla, 6' 5", worked off the post with graceful and amazingly accurate left- or right-hand hook shots. After Denver, he played with the New York Knicks and later returned to Denver, where he helped establish the Denver American Basketball Association franchise and later the Denver Nuggets. It has been these fifty years later that I realized what an amazing opportunity I had watching such a great player. At the time I was at Denver, I was just happy to take my wire recorder to the gymnasium and record the games coached by Hoyt Brawner who later became the athletic director. Today, Denver honors him with the Brawner Memorial Youth Basketball Tournament.

I had found the chance to prove, at least to myself, that I could call these games. One of the radio professors even commented that though he had never done it, he thought I was very good. That was a huge compliment.

While working through the radio department, I also met my journalism requirements. I signed up for a double major: radio and journalism. A reporting course demanded that we cover various breaking events, such as trials and the state legislature, and write feature articles. I had little or no experience interviewing anyone, maybe a couple of football and basketball players, so the day I was in the elevator in the state legislature going up to act as a reporter, I was suddenly struck dumb. The governor of Colorado stepped into the elevator and there we were alone. He smiled at me, said hello, and I believe I nodded. If I had tried to utter a word I probably would have fainted. There was the chance for an exclusive and I blew it—but I have never forgotten it.

Our radio announcing instructor was a broadcaster from KLZ, one of the major stations in Denver. I did quite well in the course and this gentleman seemed to think there was some possibility in this raw talent. Preparing to graduate, I was offered two opportunities for jobs in radio. One was an audition at KLZ, and the other as "news director" (the only newsman!) at KCOL in Fort Collins, a lovely town north of Denver.

My KLZ broadcaster friend arranged an audition for an announcing job, and I was pumped for it—too pumped. I raced and screamed through the audition copy and ruined a perfectly good chance to start my career in a major station in Denver. I was embarrassed for my instructor who had such faith in me. However, I have never been able to be confident in auditions. I have blown a lot since.

I went to KCOL, December 1949, and worked as hard as I possibly could to do the job, morning and afternoon split news shifts as *the* newsman. Later, I had a source who called me about a shooting that had just occurred in downtown Fort Collins. Then the police chief called me and asked how I could put it on the air before they knew about it. Ah, those great reliable sources.

Then there was one of those alleged budget cuts and the entire news department was cut. Me. The general manager of KCOL owned KOKO in La Junta and I worked there for a couple of months, where the most exciting time of the day was when the Santa Fe Chief came by and blew its horn. Then it was on to a station in Galveston. These two jobs were being a sort-of DJ and everything else. I decided this life was not for me, quit, and after we sold my wife's sewing machine for gas money, headed back to Muskogee, my hometown. It was September 1950.

My vague plan was to use my remaining one year of GI Bill eligibility and go to law school. However, it was too late to enroll that fall, so my wife applied for a teaching job in Muskogee. While interviewing with the superintendent, my part in Ilene's life came up. The superintendent asked what I was doing. My perceptive wife replied that I was looking to be a sports announcer. KBIX, the oldest Muskogee radio station, was searching for a sportscaster, he offered. As soon as Ilene called from the school office with the news, I raced down to KBIX to check out the possibility.

In all fairness, the KBIX general manager was not the brightest light in the broadcasting industry. He told me that the year before, he had hired one guy to broadcast football who claimed the job because he had spotted for the famous broadcaster Bill Stern, but he couldn't describe the plays. The other one ambled in during the middle of the season and kept yelling, "Where's the ball?" The GM said it was a pretty sorry season.

"So what is your experience?" he asked. I figured that if he hired those two bozos, I had a pretty good chance if I gave him my background (enhanced just a little). I had broadcast University of Denver football and basketball and worked as a news director before returning to Oklahoma—kind of indicating it was voluntary; maybe my wife wanted to come home.

I had no tapes (they weren't around then), no wire recording, and no disc for an audition, so the GM came up with a plan: broadcast the game the following Friday in Enid, Oklahoma—this was on Monday—and if I was successful, he would hire me. We would consider it an on-the-air audition, and if I was hired, I would receive $1 per hour (the going minimum wage) working forty hours a week as a disc jockey and then receive $10 for broadcasting the high school games.

On the road games, I would receive $1 for meal money. Anything over that, I would have to pay. I had a job! Well, for a week anyway.

The trip to Enid would start early on Friday. The highways in Oklahoma did not allow for high-speed travel. Here it was late Monday afternoon, and I had three days to prepare for two football teams I knew absolutely nothing about. The first thing I did was call the Enid high school and beseech the coach to send me his team roster with all of his players' names, weight, height, and their uniform numbers by the fastest mail possible. And would he please send his depth chart.

The depth chart consisted of the first unit of starting players followed by the second and third units. As young broadcasters discover even today, some high school coaches feel that we broadcasters find out information gleaned from the roster and the depth chart, which we can pass on to our own high school coaches and help them better prepare for the game. So the opponents will delay sending it until the last minute, or not at all. I am sure I am correct that no coach ever learned anything from a sportscaster!

The Enid coach complied and I had his information on Thursday. One day to make the spotting board and try to familiarize myself with his unseen players. That same Monday afternoon, I drove over to the Muskogee High School practice field, by then it was after 3:00, to introduce myself to head coach, Paul Young. I did not know anyone in Central High where I had graduated seven years before. Coach Young was a tough old bird, well over six feet, and one of those craggy guys with a look that tells you this better be good. It was much like with my episode with the governor of Colorado, half scared and half desperate. I told Coach Young what I was going to do, explained how I had some experience broadcasting and needed to start putting all these names and formations into my game preparation. He had his manager run and give me a roster and said he would give me the depth chart after practice. I had already planned to stay for practice to study the players' numbers with their names anyway. I came out to practice each of the next three days.

Coach Young became a caring, warm-hearted good friend. In my four years broadcasting the Roughers, he took me aside during the summer and explained various formations, how plays were designed, how they should work, and how important it was for the broadcaster to describe defenses. He told me I better mention what defense his team was running, and the opponent as well, or he would do *something* to me—what it was, I can no longer remember.

Young's Rougher teams of the early 1950s won district and state championships led by the Burris brothers and Max Boydston—teams that ran their offenses brilliantly and tackled hard and correctly. Those Roughers were compared to Bud Wilkinson's Oklahoma Sooners who rampaged over everyone, and most of the Roughers' star players went on to OU.

But that was to come. I still had my three days and one night to prepare for the game on Friday. About all I could do was draw out two spotting sheets, one for Muskogee and one for Enid, fill in all the boxes and information, and try to memorize as many players as possible—especially the Muskogee skill position players. Do that and don't panic, at least until game time Friday. Also read every story about the Roughers in the two Muskogee newspapers.

As I recall, it was about a five- or six-hour drive to Enid. The engineer, with the unusually heavy remote equipment, and my spotter and I were the crew. I do recall we ate a steak in Enid, and I believe I had to pay an additional fifty cents for dinner. But I needed as much energy as I could muster.

Fifty-seven years later, the game is gone from my mind, but I do recall that Max Boydston ran into the goal post scoring a touchdown and was injured and out of the lineup for awhile. Muskogee won the game, and when the broadcast was over, I dropped into the backseat of the car and slept all the way home. I was exhausted and concerned that the broadcast was not adequate for my $10-a-week fee. After all, I was self-taught with no one ever giving me some idea of how this play-by-play thing should be done.

Lo and behold, the next day my parents' phone rang several times (Ilene and I were staying with them) and people who knew about me called to say what a "great broadcast" it was. One of the sponsors was elated. He had called the radio station to locate my phone number. I was stunned. Maybe I could do this business after all! I imagined that those two guys who preceded me must have helped my effort. The KBIX station manager called and said it was a successful broadcast and I could start Monday as a DJ with an eight-hour shift. Part of the station programming was from a national network, so our on-air shifts were not necessarily continuous, but it was the eight-hour norm.

When I went to work at KBIX on Monday, I was happy and smiling and helloing everyone. No one responded. Then two or three folks appeared, went to the elevator (KBIX was located in the upper floors of the famous Bixby building), and as they stepped in, one of the males snarled and said thanks a lot. I couldn't make that out, but finally someone decided to actually talk to me and explained that the guy who was angry had been fired to make room for me. The curse of the professional life hit me for the first time. The station operated on a very low budget, and when one guy could do two jobs, someone had to go. It took me some time to convince those on the staff that I was totally unaware of the actions of the general manager firing this popular person.

I sailed through the Rougher football season and didn't exactly demolish myself trying to be a disc jockey. I think that was passable, although I did get a reprimand from the GM for interviewing one of my female high school friends who had gone to Hollywood and been in pictures. That was a big deal then, as now. The GM sourly told me that we were not to do anything but play music and read commercials—for $1 an hour!

Thankfully, there was another radio station in the community. KMUS was an independent station in Muskogee of which I knew little except that they were KBIX's competition. I had met their announcer briefly. We were discouraged from hanging out with the competition. Turned out that, years later, I found that the late Bob Murphy, the broadcaster of the New York Mets for forty years, was the "other" broadcaster at KMUS. Murphy died in 2005.

After the 1950 football season, I was called at home by Jimmy Barry, the general manager of KMUS; he wanted to meet me. He said he had listened to my games and thought I was a good broadcaster. I went to the studios of KMUS and was offered the sportscasting job, which included high school basketball and football and the greatest prize of all, play-by-play of the Muskogee Giants, professional Class C Western Association baseball team! In addition, we would broadcast key college games of Bacone, the locally famous Indian college, and Northeastern State University in Tahlequah, where I had attended school for two years. Golden Gloves Boxing was a big event that they also covered locally and at the state level. Man alive, I was stunned. And I would also be paid $65 a week, $15 more than at KBIX with my shift and football combined. I had arrived!

When I wasn't on the air with the athletic events I had a DJ shift to run. During baseball season, it turned out I worked an eight-hour shift and then a two- to three-hour baseball game for no extra money. But I was so deliriously happy it didn't even occur to me to think I was overworked or underpaid.

I am sure you can imagine the reception my announcement at KBIX received. I gave two weeks notice, but as soon as they hired someone to replace me, I was shown the door. I arrived at KMUS in time to start work on the Muskogee Rougher basketball season. I had broadcast Denver U basketball for one semester, but would not give basketball as my key factor in a resume.

If you have never played the game and had only that one uncertain year practicing basketball, then the first step to improvement is research. I purchased a set of basketball instruction books written by some of the featured coaches of the era. I read and re-read them trying to learn what I had not found on the court myself. I had done the same during the first football season, purchasing a copy of Oklahoma Coach Bud Wilkinson's *Oklahoma Split T Football*, the bible of the latest wrinkle in football philosophy. These were not "personality" books, but instructional publications. No matter how accomplished a person may think he is when starting this business, studying whatever sport is going to be broadcast is still important. After all, preparation for broadcasting sports never ends. It goes on and on every day, and without that preparation, the career is shortened.

The first basketball broadcast for KMUS happened on the night that a bitter cold front blew into town. The Rougher gym was one of those ancient places with a balcony on one side where we set up our equipment by the front railing. Oddly, someone had tinkered with the telephone remote line and we had a hell of a hard time getting on the air. Some thought my former friends at KBIX messed with the line.

That first game was fast and furious and so was my broadcast pace. I probably called every dribble, every step, every shot with full voice and high speed. I was dripping wet when the game was over and my voice was raw. Then out we go into the bitter cold wind, and for the next three days, I had no voice at all. It just shut down. I realized from that experience that there was more to a broadcast than yelling. I thought of that fellow in Denver who yelled his way through a football game. I can recall some other broadcasts where I misplaced my own advice.

My focus had really been on football, but here I was starting with KMUS, mushing through basketball and then my first-ever baseball announcing, except for those alleged re-creations back when I was eleven on the farm (for more on that, see the baseball chapter). In the spring of 1951, not only did I have to broadcast the home games live—I also had to re-create the road games. If I had known any better, I would have been petrified, not just scared. I will give you the skinny on that in the baseball chapter.

As I said earlier, Coach Paul Young had me over to his house before the next football season to educate me in offensive and defensive formations. Like Bud Wilkinson's Oklahoma Sooners team, the Roughers ran the Split T formation. Under Young, it functioned as precisely as the Sooners, and when the Muskogee kids graduated, they could easily move into the OU athletic department. We also went through the roster and he explained who was going to do what on the hallowed field of The Indian Bowl, our revered little football stadium.

I recall a radio station called us to explain that their announcer was ill and could not broadcast their high school's appearance in the Muskogee stadium. Would we feed my broadcast to them? Naturally, we did. I knew I shouldn't be a "homer" (partial to my team), but give an unbiased broadcast. Boy, did I give them a handful of drama and excitement pitched at decibels that probably blew out tubes at their end of the broadcast.

One of the major problems for me was that I had no one to honestly critique me. Everyone said I was, that awful word, "great." But someone needs to explain that there is a better voice to use in your optimum range rather than the highest pitch possible. I fear I was too "up" all of the time. There was no one to suggest that I "paint the picture"—set up the offensive formation player by player and then run the play, follow the flow, carefully to the left, right, or up the middle using the yard lines as a road map. I don't know now how well I did that then. There was no recording equipment for me to make copies of the games and listen to them as I did later when I was the Dallas

Cowboys announcer, fifteen years later. I imagine the broadcasts improved since I stayed with KMUS until going to KRLD in 1953.

During the seasons of Rougher football when the team was rampaging through the opposition to state titles, KMUS had problems with school administrations outside our district who wanted exorbitant amounts of money for the right to broadcast live from their stadiums. There was the mistaken idea that a broadcast would keep the visiting crowds away. This was prevalent in many cities. In fact, it was still a factor with some school administrations when I broadcast Highland Park High games in Dallas in the later 1950s. In Muskogee's situation there were usually more Rougher fans at out-of-town games than locals.

My biggest temper tantrum took place in McAlester in a play-off game. The school system there wanted something like $600 to broadcast live from their stadium. That was a chunk of money in those days and our GM, Jimmy Barry, went ballistic. We just couldn't broadcast the game. Jimmy dickered with them—he was an excellent horse trader—and finally came up with the plan to pay them something like $100, *but* we would have to tape the game at the KMUS studio and not start the tape until the second half of the game started in McAlester.

So off we go to McAlester, best known for the state prison, and arrive at the stadium, which was built in the manner of a pseudo castle. It had a wall-and-parapets kind of architecture. We walked into the place and, lo and behold, there was no grass on the field! They also used the place for rodeos and the field was like a desert. To add more insult to this ridiculous situation, the location of my broadcasting area was in a so-called box seat flat on the ground at the fifty yard line. How in the name of all that was football could we see anything going on at either end or side of the field? I was a raving maniac. As we were going out of the stadium, a couple of men in suits came up and asked if we found everything. I launched into an expletive denunciation of the McAlester school system, the individual idiots who wanted to charge this enormous fee and then put us down on the field, below ground level!

After we set up our equipment, two hours before the bash, I told the station of the situation and we just went live at kickoff. I explained to the listeners the facilities and, as the game progressed, a dust cloud hung over the field on that late fall evening, which made viewing and breathing nearly impossible.

The next week, KMUS received a letter condemning my vocal diatribe, the live broadcast, and the insulting remarks made by the announcer, yours truly, about McAlester during the game. The gentlemen I spoke to happened to be the school principal. KMUS was forever banned from broadcasting another game at McAlester. Jimmy Barry congratulated me on having had the first radio station he ever managed being barred from a community. Oh, the Roughers whipped the McAlester team!

After I left KBIX, they proceeded to broadcast Rougher games in a haphazard manner. One year, when both stations were doing the broadcasts, we had a trip to Sand Springs, which is near Tulsa. There was only one available closed booth for a broadcast. The stadium folks had us flip a coin, and I lost. KMUS had to sit out in the stands down in front of the press box.

I could handle that okay, but this was early fall and one of those obnoxious Oklahoma thunderstorms came barreling in before the end of the first half. The rolling clouds were black and green and frightening. The wind blew into a gale and the monsoon that followed was something akin to one I traveled through in the Pacific during the war. It rained so hard the players became unidentifiable from my location. I was wearing a suede jacket and all of the brown coloring washed down through my pants. I was wearing a headset, but took it off when the lightning caused a little tickle on my head. Some of my friends commented on the broadcast, saying I talked too much about the rain! About calling the game? You just keep identifying who you hope and think is running or tackling—but identification was impossible during the rain and because of the mud-caked jerseys in the second half. It's all just part of the fun of "never giving up" on a broadcast in any type of weather.

This was one of the greatest eras in Muskogee Rougher football. Probably no other team before or after had as many outstandingly talented players in every position. One of the pluses of covering high school football for the announcer is the close relationship with coaches and players. I hosted the luncheons and banquets and sometimes ate with the players and coaches on the road. It was a close relationship. In 1960, when Max Boydston, the Rougher fullback, joined the Dallas Texans, he and I resumed our friendship from the early 1950s.

When we thought it necessary, or a school or college desired coverage, KMUS would broadcast a game or several games—that is, if the station could make a buck or two.

It was 1952 when my two-year alma mater Northeastern State College in Tahlequah put together a winning football team. As it turned out, there was a lot of skullduggery in building the team, but that came out later. The Northeastern Redmen were rampaging through their conference with one big game left—Southwestern State out in Weatherford, Oklahoma. Interest had boomed for Redmen fans, so they contacted us about broadcasting this big game.

We made all the arrangements, sold commercial time, arranged for the installation of a telephone line for the broadcast from the Southwestern stadium, and I prepared for the broadcast with the usual rosters, depth charts, and spotting boards.

KMUS had one of those big wood-paneled Chevrolet station wagons that we took on remotes. This was a really long remote, 215 miles due west of Muskogee as the crow flies. And crows would make a lot better time than us in that station wagon on Oklahoma highways. Two hundred and fifteen miles might not sound like a long distance today, but then it was a solid five hours or more on that dear old Highway 66.

It was a two o'clock kickoff, so I planned to have everything ready to leave around seven Saturday morning and have a leisurely drive to arrive at the game site an hour or so ahead of kickoff. My wife planned to spend the weekend with my parents on their little farm a mile out of town. We drove our car and the station wagon with the broadcast equipment out after the Friday night Rougher football game.

Everyone needs a test of character and resolve now and then. Mine came that night when a huge rainstorm blew in late and continued to pound the area until morning. I was up about six a.m. making preparations to leave for the game. The creek that ran by our farm flooded across the road and halfway up to our house. We couldn't see the road or the bridge that connected our property with the road. You could correctly say panic had arrived. It became clear that it was going to be necessary to wade through the water to check out the condition of our little bridge from the property to the road. My father and I did and discovered that one side of the bridge had dropped down a couple of feet. It meant trying to drive the station wagon across the bridge, and at the wrong angle the wagon could have dropped into the ditch. I really panicked. I don't recall what all I found that I used to fill that fallen side of the bridge, but I know I was about out of my mind knowing that time was killing my chances of making that game on time.

With my poor father worrying over my state of mind after I flung boards and debris around the bridge, I brought the station wagon down running board-deep in water to make a run at it—well, a crawl at it. I had to nudge the wagon across on a couple of two-by-fours I had laid together where the bridge had dropped. My wife and mother were also watching this with much anxiety. If the boards slipped, if the rear end fell into the ditch, I would have kissed that part of my trip goodbye. I imagine I would have had sense enough to call Jimmy Barry or some other station person to loan us a car.

I slowly drove the big Chevy across and actually made it to the road on the other side. Then, it was back to the house, change out of soaked clothes, roll up the pants legs of my dry clothes, walk barefoot down to the station wagon, put on my shoes, and drive up the slippery muddy road to the city limits. I hurriedly picked up the two other members of our broadcast crew and headed west as fast as that station wagon could be pushed.

But the story is not over. We probably hit the highway well after nine a.m., a good two hours late but still with a chance to arrive a little before the kickoff at two o'clock. But then, thirty miles from Weatherford, we ran out of gas. The gauge said we had gas left; the tank didn't agree. Another round of panic absorbed me and the crew. Just as we stepped out on the highway to hail a passing motorist, a car screeched to a stop in front of us and backed up. It was the football coach's wife and some friends. One of us jumped in their car, raced to nearest station, procured the gas, came back, fueled the wagon, and headed for the stadium. It was about forty minutes before kickoff and there were miles to travel. By the time we ran up the stadium into the booth, there were about ten minutes left. When we had hooked up the remote amplifier, called the station, and I sat down to introduce the game (missing a fifteen-minute pregame program), they kicked off. The rest was fairly easy.

I really owe my sports career to those years spent at KBIX and especially at KMUS. Had the GM of KBIX not given me the chance that week in 1950, I have no idea what I would be doing now. And at KMUS, I earned a "master's degree" in sports broadcasting, having experienced play-by-play in every athletic event I would later cover in Dallas.

After I had been at KMUS a few weeks, the management told me they had forgotten to tell me about another broadcast I had to do—a monthly play-by-play report of professional wrestling at the Civic Auditorium in downtown Muskogee. Wrestling? I had never been to a match and only saw a few on television about two years before in Chicago when I was on a Denver U debate trip. They suggested that I go over and talk to the promoter, visit with a couple of the wrestlers, and let them teach me some of the holds and routines. The promoter was a pleasant fellow, and with his help, I learned some of the basic holds like the flying drop kick and gained some basic knowledge of what to say while one wrestler has the other in a hammerlock for what seems an eternity. That's where I first encountered Danny Mc-Shain, Wild Red Berry, and the Fabulous Moolah, the great woman champion. I have no idea if anyone ever listened to those broadcasts, but they were sold. In three years of those radio wrestling broadcasts, I learned quite a bit about the grunt-and-groan business. My fellow broadcaster Ed Dumit would introduce me as the "the voice of professional wrestling, Garbo Plodnik!"

Other than opening the door to Dallas, wrestling provided me with the opportunity of meeting and interviewing Joe Louis, the great former world champion. Joe's life had not been easy since leaving the ring, and to make a few bucks he acted as referee in pro wrestling bouts around the country. We broadcast our wrestling program early in the month to promote the rest of the shows for the promoter. When Joe Louis came in to referee, I arranged for him to come to the station for a taped interview. We had a little reel-to-reel recorder by then. I was alone in the station when Joe came up the steps and into the studio. He was gracious and rather shy. We started the interview and the only part I remember was when I played a cut off Ed Murrow's *I Can Hear It Now* album with Clem McCarthy the announcer calling the second Louis–Schmeling championship fight. McCarthy was calling the onslaught by Louis and then "Schmeling is down, Schmeling's down. The count is four . . . five . . . Schmeling is down! Louis won in the first round!" Joe sat there, staring ahead, visualizing every moment of his great return win over the German. So we finished the interview. I had met and interviewed one of boxing's greatest champions. And did I save the tape? Did I ask for his autograph? Did I have a picture taken with him? Nothing. I only retain the memory of sitting in that little studio in Muskogee, Oklahoma, with the Brown Bomber, Joe Louis.

Why leave Muskogee for Dallas? Well KRLD-AM was a fifty-thousand-watt station as compared to KMUS with its one thousand watts. Muskogee's population was thirty-two thousand and Dallas was, well, Dallas! And there was that animal—television—that I had absolutely no idea how to handle. For a while, I thought it would devour me.

KRLD-TV had gone on the air in December of 1949, so it was a relatively new station when I joined in 1953. In the fall of '49, they were building and planning for the start date and took their "bread truck" mobile TV unit out to the Cotton Bowl to shoot an SMU–Notre Dame football game. Howard Chamberlain, an engineer who was with the station from the beginning, recalled they used their Dumont cameras, which had three-lens-turrets. No zoom lens. To change from a wide shot to a closer view it meant turning and locking the turret while the camera's picture was not being seen. The story goes that one of the three cameras was mounted in the end zone, and when a field goal was attempted, the cameraman kept following the flight of the ball out of the stadium until he realized it was a pigeon.

There was also sentiment among some members of the KRLD-TV management that I was too short to be a sportscaster! That was the first time I had run into that prejudice as a sportscaster. I had often been kidded in school and the Navy about my height. I was called "Peanuts" by my Navy buddies. But, of course, no one cares how tall you are on radio. I had heard this rumor when I was first allowed to become a part of the nightly Channel 4 news block, so I planned a little self-deprecation. The Southern Methodist Mustangs were Southwest Conference Champions in those years, so I invited the entire team and Coach E. O. "Doc" Hayes to the station to present them on my program. I lined them up according to height and introduced them. When I reached the 6′ 10″ Jim Krebs, I climbed a small step-ladder to be eye-to-eye with him. The station had great response about this crazy young sportscaster and I didn't hear anymore about being too short to handle sports.

After I had been at KRLD for four years, the station management realized that their days of relying on the Columbia Broadcasting System programming was over. Network radio was turning everything over to television, and high-powered local stations like KRLD, WBAP, and WFAA in Dallas and Fort Worth had to come up with creative programming of their own. KLIF, under the creative reigns of Gordon McLendon, had produced the Liberty Broadcasting Network, doing live and re-created Major League Baseball games for several years. The Old Scotchman, as McLendon referred to himself, had set the standard for re-creations with every sound effect known to man. And KLIF introduced the Top 40 music format with high personality disc jockeys like my friend and boss of later years, Ron Chapman. So KRLD suddenly branched out in 1957 with high school football. Not just any high school but the high-rolling Highland Park High Scots. I was "the" sportscaster at KRLD and, with my "vast experience" at Muskogee, took over that duty.

My dear friend Hugh Neeld, who worked with me at KMUS and recommended me for the KRLD wrestling position, was managing a station way out in West Texas in Eastland when I was in Dallas. Before the Highland Park games came along, I would take off Friday afternoons and drive out there to broadcast his games when he needed me. It kept me in practice even though it was a long journey. Sacrifice of time can be a plus. The Highland Park experience was the foundation for my play-by-play work in the North Texas area. KRLD was heard all over the state and my reputation would be made or broken in that era. Scots football was the catalyst for my later broadcasting.

After a few years at KRLD, the town of Denton, thirty-five miles north of Dallas, became an important part of my life. When we were broadcasting Highland Park in Denton, the Denton Broncos played at their little stadium across the street from the school. The press box was so tiny that the writers, public address announcer, and both team's broadcasters sat side-by-side in the little facility. I would put my color commentator, Jack Dubberly, between me and KDNT, the

Denton station's announcer. Still, it was a mess with the newspaper guys yakking and two, three, or four broadcasters going full blast.

I had noticed that the top of the Denton press box was flat. There was also a wooden ladder attached to the side of the building so photographers could climb up and shoot their game film from up there. After my first experience in that chicken coop of a press box, I asked the athletic director if Jack and I could set up on the roof for our next game in Denton, which occurred every other year. We brought along a card table and two chairs, ran our telephone line from the press box up there, and settled in for the broadcast just as a cold northern blew in. There we were with no protection, huddled up broadcasting from high atop Bronco Stadium. Fortunately, no heavy downpour followed—we just lightly froze, but it was better than down inside the community press area. At least, I kept telling Jack that.

I must interject here an event that occurred that, as they say in psychological circles, changed my life—forever. I was producing and hosting the evening sports show during the ten o'clock news segment. There was no six p.m. newscast, as CBS had Douglas Edwards, later Walter Cronkite, on a fifteen-minute evening newscast and Perry Como had a fifteen-minute songfest.

Covering sports in Dallas in those days consisted of Southern Methodist University, the high schools, Devil's Bowl auto racing, and whatever else one could put together. We also had Texas Christian in Fort Worth, but there was no great love lost between the two cities, so we pumped up everything Dallas.

One evening in the late summer of 1957 before Highland Park football, checking the newspaper's sports pages, I noticed a small box story announcing the beginning of fall football practice at North Texas State College. They didn't put in the location, so I asked around the newsroom where North Texas was located. In Denton, I was told where I was to broadcast high school football that fall. It seemed like another chance to add to the limited television sports coverage, so I called and was put in touch with the sports information office and the director, Dr. James Rogers. I introduced myself and asked if it would be possible to come up and film some of the practice and do a story for my sports show. "You bet, it would be great," Dr. Rogers said. We made arrangements and I went up to the practice field next to

Fouts Field, the football stadium, with my trusty Bell and Howell 16 mm camera with one one-inch lens.

As it turned out, I was the first television reporter, cameraman, whatever to attend a North Texas practice and shoot some film. I was introduced to Dr. Rogers's assistant, Freddie Graham, who it turned out would become a lifelong friend and sometime business partner. Demonstrating my camera prowess, I knelt on the ground a little ways in front of the offensive line. They were practicing coming off the line after the center hiked the ball to the quarterback. I had to be fairly close because when you only have a one-inch lens on a camera, you have to do a lot of physical zooming. You move in for a close-up, back for a medium shot, and way back for a wide shot—we had no zoom lens in those days. So I am down on my knees to get one of those great tight shots, and the line comes off the ball and right over me. The players picked me up, dusted me off, and everyone had a good laugh. My shots made a good story for the ten o'clock news.

You never know in this business what opportunity comes knocking or when you will accidentally open the door to that opportunity. Two years later in 1959, I became the announcer for the North Texas State University Eagles of the Missouri Valley Conference, a job I held for most of the next thirty-five years. The opportunity to broadcast on CBS radio's broadcast of the Cotton Bowl game came in 1956. Interestingly, CBS, with recommendation from their affiliate, used the local sports announcer or personality to work as the color commentator on games like the Cotton Bowl, then a New Year's Day national headline affair. I had also been working as the Southwest correspondent for CBS Network's *Tom Harmon Sports Show* that originated out of California. When the show went nationwide, they had called KRLD asking about a sports reporter. My friend, fellow reporter, and weatherman Jim Underwood at KRLD had given them my name.

I began sending in news stories to the CBS program that had no particular length of time—some two, three, or four minutes. Immediately, the producer, Sterling Tracy, began bombarding me with instructions to cut the features I was sending to no more than a minute and a half. Man, the stuff I was sending was so good it couldn't be cut! Bob Panella, the program editor, said that may be true, but you better learn how to edit those stories down—they were tired of editing them for me! So, here I was on CBS radio, finding myself in a learning process of radio story production. With Panella's teaching, I learned to quickly and clearly set the scene of the story, introduce the person I was interviewing, and then close everything within that minute to minute and a half. In the fifth year of the Harmon show, I was listed with thirteen other reporters around the nation (Chris Schenkel was the New York rep) in their colorful promotion piece: "Bill Mercer, ace sportscaster of CBS affiliate Dallas, is one . . . of the up-and-coming sports reporters in the country."

I journeyed around the state interviewing key sports figures, sending in reports in the early fall with every major college coach in Texas, flying with the print media in an old DC-3 charter. Back when Paul "Bear" Bryant was coaching Texas A&M, I drove down one hot summer day to interview him. I knew his reputation, so I was somewhat apprehensive. As I drove up to the office, there was the Bear, leaning up against the wall, smoking a cigarette. In the end, we had a dandy interview and another good story for Tom Harmon and CBS.

Sometimes, by luck, you find and report a great story. At Moody Coliseum in Dallas, Southwest Conference Champ Southern Methodist University and Kansas, winners of the Big Seven Conference in 1957 with the famous Wilt Chamberlain averaging 24.3 points per game, were in a tough NCAA regional game. I was there just to do a story for Harmon, but as the game was winding down, I started recording a play-by-play segment on my cassette recorder just for fun. Well, SMU hit a last-second shot and it went into overtime. It turned out to be one of my best stories as they took my last-second play-by-play and then the story of Kansas winning in overtime, followed by a short interview with Coach E. O. "Doc" Hayes. Now that was good luck.

SMU Coach Hayes and I worked together on his television show. Doc was one of the great characters in the state, one of the funniest guys in the business, *and* one of the most successful. He loved to tell of the times when he was playing basketball at North Texas State College in Denton. He would wait by the trolley line at the drug store across from the college hoping that future movie stars, Ann Sheridan and Joan Blondell, would come along so they could ride the trolley down to the square of Denton and back. Big date!

Twice, I covered Muhammad Ali fights in Houston and missed a great verbal battle between Ali and a reporter over Vietnam by not having my recorder on.

One of my best humorous contributions to the Harmon show concerned the opening of the turnpike between Dallas and Fort Worth. For promotional purposes, they enticed a couple of local pro golfers and a bunch of amateurs to play golf all the way from Dallas to the Fort Worth end, more than thirty miles, while the road was under construction: the longest tournament in the history of golf.

In life, sometimes you learn by losing or making mistakes. I had a nightly TV sports show, which ran after my eight-hour announcing shift. I received a talent fee doing the program outside my regular shift. I was racing around with my trusty 16 mm camera, and made a couple of costly mistakes. One of my sponsors was a paint company, and one night I did not notice while cutting and editing the film that the billboard of another paint company at the baseball park, Burnett Field, was prominent in my story. There was a big discussion about this. Fortunately, I just received a slap on the wrist.

Judgement and common sense were the name of the game. Another sponsor was a beer company, and in the daily rush to give all the sports, I mentioned that there was a large bowling tournament in town. Even though I did not mention that the sponsor was "another" beer company, my sponsor had me kicked off my program and Eddie Barker took over for the life of the beer sponsorship. Here is the kicker. I had bought a new 1956 Oldsmobile, and was making the payments with my nightly talent fee. Now, the show and talent fee were gone. In order to make those payments, only about $35 a month in those days, I increased my number of stories to Tom Harmon and used the additional $9.95 fee per story from them to pay for the car.

The Harmon production folks recommended me to work as the color commentator with the Cotton Bowl broadcast. I did that for the next seven years. One announcer I worked with was the nationally famous voice of the St. Louis Cardinals, Harry Caray—a guy I would be paired with in 1974 and '75 with the Chicago White Sox. I still have a letter from CBS director of sports Jimmy Dolan dated January 5, 1962: "All the reports I have had on the Cotton Bowl game have been good. Both you and Harry were given salutations for the job and, all in all, the whole thing came off fine."

Early on at KRLD, I auditioned to work on some of the Magnolia

High School football playoff broadcasts as a color announcer, but that was mostly reading some commercials, introducing the announcer, and covering the halftime with interviews with representatives of each school. It was also necessary to write fifteen minutes of material about the schools, players, and communities, which might be used in case of a power failure. There had been a power failure some games back, and no one could ad-lib satisfactorily to cover the fifteen-minute delay. Yes, the stadium lights were out, but not the press box. I wondered if we were supposed to provide a flashlight in case the press box went black, too. I never had to use one of those fifteen-minute essays.

The Cotton Bowl game and social events around it was one of the great events of the year in Dallas. The Cotton Bowl invited some of the best teams in the nation to compete against the champion of the Southwest Conference. For CBS, it was a major broadcast. For me, it was a glorious moment. It was also a slam-bang period of preparation for me. I needed to present myself as an "authority" in the broadcast. I read all the newspaper accounts of the teams, went back over the individual and team records (as they might come in handy), and recalled as much as the players and the game plan as the play-by-play announcer. Sometimes, people selected to handle this part of the job don't realize the preparation involved. It is just like reporting a news story that has continued for a solid year.

My wife loved this portion of my sports broadcasting because we were invited to the gala New Year's Eve dinner and dance put on by the Cotton Bowl Association. I met a number of great CBS people, including Jimmy Dolan, who would recommend me for another job later that I could not, or would not, take.

So here was a full-blown sports career taking shape: nightly TV sports show in the KRLD news block, sending stories to Tom Harmon that ran nationwide, high school football play-by-play, and the once-a-year Cotton Bowl broadcast. I was beginning to make some extra money. Our union contract at KRLD provided I would be paid for the high school games, which were in addition to my regular shift on radio and television—and the Cotton Bowl check was in *three* figures! Life was good and it was going to be better

When I added the North Texas football Saturday game schedule to my duties in 1959, most of my week was filled up. Nineteen fifty-nine was also the first year I began broadcasting the Dallas–Fort Worth Rangers Triple-A baseball team at Burnett Field in Dallas for KRLD. On the out-of-town games, North Texas sometimes flew up the day of the game. It saved staying overnight in hotels and, with the addition of African American players on the team (North Texas was the first major college in Texas to integrate), it saved the problem of finding rooms for them, as some hotels would not rent rooms to black athletes.

The star athlete of the North Texas Eagles for three seasons, 1957 through 1959, was Abner Haynes, the first black player to play in a state college in Texas. Abner led in rushing and receiving for three years and scoring for two years in the Missouri Valley Conference. He was one of the most exciting players I ever watched, even equal to my high school idol, Jack Jacobs. He went on to be the star back for the new Dallas Texans of the American Football League and for Denver, Miami, and New York.

In 1959, North Texas was gaining national attention for its success on the field with Haynes. Five games into the season, and undefeated, the team was headed to play the University of Houston. Fan support was so immense that the school chartered a train for the players and the fans to ride to Houston. When the team bused over from the train to the Houston hotel the night before the game, they were refused admittance because of Haynes and another black player on the squad.

Rather than follow the ignominious routine of taking the black players to a hotel in "their" section of Houston, the team voted to spend the night on the train. The Eagles went out the next day and defeated Houston, 7 to 6. I broadcast the game in huge Rice Stadium where they had a big Boy Scout celebration at halftime, with hundreds of scouts holding American flags, marching on the field. How ironic—to be cheering for America and freedom while Abner Haynes and his teammates slept on that train that night because of segregation.

North Texas finished the season with one loss. That was against Tulsa and played in the Oil Capitol on a bitterly freezing day. The Golden Hurricane won 17 to 6, the only blemish on the Eagle's 9 and 1 season. North Texas was invited to the Sun Bowl in El Paso and lost to New Mexico, 28 to 8.

Abner Haynes and his quarterback, Vernon Cole, were two-year

All-Missouri Valley selections while the guys who worked in the trenches and honored as All-Missouri Valley selections were Bill Carrico, who later became Denton High School athletic director, George Herring, and Fred Way. North Texas did not have comparable successful seasons until the era of Steve Ramsey–Joe Greene from 1965 through 1969.

By hook or crook, I had become established as a Dallas sports announcer in all sports but basketball. Even professional wrestling was still on my agenda with those infamous "Studio Wrestling" productions taped in the KRLD-TV studio.

Coming up on the sports horizon for Dallas was the development of the American Football League by Lamar Hunt of the famed H. L. Hunt family, which had enormous wealth in oil and myriad other holdings and businesses. Hunt was a 1956 graduate of Southern Methodist University where he played football. I first met Lamar when I interviewed him for my television sports show, suited up in his Mustang uniform.

Hunt realized the potential of the Dallas–Fort Worth, North Texas market and, with his healthy cashbox behind him, applied for an expansion franchise in the National Football League. When denied a franchise, Hunt worked with a series of businesspeople in seven other cities to organize the American Football League. The majority of the teams were in cities without NFL franchises, except for Los Angeles and New York. The remainder of the teams was in Dallas, Boston, Buffalo, Houston, Denver, and Oakland. The future success of the league was bolstered with the rising popularity of television and a contract to telecast all AFL games with the National Broadcasting Company. The NFL followed suit two years later with CBS-TV.

In fact, the AFL's innovations were ultimately copied by the NFL: the two point conversion, the scoreboard clock as the official game clock, the use of player names on the uniforms, colorful, imaginative uniforms (some way too imaginative!), and the wild card playoff where the second place teams in each conference played.

Following these renegade young businessmen of the AFL was the promise of another professional football team for Dallas. Clint Murchison, member of an abundantly wealthy family, was sought out by the NFL to lead in the funding and support of the Dallas Cowboys. Suddenly, Dallas, which had tried a pro football team in 1952 that ended in financial disaster, now was provided with two choices: old-line NFL teams with well-known players (the Cowboys) or the up-start Texans with new teams and new players. Both teams would play their home games beginning in 1960 in the Cotton Bowl. Dallas seemed underwhelmed.

The ensuing struggle to sign *the* best players from Texas was some-thing akin to the sharp, rancorous political campaigns today. Some players who were agreeable to signing with either team were taken off to "safe houses" where they would not be kidnapped by the other team. Players actually signed contracts with both teams. Salaries for football stars coming out of college skyrocketed, though nowhere near the escalation of today. Players with their contracts running out were wined, dined, and shown the checkbooks. Charges, counter-charges, lawsuits, and near-physical combat filled the newspapers and airwaves. It was a heady time and, you might say, the birth of today's fan—eccentric, egregious, combative, and vulgar. The Cowboys fans hated the Texans, and vice versa.

The immortal Tex Schramm took over the reins of the Cowboys, hired Tom Landry to coach the team, and proceeded to do everything in his power and more to destroy the gang of radicals in the AFL.

The Texans were managed by Jack Steadman and coached by Hank Stram. Stram turned out to be the only coach the Texans—and then, after the team moved to Kansas City, the Chiefs—had in the AFL. Stram was an innovator, and his wide-open offenses and dura-ble defenses became fan pleasers. Stram died in 2005.

The Cowboys had trouble winning a game while the Texans fin-ished second in their division of the American Football League. But first, as famed newsman Paul Harvey says, "Here is the rest of the story."

I was so busy with a high school and college football game each week, my work at KRLD on TV and radio, and Minor League Base-ball in the spring and summer that I really didn't pay a lot of attention to the structuring of the broadcasts for the two teams. There were quickly rumors that so and so was up for the Cowboys job, and what-ever team arranged to have its games broadcast on KRLD might provide an opportunity for me to be a part of the announcing staff. I also was not real smart about jumping in and contacting people, sending resumes, and audition tapes. But out of the blue, I was called by Bob Halford, the media director for the Texans of the AFL. He asked if I would be interested in working their games, which would be on KRLD.

My assignment would be as the color commentator on home games and some out-of-town assignments. They had hired Charlie Jones to be the play-by-play announcer. Charlie had graduated from the University of Arkansas with a law degree, but had this deep-down desire to be a sports broadcaster. He had heard of the Texans broadcast position, caught a bus, rode from Fayetteville to Dallas with an audition tape, went to the offices of the Texans, and beseeched them to give him an audition. By his sheer personality and determination—and, undoubtedly, his natural talent—he was hired. Like most talent fees those days, I imagine the Texans hired him for a "reasonable" fee. Then the Texans helped Charlie land a spot with the NBC television network broadcasting all the AFL games, and he also snared the sports director's position at WFAA-TV in Dallas.

Charlie helped bring me into the broadcasts. I would read some commercials if necessary (promotions, of course), keep game statistics, spot for Charlie, and provide moments of brilliance with my analysis and color, and do the play-by-play when Charlie was working the TV network. There were only two of us, and we were saddled with a tight budget. My duties would keep me busy on a Texans broadcast and on football weekends with a high school game Friday, North Texas on Saturday, and the Texans on Sunday.

I wouldn't suggest that broadcasting three football games a week, in three different levels, is the best policy for anyone. However, I was eager to do everything I possibly could in the business—and the opportunity was there, so I took it. The preparation was not as difficult as you might believe. For each of the teams I covered weekly— Highland Park, North Texas, and the Texans—I had a basic spotting board for each that I updated each week. Preparation for them and the opponents meant spending long evenings at home working on each separately. The high school preparation was the easiest, with little statistical or biographical information available in those days. North Texas's opponents had considerable information, and then the Texans were the most involved. I might say, my ability to memorize was pretty keen fifty years back. I worked memorizing the skill positions first and then key defensive players like linebackers, corners, and safeties.

Separating the teams from game to game was no problem. I just shut out the preceding game. I learned early on to use binoculars to set up the play and follow the passer or runners. In order to do this, it was and still is necessary to *know* the players by their numbers. Actually, after a few games with the binoculars, I identified the players of my teams by the way they looked physically and moved. Every year when I teach sportscasting, I have to impress on the students that they use the names of the players, not their numbers. The numbers are for the people in the stands. Radio must identify by name.

There were some harrowing travel adventures—flying nearly all night on those red-eye flights, driving like mad from one afternoon game to a night game—but the funniest one happened between a local high school game and North Texas playing in El Paso. I had a Friday night high school game that was a far driving distance from Dallas. For some reason I don't recall, I had a shift on Saturday, so it was necessary in order to make the Saturday North Texas game to work a deal with one of the other announcers to cover me at KRLD. My friend Jack Dubberly would ask me at the beginning of a week what five football games I had that week.

Here is the scenario. I drove back from the high school game into Dallas after midnight, went to KRLD, and slept on a couch in the ladies rest room. It was the only couch available. I then went in to work on the six a.m. shift until eight a.m. when my buddy relieved me. I raced out to Love Field, the main airport at the time, to board a plane for El Paso. Earlier in the week, I had the brilliant idea of calling the El Paso police chief to ask, due to my tight schedule, if one of his cars could meet me at the airport and hustle me over to the Sun Bowl Stadium. Surprisingly, he agreed.

So at Love Field, the plane was delayed from its nine a.m. departure. We finally boarded and then sat on the runway for about thirty minutes before takeoff. Leaving at nine, I had a nice cushion to work on for the two p.m. kickoff—1:45 pregame broadcast. Leaving at ten, my cushion had shrunk to about forty-five minutes prior to kickoff.

By the time the plane landed in El Paso's airport, my cushion before the kickoff was less than thirty minutes. The stadium was on the far west side of El Paso, the airport on the east side. When I hit the tarmac, there were two policemen waiting at the doorway. I trotted up to them and introduced myself. They said, "Let's hit it—we don't have much time." The policeman driving didn't turn on the emergency lights, but he put the pedal down and we moved! At one point, his partner said, "Don't kill us—it's only a football game." To him, maybe!

We reached the stadium with a few minutes to spare before kickoff. I thanked them profusely and raced with my briefcase through the gate toward the press box just as the National Anthem started. My broadcast partner, North Texas Sports information director Fred Graham, had brought the broadcast equipment with him the day before when the team came out. He had the local station engineer set it up for him. I had missed the pregame program, a fifteen-minute affair, so Fred was trying to fill the time as best he could. Fred could write the greatest sports stories, but this ad-libbing or reading my pregame copy was certainly a new task.

I am very patriotic—three years in the Navy overseas in World War II proves that—but this time, I did not stop for the anthem. I ran around the field, up through the stands, and to the press box. Folks looked at me with varying expressions. When I trotted into the broadcast booth, Fred looked relieved and said, "Here is Bill Mercer." I then realized I had been running in a higher altitude and had no wind and no voice. We took a commercial break, but it took me sometime into the first quarter before finally having enough breath for my optimum broadcast voice.

A similar incident occurred when North Texas played Southern Illinois University in Carbondale, Illinois. It, like Jonesboro, Arkansas, is a place you just cannot go to—directly, at least. It is necessary to drive from an airport to either of those cities. This time, I drove a rental car with great haste from Paducha, Kentucky, where I had the best plane connection. It is about a hundred miles as the crow flies, except the crow doesn't have to follow all those curving highways. I gauged from looking at the map that it would take me at best an hour and half, but it was more like two hours. As I drove up to the stadium, I saw Fred leaning out the radio booth window on the lookout for me. I made it by about two minutes prior to pregame.

The Texans were the more exciting team of the two teams in Dallas that first year. The Cowboys had to contend with all of those power-ful, seasoned teams in the NFL, while the Texans and the AFL were new, young, brash, and wild. In 1960, the Cowboys won 0, lost 11, and tied 1. The Texans finished 8 and 6 in second place in the Western Division.

The star running back of that first Texans team was Abner Haynes. Boy, what a coup that was selecting this electrifying back from North Texas State who I had followed the year before. Old Baylor quarter-back Cotton Davidson ran the offense. The hapless 1960 Cowboys were quarterbacked by the veteran Don Heinrich and 5' 7" Eddie LeBaron. Eddie and I stood nose-to-nose in interviews. L. G. Dupre from Baylor was the leading running back, Don McIlhenny of SMU at fullback, and there was another quarterback from SMU named Don Meredith who played with the Cowboys through 1967.

One Dallas sportswriter wrote after a game, about either team it didn't matter, that "you could fire a cannon through the Cotton Bowl and not hit anyone." The Texans averaged about 24,000 fans that first year in a stadium that held 65,000, but Charlie and I had a ball broadcasting these wild, wide-open games. The long pass was a fea-tured attack mechanism. Wild and crazy defensive play resulted in probably a record number of team fights in those formative years of the Texans.

Watching the Texans' Abner Haynes in 1960 as the leading rusher rolling up 867 yards and nine touchdowns was like a continuation of my first year work with North Texas. Jack Spikes, a former TCU Horned Frog, was the fullback. Davidson finished fifth in the league. Cotton's passing completion percentage of 47.2 was the second best in his career that ended in 1968 with Oakland. Abner also finished fifth in pass receptions with 55. The main wide receiver was Chris Burford, who caught 46 passes and scored only 5 touchdowns.

There were a number of future stars debuting that inaugural AFL year. Frank Tripucka led the league in passing and yardage and was second in TD passes. Future politician Jack Kemp was in Los Angeles, then moved with the team to San Diego in 1961, and on to Buffalo, where he remained for the rest of his career. Vito "Babe" Parilli had been around the NFL since 1952, but played with Oakland in 1960 and then moved on to Boston, where he stayed through 1967. Tom Flores, who later coached Oakland, was an NFL castoff when he joined Houston in 1960 and later played in Oakland. The greatest career story was that of George Blanda. He had started in the NFL in 1949, joined Houston of the AFL in 1960, played there through 1967 where he led the Oilers to the first two AFL championships, and then finished his storied career in Oakland in 1975—twenty-seven years in professional football.

The team and support staff journeyed to the out-of-town games on chartered four-engine prop planes. These were relatively noisy by today's standards and when there was bad weather, it was as rough as riding on a wild roller coaster. Even on good weather days, many of the players were not comfortable with flying and went white-knuckled to and from game sites.

The stadium facilities around the league were good. The Cotton Bowl one of the best, to terrible at the old Polo Grounds in New York. The Houston Oilers played in a high school style stadium, Jeppesen Stadium. The Boston Patriots played a few games at Harvard, some at Fenway Park, the hallowed turf of the Red Sox, but most were played in the old Boston Braves field. Denver moved in with the Denver baseball team at Bears Stadium, a nice facility but better set up for baseball. The Los Angeles Chargers played that one year in the venerable old Memorial Coliseum where the Los Angeles Rams of the NFL held forth. The Chargers drew light crowds in 1960 and moved to San Diego the next year. Late in the year, everyone shuddered about going to Buffalo where snow was anticipated and would make the going rough in the old War Memorial baseball stadium in that city. Oakland actually played their games in San Francisco at Kezar Stadium the first two years and then moved to Frank Youell Field in 1962.

That takes me back to phone lines and installation. I had a solo game at the Polo Grounds, with Charlie off doing his TV thing. We always were in the park two hours before the game. That gave us time to find any surprises that we might have to correct.

For this game in the ancient Polo Grounds, where the New York Giants Bobby Thomson hit his famous homer, we were given information regarding where the broadcast was to be—in a spot across the field from the home announcers. We found the pigeon-stool-splattered location. These booths—actually, they were more like baskets hanging on the facade of the stadium—were open to all creatures and weather. We set up the equipment, tied into the line, and could not find a sound. The line was dead.

Visiting radio and TV personnel are well-directed by the media folks in today's professional franchises, but that wasn't true back then—especially New York, where you were so distanced from the media area it took a search team to find it. The Titans were owned by former sports talker Harry Wismer, a self-promoting type who had put together the financial group. It was a poorly run outfit. No official was around to give us aid in the cavernous Polo Grounds.

The Texans' media guru, Bob Halford, started stalking the press area looking for someone to help us while I ran around like crazy looking for a phone to call the telephone company—but fat chance figuring out who to contact in that enormous city.

About ten minutes to airtime, we still hadn't located anyone to help us. I had called the radio station to alert them to our problem since it appeared we would be late going on the pregame program—if we went on at all. Suddenly, a guy runs up and says we were to come around to the Titans' broadcast area where they had set up a spare line and equipment for us. I grabbed my briefcase, spotting stuff, and binoculars and started running around the Polo Grounds' old dilapidated stadium. It was an oblong affair and a far piece from one side to the other. As I was racing around the long curving end of the stadium, Lamar Hunt came into view and asked where I was going. I didn't pause, just yelled, "To broadcast!"

When I leaped into the new location, there was the Titans' Bob Murphy, who had been in Muskogee prior to my broadcasting days at KMUS, smiling and pointing to our spot. The Titans' radio folks had learned of our misfortune and taken care of the problem. If you ever have a phone line problem, or any other problem, it is usually the best policy to have good relations with the other broadcast crew.

I have mentioned Bob Halford, the head of media relations for the Texans. In one of those convoluted relatives scenarios, we are vaguely related—not blood relatives, just in-law types. Anyway, Bob is still a good friend. He refers to me as "the whip" because of the description I used in describing the swing of a baseball player. Bob recalled the stadium locations in Boston and we remembered, without much fondness, the Texans–Patriots game of November 18, 1960, when the Texans won 42 to 14. But that day, Bob had nothing better to do, so he spotted for us. Charlie and I worked that one together. I know because that morning of the game in the hotel room, I was reading a paper and Charlie was in the bathroom when I noticed it was snowing lightly. I mentioned that to Charlie and he proceeded to start gagging. Charlie had a sensitive stomach.

So the three of us were in the booth in that old Boston Braves stadium, Bob spotting for us. It was cramped, cold, and tight when Bob announced he wasn't feeling well and had one of those sudden vomiting eruptions. Charlie, with the weak stomach, took a lot of antacid pills, and I gagged just thinking about changing baby diapers, so we suffered the most horrible broadcast situation possible. Let me assure you there is very little worse than trying not to breathe while broadcasting at the same time.

When the Texans visited Buffalo, I had a baseball friend there, pitcher Marion Fricano, who would spot for us. Marion had pitched in the majors and at that time was with the Dallas–Fort Worth Rangers, which I broadcast in the summer.

As we journeyed around the league during the initial season, we set up a network of guys who loved to work around the games in whatever capacity was needed. Usually, it was as a spotter, following the home teams on the field and pointing to the person on the spotting board who ran, passed, caught, kicked, and tackled. We had our Texans memorized so thoroughly we only needed a person for the home or visiting team. Early on, they would do this just to see the game. They were just pleased to have their name mentioned on the air. As we progressed in the business, we would pay them—it seemed to start at $10, and I suppose it is much more lucrative today.

Years later, when I broadcast a lot of Texas A&M football with my young color commentator Steve Fallon on the Mutual Radio Network, we had a fellow who was such an avid Aggie and so dedicated to seeing the games he would pay to travel to out-of-town games so he could sit in with us, spot, and watch the game. Of course, I left him a press pass and he had free admission. Mutual gave us an expense account, so our spotter also made a few bucks.

The Dallas Texans went into a losing tailspin in the middle of the 1961 season dropping six consecutive games. Though they won three of the last four, the Texans finished 6-8-0 and out of money. Abner Haynes was again the key offensive player with 841 rushing yards and nine touchdowns, but just three TDs out of his thirty-four pass receptions. The running game was opened up with fullback Jack Spikes, the key blocker (also 324 yards rushing), and wide receiver Frank Jackson added nearly 400 yards on 65 carries, mostly on sweeps.

The passing game was still not producing enough touchdown momentum. Chris Burford improved his statistics with five scoring catches out of the fifty-one completions, Jackson caught two TD passes, and my old friend from the Muskogee Roughers High School days, Max Boydston, came in as a wide receiver and scored once in twelve receptions.

This was to be Cotton Davidson's last year with the Texans. Cotton was an outgoing, friendly guy who would remind you somewhat of Don Meredith over in the Cowboys camp. Cotton was loose, easygoing, and funny. E. J. Holub, the huge West Texas linebacker, had joined the Texans and became an awesome force in the AFL. In a game in Oakland where the tension was always prevalent between the two teams, the Texans claimed a 42 to 35 victory. Just before the end of the game, a huge fight broke out on the Oakland side of the field. Holub was the instigator, and led the battle into the Raiders bench, swinging his helmet, sending noncombat players running for their lives. I was watching this mayhem unfold and glanced over to the Texans' side of the field. There was Cotton Davidson standing holding one of the ten yard markers while everyone else ran over to join the fray or just watch. We asked him after the game what he was doing and he said the guys holding the sticks wanted to watch the show, so he obliged by taking over—all said with a twinkle and laugh. Cotton was also careful about his relationship with fans, especially younger ones. After a game, we were standing around near the bus waiting to leave; Cotton was sucking on a cigarette when he spied some youngsters coming his way. He quickly put out the cigarette, commenting that it wasn't good for the kids to see anyone smoking, especially an athlete. Good guy. His last year, Davidson completed nearly 46 percent of his passes and threw 17 touchdown passes. He also rushed for 123 yards and made a touchdown, which we thoroughly enjoyed.

The Texans' defensive team was taking shape, with Holub and wild man Sherrill "Psycho" Headrick as linebackers, Paul Rochester, Dave Webster, and Mel Branch as defensive backs, and Bobby Hunt and the late Jerry Mays in the defensive line. Nineteen sixty-two was the culmination of the Texans building plan. The Texans added the giant Jim Tyrer to the offensive line, and with Marvin Terrell, Sonny Bishop, Jerry Cornelison, and veteran Joe Gilliam, they swept away the opposition. Hank Stram found an NFL castoff quarterback named Len Dawson who took over for Cotton Davidson and became a legend with the Texans that final year, and later with the Kansas City Chiefs.

Added to the ability to strike fast and hard on the ground was a massive fullback, Curtis McClinton. He opened more territory for Abner Haynes who rushed for 1,049 yards and 13 scores while catching 19 passes, 6 for touchdowns. Wide receiver Chris Burford scored 12 touchdowns and newcomer Fred Arbanas, the tight end, scored 6 more TDs on his 29 catches. The Texans took this awesome juggernaut out and demolished the AFL with 11 victories and 3 losses. The offense scored the most points in the league and the defense allowed the fewest. This was a solid championship team with the greatest achievement to come.

Len Dawson, who completed 61 percent of his passes with nearly 2,800 yards and 29 touchdowns, also was a competent runner, scoring 3 touchdowns out of his 252 yards rushing. For the third straight year, Houston's Oilers won the Eastern Division and were seeking their third straight overall championship, led by George Blanda and LSU Heisman Trophy winner Billy Cannon, plus Charlie Tolar as running backs and Charlie Hennigan as wide receiver.

The 1962 AFL championship game between the Texans and the Oilers at the time was the longest and is still described as one the best professional football championship games ever played. The game was played in little Jeppesen Stadium in Houston. In a few short years, the Oilers moved into the Eighth Wonder of the World, the Astrodome and its covered roof. The Texans led 17 to nothing after the first half. Abner Haynes had scored the two touchdowns, one on a pass from Dawson. Then the Blanda-led Oilers stormed back in the second half to tie the game and send it into overtime. This is the moment when Haynes, the Texans' captain, made what could have been a fatal decision— whether to kick or receive after the Texans won the coin toss for the overtime. He indicated the Texans would take one end of the field, probably assuming that meant the offense with the wind. It turned out it was the Oilers who had the ball in the sudden death game. Fortunately, for Haynes's life and reputation, the Oilers couldn't move into field position for a field goal and the game went to double overtime, the first in professional football history. Tommy Brooker kicked a 26-yard field goal for the Texans' 20-to-17 AFL championship.

The sad thing about reliving the championship game was that Charlie and I did not broadcast it. The network controlled the TV and radio broadcasts and used their own announcing teams—but what a finish to three years in Dallas.

Lamar Hunt's vision for the new league and the success of the Texans was realized. Seeing the continuing dispute with the Dallas Cowboys benefiting neither team, he moved the Texans to Kansas City where they are still the Chiefs. Lamar is one of the most interesting men I have ever met and undoubtedly the richest. He seemed somewhat shy at times, but was generous and loyal. There are amusing stories about Lamar and his failure to carry pocket money—one, of many, recounts walking through a city and everyone stopped to buy an ice cream and Lamar didn't have change, so the PR guy paid for all of us.

In those festive, carefree years with the Texans, we young journalists, radio-types, and the media staff would journey out for dinner and drinks afterward. On one occasion, we had a riotously good time at a bar. Upon returning to the hotel, we took the elevator up where we stepped off to find Lamar standing there. A media type, a bit overly sloshed, patted him on the back and said, "You are a rich SOB, but a nice one!" and laughed as he headed for his room. Lamar just let it pass.

Another time in Buffalo, we had a fine Yankee dinner, a considerable fellowship at the bar, and then decided to go over and look at Niagara Falls—at night. Somehow, we ended up on the Canadian side searching for the famous falling water. It was very late when we stopped and asked some folks where the fool thing was. Five of us were driving around in the dark until one guy thought he heard it. Stumbling around in the dark, we figured we had the right direction, followed the sound, and then we literally crawled over and still believe to this day we had a midnight look at the famous waters.

I have always felt privileged to have been a part of the Texans those three years in Dallas. I still have my bright red jacket with the Texan

logo, which was designed by Bill McClanahan, and a Zippo-type cigarette lighter with the name of the team and the club logo. The early
philosophy of a fun league, with wide open football, colorful and
zany, seems to continue today thirty-eight years after the NFL-AFL
merger.

One of my major disappointments was being unable to join the
Kansas City Chiefs some twenty-plus years later. I was working at
KVIL when the general manager of the radio station in Kansas City
called me for a meeting while he was in Dallas. He wanted me to
work for his station with morning sports like I was doing at KVIL
and broadcast the Kansas City Chiefs football. I was ready to jump
when he mentioned the pay—it was the same amount I was making
at KVIL for *both* jobs. I explained to him that didn't make sense. He,
a very nice man, thought it did. I explained that I was making twice
what KVIL paid me through all my other broadcasting and teaching,
and with two of my four children in college, I couldn't take a cut. We
discussed this a few weeks later, but he had no more money available.
Of course, it was a great opportunity to be back broadcasting major
league football, but some family responsibilities had to be factored in.
A few weeks later, Lamar Hunt called me and asked why I couldn't
take the job. Lamar said he was sorry, but he understood the financial
problem. What he didn't mention was that twenty years after the Dallas Texans, he still respected my work and recommended me.

Back to 1961. The Dallas Cowboys were improving. In '61, they
won four while losing nine and had one tie. They added another to
the win column in 1962. It wasn't until 1965 that the Cowboys had a
five hundred season and I was with them then. More about this later.

As it turned out, 1963 was the last year I broadcast the Dallas–Fort
Worth Rangers baseball. In 1964, KRLD decided not to renew another five-year contract.

When I remember 1963, my emotions still react with a shudder. It
was a great year until November 22. Part of my job at KRLD, in addition to sports, was as a newsman. Several of us were interviewers on
a program called "Comment" that news director Eddie Barker had
designed. In addition, I was editing, producing, and announcing the
noon news on Channel 4.

Then, President Kennedy was killed and our professional lives were
tested. I suggest you read a book that four of us wrote about that day

and our response. It is called *When the News Went Live*. One note about that fateful weekend. Every sports venue in the country cancelled games for the weekend following the assassination, except the National Football League. There were excuses, but none sufficed as far as I and millions more were concerned. It was a black mark on the NFL.

There are turning points in your life and career that you will never forget or, in my case, never have your family fail to remind you of. I had no baseball that summer. As I said, KRLD did not renew its contract to broadcast the minor league team. But I was hired by the Rangers' owner, Ray Johnston, to handle their public address duties at the ballpark. The 1964 team was the worst baseball team I have ever seen. The only major league affiliation Mr. Johnston could acquire was with Charley Finley and Kansas City. Charley didn't have much in his minor leagues then, or else he sent the bottom of the baseball barrel to play in Dallas. However, Finley moved to Oakland in 1967 and there began a baseball dynasty.

I can drop this bit of personal pride in here because the basis of my work was play-by-play. I was preparing to leave KRLD late one afternoon and go to Burnett Field for my public address job, located just across the Trinity River from downtown Dallas, when we had an alarm that the new county courthouse just barely under construction was on fire. All the reporters had finished their shifts and everyone else was preparing the six p.m. news block, so Eddie Barker asked me to take a mobile unit with the two-way radio and call in reports from the fire. I called the ballpark and suggested I might be late.

The new courthouse was under construction at Houston and Commerce, just a stone's throw across the river to the baseball park. The steel girders were up on the building and they had placed the wooden frames around the steel to fill in with concrete. Somehow, those wooden frames ignited, and with a fairly stiff south wind, which blew most of the time, the fire was racing all around the structure.

Firemen and police were everywhere. One of the police was chewing out another TV crew for driving over the fire department hoses lying all over the area. I took a look at the fire, and it came back to me that what I was watching was the same scenario that I watched in the movie cartoons when I was a kid. Those cartoons would have the fire take on a human appearance and run or jump to the narration.

My broadcasts from the site were play-by-play. "The fire is now on the third floor, racing up the wooden pilings to the fourth floor. Further down on the fourth floor, the firemen are chasing the fire that now has found another piling and is tearing up to the fifth floor. About the time the firemen seemed to have the fire stopped, it breaks free and races for more territory." Something like that. On several live reports to the station I was using the fire as the offense and the firemen as the defense. It was accurate and descriptive.

I am proud to say I received the Outstanding Reporting Award for that month and a $50 bonus. I also made it to the ball game that evening.

I had been at KRLD for eleven years. Thanks to the opportunities afforded me, I had become a recognizable member of the sports broadcasting community. I had been fortunate that so many athletic innovations were developing and I had been in the right place at the right time. But, there were some strained relationships. I was the American Federation of Television and Radio Artists union representative at the station. That is never an easy task and I still support that union totally. It is one of the best in the country.

So about three weeks before Christmas of 1964, I became angry about something at KRLD (although I can't remember what) and gave my two-weeks notice in writing. That's why my family reminds me of my hair-brained decision now and again: I did this right before Christmas.

As I stumbled into 1965, I found work at KLIF broadcasting the evening news, tried my hand at the advertising business with Paul Berry (I am not a good salesman!), and then my guardian angels called. Joe Macko and Dick Butler called to ask me to broadcast the new Dallas–Fort Worth Spurs baseball team that would play at a new stadium being built in Arlington, halfway between Dallas and Fort Worth, for the summer of 1965! Joe was a former Texas League star player and Dick had been the president of the Texas League. They were both good friends. And my former partner with the Dallas Texans, Charlie Jones, would be my partner with the Dallas–Fort Worth Spurs on WFAA-Radio. I cover the details of all this in chapter 2.

You see, you do one thing and, like mushrooms, several other things pop up. I am back in baseball in 1965. I met with my good friend at North Texas, Dr. Reg Holland, after a ball game. He demanded that I come up to North Texas and attain my master's degree in one year and then teach in the radio/television department. I would also teach while working on the master's and receive a small pittance, but I had to finish the master's by the end of the summer of 1966. I had taught some radio courses at a private broadcasting school in Dallas, at Elkins Institute, a few times, so this sounded like a nice career change. I agreed.

I would enroll at North Texas in the fall, but baseball season starts in April—and this mysterious guardian angel in my life went bonkers. Jay Randolph, the broadcaster for the Dallas Cowboys, gave me a call. Jay said they were looking for a person to handle the color analysis for the Cowboys. He had heard my work with North Texas and wondered if I would consider taking the job. Why not? So I entered the multiple job category again—baseball, North Texas football, studying for a master's degree, and working with the Cowboys!

Jay Randolph was and is one of the finest gentlemen in this business. He came by his gregarious nature from his father, the former senator from West Virginia. Working with Jay was as pleasant an experience as anyone could hope for. I spotted and kept stats; he did the play-by-play. He is a superb announcer.

Since 1960, the Cowboys had not had a winning season. Under Coach Tom Landry, they had won five games twice. But 1965 was to be the turning point. With Don Meredith at quarterback and Don Perkins and Dan Reeves at running back, the offense was ignited by the fastest human alive, Bob Hayes at wide receiver. Hayes joined the steady veteran Frank Clarke for a passing offense not before seen in the NFL. Hayes scored thirteen touchdowns on just forty-six pass receptions. Danny Villanueva anchored the punting and field goal duties and the defense was still under construction, led by Bob Lilly, George Andrie, Lee Roy Jordan, Mel Renfro, and Jethro Pugh.

The Cowboys opened at home with victories over the New York Giants and the hated Washington Redskins. Then they played to their past years' form, losing five straight (four on the road) before winning a couple more games at home, one which remains a classic—the Cotton Bowl with the Cleveland Browns, the NFL's elite team with a 7 and 2 record and the fabulous running back Jim Brown. Brown held every rushing record that one person could amass at that time, and it was his final year in the league. A record Cowboys crowd of 76,251 filled the Cotton Bowl. The Browns won 24 to 17 in a game where Meredith passed for 200 yards and 2 touchdowns but had 3 costly interceptions. Jim Brown rushed for 99 yards and ran through seven would-be tacklers to score a touchdown.

Washington hosted the Cowboys the following week and the Redskins won by only 3 points. Things were changing.

It came down to the final three games: in Philadelphia, at home with St. Louis, and then New York for the final game. The record was 4 and 7. The first Cowboys road win of the year happened against the Eagles as Dallas eked by on a nail-biter 21 to 19. Now the record was 5 and 7. Dallas came home to put a 27-to-13 whipping on the St. Louis Cardinals; the record was 6 and 7 with the Giants' road game left.

The Cowboys mastered New York 38 to 20, and for the first time since their winless inception in 1960, the Cowboys had a .500 season: 7 wins and 7 losses. Move over NFL—the Cowboys who would later be called "America's Team" were poised to start their rampage in the league.

The flight back from New York was a wild and raucous occasion on the venerable Braniff Airlines charter. Beer was served to the players, but somehow there seemed to be an added supply of other alcoholic beverages. Nobody slept; nearly everybody played, yelled, laughed, and stormed around inside the plane. The stewardesses (they were called that then) were trying to avoid physical contact!

Approaching Dallas, the pilot called back that the players should be prepared—there was an estimated ten thousand fans at Love Field waiting for the plane. After landing and taxiing to a rather secluded spot from the terminal, the front and rear doors to the old plane were opened. I sat way in the back with Jay and we headed for the rear exit under the tail. I was squeezed in between a couple of huge players and, as we hit the ground, the fans tore down the chain link fence separating them from the plane. Thousands of fans stopped everybody coming off the plane in their tracks. There was a wild, screaming roar—and the Cowboys appreciated the reception, but at the same time, tried to escape the danger of this enormous, loving crowd.

It had been a wonderful year with Jay. He knew every major city in the league from his senator-father's travels and we visited the best and most memorable places. While in Washington, we stayed at his parents' home, where I had the pleasure of meeting the senator and Mrs. Randolph. During that weekend, we hit a few nightspots and ended up in Arlington Cemetery shedding tears standing at the graveside eternal flame of the slain President Kennedy.

That year, Jay and I experienced a sad spectacle at St. Louis. We finished our broadcast and prepared to leave our booth down in the seating area of old Sportsman Park or Busch Stadium, when we noticed a lady and two children with security personnel above us. The husband/father of this family had suffered a fatal heart attack and was still lying in the seats. Today, the emergency equipment and personnel are well trained and act quickly in such cases. That was not the case in 1965.

On a lighter note, the day before when the Cowboys came out to practice, the equipment manager had forgotten to bring the footballs, so the players ran the drills without touching a ball. The Cowboys lost the next day by a touchdown.

One of the least fun things to do then was attend the Playoff Bowl for teams that finished in second place in the two conferences. Early on, though, the Playoff Bowl drew big crowds and cash for the NFL. For the 1966 game, Dallas tied with New York with 7 and 7 records, but the Cowboys qualified since they had beaten the Giants twice.

Baltimore finished tied with the Green Bay Packers in the Western Division at 10 and 3 and then lost 13 to 10 in a playoff. Baltimore qualified for the Playoff Bowl, while Green Bay went on to defeat Cleveland in the World Championship game.

There was but one seat for a broadcaster on the Cowboys' charter to Miami for the Playoff Bowl, so Jay was the one to go. They went down a couple days ahead. The next afternoon, Jay called to tell me he had arranged a seat for me on a private charter that a group of fans had ordered. They were leaving late that afternoon. It was free and I could stay in his room. I tossed a few things in a bag, grabbed my working gear—binoculars, legal pad, notes, and pens—and took the flight. The next morning, the day before the game, Jay and I worked on game preparation and at noon went to a reception by a corporate sponsor. We had to catch a Miami city bus and it cost me a quarter to ride. A whole quarter.

There was a fabulous layout of every kind of food imaginable. I lived by the cold shrimp area. These events always attract the beautiful people. There are execs of various sponsors and lovely young ladies who could pass for high-dollar models. For a married guy with four children, it was a sight to behold. We spent the afternoon eating, drinking pleasant drinks, and visiting with anybody and everybody. Jay seemed to know just about everyone in the room, so it was an education for me on public relations, schmoozing, and remembering the "right" people.

Late in the afternoon, we made contact with a group of Dallas Cowboys fans right out of a Texas novel. They wore cowboy boots and hats and were big fans of the broadcast. They heaped praises right and left and invited us out to have the biggest steaks in town that night. They dropped us off at our hotel and picked us up later. We were treated to a grand evening.

All in all, on my trip to Miami, I had taken a charter plane for free, stayed with Jay at the hotel for free, had the finest cuisine and company for free, worked the football game the next day (the Cowboys lost 35 to 3 to Baltimore), and spent a quarter for a bus ride—that was it, one quarter. Plus, I got a small paycheck for my broadcast duties. You can't beat that.

I have mentioned that Jay was a profoundly professional broadcaster. He was always under control, recognized the players instantly, and followed the play with beautiful fluidity. I determined that my part was to fill in the blanks that Jay, or most every play-by-play person, could not call during the course of a play. I backed up his runs and passes with the identity of the players throwing key blocks or, if a play failed, the defensive player who interrupted the flow and how he did it. I have little patience with ego-driven color/analysts who can "coach" a game from a broadcast booth several hundred feet from the field complaining about decisions, player's efforts, and a myriad other things with an "I would do it this way" attitude. Paying attention to the offensive blockers and the defensive players completed the picture we were painting for the radio audience, and all the players appreciated having their efforts acknowledged. To me, the color portion of a broadcast is finding little known facts, stories, and sidelights of the players and the team and dropping them in during the broadcast. Many radio broadcasters today are calling a television play-by-play that paints no picture for the radio listener—they don't set up the offensive players before the ball is snapped, don't mention the defensive alignment, spend most of the time talking to their fellow broadcaster, or talk about nothing in particular after a play.

Following the 1965 season, Jay Randolph was hired by KMOX-Radio in St. Louis, one of the most respected broadcasting stations in the country. KMOX carried the St. Louis Cardinals, announced by Harry Caray and Jack Buck. They carried every major sports event in St. Louis and had some of the most prominent broadcasters in the day-to-day operation of the station.

Naturally, I threw my hat into the Cowboys ring as the successor to my partner, but I also understood that this was not the usual process, color announcer to play-by-play. Well-known broadcasters who were between jobs or dissatisfied with their current assignment sent in their resumes. Highly qualified announcers with other professional or college teams applied. Today, a Major League franchise can expect hundreds of tapes flooding their offices when a broadcasting change is made.

I found out I was being considered for the position—even pro teams have leaks—but I also knew they were interested in a broadcaster I knew who had professional and college experience. I mentioned to the Cowboys' source that I also had those attributes.

As I mentioned earlier, it seems that jobs come in bunches. I was anxiously waiting for the notice whether I have been selected or not for the Cowboys when I received a call from a person at CBS-Television asking if I would be interested in hosting a scoreboard show. I said I certainly would, and he advised me he would get back to me. I suppose a couple of my friends with CBS-Radio had been involved, but someone had to have seen me on television to determine I was acceptable.

A day or two later, the Cowboys called and offered me the play-by-play position. I was elated. Now I had a college game and a professional football game again each week, plus the Minor League Baseball Spurs during the summer. Then CBS called back and said they would like for me to take the job. Here, truthfully (and it would happen again) I blew my chance for a network position. For one thing, I didn't even think fast enough to ask if I could do the job while also broadcasting the Cowboys (and there was North Texas) or inquire about the details of the position. I just said I couldn't take it because

I was to broadcast the Dallas Cowboys. The guy was incredulous. "You are turning down a network television position?"—and he said it with a good deal of anger. I told him I wanted to focus on radio play-by-play and was sorry I felt I could not do the other. One factor in my decision was that I would be giving up all my work in the Dallas area to sit in a studio, read, and highlight football scores. Frankly, I didn't like television that much. Later, I thought I could have at least carried on some kind of dialogue that would not abruptly preclude me from *ever* being considered for even a spotter on CBS—but, of course, hindsight is flawless.

My duties with the Cowboys were varied. I handled the play-by-play, was available for public relation appearances, and emceed the weekly Cowboys luncheon for the high-rolling fans. All that and in my first year as the Dallas Cowboys radio voice, I was paid $75 per game. This wasn't a bad rate at the time. Kind of makes your head spin! To be fair, I received a small raise each year I worked with them.

In Los Angeles in 1966, we had an eight p.m. preseason game kick-off. After the game, I was to run by the CBS television station and pick up the two-inch wide videotapes of the game (contained in large, awkward, and heavy tape cans) to bring back to Dallas for viewing on Sunday. Those cans probably weighed twenty pounds apiece. I had a rental car, left the coliseum after the game, raced over to pick up the tapes, and realized that my late flight and I were going to be hard-pressed to meet. As I drove to the terminal at LAX, I was running down to about five minutes before the plane left. With no time to put the car in a lot, just pulled up in front of the terminal, grabbed the cans and my briefcase, and, as I ran by the ticket counter, tossed them the keys and yelled to them to turn in the car—that I had to catch the plane to Dallas or die trying. There is, or was, an interminably long concourse to the steps leading up the boarding area. I ran with those two videotape cans tearing up the steps and, as I approached the gate, the attendant waved me on. I tore through the door to the jetway, they shut the door, and I stumbled into the plane. The guy at the counter had called up to say some fool with two big cans was running for the plane. They held it and, by the time we reached Dallas, I was breathing normally again.

The next day on Channel 4, with the game play-by-play sheets in hand, I followed the tape and rebroadcast the game, this time in my "television style" play-by-play, not revealing that I knew the outcome. Fun stuff.

Heading into the summer of 1966, I had a few things on my professional plate. I was writing my thesis for the master's degree in communication at North Texas. It would be a how-to thesis on broadcasting sports. It had to be finished and approved along with my year's grades before the start of the fall semester of 1966 so I could begin teaching.

Of course, it is wonderful to have all these broadcasting responsibilities and expectations, but there are severe problems as well. There were five preseason Cowboys games during the summer while the Spurs were playing baseball at Turnpike Stadium—and both announcers were tied up with professional football, Charlie Jones with the television network and I with the Cowboys. That meant that one or both of us would miss some baseball games. Prior to the first preseason Cowboys game, it was necessary for me to attend the training camp in Thousand Oaks, California, for several days. That left Charlie with the Spurs. No one likes their business or professional sport to be considered second best, and I know that Joe Macko and Dick Butler were a bit irritated that we had to call in some backup to fill the Spurs games while we were gone. But it was a plus for them that their two announcers were "important" major league announcers. However, this happened every year that I was with the Spurs and Cowboys through 1971, so we all became accustomed to it. A former Southwest Conference and baseball broadcaster, Eddie Hill of WRR-Radio in Dallas, filled in for us. That didn't bring into the equation the North Texas football team, but they were understanding and also gained some pleasure in having the Cowboys' announcer on their broadcast. I missed few Eagles games, but had an excellent young backup announcer who worked for the Denton radio station KDNT. Ted Davis was mature for his age—he was in high school and I thought he was in college. He also became a major league announcer.

Let me give you a little insight into what can happen when you are juggling a number of professional balls in the air. I would write my thesis when I came in from the nightly Spurs broadcast and again in the morning, prepare for the Spurs broadcast, and repeat the process each day until I was mentally exhausted. As the time came, in July I had to prepare for the Cowboys' first game.

I had completed my first draft of my thesis on how to broadcast sports, left it with Dr. Ted Colson, my advisor at North Texas, and flew out to California to Cowboys camp. After I had been there a couple of days, Ted called to inform me that the first chapter was the most poorly written paper he had ever read. I guess I was still writing as a radio reporter rather than an academic, which I knew nothing about. That bit of news certainly jolted my mind while I broadcast the San Francisco 49ers game at Kezar Stadium in the beautiful city by the bay.

Until the noted Dallas sports columnist Blackie Sherrod joined me the next year, I did not have a regular color/analyst at home and certainly not on the road. Former Cowboys player Jerry Tubbs worked a few games with me at home before he rejoined the team as an assistant coach. My friend and KRLD reporter Jim Underwood also handled a few games. On the road, we had contacts with local broadcasters and called in various ones in each city to sit in with me. KLIF was our local broadcast outlet and had no network affiliation, so we could pick and choose guys with good reputations with network stations on road games.

At times, the most unnerving situation involved a technical engineer who was to provide the necessary broadcast equipment for the road games. Like announcers, there were good ones—and then there were others. I had the responsibility of the pregame show, which was just thirty minutes then (where now it runs an hour or two). The pregame included an interview with Coach Landry and a player, which I recorded prior to the game on a cassette recorder. Once I handed the tape player to the engineer on the road and explained that it included the pregame interviews, he asked me how the thing worked! I did the engineering of the tape machine from then on.

The Cowboys won every preseason game in 1966, including a 21-to-3 victory over Green Bay before 75,504 fans at the Cotton Bowl. I was sure I had made the right decision in turning down CBS-Television. I finished my thesis and obtained my master's degree at now North Texas State University. My father and mother were on hand to witness this marvel in our family. My father had finished only the seventh grade and my mother had attended college, so they were quite elated. As far as I know, I was the only member of my small extended family to attain an advanced degree.

One of the great early-day sportscasters, Red Barber, wrote several books after his retirement and before his death. I use two chapters on how to broadcast from his book *The Broadcasters* for my sportscasting class at the University of North Texas. Red said there are six important areas to remember: preparation, evaluation, concentration, curiosity, impartiality, and imperturbability. Before Red's book, with the experience I had accumulated, I was aware of the need to prepare, and probably was becoming somewhat expert in the other five key words.

In the fall of 1966, I began a strict weekly practice of preparation that I followed throughout my career. After a Cowboys game on Sunday, I dropped by KLIF-Radio on Monday on my way to my teaching duties. Since the game was on reel-to-reel tape, I sat in a booth, listened to the game, and made notes on a legal pad of the areas I needed to improve, such as player recognition and setting the offense before the play (running backs Perkins and Reeves in the various formations, etc.). I carefully followed the play from the quarterback to running back, watched its direction left or right, and examined the yard lines for progress—or the pass to a receiver, whether it is caught or incomplete, and who caught it and where. The *where* had to be the team yard line, not just a yard line. Then the tackler: review the play (evaluate), be curious about its success or failure, and start over. I could fill up several pages of notes by listening to my broadcast recording each week.

Next, I would drop by the Cowboys' office to pick up the newest information on next week's opponent, noting any changes in the lineup, injuries, and new players—whatever affected the team. I would go home and start correcting the Cowboys' spotting board with any depth changes in the line, backfield, or defense. Also, I would take white label paper and cover the statistics beside the various players from the week before. My great niece, Sarah Elizabeth Lowry, watched me covering the previous games stats on a spotting board. Looking at me seriously, she asked, "Uncle Bill, are you covering up your mistakes?" Sarah and I were great debating pals. She always had the last and best word.

Tuesday was the Cowboys luncheon in Dallas, which I emceed. I would make a hurried trip from Denton to Dallas, do the luncheon, stop by the Cowboys' office, and pick up the next opponent's volumes of player and team information and return to my teaching obligations in Denton. Tuesday night I would prepare the opponent's spotting board. This would take several hours after dinner while spending some time with our four kids.

Wednesday, I dropped by the Cowboys' office to watch any film available of next week's opponent accompanied by the new spotting board to practice recognition, discussing news that some of the assistant coaches would offer on the opponent. I also read every word in the opponent's media guide and other biographical information in newspapers and sport magazines for colorful, important personal information about the players, the organization, and whatever historical importance the upcoming game offered, making notes of these facts on the spotting board.

On Thursday, I would begin the spotting board and team information for the college game that week, continuing the process on Friday, taking time out to attend the Richardson High School football game to watch my sons, David and Evan, perform in the band at halftime. They took after their father and were not football types. Saturday was college day. If the Cowboys were out of town, I had to find a flight I could take after the North Texas game, whether at home or on the road. Sometimes, there were middle-of-the-night adventures on those red-eye flights, but having the Cowboys at home on Sunday made the end of the week a snap. Interestingly, there were few real travel problems over the seven years I broadcast the Cowboys. On those occasions when there was no way to broadcast North Texas and make the Cowboys games, Ted Davis covered for me.

If I traveled with the Cowboys on Saturday, we would usually take a tour of the city we visited, then have dinner and socialize afterward. I had an ironclad resolution: I checked out of the Saturday-night partying (and permitted myself only one drink) and went to bed at midnight. Up at eight a.m., I had breakfast in my room and studied the two teams prior to catching the first team bus at least two hours before the game.

Plunging out of an exciting Spurs baseball season into finding my teaching legs at North Texas while broadcasting the Eagles games and establishing myself with the Cowboys was a huge assignment in the fall of 1966. But a major development brought the NFL and AFL into a merger in 1966. Cowboys General Manager Tex Schramm and the

AFL's Lamar Hunt concluded two months of negotiation, agreeing to a merger of the two leagues on June 8. They agreed to operate a common draft and to have a championship game between the two league champions. Later, this would become the Super Bowl, named by the AFL founder Lamar Hunt. Thus ended the bitter financial struggle between the two leagues, although the rivalry continued as they met in the championship games each year. The rivalry between the two leagues prior to their merger involved the national media as well as within the cities with two franchises. CBS-Television carried the NFL games and failed to give AFL game scores on its broadcasts. Other print publications such as *Sports Illustrated* published color photos of NFL action while giving the AFL black and white prints. Putting the AFL in a less-than-acceptable light continued even after 1966, but grudgingly became acceptable after the New York Jets defeated the Baltimore Colts in the famous Joe Namath quarterbacked game. Tex Schramm was elevated from general manager to president of the Cowboys and began a remarkable tenure building the Cowboys into a nationally admired football team. There is still strong AFC–NFC rivalry today.

The saga of the two leagues vying for important college players culminated in the final decision on Oklahoma tackle Ralph Neely whose signing with both Dallas and Houston had been in court since 1965. It was resolved out of court. Neely stayed with Dallas and Houston received the Cowboys first-, second-, and two fifth-place picks in the 1967 draft. Tom Landry signed a ten-year contract in 1964, so everything was in place for the Cowboys' surge to fame and fortune.

The on-the-field performance of the team also brought about a surge in television and radio station acceptance. CBS-Television had twenty-eight affiliates carrying Cowboys games in 1966; Jack Buck and former Cowboys quarterback Eddie LeBaron were the broadcasters, while seventy Texas radio stations carried the broadcast. Yours truly was listed as the play-by-play announcer.

The Cowboys followed up their best season in 1965 with their first crown jewel in 1966. The Cowboys went 10-3-l, led by Meredith, Reeves, and Hayes offensively and the burgeoning "Doomsday Defense" dominating NFL offenses. The Cowboys–Washington Redskins rivalry was as intense as football could be without fatalities. This dated back to an early attempt by some Cowboys financial founders to allow several hundred chickens loose on the field in Washington. That was foiled, but there were always moments that dramatized the effort to humiliate the other.

In 1966, the teams split, Dallas winning in Washington, the Redskins at the Cotton Bowl. The D.C. win was 31 to 30, highlighted—no, that's not a strong enough word—*emblazoned* in sheer drama by Meredith and Hayes. The Cowboys were leading 14 to 6 in the first half when they were pinned back on their own five-yard line. Don Perkins and Danny Reeves lined up behind Meredith; Pete Gent and Hayes were the wide receivers. Meredith dropped back, faked to one of the running backs, and launched a pass downfield to the streaking Bob Hayes, who caught it in full gallop, easily running untouched for the touchdown ahead of the rampaging defensive tribe: 95 yards on a first down pass! A Cowboys record and a "take that, Redskins!" I probably still have that call on tape somewhere, with my optimum voice raised a few decibels.

The Cowboys' fan base had been expanding from an average of just over 38,000 in 1964 to over 67,000 during the 1966 season. The Cleveland Browns appearance at the Cotton Bowl brought out over 80,000 delirious Blue and White supporters who celebrated a 26 to 14 Cowboys victory. Impressive NFL league statistical honors went to Meredith, Reeves, Perkins, Hayes, and solid kicker Danny Villanueva. The offense had arrived. Mel Renfro made the list with his kickoff and punt returns.

That ten-win season also gave Dallas its first Eastern Conference championship and began a frustrating series of NFL championship games with the Green Bay Packers. Before 75,000 fans at the Cotton Bowl, Dallas lost 34 to 27 to the Packers and the championship. Quarterback Bart Starr threw for over 300 yards, with four touchdowns and no interceptions. Meredith threw for just one touchdown to Frank Clarke late in the game. Dallas trailed early 14 to 0 and fought back to the final score. With just one minute remaining, Dallas had a fourth down and goal from the Packers' two. Meredith was chased by the Packers' Dave Robinson and, spying Bob Hayes in the end zone, fired a pass that was picked off by Tom Brown in the zone. That interception rested in the craw of the fans; nearly everyone thought Meredith could have run in the touchdown that would have won the game. But they were hailed by columnist Arthur Haley: "If ever a team attained tremendous stature in defeat, it was Dallas."

Pete Gent, a 6' 4" former Michigan State basketball player who had the record of second leading scorer in that school's history, joined the Cowboys in 1965. He caught 16 passes as a wide receiver, including a touchdown against the Cleveland Browns, but improved to 27 receptions in 1966. Pete and I became close friends and television "stars" in 1967, which did little good for my association with some Dallas coaches and the administration.

Earlier, I mentioned one of my duties as the play-by-play announcer also entailed being the host for the weekly Cowboys fans' luncheon. This Cowboy Club started way back in 1961 as a kind of buddy-buddy affair that few attended, but let me quote from a column that *Dallas Morning News* sports columnist Sam Blair wrote in September 1967:

> That was 1961, when the Cowboy Club was organized with a flourish [held in a cloakroom]. A large number of prestige members were signed . . . John Wayne, Dean Martin, Mickey Mantle. . . . They shared a common bond with the fans. They didn't come to the luncheons either. Nearly any autumn Tuesday [in 1967], you'll find 400 or more fans flocking to one of the [Hotel] Sheraton's largest halls to hear Landy and key players relive last Sunday's adventure. It may be the most popular affair of this type in pro football.

Sam also threw my name in and some of the players we interviewed. He closed with this story: "And to leave them laughing, they closed the player interviews with last Sunday's clutch-catching casualty, Pete Gent." Pete had leaped for a pass at the goal line and was nearly torn in half by a defender. Pete spent a day in the hospital. Blair continued:

> Mercer noted, "You look kind of peaked, as my mother would say."
> "Well, they wouldn't feed me in the hospital," Gent said, "so I came over here to get something to eat."
> "Actually, I gave birth to a 12-pound baby girl last night."
> "Pete, you're described in the Cowboy press book as the team's morale guy," Mercer said.
> "Oh, I thought that was moral," Gent shrugged.
> "And if there is one to this column, it's that you may hear anything at

a Cowboy Club luncheon these days. That old cloakroom was cozier but not nearly so entertaining."

I had nice support from the writers of both the *Dallas News* and *Dallas Times Herald*. The *Times Herald*'s late Steve Perkins mentioned in a column later in 1967: "Bill Mercer stands up throughout the contest to give you the play-by-play of Cowboys games on KLIF. Can't see over the lip of some press boxes, also the esophagus is more baritone when erect." He was correct on both counts!

This is a good place to connect to the famous (or, in the opinion of some corporate folks, infamous) Pete Gent TV show. I think Pete realized I was something of rebel (although sometimes unsuccessfully), and we were great friends. Whenever he would be in the hospital, I would visit. He was always going all out when he played to secure a starting job with the Cowboys, and physically paid for it.

Pete, and every other receiver, was overshadowed by the World's Fastest Human, Bob Hayes. Gent had battled Buddy Dial for the flanker spot in 1966, and in 1967, when Dial went down in training camp, it looked like Gent was in—but Lance Rentzel swept past him for the starting spot. He played sporadically in 1967. In a Giants game, he caught four passes and a touchdown, but was put out of action with a linebacker knee to the back. He rested it off for a couple of weeks.

In the next-to-last game of the season, Bob Hayes was rested because of a pulled muscle, so Gent was to start in his place against Philadelphia. The headlines read: "World's Fastest Human replaced by World's Slowest Human!" At a news conference, Coach Landry laughed and said Gent "actually wasn't the world's slowest." So Pete started, along with Rentzel, and caught four passes in the game.

The television program was arranged with an old friend at KRLD-TV, Nevin Lyerly. All I really had to do was open and close the five-minute program, which ran at ten thirty each evening after the news block. We tried to tape most of the programs. Usually, the Monday show was live due to the Sunday football game, and then we taped the nightly shows for the remainder of the week.

Craig Morton, who had joined the Cowboys as the backup quarterback in 1965, Meredith, and Gent were close friends. Gent and Morton, both bachelors, roomed together and owned a big handsome English sheepdog who would stray away from their house and remain lost for a week. On one show, Craig and Pete extolled the virtues of their dog and had a poster made asking the dog to return home. Thanks to the show, the dog was found. He came down to the program and sat between Pete and me while we talked about whatever. As Pete signed off, the dog kissed both of us, and it was a wonderful crowd pleaser. Much of Pete's time was spent stressing how little he was allowed to play, while drawing formations on a blackboard showing all the players on the field. Pete was on the bench.

In one of his columns in the *Times Herald*, Perkins pointed out: "The other night on Gent's KRLD-TV vignette show he demonstrated the pro's uniform and explained a pair of loose-fitting pants: 'I usually fill mine with tapioca.'" One week, Meredith was invited down. We recorded three programs for three different nights with Meredith sitting between Pete and me. He was completely ignored all three nights until the final show, on Friday, when Pete turned and said, "Thanks for being on the show, Don." Meredith replied with a quiet, "You're welcome."

When Pete was named to start that Eagles game late in the season, he mentioned on the Friday program before the game, "When Mercer found out I was going to start this week, he went searching through the game movies and put together a sort of highlight film of my best plays—it lasted eight and a half seconds."

One segment of the show each week was the player look-alike contest. One week, it was LeRoy Jordan, another Bob Hayes, and so on, for whatever failed reason Pete decided on. And every week, the winner was Benny Molina, the KRLD-TV studio floor manager who was in charge of giving cues, handling sets, and doing every darned thing imaginable. He was (and is) about 5' 6" and rather plump. If the player look-alike was to be 6' 7" George Andrie, here was Benny coming on the set dressed in a Cowboys uniform and helmet. When Pete or I would ask him questions, Benny would answer in a sort of Mexican accent, "Chesss."

Pete had an acerbic humor and was not loath to make jokes about his coaches, the National Football League, and whatever else crossed his mind. He even took shots at Coach Landry, particularly question-ing why he didn't give Pete more playing time.

The Cowboys organization was, to use a political term, conserva-tive. They were very protective of the image of a well-organized, per-fectly run team and front office. Tex Schramm was not shy about calling and chewing out a print columnist or radio or TV reporter if a story was incorrect or considered a slur against the Cowboys. So here is Pete Gent, a part of the "franchise of perfection," making re-marks, jokes, and slurs about the NFL and, occasionally, his team. By my announcer status on the program, without ever uttering a word editorially, I caught some of the flack.

We were in San Francisco having our usual sumptuous dinner and party with the coaches and media the night before the game. Ermal Allen was the offensive line coach, and football literally was his life. He was a University of Kentucky quarterback and played with the army football teams during the war and the Cleveland Browns in 1946. He coached under Bear Bryant and Blanton Collier at Kentucky before joining the Cowboys in 1961. Ermal was a fun guy. I liked talking with him—discussing football, offensive lines, whatever—except he didn't think much of the Pete Gent show. In fact, I can't repeat the words he used to describe it, and that night in San Fran-cisco he shouted at me in the restaurant that I should be ashamed to be on the show. The show and I were insulting the Cowboys and pro football, and maybe he or someone should whip my and Pete's ass. Ermal always enjoyed his libations, many times way beyond what was consumed by the rest of us, and that evening he was swaying a bit as he stood. The other coaches sat him back down. In fact, I imag-ine the other coaches agreed with his assessment of the program.

About the time Pete was to start against Philadelphia, the question of long hair on athletes became a major controversy. The hippie movement was rampant around the country, particularly on the coasts, and since Pete had that seething antiestablishment core, he began to let his hair grow—emotionally simmering while warming the bench. In a Steve Perkins column, the story went that someone had asked Pete if he was going to let his hair grow until he became a starter again. "If I'd done that," Pete said, "I would now have 4,200 pounds of hair."

With his various injuries, I once visited him in the hospital, and he told me I was the only person who had come to see what was left of him. He caught only nine passes in 1967. He came back in 1968, played in ten games, and caught sixteen passes. He twice tried carrying the ball on end-around plays and had a total of minus five yards. Then he was gone. Over his career, he scored four touchdowns. One former NFL publicist told me if he had one kind word for Pete Gent, it was "tough."

Pete was a lightning rod for NFL purists who didn't see the humor in many situations. Pete did. In a game against Pittsburgh, he caught a pass on the dead run and beat the defensive back Paul Martha down the sideline. He was asked about his apparent increased speed: "If I can't outrun someone named Martha, I shouldn't be in this league."

Pete retired, probably on a medical discharge, and became nationally famous when he wrote *North Dallas Forty,* a thinly veiled satirical story of a Cowboys-type franchise. What really upset many NFL corporate types was the revelation of the use of various drugs—uppers and painkillers—that the players used to "play hurt." Though it was disparaged at the time, Pete's story turned out to be too true.

The last time I saw Pete, he stopped me at Love Field. I would not have recognized him with his long hair and hippie glasses and attire. He asked me if I noticed he used my name in the book. One of the character's first name was Mercer. A few years ago, I called Pete at his mother's home in Wisconsin, where he was living and still writing. I have fond memories of Pete Gent.

The announcer who preceded Jay Randolph was Frank Gleiber—the late Frank Gleiber who went from the Cowboys' play-by-play announcer to one of the best CBS sports broadcasters in any sport. Frank had been hired by CBS away from the Cowboys while he was sports director of KRLD-Radio and TV, my old station. When I moved into the Cowboys' radio seat, Frank took a job in Cleveland television for more money while still working for CBS, which left me with the pleasant task of hosting the weekly *Tom Landry Show* on Channel 4. Most people view Landry as the cold sideline general who rarely changed expressions and always wore a hat. Away from the field, the real Landry was humorous, pleasant, and out-going. We traded jokes prior to taping the TV show; he would read the paper and make humorous comments about various subjects. On the show, he was a little stiff, but always generous and never caustic or insulting, like some sports stars. I found an old copy of one of the formats that we used for the director and floor managers. We opened with a discussion of the preceding game, talking about some of the key plays and players, then after a break ran through the highlights of the game with Coach Landry handling the narration. We would then discuss some particular play that might have been a key in the game or one that was unusual. It was basically a discussion of football as it was played each week. We also discussed that week's NFL schedule, but Coach didn't pick winners.

Landy held press conferences every week and quickly built his reputation of answering every question, no matter how ridiculous. It also became apparent that for some questions, he had exactly the same answers, but he never displayed anger, was always gracious, and always displayed his sense of humor—which many times went over the heads of the assembled "ink-stained wretches" of print media and the so-called Golden Throats of radio and TV—as Blackie Sherrod, the sports columnist, called us on radio sports.

Nineteen sixty-seven was most dramatic for the Cowboys, with a classic National Football League Championship game loss and a defining moment for me—and my relationship with the Cowboys organization. Equally important was the hiring of Blackie Sherrod, famed local sports columnist, to work as my color man, at home and on all the road games.

Blackie had a devilish sense of humor and has been, for more than fifty years, one of the best sports reporters/columnists in Texas and the nation. I suppose Blackie would not mind my saying that he also could be the ultimate curmudgeon. We radio/TV folks caught the brunt of Blackie's columns when he took on our portion of the media. Every now and then, but assuredly at the start of the football season, Blackie would write some humorous to scathing column about us Golden Throats. And if the Cowboys thought they could hire Blackie and control his reporting, they were, as the old cliché goes, sadly mistaken.

Blackie did not have a broadcast voice—he was no golden throat. But he had the ability to observe and report quickly, and only when he had something important to say. Our timing together, our relationship together was excellent. I enjoyed having him with me. We handled the preseason games first at San Francisco and Los Angeles. Then there was the first home game with Green Bay on August 28. It usually turns hot in Texas in June and doesn't give us respite until late September. That first game was a scorcher in the Cotton Bowl. Blackie asked about the halftime plan, and I laughingly told him I went out to cool off while he interviewed whoever the Cowboys had arranged for us. Blackie and I worked the half together.

I was very comfortable with my broadcasting in the first full year. There were many things to improve on in terms of my overall performance, I am sure, but it was, to me, a solid start.

The Cowboys tossed me five projects to see if I could go out and hustle them in the broadcast community, in particular. I handled all of them successfully, but the one to put me in strongly with the organization was arranging for a thirty-minute *Tex Schramm Show* on KRLD-Radio. Tex, without question, was the man who ran the business of the Cowboys. He was the image maker. He had the answers just as Coach Landry had the answers for the team. It was surprising to realize that Tex was not on the air in the seventh year of the Cowboys' existence. Tex Schramm was a strong communicator. He didn't pull punches; he didn't shy away from conflict. The show was a great success and ran for many years.

I really felt comfortable handling my various assignments outside of play-by-play, and then Charlie Jones left WFAA-TV as their sports director for a full-time position with NBC-TV, where he stayed for more than thirty years. You never expect to be blindsided by someone taking another job, but it happened. The 1967 season was underway when I was called into assistant general manager Al Ward's office. Al was a pleasant, friendly man who handled whatever Tex tossed his way. Al explained that there was an opening at WFAA for sports director, and the Cowboys wanted me to take the job. My first thought was, how can they just declare that they want me to take this job? But quickly, I realized Tex had a strong relationship with the local media and this job was already arranged.

Now I had spent a great part of my eleven years at KRLD-TV producing sports shows. It's not a disagreeable job, but it is not on a par with play-by-play. As I listened to this sermon from the Cowboys' mount, I went over all the activities I had: Cowboys play-by-play as well as North Texas State University football and Minor League Baseball. I had just completed my first year of teaching at North Texas after a furious session of studying for my master's degree. If I go to WFAA, that's the end of everything but the Cowboys. I had already refused a job from CBS for essentially the same thing, sitting in a TV studio.

Without much thought (you might say, as usual), and with no inquiry into how this might affect my financial status or future professional career (no baseball was the key), I said I appreciated their offer, but I preferred my life as it was currently being run. I also explained what I mentioned earlier, that I had done that sports-in-the-news block thing and wanted no more of it. Ward reiterated that the Cowboys (mostly Tex, I am sure) wanted me to take the job. I knew how Tex valued having the close relationship of the key sports people on television, some on radio, and the top sports columnists at the papers. There were two Dallas papers, *The Morning News* and the *Times Herald*, and they sent their reporters on the charter airplane. The media types and the corporate folks, friends, and wives sat in the front section of the plane, with the players in the rear.

After I told Ward that I no interest in the Channel 8 sports job, he looked at me and said, "If you don't take the job, then we won't help you"—with what, he did not spell out. As you read this, you might be murmuring that now is the time to go see Tex Schramm. I know Nevin Lyerly at Channel 4 would tell me that I should go talk with Tex. Well, I didn't. For one thing, I didn't have much time to do anything except follow my schedule and, for the other, I felt Tex viewed me with some skepticism—probably rightfully so since I was young, carried the Cowboys' radio image on my back, broadcast baseball (which Tex viewed with disdain), and was the president of the local office of the American Federation of Television and Radio Artists union. Tex never showed much enthusiasm for the work I did as emcee of the Cowboys luncheons. This sounds like paranoia, doesn't it?

So that was that, I figured, with WFAA-TV—and it was, except when we all trudged out to take the airline charter on the next road trip Ward, who greeted everyone at the doorway of the plane, greeted me with a cold, hard look. "Bill, you sit in the back of the plane with the players." Ah, I was demoted from the "elite" front section with all the other media and staff. It hit me then that my time with this team was probably in question. They were not only not going to help me; they were going to punish me. I was relegated to the player's section from that day through my last game, the Super Bowl in 1972. But, you know, I came to enjoy being with those guys much more than sitting up front. It was kind of odd that my color man sat in the first-class section, but I had lost my rank.

The efforts of the Cowboys to replace me surfaced every now and then. A good friend and former co-baseball announcer with the Dallas–Fort Worth Spurs, Bill Enis, called me with the revelation that the Cowboys had offered him the job. It was some kind of coannouncer status the first year, and then I would be the color announcer from then on. At any rate, Enis was making his name in Houston and on the network and did not accept the offer. It was generous of him to let me know. Then Bill Enis, age thirty-nine, came home from the TV studio one day, sat down in his easy chair, and died. He left a great family. I was one of the pallbearers. Bill, whose handsome image was and still is on a national brand hair spray, could have been one of the major national sportscasters. He was terrific.

I must say the episode of the WFAA-TV job was never again mentioned and there were no other outward signs of the Cowboys displeasure with me. It seems now that if they had really decided to kick me out, there were plenty of highly qualified announcers who would have gladly taken my place. I attended all the functions at home and on the road, was invited to Tex's home for parties, and became somewhat closer to him, especially on road trips. We would talk about things such as what he thought I, as a union leader (heavy term for "the Dallas local"), would expect the NFL to do in case of a player strike. I explained I had little to do with strikes since Texas was one of those "right-to-work" states (what a misrepresentation of a term!)—but if I were in his position, I would take all the players who would cross the picket line and then invite all the players who had been cut to play. "Scabs," we call them. I can't take credit for what ultimately happened in future labor problems. But enough of my travails riding in the back of the plane.

The Cowboys won three of their first four regular season games in 1967. Emerging from the shadows were young quarterbacks Craig Morton from California and Jerry Rhome from Tulsa. Morton was 6' 4" with a very strong arm. He had also been a pitcher in college, and when some of the Cowboys came out to play an exhibition game with the Texas League Spurs at Turnpike Stadium, Morton was the pitcher. He could face the professional players with confidence and had a very hard fastball. Some of the Cowboys players were a bit shy at the plate, not relishing a collision with that hard white ball.

Rhome was a six-footer who had led Tulsa to great seasons with his running and passing. Jerry was a great competitor, but never quite attained a prominent status with Dallas. While Meredith was undoubtedly the number-one quarterback in '67, Morton threw for nearly a thousand yards and ten touchdowns. With three stellar performers, this gave the Cowboys plenty of injury insurance.

There were two major additions to the '67 team—Lance Rentzel, the wide receiver, and defensive lineman Rayfield Wright. Both became vital cogs in the Cowboys' drive to the future championships.

In 1965 and 1966, the Cowboys first offensive play was always a Meredith handoff to fullback Don Perkins who ran somewhere with the ball, usually up the middle. Prior to a game in 1967 when I was down in the Cotton Bowl dressing room, Don yelled at me to come over to his locker. In a conspiratorial tone of voice, he said, "You know how I always hand off to Perk, on the first offensive play?" Naturally, I knew. Then he said, "I am going to make you famous today. You tell your radio audience that you have a feeling that Meredith is going to change up the routine and not hand the ball to Perkins, but drop back and pass. Then I will do just that and everyone will think you are a football genius!" We chortled over this revelation, our very big secret. I promised I would carry out my part of the plan.

So in the game, which one I cannot recall, as the Cowboys came up for their first offensive play, I broke into this deeply intelligent evaluation of all the times it had been Meredith-to-Perkins, and today I believed, strongly, that there would be a change. Meredith would pass. Sure enough, Don faked to Perkins and dropped back to pass. Well, my cohorts in the booth were all offering congratulations on my sudden coaching knowledge of the game. It came up that maybe someone told me, and finally after a few plays and some on-air harassment, I told the truth.

Speaking of the Cotton Bowl broadcast booth, my Cowboys spotter was SMU swimming coach George McMillan, my statistician was Dr. Reg Holland (my friend in the North Texas radio/TV department, an engineer/producer from KLIF who kept track of needed commercial and station breaks for the big network of stations), Blackie Sherrod was the color commentator, and on alternate game weeks, one of my teenage sons, David or Evan, spotted the opponents. Take a look at the Cowboys' broadcast booth the next time you are at the Irving stadium in a huge crowd. Of course, I think their pregame now is an hour or longer, while ours was thirty minutes. We didn't have live reports from the field before or during the game, and only when Verne Lundquist joined the broadcast from the dressing room after the game. Now there seems to be live reports and voices all over the place.

Over the season, Meredith had missed a couple of games due to injuries, while Morton and Rhome picked up the slack. Over the last five games, the Cowboys won two and lost three, finishing with a 9 and 5 record and, capitalizing on the new four-division alignment, were easily champions of the Capitol Division. One of their finest days occurred when the Cowboys tromped the Cleveland Browns 52 to 14 before seventy thousand fans in Dallas the day before Christmas. Meredith, discarding a mask he had been wearing for a broken nose, threw only twelve times, but completed ten, including touchdowns to Hayes (one of eighty-five yards) and newcomer Craig Baynham. Baynham replaced the injured Dan Reeves in the backfield and scored two of four touchdowns rushing.

This set up the most spectacular game in the history of the franchise, the Ice Bowl with Green Bay. Years later, whenever Dallas played on a wet or cold bitter day and lost, it was a sure sign that the Cowboys were a "fair weather" team—or when they couldn't win wearing the blue jerseys, or was it the white, whichever, these myths do grow.

December 31, 1967—one only has to say "Ice Bowl" and, like most great emotional events, a fan can remember where he or she was at the time. Just as Dallas is an oven in the summer and early fall, one expects Green Bay to be cold in winter. Green Bay knows that better than most, so that year they had installed the latest technology under the playing field that would keep the field, if not warm, at least playable on the worst of the cold days—best-laid plans and all that.

As usual, we traveled to Wisconsin the morning before the game. It was pleasant overcoat weather. When the Cowboys worked out in Green Bay Saturday morning, it was hovering around twenty degrees—cold for Dallas, balmy for the Packers. That afternoon, the Packers' coach Vince Lombardi, along with an executive of the company that had installed the heating system under the playing field, took us on a tour of the stadium and a walk around the perfect field. Even though it was twenty degrees, the field was soft underfoot and ready for a great game on Sunday. I invited the company representative to drop by at halftime and describe the workings of the technological marvel. After dinner, several of us, including Blackie and Frank Luksa of the *Times Herald*, walked around the city. It was comfortably cold when wearing a hat and overcoat.

When the phone rang with the wake-up call Sunday morning, the operator said it is 8:30 and thirty-five degrees below zero! Now that is a message that grabs you and shakes you. I leaped into my clothes, tore downstairs, walked through the revolving doors to the outside of the hotel, and keep right on going back in as that knife-like cold riding on a twenty to thirty mile-an-hour wind penetrated everything in that few seconds! It was damned cold—colder than I had ever felt, even when I spent a winter in Farragut, Idaho, my last few months in the Navy. As we ate breakfast, the discussion centered on survival—and whether the NFL would allow the game to be played in death-defying cold.

Ultimately, we packed our gear and headed for the frozen Arctic that had escaped from the North Pole and landed in Lambeau Field. The bus took us to the field, and then there was the walk from the east side of the field up to the press box on the west side. I was wrapped up with everything but gloves. I had forgotten to bring them, so I carried my valuable broadcast information briefcase in one hand until it began to hurt and then switched while hunkering over against the vicious cold wind. On a windy cold day in Oklahoma in my youth, my mother would say that "the cold wind goes right through you." That was absolutely the truth on that day in Lambeau Field!

Once in the pressbox, all was mayhem. There was no heat, the windows were icing over—and, by the way, that marvelous heating system under the football field? It failed totally and completely and the field was frozen like a parking lot. The gentleman I invited to discuss the device at halftime never showed.

There was coffee in the press box, but it turned cold in a cup in about a minute. Our broadcast booth was large enough for four people to sit or stand in front. But as I was placing my spotting boards in front of the lower part of the windows and checking the various parts of the broadcast, calling KLIF to give them a voice air check and keeping my hands in my coat pockets, the windows began to ice over from the breath of the five people in the booth. Soon it was going to be impossible to see much of the field. The young man who was spotting the Packers for us suggested we needed some windshield de-icer to keep the windows clear. On every other occasion in the league, I opened up the broadcast booth windows, hot or cold weather. But today, the windows would not be opened. They were frozen shut.

So this local Packers spotter volunteered to go over to a convenience store across the parking lot behind us for de-icer. On a normal day, he would probably trot over there and back in fifteen or twenty minutes. About forty-five minutes later, the poor guy came back really hurting, face beet red, ears frozen, and with two big cans of de-icer. We were just about to go on the air as we cleared our windows. We used the entire contents of the two cans during the game. I hope I gave that young man a well-deserved bonus payment.

Unbelievably, the stadium was packed with fans, bundled up in every layer of cold-weather gear they owned. At even thirty-five degrees in Dallas, you have a giant migration away from an outdoor event—but, resolutely, Lambeau was packed. The band members couldn't play because their lips would freeze to the instruments and the officials couldn't use their metal whistles.

There were heaters behind the benches. The players were trying everything imaginable to stay—well, "warm" is not the word—alive and not frozen. Still, many of them suffered from frostbite years after game. Bob Hayes caught all of three passes in that game for sixteen yards as he trotted around with his hands stuffed down in his pants. Lance Rentzel caught a fifty-yard touchdown pass, the only one that day by Dallas.

When the game started, it was twenty-seven degrees below zero. I had broadcast games with snow and ice, rain and sleet, but never had the temperature been so uncomfortably miserable. The only thing to do was use the Red Barber idea of imperturbability and broadcast. Standing in that booth with overcoat, hat, and no gloves, we proceeded. My style is to use binoculars to set up the players as they come up for the offensive play. The binoculars were cold and so were my hands, but at some point you ignore the difficulties and "warm" to the task. Blackie didn't interject often, so I was given the opportunity to really stomp around, wave my arms, try to keep warm, and follow the play. I have listened to the tape a few times. It isn't bad. I didn't sound cold, and on the one Dallas touchdown pass, I was right on top of it. My friend Mike Capps, a former CNN news reporter and now play-by-play voice of the Pacific Coast League Round Rock Express, says it is a fine example of a technically accurate football broadcast. I hope he is right. Only rarely did we mention the cold; we just followed the action and tried to report it to the best of our ability. I don't recall our halftime guests, but they must have been someone in the press box, because no one was coming up there from any other location. I was so disappointed in the outcome of the game and what I imagined my broadcast to be I did not listen to it for several years. I began to receive requests from the network and individual stations asking for excerpts or, in the case of KLIF in 1997, to broadcast the entire game on its thirtieth anniversary.

Green Bay was a smooth machine on any day. Even on this bitterly cold day, the Packers drove eighty-two yards and scored a touchdown on their first possession. Boyd Dowler, who scored two in the game, caught an eight-yard pass from Bart Starr with nearly nine minutes gone in the first quarter. Don Chandler kicked the extra point. Side note here. When I was in Muskogee, Don Chandler and a brother played football with Bacone College, the nation's oldest Indian college. Chandler then played his final two college years at Florida. He was one of the NFL's premier kickers for years. In the second quarter, seemingly unperturbed by the Arctic day, Starr hit Dowler for a forty-three-yard touchdown, and the Packers led 14 to nothing with just over twelve minutes to play in the half.

Dallas offensively was immobilized by the cold, but the great developing Dallas defense started to respond. George Andrie and Willie Townes knocked the ball out of Starr's hands on the Packers' 26 and Andrie picked it up and marched seven yards for the first Dallas touchdown. Danny Villanueva kicked the extra point.

Just before the first half ended, the Cowboys' Phil Clark recovered a Packers' fumbled punt on the Green Bay 17. Dallas couldn't move for even a first down, but Villanueva kicked a twenty-one-yard field goal, and the half ended with the Packers leading by 4.

Dallas missed a chance to add points in the third quarter when they fumbled on the Packers' 22. On the first play of the final quarter, Meredith stepped back and threw a swing pass in the flat to Danny Reeves, the former college quarterback, who then fired a pass to Rentzel, a total play of fifty yards for the go-ahead touchdown for Dallas.

With the Cowboys leading 17 to 14, the Packers had the ball in the fourth with 4:50 remaining on their own thirty-two yard line. Starr then engineered a brilliant twelve-play drive, mostly tossing the ball in the flat to receivers running straight ahead by grasping Dallas defenders. The Packers drove down to the one-yard line of Dallas. After the famous timeout, Starr punched the ball in from the one-yard line for the 21 to 17 victory in the coldest game ever played.

Sitting on the Cowboys' charter in the seat behind Meredith, I listened to him in tears take the blame for the loss. That was not the case. But the fans had begun to blame Meredith for various losses and failed plays, even though the Cowboys had journeyed far under his direction.

The Cowboys continued to run up great regular season records in the following years. In 1968, they were 12 and 2, winning their first six games of the season before losing to the confounding Packers in Dallas. One episode that stands out in my memory of the 1968 season was one of the rare games Dallas played in Chicago against the Bears. There were at least three interesting asides in that 34 to 3 Cowboys win—playing in Wrigley Field, the rabbit, Dick Butkus, and one of the last two years that Brian Piccolo played. Soldier Field, the ancient edifice where the Bears normally played, was about to fall down, so the team moved to Wrigley while it was being repaired.

It is true that baseball fields are not laid out so that one can just squeeze in a football game. There were tarps at various places around the field so people couldn't go on the field during the game. It was another one of those damp cold days and a not very exciting game. The Bears were in the midst of four so-so years, finishing 7 and 7 in '68 and going 1 and 13 in 1969.

We were all interested in Butkus; we had read reams of copy about his wild play, physically hurtling himself around and over the players, every sort of kamikaze-type action that could be reported or made up. Many players figured he was taking one (or more) of those "uppers"—pills that encouraged excess enthusiasm. He lived up to his promotional copy, eyes wild in his head, going like crazy on defense.

Then there was Brian Piccolo, a back-up running back who was a close friend of the famed running back Gail Sayers, felled by a devastating knee injury. Piccolo played in that game, but like the rest of the Bears, didn't accomplish much. The next year, his bout with cancer took him out of the league and Piccolo died June 16, 1970. *Brian's Song* became a bestseller and even hardened athletes cried when the movie came out.

Oh, the rabbit. We were following the game along, dully executed for the most part, when we spied a cottontail rabbit running around the field. The rabbit tried to leave the field, but those tarps I mentioned prevented him from doing so. So little Mr. Brer ran up and down the sideline and out on the field and then scampered back when players came thundering down on him. It was a strange day, broadcasting a football game in storied Wrigley Field with a rabbit the feature attraction.

Dallas finished that season winning the last five regular season games, the Capitol Division again, but lost the Eastern Championship to Cleveland 31 to 20 after soundly beating the Browns earlier in the year. If there was any solace, which few cared about, the Cowboys defeated Minnesota in the Playoff Bowl, 17 to 13 before a few fans in Miami.

After he was drafted number five by the Cowboys in 1966, Walt Garrison, a nationally acclaimed running back from Oklahoma State, began to hit his stride in 1968 with five touchdowns scored on just forty-five carries. In 1969, Walt, a prominent rodeo performer prior to his pro football days, rushed for his personal high of 818 yards— hard won yards! This six foot, two-hundred-pounder was probably the toughest guy in the league at that height and weight. The only other I could think of was Larry Wilson, the free safety in St. Louis.

I recall a game in New York when Walt battered at the line until he had to be carried to the team plane, he was so physically beat up. He was back the next week! Walt had one of those Texas drawls, pure cowboy, and at times his buddy Danny Reeves had an almost unintelligible Georgia drawl. They were a rare, beautiful pair of overachievers who gave everything they had every game. They also loved country-western music, humming and singing those plaintiff songs when not busy crashing around in Cowboys games. So on a preseason game trip to San Francisco, I put the two of them together on the team charter and introduced them as the country-western stars of the Cowboys. I asked if they would sing one of their favorite songs twenty thousand feet over California. Danny told me the name of the song, and with that Georgia soft twang I couldn't understand him, so I asked him again. He said, "Bill, caint youall unerstand English?" It was hilarious. They sang and the team applauded. I still have the tape somewhere. It was a classic, though some of my more stern Cowboys execs asked why I was doing a recording on the airplane.

Garrison finished out his career with the Cowboys and in the last three years—'72 through '74—scored twenty-four touchdowns, rushing and pass receiving! All the time he was with the Cowboys he, as we say in the South, dipped snuff. They call it smokeless tobacco now, I believe. Following his football career, he ran a rodeo office for Copenhagen snuff in Lewisville, Texas, his hometown, and was married to a member of the famed Phillips' ranching family of Texas. He figures prominently on a website, Smokeless.de, most of which is in German.

The Cowboys luncheons were filled to way overflowing with the success on the field. The sixteenth pick of the Cowboys in the 1968 draft was a big, blonde lineman named Larry Cole, who I immediately recognized as a facsimile of the cartoon strip *Joe Palooka*. Larry was such a nice, quiet fellow he took no umbrage at my comparing him to the famous character. There may be an argument here with some media-types over recognizing this Cole-Palooka look-alike (which we used on the Pete Gent Show), but I am sure I saw him first.

As I have mentioned, my association with Pete Gent on his show was not good for my reputation with the Cowboys—but then came the 1968 Democratic National Convention. Let me just set up this scenario by saying that a great number of folks were convinced that the media was not telling the truth about the student riots and the police brutality outside the convention in Chicago. We were taking the bus in some other city, not Chicago, from the hotel to a game site—a bus with coaches, media, and no players. I recall it was Ermal Allen again who was leading a loud discussion about the phony pictures and reports about all the activities outside the convention, when he turned to me and posed a question and statement all in one: "Mercer, it's true, isn't it, that those guys with TV cameras can block out part of the picture they don't want to show and put in other scenes to make the picture they want? Right?" I replied that a cameraman with three different lenses could take long, medium, or tight shots, but they couldn't select the pictures or edit while shooting. In order to change the story, other scenes would have to found and inserted in an editing studio, if it was done at all—I knew this wasn't the case after watching the Chicago Cops and rioters going after it. That wasn't the answer he expected. So then he mentioned the fact that we media people stuck together, made up stuff, and, since I was a union guy, I probably was on the rioters' side. I tried once again to explain the operation of one of those large cameras but, much like today, it was the "liberal" media—or just plain old media—that was cooking the story. Just another day in the life of those riotous 1960s and 1970s.

Our 1968 radio network grew from seventy to a hundred stations, including Louisiana, Oklahoma, Arkansas, and Texas—oh, I don't take *all* the credit for that dramatic increase. A new face appeared in Dallas television sports, Verne Lundquist, who took the Channel 8 job I passed on. Verne came up from Austin and was almost immediately selected to join us on the Cowboys' radio broadcast. He handled some of the pre- and postgame events and halftime. Vern and I became solid partners as the broadcasts progressed. He came on as the color announcer in 1970 after Blackie left and continued through the Super Bowl of 1972.

Let me take the occasion here to describe the various near-disasters and some dandies that we had with our "high-powered" technology back then. As I have mentioned, we were using cassette recorders to record the pregame interviews. With Verne aboard, we then added in a live postgame interview program from the Cowboys' dressing room, win or lose.

Basically, all we had for the booth broadcast was a microphone amplifier with three, maybe four, microphone pots, the poles to attach the outgoing telephone line, and a line to the dressing room. That pretty well filled up our technical capacity.

Fortunately, I didn't have anything to do with ordering the lines as I did with the North Texas college games. When we arrived at the stadium a couple of hours prior to the game, we started checking out as much as possible to be sure, first, we had a broadcast and, second, that the other broadcast possibilities existed. Remember at this time we relied on engineers who were hired in the various cities.

Once in Philadelphia, we completed the broadcast and started checking the line to the dressing room. There was no reply. The sounds of a dressing room were there, but there was no way to communicate with Verne. Finally, the engineer realized that a two-way line had not been put in so we could talk to Verne. He didn't have a clue as to when to talk, and we couldn't cue him. There's one postgame report, dead.

Becoming much smarter, in Washington, D.C., we checked out the line in the dressing room prior to the game. We "tried" to check it out, but the line was nowhere to be found. After dashing around hither and yon, we came up with the plan to use a regular telephone in a coaches' office nearby. Here's the way this postgame thriller would work: after the game, when I was on a break or when Blackie was giving postgame analysis, I would pick up the phone in our booth, call on another line to the coaches' office and tell Verne to stand by. By then, he would have called the station, feeding the network on a separate line, advising them that when I cued the postgame show on the air and by this telephone to the office, Verne would then interview on the other phone to the network. You may have to read that again to get the gist of it—it worked. I cued the interview simultaneously on the air and on the telephone, and Verne dropped that phone in one ear and used the other phone to interview players to the network. Boy, were we pros!

When I walked into my sportscasting class on Monday, they all proceeded to ask why the postgame wasn't on KLIF in Dallas. Why did KLIF just play music for about ten minutes? Then it hit me—KLIF did not take the network feed, but had their own line direct from the phone company bypassing the network, and they couldn't call me during the time we were doing the interviews because I had the phone tied up to the dressing room office waiting to hear from Verne that he had finished the interviews. This is where a nonbroadcasting producer would have been able to have all this information and avoid some of the problem. That's what the current Cowboys' broadcast has among dozens of others sending the signal to KLUV in Dallas.

One more disaster. We were in San Francisco. It was the fabulous 1970 NFC Championship game that Dallas won 17 to 10. Verne stayed in the booth as long as possible watching the game play out, and then he rushed to the dressing room for the gigantic celebration that would be aired on more than one hundred stations. I did all my usual postgame reports of scores, stats, and stuff and awaited a call from the dressing room. We had carefully checked out the two-way line and all before the game (see, we *were* getting smarter and smarter) so we knew Verne would be with us any moment. Then the moments passed. I had several breaks back to the net and then began interviewing people in the press box area vaguely connected to the Cowboys or the game. Still no Verne. After about twenty-five minutes of scintillating comments from anyone who could talk, we decided Verne had met with personal disaster and closed the broadcast. Verne later came limping (figuratively) into the booth, furious about everything. When the players roared into the dressing room, they threw all of their dirty uniforms, towels, and whatever into a corner of the room, exactly where the remote equipment was plugged in. Under this huge pile of laundry was a postgame show that never aired. By the time anyone sorted all this out, we were long gone off the air.

We had some very funny personal experiences roaming about the NFL world in those last three years. Again in San Francisco, we had attended a party and then headed for our hotel a few blocks away. Verne smoked, I didn't. Verne was smoking as we walked along and, for whatever reason I don't recall, had to look for something in his pockets. Whatever it was, he found it and we continued on—I noticed smoke wafting from his suit coat pocket. He had put his cigarette in the pocket when he began the search. He didn't go up in flames, but he certainly had to get his coat repaired.

Speaking of coats. Whenever we went to Cleveland and played in that mammoth Municipal Stadium by the lake, it was wise to dress almost like going to Green Bay. That wind off the lake on a cold day turned bone marrow to ice cubes. Plus, our so-called broadcast booth rested on top of the roof, at the very edge, where we peered down on the action on the field hundreds of yards below. To reach that little aluminum shed, which featured an electric light but no heat, one had to climb miles of steps on the second level to a ladder/stairway onto the roof.

This particular game, I had made my way up to the crow's nest before Verne. It was cold. There was a hard wind blowing off the lake through the open end of the stadium—I even bundled up in my heaviest overcoat, hat, and gloves but was still chilled. Here comes Verne, ready for the pregame with only his suit coat on—no overcoat, no gloves, no hat. I asked him where his warm gear was and he said that he didn't know—he had lost it. So Verne sat next to me the entire game shaking and shivering, and with that going on, I too was miserable.

There were personality idiosyncrasies rampant among the media faithful who had followed the Cowboys. Dear Frank Gleiber, who died while running in a Dallas workout in future years, loved to eat. Frank was always going on a diet and then going off, depending on his appearance on CBS-Television. But this on-and-off diet plan didn't help his health. When we were out for our night-before-game meal, Frank would suggest that if someone didn't want his baked potato, would he mind handing it over?

Then there was the former sports columnist of the *Times Herald*, Steve Perkins, who was at the time of this episode editing the Cowboys' newsletter, a major undertaking as the Cowboys became more successful. It was the first regular season game of the 1971 season at Buffalo, one of the original members of the American Football League. Having been to Buffalo with the Dallas Texans, I was considered an expert on the community. Well, I had crawled to the edge of Niagara Falls one night. As part of the entertainment on this Cowboys trip, they had supplied us with a city bus to drive up and actually see the falls in daylight. We also naturally had spent a good deal of time with refreshments.

We saw the falls and rode back to the city toward our hotel. Steve Perkins had fallen asleep. Steve had this idiosyncrasy of eating and drinking and then, before leaving the restaurant, he would fall asleep. On our bus trip up and back, we probably had a few more drinks, and when we reached our hotel, Steve was sound asleep on the bus. So we quietly filed off the bus after one of us advised the driver to go on to the car barn, which he did with Steve. You may think this a monstrous trick. We hadn't really stopped laughing about thirty minutes later when Steve joined us at the bar totally unconcerned. We were a tight group. Dallas beat Buffalo 49 to 37 before forty-six thousand fans the next day.

Before the 1969 season, two of the great stars of the Dallas Cowboys retired. The last of the original Cowboys, quarterback Don

Meredith, announced his retirement on July fifth. On the eighteenth, the day the veterans were to report to training camp, the all-time rushing great Don Perkins officially retired. No more hand offs from Meredith to Perkins on the first play. The day Don retired, we were told to go to the Cotton Bowl for an announcement. As I stepped on the press elevator, Don also got on. He looked down at me and said, "You are the first to know, Bill—I am retiring." I haven't seen him since, except on Monday Night football with Gifford and Cosell. Don keeps a quiet life in New Mexico. Like Pete Gent, I remember Don with great affection.

As Meredith left, Roger Staubach, a quarterback the Cowboys had been shepherding through his Navy years, put on his uniform in 1969. Craig Morton's tenure as number-one quarterback was to be quite short. I vividly remember the great game Staubach played for Navy in the 1964 Cotton Bowl game I was fortunate to broadcast. Navy lost, but not because of anything Roger failed to do. The Cowboys grabbed up Roger and waited until he finished his five-year Navy commitment.

Before those two football greats retired, there was a Cowboys newcomer on the horizon. After several years of political and business battling in Dallas, the Cowboys broke ground January 25 for the new Texas Stadium in suburban Irving, squeezed in between the highways that intersect 183, which runs from Dallas to Fort Worth. It wouldn't be ready until 1971, so we still enjoyed the venerable old Cotton Bowl with all of the various wonderful memories: the beautiful frolicking Grambling Band at so many halftimes, great victories, stunning losses, but always the home of the two pro teams, the Texans and the Cowboys who vied for fan support in the same years. The famous Cotton Bowl college game would continue, but even its luster was lost when the ridiculous college bowl system controlled what bowls were important and which weren't in the late twentieth century.

The Cowboys rampaged across the NFL in 1969 with an 11-2-1 record, the Capitol Division championship, and once again lost to their other nemesis, the Cleveland Browns, 38 to 14 at that same old Cotton Bowl in the Eastern Championship Game. That old cliché about how coaches "get up" their teams before a game seemed to be of great interest in those days. Maybe we have learned more about player personality today and it isn't so widely discussed. But I recall I interviewed Blanton Collier, the longtime coach of the Browns, a couple of days prior to the game and explained this "getting the team up" refrain was popular with fans and wondered what his thoughts were on it.

The kindly but tough Collier said frankly he didn't have any idea about that. He said he couldn't tell if he was getting the team up for the game; he just prepared them the best he could. If they were ready, they would go out and play well. "Attitude summarizes everything," he had said earlier. "Individual attitude, squad attitude. Ability minus attitude equals loss. Ability plus attitude equals win." The Browns romped over the Cotton Bowl the following day, evidently with the right attitude. The Cowboys lacked much attitude as they lost 31 to 0 to Los Angeles in the sickly Playoff Bowl in Miami.

There was an outfit in Dallas called Metro Sports News that ran a poll of twenty-five hundred area sports fans who cast their ballots for their favorite sports personalities, broadcasters, and writers of 1969. Jerry Levias of SMU was the top college athlete, followed by Joe Greene of North Texas State; Don Meredith was the top pro favorite; Sam Blair was the leading sports writer; Darrell Royal, the University of Texas coach, beat out Tom Landry by 11 votes; and I, your short sportscaster, beat out Gene Elston of the Astros, Frank Glieber of the Cowboys (TV), and my friend Bill Enis of the Houston Oilers. I never made that National Sportscasters and Sportswriters Association regional and national honorees in Salisbury, North Carolina, while with the Cowboys. They undoubtedly were true to their word in not helping me.

There was one other retirement that year. Blackie Sherrod decided to leave the broadcast booth after the '69 season. He and I lunched earlier in the season and he told me he was tired of the management trying to pressure him on what to write in his columns. He said he was aware why they placed him on the broadcast. I am sure that the weekend of December 6 and 7 would have been the end anyway.

The Cowboys were coming off a loss to the Rams and a tie with San Francisco after compiling an 8 and 1 season record. The final three games of the season started with a visit to Pittsburgh at old, dark Pitt Stadium on December 7. Meanwhile, Blackie told me he was going to Fayetteville to cover the two hottest college teams in the na-

tion, number one Texas and number two Arkansas. He would probably be in Pittsburgh very late Saturday night/early morning.

That was the nail-biter Texas 15 to 14 win over the Razorbacks.
We had heard about the game and marveled that Texas set up the win-
ning touchdown on a pass from James Street to Randy Peschel. Darrell
Royal noted once that two things can happen when you pass and both
are bad. Noted for their strong running game but stymied by a great
Arkansas defense, Royal pulled out the play and Street executed it.

It was a cold, damp day in Pittsburgh that December 7—some light
rain, snow, and pretty good wind. We hadn't heard from Blackie that
night and he hadn't arrived by the time we left for the stadium about
noon. After checking out the radio location, which was a couple of
plywood boards stuck up outside the regular press box, and our
engineer, I headed to the dressing room for some medication for a
headache. Coming back across the field, I took a last look at this
black-sooted old behemoth of a stadium. The steps were worn down
so that they were almost round. The place was way beyond its best
days.

As we reached the top of the steps and started for the press box,
there, hunkered under the stairwell, was Blackie. He was waiting for
us after just having arrived in town and at the stadium. I can't recall
all the names and places, but his journey went something like this:
After the game, he and three other sports reporters headed for their
rental car to drive to the Little Rock airport, south of Fayetteville,
which had little if any airline service then. They stood around the car
while the reporter driving was looking for his keys. He had locked
them in the car. It was about eleven p.m. on December sixth. After
some time, they managed a ride to Little Rock, where they had missed
their scheduled flights. Now they were into Sunday, December seventh, looking for flights to anywhere. Blackie, as I recall, found a
plane that took him to, say, St. Louis, where he had a layover, and
then to Chicago and on into Pittsburgh, and there he was. Up all
night, absolutely beat, hungry, and here to broadcast, Blackie and I
went up the "chicken coop" booth as the light rain turned to snow.
There was no window in the booth, no place to keep my spotting
boards out of the snow. About that time, Mrs. Alicia Landry and Mrs.
Marty Schramm, wives of the coach and president of the Cowboys,
respectively, came into the regular, well-constructed booth next to

ours. I noticed that they carried some clothes with plastic covers, so I asked if I might borrow the plastic to cover my spotting boards so the ink and numbers and names wouldn't wash away in the snow. They came over and looked at our set up and gladly provided the plastic—two truly lovely, delightful ladies. This was our last road game together—two home games left, and the ridiculousness of Blackie's journey, the weather in this old stadium, and a lackluster 10 to 7 Dallas win probably provided the most humorous broadcast we ever had.

Blackie is still remembered for his observation in a late-season game in Philadelphia. At halftime, well before Christmas, they had Santa Claus riding around the track waving to the fans and probably throwing candy. Blackie watched this spectacle for a few moments and then commented: "They even boo Santa Claus in Philadelphia!" which, of course, they were doing. Tough fans in the City of Brotherly Love.

Years later, Blackie had a special sports show on KVIL and I was the morning drive time sports announcer with Ron Chapman. Blackie broadcast and wrote stories, and even though he wasn't a Golden Throat, he had a huge following on radio. Upon Blackie's eightieth birthday, he told a reporter that he hated every minute of those three years on radio. I was just the opposite—I enjoyed working with him every game.

Nineteen seventy and '71 were the pinnacle of success after the long journey from 1960. The Cowboys won their last five games in 1970, which included Washington twice, even Green Bay and Cleveland. In their 10 and 4 record, two opponents emerged as new dangerous threats: Minnesota Vikings and St. Louis Cardinals. Dallas lost badly to St. Louis twice.

There were two unusual games that year, two defensive gems, which most fans abhor. Dallas slipped by the Browns in Cleveland 6 to 2 and mustered little more offense in a 5 to 0 stomping of Detroit in the divisional playoff in Dallas. Following their biggest prize in eleven years, a 17 to 10 win over San Francisco for the NFC Championship (where the players buried our postgame interview show under their uniforms), Dallas made its first appearance in a Super Bowl (number five), only to lose to Baltimore 16 to 13 in a sloppy offensive game by both teams. The depth of the offensive morass was evident as the

MVP award went to Cowboys linebacker Chuck Howley, who intercepted two passes and caused a fumble.

In 1970, I began a two-year association with Verne Lundquist as my sidekick, color analyst, and friend. Verne was young and enthusiastic, but quite disciplined working a game. So many color announcers talk over the play-by-play man or give him little time to set up the next play. If Verne had nothing to contribute following a play, he didn't "grab the mike" just to be heard. When he was ready to provide some insight, he usually held his hand up to be sure I saw him and brought him in. We rarely if ever "stepped on each other."

The Cowboys, on the other hand, had a newcomer in 1970 who became a lightning rod by later refusing to talk to anyone. Duane Thomas was the number-one draft pick of the Cowboys in 1970. Duane took his new job seriously, finishing the year with 803 yards rushing, a rookie club record, and a touchdown in Super Bowl V. The next year, Duane had fewer rushing yards at 793, but he led the league in touchdowns with 11 and rush/receiving touchdowns with 13. It was his second and final year with Dallas.

The other sensation in the Cowboys backfield was Calvin Hill, an intelligent young gentleman from Yale, who covered the field in long, hurtling strides. Hill had been drafted in 1969, another first choice, and scored eight touchdowns on just two hundred carries in 1969, and eight in 1971. Hill surpassed the one-thousand-yard mark rushing in 1972 to '73, and then he was traded to Washington in '76, where he never regained his earlier form.

There was another draft choice of 1970, a linebacker name Steve Kiner, who never made it big but figured in an amusing story with me in 1970—flower child time. I suppose the first one on the Cowboys was Pete Gent a couple years before, but the effects of the movement were beginning to be felt in the NFL. During this period of free love, long hair, and whatever kind of clothes, Dallas had played a game in Kezar Stadium in San Francisco, and were driving in their bus through the Haight-Asbury Park area—*that* was an eye-opener. The players were straining watching couples making love, smoking pot, playing music, and all other manner of hippie lifestyle choices. Suddenly, in a quiet moment, Bob Hayes announced, "There is a hippie guy with a little hippie dog!" He broke up the bus as they watched the longhaired guy with his little longhaired pooch sashaying through the park.

Duane Thomas was an enormously talented back who had a four-year career in pro football, only the first two worth mentioning. He was mentored by the former Cleveland great Jim Brown in the period of free spirit and evolving racial freedom. Another free spirit, Steve Kiner, now a member of the University of Tennessee Hall of Fame, came in 1970 as an All American linebacker prospect, but quickly became a player who refused to obey rules, drove an old beat-up car, and stayed with Dallas only one year, never to be heard of again. Kiner was in the coaches' doghouse most of the time while Duane was silent, not talking to the press and presenting difficulties for the coaches.

During one road trip in 1970, I headed for my usual Siberian location in the back of the plane and found an empty seat between Kiner and Thomas. I thought this would be the quietest trip I had ever taken, but as it turned out Steve and Duane and I discussed our families, schools, football, politics, race—just about everything that could be discussed in two or three hours on a plane.

When we left the plane and I caught up with the front-of-the-plane privileged media friends, they asked me who I was sitting with. It became a point of interest after each trip because I was the only media person in the back. I nonchalantly said, "Oh, I sat between Duane and Kiner." They laughed and said that must have been quiet. Oh no, we talked all the way and I laid out all the subjects. "*You* talked to Duane!" they said, like I was one of the apostles who had access. It was a huge laugh as they couldn't believe my conversational success, nor did Verne when I mentioned my seat partners on the broadcast the next day.

After ten years of steady growth, 1971 was the ultimate year for the Dallas Cowboys. Duane Thomas would make some comment about that in Super Bowl VI, but not before he nearly drove Landry, Tex, and everyone else around him insane. Thomas started his strange mental spiral earlier in the 1971 training camp, demanding a new contract and more money. It was denied him and, after refusing to attend training camp, the Cowboys traded him to New England where he incurred the wrath of the coach and was dismissed. In October that season, he showed up in Dallas and proceeded to play as though he had never been gone. There is a detailed account of the Thomas brief encounter with pro football in Bob St. John's book, *Landry: The Legend and the Legacy.*

Speaking of "The Saint," as everyone called him, there were some great characters in Dallas sports reporting such as Blackie, Sam Blair, Steve Perkins, and Gary Cartwright. I was coming into the Cowboys' upstairs office on Central Expressway one afternoon. Rolling down the stairs is one of the area's Golden Throats. He and Gary had a fight and Gary knocked him down. There are some other stories of Gary's unique personality, but undoubtedly someone has chronicled them in a book.

After the first six games of the 1971 season, the Cowboys opened their new home, Texas Stadium, playing field with three-fourths of a roof in Irving. On October 24, 65,708 fans turned out for the opening game against the New England Patriots. They had only to wait two minutes and sixteen seconds after the opening kickoff for the first score. Duane Thomas raced fifty-six yards for the touchdown. Dallas went on to win 44 to 22, one of its eleven victories against only three losses that year.

That roof at Texas Stadium was a blessing and a headache—fine for the fans when it rained and they avoided being soaked, but the sun shone through in various places and, in others, there was dark shade so that the television cameras went crazy trying to adjust to the sudden changes in light. It was often discussed why they put an "almost" roof on the stadium that they didn't finish closing, and why they didn't air-condition the place—cost, it was presumed, was the overriding factor, but in Texas's renowned blazing heat, even a partial roof in August and into September was better than none at all.

Now, the new owner of the Cowboys, Jerry Jones, is watching his new stadium in Arlington take shape. Arlington is the center of pro sports in North Texas with the Texas Rangers and now the Cowboys. In letters to the sports editor, I suggested that the name should be changed from Dallas Cowboys to Texas Cowboys with Willie Nelson their mascot. Downtown Dallas has the NBA Mavericks and the NHL Stars. Dallas leaders failed in the sixties with the opportunity to replicate St. Louis with a downtown stadium. Then they failed again to build the new Cowboys stadium in Dallas. Credit Jones for part of that problem.

The sight lines at Texas Stadium are excellent and the original press box for radio and television broadcasters was the best in the NFL, but those have been moved to allow more expensive boxes for patrons. The radio folks now sit up under the roof, a nosebleed away from the field. Progress does take its toll sometimes. Jerry Jones would have put the media up in a hole in the roof if he could sell more expensive boxes.

For the Cowboys, 1971 was *the* year of their existence: their sixth straight year to make the playoffs, their second consecutive National Football Conference Championship, and the first World Championship in Super Bowl VI. The preceding two years had been Craig Morton's to quarterback the team. Nineteen seventy-one belonged to the U.S. Naval Academy's 1963 Heisman trophy winner Roger Staubach—and except for 1972 when Morton regained command when Staubach played only four games due to an injury, he remained *the* man until his retirement in 1979. He was among the league's top ten quarterbacks for his full eight years as the Cowboys quarterback.

The 1971 Cowboys, winning fourteen games and losing only three, were overflowing with offensive and defensive talent to become "America's Team" headlined by the "Doomsday Defense."

Super Bowl VI was my last broadcast with the Cowboys. It had been announced in the fall of '71 that the Washington Senators of the American Baseball League were moving to Arlington to become the Texas Rangers. Shortly before the Super Bowl, I had been picked, thanks to the efforts of Arlington Mayor Tom Vandergriff, who was the architect of the ball club move, to be the first radio announcer, along with the future Hall of Fame pitching star of the Los Angeles Dodgers, Don Drysdale.

Verne and I broadcast the brilliant 24 to 3 victory over Miami in the Super Bowl. It was in old Tulane Stadium in New Orleans and we were crammed into a booth just big enough for two. Leaning forward on one of the old wooden windows prior to the game, the thing suddenly broke loose and fell into the crowd. Fortunately, no one was injured, but New Orleans fans were emotional, to say the least—so we did some waving, smiling, and gesturing to indicate the thing fell on its own. We hadn't attacked anyone.

Mike Ditka (the old Chicago Bear), Lance Alworth, and the inimitable Duane Thomas scored touchdowns in the Cowboys' Super Bowl victory. Thomas, Walt Garrison, and Calvin Hill set a Super Bowl record with 252 net yards rushing and 5.3 yards per carry. Roger Staubach was named Most Valuable Player. But it was Thomas who actually had the last word. I believe it was the alleged sports-type Tom Brookshier who mentioned to Duane after the game that this was the ultimate Cowboys win. Duane quietly replied, "If this is the ultimate, then why play another?" For Duane that was about it. For me, that was it—my last game after spending seven years with the Dallas Cowboys.

Like working for the Dallas Texans, this span of work with the Cowboys was thrilling, dramatic, and so rewarding. That the Cowboys management had little respect for my desire to pursue my professional career in my own fashion bothered me for some time. But, it is difficult to separate the talent part of broadcasting from the business end. And with the Schramm-run Cowboys they, of course, had the final word. I must strongly comment here that I never ceased in my program of weekly preparation for every game I broadcast, right through the Super Bowl VI!

It was an honor and a privilege to have broadcast the rise of the Cowboys team, to have enjoyed the relationship of the players and the coaches, particularly Tom Landry, and to have been a part of the first pinnacle of their future successes. Before the Super Bowl broadcast, I told Verne that this was my last game—that I was going into Major League Baseball. I told him I had not informed the Cowboys as yet. He asked if I would mind if he went in immediately after returning to Dallas to ask Tex Schramm about replacing me. I agreed he should do just that.

At the time, it seemed Verne had an offer from a Los Angeles television station to become their nightly sports anchor, but, much like my decision with CBS, he would prefer working with the Cowboys. As it turned out, he was hired. The interesting part of this is that Verne had never called one down of play-by-play of any sport. I imagine that Tex figured with his excellent reporting abilities on TV sports shows and his personality, he could learn the business. And, of course, I knew that the Channel 8 sports reporter position was as important, or maybe more so, to Tex than the radio play-by-play. At least, it was important enough that I rode in the back of the plane throughout my tenure.

When Jack Buck was the announcer on the CBS telecasts of Cowboy games, he inadvertently mispronounced Pettis Norman as Norman Pettis and received a lot of fan antipathy and notes in the local papers about the gaffe. Fans swore allegiance to listening to the radio while watching the game. Fine with me. In fact, I wrote Jack, a good broadcast friend, a note and suggested he keep calling Pettis that way and add another player or two to help my broadcast! Radio is important.

I know Verne must have worked hard over the spring and summer to prepare for the radio job. I had spent fourteen years trying to master my technique to that point. To Verne's credit, he stayed with the Cowboys for years and today is a respected broadcaster for CBS-TV Sports. He pretty well summed up this business/talent meshing by saying once in an interview, "I will do anything Tex asks me to do." It certainly paid off.

North Texas State University. When I began my thirty-four-year tenure with North Texas football, the technical part of broadcasting was still simple, at least with the equipment supplied by our sole radio station, KDNT. Owned by a former undertaker, Harwell Shepherd, the station operated like his penny-pinching personality.

In 1959, when sports information director Fred Graham and I started our long journey as on-the-road broadcasters, we carried a cardboard suitcase with us that was a visual disgrace, held together with tape. Inside was a homemade piece of equipment that had one microphone outlet. I would talk and, when Fred had something to say, stick the mike under his nose.

The amplifier looked like something that an enterprising high school electronics phenom might have put together from a kit—and it worked! We would slip into a stadium hiding the dreadful-looking suitcase, sneak into the visiting radio booth, attach the telephone remote line to the amplifier, and go find a telephone to call KDNT to tell them we were hooked up and they should listen to whichever one of us was talking on the mike at that time. As our time for the broadcast approached, I would give a minute-by-minute countdown so the KDNT board operator could put on the opening commercial billboard and we, flying blind, would start the broadcast at the advertised time. We never knew if we hit all these pegs of modern 1959 broadcasting on time. Fred became so embarrassed carrying the ugly little suitcase with its faux plaid cover and tape that he scraped up enough money to buy a new one for the same sad piece of equipment. At least, we didn't try to hide the case when walking in the stadium.

Sometimes we would come back from a trip and there would be a note that we went off the air before the game was over. News to us. One time in Louisville, we were flying along when the cable fell out of the foot-long old microphone we were using. I pushed it back in, but it didn't work. We knew that broadcast ended early.

Speaking of going off the air early. It was a Southern Illinois game in Carbondale, undoubtedly 1966 when North Texas was a power, that Mr. Shepherd walked into the KDNT studio and, finding that the Eagles were leading 53 to 0, ordered the broadcast shut off. He figured no one listening to such a lopsided game, so might as well play music.

While engineering/broadcasting the road games seemed to be a miracle if successful, following the Eagles was a wonderful experience. The school was about five thousand students then, a small campus where everyone seemed totally dedicated to the betterment of the school. It was heading toward the end of the era when female students were required to wear dresses to class, had a ten p.m. curfew to be in the dorm, and dreaded to face the wrath of the Dean of Women Students, Imogene Dickey. There are friends of ours in their sixties who still cringe when Dean Dickey's name is mentioned. Actually she was a wonderful, intelligent lady, but strict in the manner of the day.

When last we mentioned North Texas, the Eagles had completed their 9 and 1 season record and lost to New Mexico in the Sun Bowl. Abner Haynes and the core of the team graduated, and the Eagles immediately fell on hard times until 1966.

Coach Odus Mitchell had led the Eagles since 1946 when he ran off a string of seven consecutive winning seasons. There would almost be a predicable pattern afterward of a few years of great success and then a spate of years when the record would dissolve to 2-7-1 as it did in 1964. But Coach Mitchell was the kind of person a father would wish his son to play for. He was honest, dedicated, and ran a disciplined team. When former players came back to visit, they would address him as Coach Mitchell, never smoke in front of him, and heaven forbid they should ever curse.

One player recalls the day he was having a particularly bad day on the practice field when the trainer came up and told him to go to the dressing room and not come back that day. The player had been busting his behind, so he was confused over the order. After stripping off his uniform, the trainer walked in and the player asked why he was sent in. The trainer merely asked, "Did you swear on the field?" A lesson learned.

In the feast and famine life of North Texas football, there were players who excelled, although the overall team did poorly. The 1961 team featured three-year quarterback Billy Ryan, who later coached at Denton High and was so beloved they named the new high school for him after he died of cancer.

There were the African American running backs Bobby Smith, A. D. Whitfield, and Arthur Perkins, who followed the lead of Abner Haynes and played several years of professional football. Bobby Smith taught me a lesson in 1961. This talented running back, in the on-the-field style of Duane Thomas or Calvin Hill, had been injured and returned for a game at Fouts Field in Denton. I had a particularly hard week, a big Friday night high school game and came out that Saturday afternoon bone tired. As the game progressed, Bobby Smith took a pitch from Billy Ryan and started around left end. I can still see the play—he broke a tackle at the line, spun off another potential tackler downfield and then, honestly, was hit, did a forward flip in the air, landed on his feet, and kept running. Laid-back and tired, I called that play, step-by-step, falling behind but maintaining the flow of each of his beautiful gyrations. A light went on in my mind that this was the way to call a play—stay with it, visualize it as it leaves you, keep talking, and don't rush to catch up, just keep describing it. Many years later at a North Texas Hall of Fame banquet, I visited with Bobby and we recalled that run and my call. Bobby Smith played pro ball with the Buffalo Bills and Pittsburgh Steelers.

Those were tough years for the black players who were verbally spat upon, and probably actually so, when they played in some of the out-of-town stadiums. Fred and I hated Memphis and old Crump Stadium where the racist fans never let up on the black players. The language hurled at the black players and applause from the fans when one was injured was unthinkable. Fred and I routinely waited until the fans were gone from the stadium before we left the press box.

Carl Lockhart was a phenomenal receiver in 1964 and went on to have a long, illustrious career with the New York Giants. Duane Bean, an old-fashioned rock-hard-headed running back in '62 and '63, later served as my color commentator on our broadcasts. He is long remembered for observing on an extra point attempt: "Jesus Christ, he missed it!" Duane was fun if not a little out-of-control at times.

Just before the immensely successful years of quarterback Steve Ramsey and a big kid named Joe Greene, there was a large quarterback named Vidal Carlin who threw 341 passes, leading the Eagles to a 3 to 7 record in 1965 and then tossed 24 interceptions in 1966 while his team scored an 8 and 2 record. Stats don't always make sense.

In addition to working with a piece of highly suspect broadcast equipment from KDNT, we had the added pressure of being assured the telephone lines were ordered and then actually installed and, in the case of those already in a booth, activated. I learned very quickly that it was absolutely essential to arrive at the stadium at least two hours before the game and hope that the line was in and active. After some nonfunctioning line disasters, we always called ahead the week of the game to find the telephone number for repairs and installations in that city's telephone office, along with a personal contact there. Going in cold a few times and trying to make a person who just happened to be in a telephone office interested in our plight of a dead line was part of the education.

Nineteen sixty-six was the beginning of one of the most productive and exciting four-year periods in Eagles football. It was also the final year of Coach Mitchell's tenure. Coach Mitchell's greatest recruit, Joe Greene, burst on the scene with stunning speed and strength leading the defensive team. Greene, along with Burkley Harkless (whose name I consistently reversed in the broadcast—Jack Buck would have been proud), Henry Holland (the big redhead who committed suicide years after leaving North Texas), Ed Brantley, Charles "Hatchet" Beatty (became the mayor of Waxahachie, Texas, in the 1990s), Paul Draper, Glen Holloway, and Cedric Hardman—all became All-Missouri Valley Conference offensive or defensive lineman for North Texas. Most if not all played pro ball. The key running backs in that period were Vic Williams, who became a minister, and Leo Taylor.

This Eagle's team depth was epitomized by the defensive secondary play of Ret Little (still a teacher in the Richardson, Texas, school district), Leonard Dunlap, Billy Woods, and Bernie Barbour. This period was dominated by defense led by Greene and a passing game that became nationally famous. Not fleet afoot but with a powerful body and laser-like arm, Steve Ramsey set every school passing record throwing to the likes of John Love, Barry Moore, and Ron Shanklin. Shank later became my color analyst, a North Texas and professional coach before his recent untimely death.

The highlight of the '66 North Texas season was the final game against Chattanooga, the final coaching assignment of Coach Mitchell after forty-two years on the field. Coach did not like to run up the score on other teams and cleared his bench when it was obvious his opponent was unable to mount an offense. So it was an anxious Mitchell who watched his team unleash an offensive blitz against Chattanooga highlighted by John Love catching three touchdown passes. The players worked on all the various scoring options to ring up a 42 to 7 victory. Forty-two points for forty-two years, all that a great coach and human being like Coach Mitchell deserved. Mitchell compiled a 122-85-9 record, the winningest coach in North Texas's history. His teams won or shared ten conference championships and played in three bowl games. Coach Mitchell died at the age of ninety in 1989.

The perils of coaching at any level are well known. When Rod Rust came in to replace Odus Mitchell, we all thought it was a perfect fit. Rod was outgoing, humorous, had an outstanding coaching background and a team that any new coach would die for. But what most of us did not realize was the displeasure of his assistant coaches, left over from the Mitchell era, who were furious that they had been passed over. Rust's career was effectively over after three short years. He finally left after his fifth year with a record of 1 and 10. As any head coach will tell you, recruiting players is only as successful as the support of your assistant coaches. I recall meeting one of the assistants the day Rod was released. He smiled and said, "Well, we finally got the son of a bitch." Rod Rust has been a successful defensive coach with several professional teams, his last the New York Giants.

When I was at Channel 4, I freelanced the production of the television program of Texas A&M Coach Hank Foldberg. My friend, a future employer for a brief time, Paul Berry was a first-rate Aggie and owner of an advertising agency that sponsored the program. Each week, Paul would meet me Sunday morning at Love Field, fly us in his private plane to College Station, home of A&M, pick up the black-and-white game film, then fly on to Houston. There I would edit it down to the required fifteen to twenty minutes of highlights and then host the taping of the thirty-minute show with Coach Foldberg. This Sunday's production plan demanded a tight schedule; pan the film through the viewer, cut the plays, tape them to the front of the edit table, splice them together, race into the studio, and do the show. One Sunday, as Foldberg and I were commenting on the film during the taping, I noticed I had the film turned around so that the numbers were backward! I said nothing about it and that was the way we presented that one program.

I was paid a nice talent fee. Unfortunately, the show just lasted one year and Coach Foldberg was fired. Visiting the A&M campus was a treat in those days when every student spoke to you with "Howdy!" But that led to my working with Southern Methodist University basketball coach E. O. "Doc" Hayes on his fifteen-minute TV show. I took my trusty sixteen millimeter camera with the one-inch lens and shot the Mustang home games just on the "feel" of the shift of momentum that happens in basketball. I edited that film and Doc and I did our bit for Mustang fandom. When Hayden Fry was head football coach at SMU, I worked with him on a coaches' interview show on KRLD-Radio.

All this to say I had quite a bit of experience hosting coaches' shows when Fred Graham and the sponsors put together a plan to have a *Rod Rust North Texas Show*. Same format as the Foldberg program. The shooting of games and any features had to be done with film. We had no access to a sound film camera, so we just ran the highlights of the game and sat in the studio talking about the game. Rod was, as I have mentioned, a wonderful individual with a great sense of humor; he thought Fred and I were, I could say, unusual. We did have a great time doing what we were doing.

After the shows that were taped and ran on a Dallas independent television station, we would stop by a club on Harry Hines in Dallas and play some pool—and drink a couple of beers, too. This part of Dallas was one of those streets considered pretty sleazy, with all sorts of rough clubs and dives. One night, a football-scout-friend of Rod's (a big tall guy like Rod) joined us for the pool game after the show. As we were playing along, a young punk, pretty well oiled, walked up and demanded to play the winner. We said we were just playing for fun and declined. The guy walked back over a little later and once again demanded forcefully that he play. I am 5' 7" or so, not a physical force, and should know better, and this irritated me. So I turned the pool cue around, holding the heavy part like a bat and told the guy to get the hell lost. Had it been just Fred and me, we probably would have been mauled, but the two big guys were there so the kid left. Rod smiled, looked around, and said, "Why is it always the little guys?" referring of course to me and the punk. But there was no fight.

There is one more story about our Rod Rust television extravaganza. During one particularly unfortunate game that North Texas lost, Fred and I decided to have some fun with Rod. We set it up with the director before shooting. The billboard rolled and they came to the studio with Rod and me facing the camera. I welcomed the viewers to the show and then turned to Rod and said, "Coach, would you say that in yesterday's game, North Texas farted, fumbled, and fell?" Rod didn't even flinch; he merely said that he wouldn't characterize it that way and then went in to his game analysis. Well, of course, I couldn't hold it and burst out laughing. Rod then quit talking and joined in the fun. We then rolled tape again.

Under Rust, Steve Ramsey passed for a record 7,076 yards and 69 touchdowns; Ron Shanklin caught 144 of Steve's passes for 2,465 yards and 31 touchdowns, still a school record. Shank, John Love, and Barry Moore all caught 3 touchdown passes in a game from Ramsey. It was one of the nation's top passing offenses.

By this time, our broadcast equipment had been updated to a modern microphone amplifier and our broadcasts were the best ever. I occasionally had a conflict with my Dallas Cowboys assignments and young Mr. Ted Davis filled in admirably. Here I thought Ted was a college student, working with KDNT, when actually he was still in high school. Ted was one of those remarkable talents that come along rarely and we had a long association with North Texas. He would become just a bit agitated (rightfully so) and always correct me when I inadvertently called him Jeff Davis. Ted and I later worked together at KVIL-Radio, he then with the Dallas Mavericks and now with the Milwaukee NBA team.

Every game in this four-year span held the promise of something special with the Greene-led defense (which was dubbed "Mean Green" by Sidney Sue Graham, wife of the sports information director Fred Graham, my road partner) and the Ramsey rocket offense. Let me highlight a few of the key games in that period.

In 1967, North Texas defeated every Missouri Valley team except Memphis, which scored another heartbreaking victory of 29 to 20. North Texas and New Mexico, the 1959 Sun Bowl opponent, tied. The last time I looked, Memphis had won fifteen games and North Texas four in the series that ended in 1980.

The game in Cincinnati that year had a pregame drama riding on it. North Texas rode a Convair charter plane, a twin-engine workhorse of the airline industry, to this particular game. As the team was crossing the Texas–Arkansas line, my partner, Fred Graham, sitting by the window noticed a small river of black oil pouring over the starboard wing. He checked the wing again in a few minutes and it seemed that the river was widening. Fred mentioned it to Coach Mitchell and about then the captain of the plane came back. He told Mitchell that they were having a problem and might have to land before they reached Cincinnati. Coach told the pilot that he and Fred noticed the oil spill and he was somewhat frightened. The captain said he was too! Well, that did it—it was a white-knuckle flight from then on. Quarterback Steve Ramsey rushed to his seat when they announced that everyone put on the seat belts and sat on his horn-rimmed glasses. This tension lasted across Arkansas until the plane was brought to a safe landing and repaired in Memphis.

There were two huge disappointments in 1968 and five magnificent successes. Another disappointing loss to Memphis, 30 to 12. That came after the Eagles beat Colorado State 17 to 12. North Texas knocked off Tulsa, Louisville, and Wichita for three satisfying wins. Then the loss, that to this day when those now graying veterans of 1968 come together, is forever cursed. I am sure that Ron Shanklin might have thought of that game just before he died. It meant that much to him.

It was Arkansas at Fayetteville. It was North Texas playing a high profile Southwest Conference team. With the Razorbacks leading 17 to 15 late in the fourth period, Ramsey called Shanklin for the play of the game. Shank split wide right, ran deep, and then cut across to his left to the end zone where he went to his knees to catch Ramsey's low pass. Touchdown! No, waved off by the Southwest Conference official. Shanklin trapped it, the official motioned. We were looking from our booth right into the play that Shank had made many times. To this day, the team and Fred and I are sure North Texas defeated Arkansas that afternoon. You won't find it that way in the record book.

Cincinnati ranked second to Memphis as the team most despised in the Missouri Valley Conference. This particular home game came right after the Theft-in-Arkansas, so it was very possible that the Eagles were having a hard time getting their dauber up for the Bearcats—that and North Texas had beaten Cincinnati the last three consecutive years.

A huge storm came barreling out of the southwest—black and green clouds, rain, and high winds—just as the homecoming game started, running off many of the eighteen-thousand-plus at Fouts Field on the North Texas campus. By halftime, Cincy led 34 to 0. Coach Rust was not a gung ho, yell-at-the-top-of-his-voice kind of guy, but whatever went on in the dressing room ignited the Eagles. Ramsey threw five touchdown passes (he did the same a week later against University of Texas–El Paso) and led the Eagles to a momentous 55 to 34 victory. This might well be the greatest comeback in the history of the school.

The following week, with the field goal kicker injured (North Texas had connected on only one point-after-touchdown kick), North Texas came down to the final moments in El Paso against UTEP with the game tied at 31 to 31. With little or no experience kicking, hard-nosed defensive back Bernie Barbour trotted out on the field and kicked a thirty-yard field goal for the victory, 34 to 31.

Joe Greene was named an All American after the '68 season by every national organization voting for the award. He was drafted by the Pittsburgh Steelers and led the "Steel Curtain" defense that helped provide four Super Bowl Championships before he retired in 1981.

In my mind, I always see the game against Memphis when Joe Greene was playing on a badly sprained ankle. Being in the trenches with Memphis was always a bruising battle. Joe hobbled on and off the field, retaping his leg, and going back out to do more battle with the Tigers. Then, with North Texas victory in sight, Memphis kicked a field goal, by a guy who had never kicked one, like NT's Barbour, and won the game. The Eagles sat on the field so long that Fred and I were in the dressing room when huge Henry Holland and another player brought in Greene, draped over their shoulders. Everyone was in tears, the players, the coaches, and, if someone had said anything to me, the broadcasters also. It was the most emotional game I have ever seen.

As the team bussed out toward the airport to catch the charter, Vic Williams stood and starting singing the song they had made up, "We are the mean green, shooby doo," and everyone perked up a bit. I know that other teams have had eras like that, but I have seen few. It ranked with the loss after the Ice Bowl.

The last great year of the Ramsey era was 1969. Another close loss to Memphis followed by a six-game winning streak featuring a brilliant 31 to 30 win over Cincinnati on a sleet-covered field in Ohio. The last game of that season was against San Diego State, which won 42 to 24 and lasted about four hours.

In that four-year span, North Texas won the Missouri Valley Conference once outright, tied for it once, and finished second in '68 and '69. North Texas went into a dismal tailspin in 1970 through 1972, the year Rust was fired. How bad was it? The first two years were 3 and 8, and the third was 1 and 10. The passing attack accounted for 16 touchdowns in those three years and the running game 11. Ramsey had thrown 24 touchdowns in one year; in the next three, the total offense had 27.

I recently asked Rod Rust his recollections of that era of North Texas football. "My recollections lately have been marred by not having known about Ron Shanklin [his death] until this past winter. I had every intention of hiring him at New England after the first year was over and then it was over for me as well. . . . This [North Texas team] was a remarkable bunch. The best part of that experience for me was to witness the tremendous interaction between the players and real affection and respect they had for one another. And a really diverse group of individuals."

I did not broadcast the games in 1972; I was off trying to be a major league broadcaster with the Texas Rangers. Actually that Rangers team would have had a hard time beating the old Dallas–Fort Worth Rangers of 1959, if they could at all. Brad Sham and Norm Hitzges, two young, highly motivated sportscasters, took my place in what looked like my last days with North Texas.

There are still those hanging around who believe the six years under Hayden Fry were the ultimate (ask Duane Thomas about that!) in the history of North Texas football. Hayden Fry had been fired at Southern Methodist University and was available when Rod Rust was relieved of his misery. Fry came in with his usual high-profile personality and an ego that is pretty hard to imagine. Hayden is an enigma. I had known him for a long time and we enjoyed a healthy relationship. He had taken SMU to the Bluebonnet Bowl in December of 1968, a new endeavor in Houston, and scored an upset victory over Oklahoma, 28 to 27. The elation over that victory carried through 1972 at SMU. He was head coach at SMU for eleven years, but had just three winning seasons, two with 8 and 3 records and his last in 1972, 7 and 4.

Not satisfied with the humility of leaving one job and stepping into another thirty-five miles away, Hayden blew into North Texas as both athletic director and head coach with grandiose plans. First at a public fans' meeting attended by a number of ex-players, Hayden announced that there had not been a history at North Texas before he arrived and all that would change. That kind of blindsided a number of alums and exathletes who had some deep feelings for the history of the past sixty years. Hayden promised to take North Texas to a bowl game and make the athletic program "The Notre Dame of the Southwest" by dropping out of the Missouri Valley Conference and becoming independent with the promise of being highly ranked in the polls and appearing on national television. Fry also kept a running dialogue going through his tenure demanding North Texas be admitted to the Southwest Conference.

The only one of those that occurred was the independence. That took North Texas out of future grandfather clauses when the Missouri Valley finally morphed into Conference USA. The independent feature eliminated any chance of winning championships and ultimately took a toll on attendance by not having anything to win. It virtually destroyed North Texas basketball for years.

Let me be fair and say Hayden Fry and his outstanding staff could recruit and coach. He set up SMU on the '74 schedule and lost 7 to 6, a moral victory for Eagles fans. There were only two North Texas victories that year, but the fans were in high hopes of great years ahead.

I pointed out the various promises Hayden Fry made for North Texas and the fact that there had been "no history" until he arrived. Well, he added some new color to the program, changing the dark Forest green of North Texas to a light lime color that we privately referred to as "puke green." A perennial hanger-on at North Texas convinced Hayden that he needed a new emblem for the athletic department, so he designed an elongated looking eagle with wings. We dubbed it "The Flying Worm." When I want to frighten people, I put on my old lime green jacket with flying worm emblem. The football team was then decked out in lime green headgear, jerseys, and pants. When they played in the Cowboys' Texas Stadium, you could barely make them out because they blended into the green of the artificial turf! My broadcast spotters had an easier time with the opponent than trying to distinguish the North Texas players from the turf. However, I always used binoculars while broadcasting, and I had the Eagles memorized. At least the numbers on those ugly uniforms were white.

Nineteen seventy-five was one of those years with a couple of games that the Green and White folks still rejoice about. By the way, in 1973, I handled many of the games while finishing out the second year of baseball. I managed to work in most of the '74 and '75 season also. In 1974, Hayden turned around the 2-7-2 record. The Eagles won seven and lost four. The two memorable games were against Houston of the Southwest Conference and the Tennessee Volunteers of the Southeast. After soundly beating San Diego State in the third game of the season, North Texas was humiliated at Oklahoma State, 61 to 7. Fry was apoplectic about the Cowboys running up the score.

After another loss, to Memphis State but only 21 to 19, North Texas gained stature with a remarkable 28 to 0 victory over Southwest Conference Houston. In that game, Walter Chapman, junior defensive middle guard, won AP lineman of the week award. Other players who gained national attention were linebacker Pete Morris, punter Don Fechtman, punt returner and wide receiver J. T. Smith, and field goal kicker Iseed Khoury. Khoury still respects Coach Fry even if Fry's decision not to take his valuable kicker to Memphis in 1977 nearly cost him the game. Fry left Khoury home for another defensive replacement and the North Texas backup kicker missed a field goal and an extra point. North Texas still won 20 to 19. Once, Hayden also told Iseed during a game to stand beside him because the photographers took so many pictures with the famed coach that Iseed would be sure to have an historical picture.

Following Houston, and a respectable three-point loss to Mississippi State, North Texas faced the acclaimed University of Tennessee in their beautiful riverside stadium. The Volunteers' colors are orange and white—a lighter shade of orange than the University of Texas, but orange anyhow. One of those orange teams North Texas ached to play.

It was a gorgeous day, a late fall afternoon with the stadium crammed with seventy-three thousand Tennessee fans. They arrive by plane, train, bus, car, and boat for the games. People came up the river, tied up their boats, and climbed to their seats. The Volunteer fans will say their team was in a down year while North Texas fans remember a surging Eagles team that would win the final three games of the season after this one.

It was a wonderfully balanced game. North Texas led 14 to 7 going into the fourth quarter. With very little time left on the clock, Tennessee scored, and it was tied. Then Tennessee kicked off and a large and not-fast running back, Sears Woods, took the ball at the North Texas two, broke through the middle of the defenders, and ran ninety-eight yards for the touchdown that gave the Eagles the 21 to 14 "Greatest Victory in the History of North Texas!" So read the headlines.

My color announcer that year was a former football player friend of Hayden's who he had "suggested" I use. The guy was nice enough, but had no idea about broadcasting. As Sears took the ball and broke through behind his blockers, the guy began to yell at the top of his voice, "He's going to score! He's going to score" a good seventy yards from the end zone. I doubt anything I said about Woods' progress was heard. He sure killed a dramatic moment.

I tell you, though, the Tennessee fans are courteous. As we were leaving the stadium, we observed people handing their players envelopes as they came out of their tunnel. I thought it a nice gesture, and as we walked across the area to the parking lot, we were invited by some nice folks to enjoy their barbecue. We explained we were from North Texas and they said that was fine—the team made a great game of it and we should have some quail! Quail is good washed down with the pride of Tennessee's famous liquid.

For four years, I managed to broadcast Texas Rangers and Chicago White Sox baseball. In 1975, during a financial recession, the White Sox were sold, my contract nullified. In 1976, I went to work as the morning sports reporter on KVIL, resumed my activities with North Texas, and started reestablishing my career.

Before the 1976 season, Hayden Fry, Fred, and I discussed our radio situation. KDNT had been handling the sales and broadcast forever, but there was no way anyone outside of Denton could hear the nearly closed-down signal at night. So Hayden, ever thinking progressively, told me my mission was to find a Dallas or Fort Worth radio station that could also carry North Texas football. This had never been done before, so I walked the plank to procure a major station.

A bunch of my friends were associated with WFAA-Radio, one of the three most powerful stations in the Metroplex, so I went over and pitched the deal. Lo and behold, they took it and they sold the advertising—something I dreaded. In 1976, North Texas football on WFAA had the highest rating of all other programming on the station. We were amazed.

One thing that improved the opportunity to have wider coverage was the stronger schedule with Southern Methodist, Tennessee (the only game ever played between the two) Houston, Texas, and other nationally recognized teams—again, a Hayden Fry accomplishment.

Ken Washington had been the quarterback in 1974 and then returned to take over the reins again in 1977. He just darned near led the team with running back Michael Jones to an even greater year under Hayden in '75. Washington was a small sprint-out quarterback who scored ten touchdowns passing in '77 while Jones ran for twelve, the most rushing touchdowns since Abner Haynes' fourteen in 1959!

With four TDs added by pass receptions, Jones's ninety-eight points surpassed Abner's ninety in the '59 season.

In the third game of '76, the "other" orange team, University of Texas, hosted North Texas in Memorial Stadium in Austin. As usual, the North Texas band (with its real musicians) won the halftime, and the Eagles led the Longhorns 14 to 10 in the middle of the fourth quarter. The acclaimed Earl Campbell had been out of the Texas lineup due to an injury, but with Texas pride on the line, Campbell returned. The huge, extremely fast Campbell, limping and all, raced out of the grasp of the Mean Green defense for some sixty yards and a touchdown and the Longhorns came away the winner 17 to 14—another great moral victory for the Green and Fry.

The next week, Hayden's Greenies played SMU and lost by a touchdown, then a six-point loss to Oklahoma State (some revenge for the terrible pasting the year before) and North Texas finished the season with a comfortable 7 and 4 record.

As we did with Rod Rust, Fred Graham and I produced and hosted the Hayden Fry show each week—same format of game film edited down to key plays and drives, and discussion with Hayden on the high points of the game and next week's opponent. In one episode, Fred somehow came up with a reel of footage of Coach Fry playing high school football. We surprised Hayden with the footage and ran several plays, the final one a sweep around right end and, as he was tackled, he fumbled. Most guys would just laugh and make some amusing comment; Hayden was not one of those guys. He contended that was his only fumble of that year!

Washington, Jones, and a dogged defense rampaged through a strong schedule in 1977, but even finishing with a 10 and 1 record (North Texas also lost to Mississippi State, but it was put in the win column by a forfeit for illegal practices), there was no television and no bowl game. North Texas defeated SMU, only the third time in the history of that rivalry. The coup de grace was a 20 to 19 victory over Memphis and decisive wins over New Mexico State and Louisiana Tech. The only official loss was to Florida State, 35 to 14 at Fouts Field which was struck by a late fall snowstorm before the game. Florida State players had a wonderful time playing in snow, something they saw infrequently, while running over North Texas.

Hayden Fry's final year at North Texas was 1978 when his team finished 9 and 2 with decisive victories over Oklahoma State, Southern Mississippi, and Memphis. A trip to Austin left North Texas with another loss to Texas, 26 to 16—a team the Green has never defeated.

A young man named Jordan Case engineered the Eagles in 1978 and '79 under two different coaches. Jordan was one of those dedicated, overcome-any-obstacle kind of quarterback. After losing to Texas that year, he led the Eagles to four straight wins, including the Southern Mississippi and Memphis games—but the most vivid victory in my memory was New Mexico State game.

Las Cruces is a delightful desert town out in the middle of nowhere and the home of New Mexico State. Nestled in with the city is the famous old western town of Mesilla, where the stagecoach stopped after a long, tough journey from El Paso. It has some really great Mexican food. These trips to New Mexico State also meant a trip across the border from El Paso, where we stayed, to Juarez. When the team came back from one these trips, there were piñatas, dolls, big hats, and all sorts of stuff the players and staff (and Fred and I) brought back.

In 1978, New Mexico State had completed construction on a brand-spanking-new football stadium and North Texas was the team to inaugurate the new era. The Aggies had long been a rival of North Texas and, in the last home game of the '77 season, 18,500 fans packed Fouts Field for the Eagles 45 to 17 victory in that 10 and 1 season. That was the fifth largest crowd to attend a game at Fouts Field at the time.

So here is '78 and an important game for Las Cruces' home folks. The two battled furiously and New Mexico State led 21 to 15 with less than a minute to play. North Texas had the ball driving down to the five-yard line, hurry up call, and Jordan Case, a runner as well as passer, rolled right, faked a pitch, swung around right end, was hit just inside the one, and catapulted himself toward the end zone, ball outstretched! Jordan forced the ball across the goal line as he was hit, and the official standing right over the play signaled for a touchdown. Had the official been in any other position, he might have missed it. North Texas won 22 to 21. Jordan Case, the personable winner, is now president of the Park Place automobile company in Dallas.

There was an amusing sidelight to that premier game at the new stadium in Las Cruces. There was a comfortable press box and a suitable visiting radio booth. We had a flawless technical situation in a brand new stadium and the climax of the game made it a favorite in Denton. The next week, I received a phone call from Dr. James Rogers, the man who was first involved with my association at North Texas, and he said he thoroughly enjoyed the exciting game, particularly the classical music playing in the background during the entire broadcast. Seems the stadium was built next to the tower of the New Mexico State campus radio station, which bled into our equipment. I hope the "1812 Overture" finale was playing on that winning touchdown!

Hayden Fry left North Texas after the last game of the '78 season for the University of Iowa where he created a remarkable record of victories and bowl appearances. He is rightfully a legend all over the cornfields of that state. This was a difficult time for North Texas. The antiwar student movement had reached the campus some years earlier and a sort of malaise had settled over the institution. After the long-reigning president J. C. Matthews resigned (he led the integration of North Texas in 1954), there followed a succession of presidents: John Kamerick and then John Carter, who acted as interim president. A rather young man, C. C. (Jitter) Nolen became president without great academic qualifications. He had been a cheerleader at Texas Christian University, a position his detractors kept reminding everyone of. Nolen was ousted in a state political coup; Carter came back as the interim, and then the most unfortunate selection of Dr. Frank E. Vandiver occurred. With an Oklahoma University booster Eddie Chiles (owner of the Texas Rangers for awhile) on the Board of Regents, nothing much happened except for a drop in school morale among the faculty and student body. Chiles once admitted he cared nothing about North Texas—Oklahoma was his school. During this period, there was little done to improve the athletic image. In fact, more and more faculty members and students called for an end to football.

With all of this administrative turmoil, the athletic complex crumbled. The football field was badly kept, the buildings and facilities deteriorated, and very few people sat in Fouts Field seats. During this period, a highly qualified friend of Fry's, Jerry Moore, was named head football coach in 1979—but was then offered the top job at

Texas Tech University in the Southwest Conference, which he took following the 1980 season.

I will mention that in 1981, the university hired the former head coach of Mississippi State, Bob Tyler, as athletic director and football coach, but I have nothing else to comment. If ever there was a department with no morale or redeeming value—well, this was the worst a university could have. The record was 2 and 9 with North Texas shut out three times. Tyler was booted after one year. My friend of twenty-two years, sports information director Fred Graham, warned the board about hiring Tyler. When they hired Tyler, Fred retired. The only positive acquisition that year was Doug Ray, who replaced the sports information director. Ray served the university well for the next thirteen years. During this time, Ron Shanklin, the former great receiver, became my broadcast buddy.

My duties at the university were split between teaching the sportscasting course and handling some radio and television promotion at the news and information office while broadcasting North Texas football and basketball, hosting and producing the coaches' show, and a few other assorted chores. Due to various circumstances, the ability to connect with a Dallas or Fort Worth radio station was difficult. Stations willing to carry sports came and went depending on their formats and on the success or failure of the North Texas program. I incorporated our broadcast on the university noncommercial station, KNTU-FM, which had reached a hundred thousand watts and could be heard up into Oklahoma and far south of Dallas, along with the old Denton reliable, KDNT. We produced the broadcasts, selling grants to local businesses for airing on KNTU (just name-mention several times during the broadcast), and took care of all expenses. KDNT took the broadcast off the air from KNTU. It saved us money on a crosstown telephone line and they ran our commercials that couldn't run on KNTU.

In 1978, Fred and I approached Harwell Shepherd's new hotshot general manager, a different personality for the old owner, about putting the North Texas games on KDNT's FM station, which was almost totally unknown. FM was just beginning to bloom in popularity and the Denton FM, a powerful station, would be great for our needed sports coverage. The new general manager kept us in state of anticipation—they were checking on the best way to provide the coverage and other vague promises. Then one day it was announced that the KDNT-FM tower had been moved to the Dallas County line, as close as it could be to Dallas, and sold. It was the beginning of the proliferation of frequent radio frequency moves all over the North Texas area and many ownership changes.

Furious at the deception of the GM (who, it turned out, was hired by Mr. Shepherd for the express purpose to gain permission from the Federal Communication Commission to move the tower toward Dallas and a more lucrative market), Fred and I began a campaign to find a new frequency for Denton County. Thus began a ten-year journey, which ended with the birth of FM frequency 99.1 and KJZY. Maybe that's a story for another book.

In 1980, the Mutual Broadcasting Company attained the broadcast rights to the Southwest Conference games. John Butler, a friend of mine at KRLD, was the Texas manager and I was hired to work a number of games, mostly Texas A&M, football, and some game-of-the-week basketball. So I ran the North Texas radio network, broadcast their games, and added more trips with Mutual. A dear friend, John Hicks, managed the Denton County airport and also bought and sold planes. Without him and his professional pilot experience, I would never have been able to pull off this double duty. We flew to College Station for a day game, and then we flew back to Denton for a North Texas night game. We also pulled this off going from College Station to Shreveport for another Eagles game. John also spotted for me on these trips. I bought the gas.

One of my fellow broadcasters in Texas for whom I had the greatest respect was the late Frank Fallon. Frank broadcast Baylor games and ran their radio department sports entity much the same as I did at North Texas. You may recall Frank's voice as the public address announcer for years on the NCAA basketball tourney championships.

When I worked a couple of years with Mutual, my broadcast partner was Steve Fallon, Frank's son and a promising sportscaster. Steve and I had a smooth relationship in the booth, much like that of Verne Lundquist. Steve was not forceful coming in with comments during the games, so I talked him into the process and we developed, in my thinking, a pleasant rapport. One of my favorite trips was a flight to Penn State University when the Texas Aggies played and lost to the Nittany Lions. Joe Paterno is one of the few deeply honorable people left in coaching and always a favorite of mine. Steve and I flew into Pittsburgh, rented a car, and I drove in a downpour to the school and the next day's game, where the Aggies lost.

There are colleges and universities that have a high profile, a recognizable color or mascot, and great student and alumnus support, but I must admit that none of these things make goose bumps on my arms like that at Texas A&M. When the Aggie band enters Kyle Field with their precise military music and marching and all those Aggies are standing and swaying to the music during the entire game, you will be almost impossibly hard-pressed to find an equal. The students kiss on every touchdown!

Out of this association with Mutual, Steve, and Texas A&M came a phone call one day from a person who said he was the broadcast supervisor of the Los Angeles radio stations handling the LA Rams games. He told me, while the Rams were playing the Cowboys in Dallas, he had heard a game that I had broadcast with Steve and was impressed by the way I worked in the color commentary. Along with other compliments, he expounded on the fact that very few broadcasters could do that. Then he hit me with, "Would you be interested in broadcasting the Rams games?" Huh? Wasn't that where everyone wanted to go, California? I said I would indeed be interested, so he asked me to send him a tape of one of my Cowboys games and another Aggie game. He would be back in touch.

A couple of weeks later, he called again (I had verified his position with the station) and he was elated with the tapes. He presented me with another plan. Since I taught sportscasting and recommended students for jobs and such, would I mind listening to a tape of the current Rams broadcaster and give him a critique? "Critique?" I asked. "Yeah, tell me what you find good and maybe not-so-good about the broadcast—what you see as a problem." I agreed, thinking that maybe I was making progress into this new job.

The tape arrived and I sat in a booth at the North Texas radio station listening carefully to the game, taking it apart as I did my student's taped games. I wrote out a detailed account of what I heard and what I considered good and lacking in the broadcast. He called me, proclaiming that was exactly what the management was troubled with. He would get back to me soon.

Near the end of that season, he called and said they would make a change. Would I accept the position as the Los Angeles Rams radio broadcaster? (Did I have to think about it?!) I wouldn't have to move out to LA right away. They would provide me all the information I needed to prepare for the broadcasts, and on Fridays they would fly me out for the games, at home and away. This way, I could continue working at KVIL and the University of North Texas. Later, once this was established, I might want to move to California. We did not talk money. I suggested that I would fly out and discuss a contract, but he said there was no rush since this was December of that year. He was adamant: "Don't worry. You have the job! The job is yours!"

The job was not *mine*. In the following spring, the California Angels, on the same radio station as the Rams, made an announcer change. My contact called and asked if I could also handle baseball. Can a monkey swing from tree to tree? Of course I could—ask Don Drysdale. I sent him a tape, but higher powers than my man made a corporate decision; I was out and another veteran broadcaster was in—for both jobs.

I never again was contacted by the executive who told me that the job was mine. I just heard who was hired by news release. A common problem in this business, and maybe all business, is that people often don't follow through and don't have the courage to call and say, sorry but I was unable to do as I promised.

At a Texas Association of Broadcasters semiannual meeting in Dallas recently, a great deal of emphasis was placed on sports broadcasting. Sports, I feel, has more potential for graduates now than news and disc jockey work. So many local stations have eliminated news departments, or newscasts, and have syndicated programs for much of their music or talk programming. But if they want to make local money, they still broadcast sports.

The current voice of the Dallas Cowboys, Brad Sham, who has been in that position for twenty-five years, made some very pertinent comments in a speech to the gathering. He pointed out that there is no "perfect job" in this business. He noted that sportscasters, even at the network level, are always looking for that chance at an elusive position, or questioning the thinking of their supervisors, and seemingly are never totally satisfied. It isn't necessarily money—it is recognition, taking on the challenge, adding another successful item to the resume. The job is much like actors who must keep trying for the "perfect role." Brad continued that sportscasters, like other talent in radio and TV, are not in a totally secure position; they serve at the subjective decision of the CEO of the professional team, president of the college, high school superintendents, and the public.

Laura Nash, senior lecturer in business ethics at Harvard, believes "that this society's fascination with celebrities can make people feel perpetually inadequate—that no amount of money or power or success can ever be enough" (quote from *New York Times*, June 27, 2004). But money was not my fascination with the offer of these various jobs I had, or almost had. It was the fact that I had reached a position in my profession where I was recognized as one of the best. To be made the Rams offer, even though it fell through, was sufficient after the shock of the loss went away. But adding in the Angels baseball position with the Rams left me wondering: Was the talent who was given the job actually better able than I to handle both jobs? In my mind, I still don't think so. I heard him broadcast and I have sufficient confidence in my work to believe I could have done better. You see, in my mind, I am still a major league broadcaster and, even now, better than many handling football and baseball. Ego? Maybe, but I believe it is confidence in my ability to do this business. And we must have that.

When North Texas hired Corky Nelson as head football coach in 1982 and Dr. Al Hurley as president of the university, a new era of progress and even happiness began to emerge. As someone unknown once opined, happiness "is not a matter of events; it depends upon the tides of the mind." For too long, there had been little but turmoil in all aspects of the university, but now began a period of academic endeavor and student enthusiasm.

Coach Nelson came to North Texas from Baylor University where he was defensive coordinator, a perfect fit for the Eagles and their defensive football history. Nelson's greatest claim to fame was his head coaching tenure at John Tyler High School in Tyler, Texas, where he coached the future University of Texas star, Heisman trophy winner and all-pro running back Earl Campbell. Tyler won the class 4A All-State Championship in 1973 with Campbell.

Dr. Al Hurley had been chairman of the Air Force Academy's history department for fourteen years and retired from the Air Force in 1980 with the rank of brigadier general. Dr. Hurley was a native of that grand borough in New York—Brooklyn. And though he had been out and about with the Air Force for much of his life, he still had an accent that was decidedly not Texan. He also had moved up from a vice president spot in the administration and was not at all known in Texas. So with our videotape equipment and student help, I wrote and produced several television public service announcements with Dr. Hurley. They featured the new president talking about the new North Texas looking ahead to the twenty-first century with the background music of our students in the famed College of Music. These thirty-second spots were not bad, if I may boast, and my dear helpmate at WFAA-TV, Alva Goodall, found time to run those for us. Alva was and is one of the most dynamic and sincere PR people I have known in this business. She and her counterpart at Channel 4 kept the North Texas name, and my reputation as a North Texas producer, before the public for several years. Fred Graham wrote and I produced, along with the director, Duncan Engler, of the North Texas television media department, a promotional spot for North Texas that was to run in the regional telecast of a North Texas football game.

Joe Greene was then the star defensive player of the Pittsburgh Steelers and came home to North Texas to work on some requirements for his degree. The spot centered on Joe's playing days at North Texas when there were seven thousand students and now, several years later, it was seventeen thousand and growing. At the conclusion of the spot, he turned to the camera and said in effect, "North Texas, it's always like coming home." The TV game for North Texas didn't happen, but the promotional spot was so well received that it ran for years whenever there was a television opportunity.

After several years of athletic independence and both external and internal athletic deterioration, North Texas took the step of joining the Southland Conference, Division 1-AA, one step below the major colleges in Division 1-A. Now at least there was something to win!

Quickly, North Texas took advantage of the new alignment and, under Coach Nelson, won the Southland Conference championship in 1983, reached the quarterfinal round of the Division 1-AA playoffs (something Division 1-A can't provide even today!), and finished fourth in the nation in 1-AA.

The conference championship showdown with Northeast Louisiana was the first regional television appearance in a decade. In the

Division 1-AA playoff, the Eagles lost to the University of Nevada–Reno in the snow, rain, mud, and cold in overtime, 20 to 17.

During the 1980s, we were beginning to use the new television videotape cameras to tape our games and produce a new coaches' show that was sent out to cable stations around the state. One glaring problem was the inadequate lighting at Fouts Field. The lighting system had not been upgraded since its installation and, in order to have a broadcast-quality (or as close as we could get) game tape, we borrowed a collapsible tower from the grounds department at the university, placed it behind the player's bench, and shot the game with the new video tape camera twenty feet in the air. Even game film was so dark it was not worth using. It was close to the standard we needed to send to other television stations and far above what we could tape from the press box. Again, our students handled these assignments.

The best students in my burgeoning sportscasting class were incorporated into the radio broadcasts as spotters and statisticians, and the top student was my color analyst. One radio person in Dallas asked how we could afford all the voices we had and couldn't believe most were students. Our students broadcast the women's basketball games on KNTU. The top students also handled the play-by-play on our videotape of the games. We rented a fifteen-passenger van and transported all the talent and equipment around the conference. When we had to fly on charters to games, we managed a cameraman, at least one talent, and my radio staff. There were slipups. On one trip to Nevada, the cameraman forgot to bring a tripod and neglected to let us know. He shot the entire game with the camera balanced on his shoulder. You know what happens when someone tries that? A three-hour ball game becomes an extension of seasickness with the picture never remaining still. If he had told us, we could have borrowed or rented a tripod and saved the game tape. People learn early that mistakes will happen but, with honesty, can be corrected.

In 1983, I left my morning sports position at KVIL to come to North Texas full time in the news and information office, continue to broadcast Eagles football and basketball, and teach in the radio/TV department. Our commercial radio station project before the FCC was coming up soon, and we temporarily moved to Denton to give us more stature as Denton residents in our application.

Traveling with the news and information director, Susan Wilson, on a speaking engagement with Dr. Hurley, I pressed the question of obtaining funds to develop a new local cable channel that had been allocated to North Texas for a student television station. The local cable company had installed several channels in the university when they came to Denton, and one was lying dormant in the television area of the radio/TV department. I had considerable television equipment, studio and portable recorders, and cameras that could be transferred into a studio in the radio/TV department. The president okayed the needed money, and NTTV was born.

Now that we had studio space to produce the coaches' show with Corky Nelson, our videotapes of the football and basketball games could be aired over the Denton cable system. At the same time, we sent copies of the coaches' show and game tapes to a number of area cable systems. These programs also were aired on the Texas State Sports network. Now, with advancing technology, we were finally putting out the North Texas message.

As part of our endeavor to build the North Texas image, we started an hour-long noontime coaches' show on our university radio station, KNTU-FM, every week from a cooperative restaurant location in Denton. The show consisted of interviews with players, assistant coaches, and the head coach. When the university opened a restaurant on campus run by the hotel management division, we moved into that location.

During the academic and athletic calendar, my schedule kept me working seven days a week from September through the basketball season. Speaking of basketball, we started broadcasting the women's basketball games, first just at home, then also the road games. At that time, the men and women played doubleheaders with the women first followed by the men. It worked out perfectly for the university radio station. My sportscasting students earned the right to broadcast the women's games. NTTV, the university cable system, also videotaped both men and women's games. Our sports program gave the students the unusual opportunity to hone their broadcasting skills at North Texas.

In addition to the broadcasting and television production, I was the sole provider of funds for our units. Long before each sport season, I pounded the pavement selling grants to local businesses. These grants covered the expenses of radio broadcast lines and travel, and the television taping and travel. Sometimes when we could add another commercial radio station to the KDNT-KNTU-FM affiliation, I stepped over into selling commercial time as well. KDNT sold its own commercial time. Selling was the last thing I wanted to do, but through the years from 1976 until I left in 1996, the university was never approached for any support of these programs! The one area I requested aid was for radio and TV equipment, which did not occur often. What all this says is that as you learn one part of the business, another demands attention, until finally you can, as an individual, be a one-person sales, production, and talent entity. For seventeen years, that was my role, as well as teaching and promotion. Through these years, Dr. Hurley would occasionally thank me for all I was doing for North Texas. Remember that.

In those first two years Corky was coach, I received a call in 1984, from John Barger, a man I had worked for at KRLD—he was offering me another broadcast position. Barger, the general manager of WOAI in San Antonio, asked me to join their broadcast as a color analyst for the new San Antonio Gunslingers of the new spring pro football league. I thanked him, but wasn't really interested in doing color until he mentioned how much he would pay. So I joined Jay Howard as part of the broadcast team for the lowly Gunslingers on a freelance basis.

Had the league been properly promoted and financed, it seemed to have a chance. But there were a couple of franchise owners whose only idea was to force the NFL to allow them in the bigger party. Certainly wasn't the 'Slingers, owned by Texas rancher Clinton Mangus, who claimed to have millions in oil but generally missed the weekly payroll of his team. The 'Slingers and the league lasted two years; San Antonio went 7 and 11 and 5 and 13. The star of the team was an unknown quarterback named Rick Neuheisel who later became a well-known coach and an infamous one at Washington.

Jay Howard was a hard-charging broadcasting type who also broadcast the NBA basketball games in San Antonio. My desire to perform as a color analyst was not the greatest, but as I said, the money was an incentive. I looked at the situation and decided that with a new team and players no one knew, I would concentrate on talking about the blocking linemen on a play, how it did or did not work, and the defensive players who also succeeded or didn't. If you can follow the plays with binoculars, you will see how a lineman breaks down or what makes a play successful. Also, I checked out all of the personal information on the players so that I could make them identifiable to the listeners. I like that better than the "if I were calling that play" color analyst philosophy so pernicious today.

We didn't expect much from the Gunslingers. The early preseason reporting indicated there would be questions and problems, but Jay and I had a great two years traveling around the country. WOAI paid us, so we were more fortunate than the players some weeks.

When flying to away games, the team hired Braniff Airways for their charters. We made a deal that I could go to DFW airport very early in the morning and board the empty plane for its flight to pick up the team in San Antonio. Then I flew home back to Dallas on the empty plane. It's kind of neat being the only passenger on a huge jet with several attendants offering coffee and rolls and such. Also, the captain was kind of a fan of mine, so I would ride in the cockpit and actually flew the plane a little—well, I held the wheel and tried to keep it level. The captain had a great sense of humor and, after landing one night in Dallas, he announced to the empty plane and crew, "That wasn't a bad landing by Bill." There was a stampede to see if I actually had landed the thing.

I was a really—as Ed Sullivan used to say, a *reaaallly*—big wrestling announcer star then. When we traveled, I would be recognized for the *World Class Championship Wrestling* show, with worldwide distribution. Jay would comment about these celebrity findings on the broadcast. It was a big deal to be standing on a football field in Jacksonville, Florida, and some folks would come up asking for my autograph—for the wrestling show, not for the 'Slingers.

In his book, Red Barber mentions how announcers should care for their voice. I took a side trip to Charlotte, North Carolina (the game was in Jacksonville, Florida), to see a friend of mine, Gary Brobst, one of the best students I ever taught, and make an appearance on his radio station. While having lunch, I suddenly felt a tickle in my throat, and by the time lunch was over, I could barely talk. When we reached the radio station, my voice had vanished. A doctor gave me some high-powered medicine to take, the kind that you start with a certain dose and then add to each day. By the time I reached Jacksonville that night, I had a squeak of a voice and in the game Sunday, enough to make a fair sound. However, that virus, or whatever, hung around for a couple more weeks, turning into a devil of an illness. You cannot prepare for that kind of thing, but it is so dangerous in this business.

From our last San Antonio trip, I can give you an idea of how poorly run this franchise was. Jay and I rented a car if we were in a remote hotel situation, and on this trip, we had wheels. Back at the hotel after the last game of the season, one of the coaches ran up to us and asked if he could borrow the car so they could go to Burger King or some such hamburger place because the team had no post-game meal! It was bad enough to haul back a hundred meals (no toys, I presume), but it was uncertain if Braniff would allow the charter to bring us all back because they were owed money for other trips. The team ate, the charter flew, and the league vanished after 1985.

The highlight of the Corky Nelson period was from 1987 through 1990 when Scott Davis eclipsed some of Steve Ramsey's passing records. Davis also could run well, so it opened up the offense. Until the current successful football regime under Darrell Dickey, 1988 was the golden year. The Eagles went to Lubbock and defeated Southwest Conference Texas Tech, 29 to 24—then, two weeks later in Austin, North Texas was in the position to defeat the University of Texas. Leading 24 to 17 late in the fourth quarter, a Southwest Conference official blatantly called a Longhorn touchdown when the receiver dove for the ball and came down out of the end zone. From my position in the radio booth, looking down to my right into the end zone, it was absolutely clear that the diving player missed the outside line of the end zone and landed out-of-bounds. This was one broadcast time I raved and, as I turned around to my left, in the next booth sat the former great UT coach Darrell Royal with no expression whatso-ever. Even Texas fans later admitted, "We wus robbed!"—same as at Arkansas those many years ago. (Oh, I never used "we" as a part of my broadcast—always team proper names.)

To cap off that Southland Conference championship season, North Texas defeated Rice in their stadium in Houston 33 to 17, and then they played Marshall in the Division 1-AA playoff and lost 7 to 0. Imagine victories over two of three Southwest Conference teams!

North Texas was riding high with sincere adoration around the

Dallas–Fort Worth area. In 1989, I as I started out to sell the radio time with our usual Denton stations, I received a call from WBAP-Radio in Fort Worth telling me they had openings on their station for five football games, which could include the Kansas State and Southern Methodist games. They would charge us $1,500 per game, and we would have to deliver the broadcast to them—that added on a small line charge. I would also have to use one of my former students, David Hatchett, who was one of their sports reporters, as my color man on those broadcasts. I would also have to pay him!

My selling depression hit a high level as I journeyed out again to add this extra $8,000 (including a fee for added talent) to my budget. Bless the Denton business folks—they came through, quite excited that they would be heard on the fifty-thousand-watt Fort Worth voice. Then, about three weeks before the fall term, WBAP called and informed me they could handle two more games if I could come up with the money. By then, I was a near nervous wreck. I am talent, not a sales person! But back I went and sold $3,000 of more time. Seven games on WBAP!

And North Texas collapsed. After winning their first three games, handily they went to Kansas State and lost 20 to 17 when the Wildcats mounted a more than seventy-yard scoring drive, keeping the drive alive twice by converting fourth-down plays in the last two minutes of the game. It was a devastating game to broadcast and it ruined the rest of the season. The Eagles could not recover and lost five of their last seven games. Obviously, WBAP did not renew its contract the next year.

In 1989, the Eagles didn't recover and finished 5 and 6. The speculation around campus and leaks from the administration was that Corky Nelson had run out of talent, or the ability to recruit by the end of the 1990 season, and he left immediately after the last game. However, that Eagles team left a legacy. Scott Davis and friends played SMU at Fouts Field and drew the largest crowd ever: 22,750 for the North Texas 14 to 7 victory. That record stood until a game with Baylor in 2003.

I happened to be on the committee to hire the football coach to replace Corky Nelson in the late fall of 1990. Prospective coaches would look at the North Texas location, thirty-five miles from Dallas and Fort Worth, and comment that it was a gold mine. Just the opposite was true, as it was extremely difficult to recruit against the South-west Conference schools while they were suffering from out-of-state college recruiters who could offer greater inducements. The South-west Conference then disappeared.

A search committee at North Texas was made up of professors, administrators, a couple of students, which included a player, and a couple of media-types like me. Naturally, many wanted to go after a high-profile coach, but those folks never applied. When it came down to trying to figure out which assistant coaches from various colleges might be of value, we were suddenly struck by the emergence of Mar-shall High School's Dennis Parker, whose team was one win away from the state championship. Parker actually flew in to be interviewed a few days prior to the championship game. After his team was victo-rious, the committee turned on its own determination not to hire a high school coach and recommended Parker.

Parker was the second Marshall coach hired by North Texas; leg-endary Odus Mitchell was the first who had also been a successful coach in that East Texas community. Coach Parker was a deeply reli-gious man who demanded his team exhibit and play disciplined foot-ball. However, he was also a pragmatist. When asked about a player wearing an earring, he smiled and said, "If he can play football, I don't really care." During his three-year tenure, there was minimal success, but few quality players were left after 1990, and Parker was trying to totally rebuild the program. Also, a group of supporters who couldn't believe there wasn't a "Bear Bryant" out there ready to give all for North Texas put considerable pressure against Parker on the administration.

We continued to build our sports broadcasting area of the radio and TV department. My former ace student, Craig Way, worked at KRLD. There were so many ex-UNT students there, in all depart-ments, that it was called the North Texas Mafia. Craig had estab-lished a high school game-of-the-week broadcast plus a statewide high school scoreboard show following the game. Craig's production of the game and scoreboard became Friday night "must-listen" radio. Over several years running, he had increased interest in high school football in Dallas. Craig also utilized my students as well as other re-porters to cover area high school games and call in reports for his scoreboard. By 1993, with KDNT in Denton covering two local high schools, plus tape-delayed broadcasts of other select high school games on Saturday and its own Friday scoreboard, I had a dozen of my sportscasting students reporting high school games and calling in reports. I will modestly say that I doubt there was any other college in the country that was providing such an education and practical opportunity for aspiring sportscasters.

Then it all ended.

I had never been to my Muskogee Central High School reunion. Now here was the fiftieth reunion of the Roughers, and I was encouraged to come and make a speech. With a former student and my color analyst, George Dunham, with me for the past five years, I elected to skip a broadcast and attend the reunion. Dunham was working at KRLD in their sports department and had been doing play-by-play for various high school games.

Returning from the reunion, I told Coach Dennis Parker that at least now my fellow students knew who I was. Early in the football season, Dunham mentioned there would be a sports-only station in Dallas coming on the air in the late fall. They had asked him to join their staff and he wanted my thinking on his making the change from KRLD. I told him he was not going to be sports director at the CBS station in the foreseeable future and the change, since he was sought out and receiving an increase in pay, couldn't hurt his career. When I returned from Oklahoma, he told me he was moving to the new station when it received FCC approval. The station would be called The Ticket.

In October of '93, the owner of KDNT suddenly sold his station to a Hispanic operator in Dallas who planned to make it a Spanish music automated station with several other small stations he owned in the area. That was the end of Denton radio except for KNTU, the university station.

When this happened, I met with the KNTU managers and discussed the fact that North Texas basketball would be solely on the university station that fall and winter, and that I would sell the advertising grants. It was practically impossible to put the basketball broadcast on any other stations. The game wasn't that popular with Dallas area radio stations.

When I returned to my office, I had a message from the interim athletic director, George Young, that he needed to see me in his office.

It was decided in 1990 that North Texas was not making any progress in its athletic programs as a Division 1-AA school. The plan was to fulfill the requirements of membership in the upper levels of college football, Division 1-A, by hiring a high-profile athletic director while making plans to expand the football stadium to meet the thirty thousand seating requirement.

The university hired Steve Sloan, a former Alabama director of athletics and a one-time Texas Tech head coach, to lead the athletic department into Division 1-A. Sloan was the person UNT supporters had been seeking for years. Meanwhile, my base of operations, the news and information office (now known as "public affairs"), had undergone a pogrom of leadership in 1991. The director, Susan Wilson, had lost favor with the president, Al Hurley, and was pushed out. Before the new director was in place, Wilson and her assistant Carolyn Barnes were codirectors sharing control and chaos.

There was enough in-fighting to make the fifteen or so staff members' lives extremely miserable. In a secret staff meeting, I was asked to seek out the current interim overall supervisor, who was head of another university department, and ask him for a meeting with the staff. Everyone considered me the North Texas broadcast legend who was untouchable. That is a real laugh. The employees were distressed, depressed, and frightened. I finally agreed, and after the supervisor had assured me whatever I would tell him would never leave the office, I gave him a brief overview of the turmoil. Of course, he immediately went over and told the two codirectors in our office that I said there were a ton of problems! My life of light hell was beginning.

The committee to select a new director (which I was a member of) had twice turned down a woman whose husband was a bureau chief for the *Dallas Morning News* in Washington. The woman was Susan Rogers, an attractive person; she had little experience in the committee's opinion, and she had no radio/TV knowledge in my opinion.

Just before Rogers arrived, my close association with KDNT (the Denton radio station with an all-news, all-talk format) provided student interns, but also helped with high school play-by-play, broadcasting some sportscast features. I also arranged for a one-hour talk show featuring in-depth coverage of various subjects utilizing UNT faculty and staff. There was a young man in our public affairs office, a graduate of Brown University, who volunteered that he would like to assist me in research for this program. He was a very bright young man.

So when Rogers made her first official visit to the office to assume duties as the director, I decided that I would clue her in on what we were doing in radio and TV. As I sat in her office, I explained my teaching, my broadcast background, and the various duties I had on campus. Then I told her I was working on this big radio program and would like to have my young friend from Brown have some free time to do research for the program. Susan Rogers looked me in the face and said, "What the fuck do you know about talent?"

I didn't respond. I just looked at her, stood up, and thanked her for her time. I had been evaluating and recommending talent for years. The first student I recommended for a job back in 1967 worked in that position with WRR for fifteen years and was currently a vice president of the Dallas symphony—and there were dozens of others. The next day, when Rogers told me to send her a plan for the radio program, I told her that it had been dropped.

After several months watching at least thirteen public affairs' staff members fired or urged to quit, I wrote a lengthy memo to the president suggesting I could better serve the university by working through the Centers for Texas Study, where I was producing a TV interview show, *Texas Books in Review*, and by working with the athletic department and radio/TV department. I moved out of my office unannounced one weekend. Rogers was enraged and stayed on my case, trying to eliminate me.

Meanwhile, Sloan began a campaign to bring North Texas into 1-A compliance with the National Collegiate Athletic Association. One 1-A qualification was to have a stadium of at least thirty thousand seats. Sloan suggested the students help fund the additional ten thousand seats, putting end zone seats in Fouts Field if they were serious about supporting the program. By 1993, there was little progress, and one day Sloan called me in and told me about a phone conversation he had with Dr. Hurley, who called from San Diego. Hurley told Sloan to advise me that I was supposed to run faculty/staff interviews during the halftime of game broadcasts—something I had been doing for years and public affairs had tried to take over. They had suggested interviews and stories I could read on the air. I told them no thanks—I would do recorded personal interviews. I may have missed one halftime because of time restraints or something. Hurley then said he knew Rogers and I didn't like each other (I wonder who informed him of a halftime omission?), but that Mercer had never said anything to him about it. Sloan suggested I should watch my back, and then he proceeded to tell me he was leaving as athletic director for a job with a college in Florida. He said he realized that Hurley was not going to fund the North Texas move to Division 1-A adequately, and it was futile to try and move forward. Sloan left, and George Young became the interim director.

So in 1993, I went to George Young's office as he requested. He informed me that the university had sold the basketball and football rights to the new sports station, The Ticket, and they would supply their own broadcasters. It didn't take a second to realize I had been kicked out after thirty-four years. I asked who the broadcasters would be, and Young said, "Your color man, George Dunham, and assisting him the sports information director, Brian Briscoe"—two of my former students. I was stunned; flabbergasted is a better word, even devastated. I called the president, went to his office, and explained what I had learned. He was very quiet and said he would look into it.

It was just a simple coup. Twice I had helped Dunham raise his grades so he could remain in college, and I supported his early family plans and then made him my permanent color analyst with the promise I would support him as my replacement when I retired. Later, I found that he and Briscoe had met with President Hurley about this new plan, and Hurley told them that it was fine—it was time I retired. In fact, I met with the president that summer before discussing my various roles, and he asked when I would retire. I told him as long as I was healthy and my voice strong, I had no intention of doing so. He suggested we all must retire at sometime, although he didn't until 2003.

One glaring problem for the basketball season was that the new Dallas radio station did not have a listenable signal in Denton at night. When the new athletic director, Craig Helwig, came in, I met with him and explained this was not a good deal; the station could not be heard in Denton at night, and it would still be necessary to use KNTU-FM. He replied that was not the case. He added that we needed a Division 1-A broadcast. I am not sure if he knew this was insulting to me, but he didn't seem to care. There was very little campus or community reaction to my dismissal from broadcasting. I had probably run out my time after all.

A few of my friends on campus had laughingly told me over the years, when many heads began to fall during the Hurley administration, that I had nothing to worry about—I was a legend. I reminded them of guys like Ernie Harwell, the "legendary" baseball broadcaster in Detroit, who had been summarily sacked by his owners after forty years of service; so anything was possible—and it still is!

Because the FCC did not okay the transfer of ownership to The Ticket by the basketball season, the new station did not start broadcasting basketball until late December. Meanwhile, we had been carrying the games on KNTU and continued the rest of the season. When The Ticket came on, we had two broadcasts for the same sport.

I finished up the basketball broadcasts in the spring of 1994 and signed off after nearly thirty-five years of Eagles athletics. My position as a teacher in the radio/TV department was secure. I realized what great friends I had there as they rallied about. I taught two or three courses a semester until May of 1996, when I reached the end of my tether. I could no longer drive to the school without some antidepression medicine. It was time to go, and I left.

I broadcast my last football games in 1994. Craig Way put me in contact with Chuck Kelly, who was a slick entrepreneur in Dallas. Kelly had the rights to the best possible high schools and secured radio stations and talent to broadcast their games. Seems Chuck had made a deal to broadcast Westlake High School in Austin but had no one there he wanted to use as an announcer. It was a good deal for my battered emotional system, and I could visit each week with my old high school friend, W. C. McCully, who lived in Austin.

I drove down on Friday, checked into a motel, visited with McCully, and then broadcast the Westlake games. This was an area of Austin much like Highland Park in Dallas—very upscale, and the football teams were successful.

I had a great year. I was planning to broadcast ten games but ended up announcing sixteen, including the state championship game in Houston that Westlake lost. That was the end of football after some forty-four years broadcasting the game.

Though the conclusion of my career at the University of North Texas was sordid, I still have the greatest love and respect for what turned out to be my professional anchor, especially at times when I sorely needed one—though I have not listened to or attended a game since I left and won't as long as Brutus is in the booth. They honored me with induction into the North Texas Athletic Department Hall of Fame in 1990; I was the first nonathlete to be awarded the honor. The Ulys Knight Spirit Award, given to an alumnus or group who has made exemplary effort to maintain spirit in the North Texas family, was also handed to me.

In 2001, my radio/TV department friends urged me to come back and teach the sportscasting course. They had run out of trained sportscasters and had the high school football games for Lewisville High coming up in the fall. Since then, I have been teaching two courses a week for nearly six years—and we have a nice stable of sportscasters again.

Around Dallas and Texas, I have been greatly honored to be inducted into the Ex-Pros Baseball Hall of Fame. Two years ago, the newly created Texas Radio Hall of Fame inducted me, Brad Sham, the late Frank Gleiber, and Kern Tipps as the first members in the play-by-play category. Recently, the Oklahoma Sports Museum in Guthrie honored me with the Bill Teegins Award, which goes to an Oklahoman who has succeeded in sports broadcasting. The award is named for the late and greatly admired Mr. Teegins, the Oklahoma State University sports broadcaster. He was killed in the plane crash that killed a number of Oklahoma State athletes and officials. The Oklahoma Sports Museum annually presents the Warren Spahn Award to the best left-handed pitcher in baseball. This year it was Dontrelle Willis of the Florida Marlins. I am forever indebted to their excellent museum director, Richard Hendricks, and my old *Dallas Times Herald* friend, Frank Boggs, for their support.

Despite this recognition, my failings were obvious to me. I didn't handle my personal relations with some owners or managers, such as Tex Schramm, quite as I should. I made some decisions too quickly and should have worked better at negotiating new opportunities, such as the CBS-TV program. However, these fifty-seven years broadcasting have been more fun than sorrow. There are other parts of my broadcasting career that I haven't even gotten to yet—the Uncle Merky kids show in Muskogee, Colonel Radar on Channel 4 in Dallas, dressing up as an elf and visiting truck stops while at KVIL, and other such delicious things that come to a broadcaster. Maybe I can put those stories together sometime.

# 2

# Romancing the Diamond

In 1900, Reginald A. Fessenden made radio's first voice broadcast. Years earlier, Alexander J. Cartwright had defined baseball. In the 1920s, radio and baseball came together in a perfect marriage. The first baseball broadcast, a re-creation, occurred on April 5, 1914, when Victor H. Laughter spoke from New York's Falls Building. The New York Giants were playing an exhibition game with the Memphis Turtles in Memphis's Red Elm Bottoms Field, from where inning-by-inning scores were telephoned to Laughter, who broadcast to the steamboat *G. W. Robertson* by either shortwave radio or telephone.

Baseball had become the national sport during the 1900s while radio was in a state of development. In 1920, KDKA in Pittsburgh and WWJ in Detroit made the first commercial broadcasts, having gone on the air after that year's baseball season. The Westinghouse Corporation built the one-hundred-watt radio station KDKA in a little shack atop its nine-story factory—really, it *was* just a shack.

Americans bought or built radio receivers as fast as producers could supply the parts. In 1921, Julius Hopp, a manager at Madison Square Garden, came up with the idea of having WJY in New York, which shared a frequency with WOR and another station, broadcast the upcoming "Battle of the Century" for the heavyweight championship between Jack Dempsey and Georges Carpentier. The promoters broadcast the match into theaters, halls, and auditoriums. Despite the difficulty of channeling radio signals into outside speakers in these places, the plan worked, and WJY had a broadcast radius of two hundred miles. Amateur radio clubs, wireless organizations, and other groups promoted the venture.

The president of the National Amateur Wireless Association, J. Andrew White, who had been an amateur boxer, was the broadcaster. He practiced his commentary before the fight while throwing punches in front of a mirror. On July 2, 1921, the fight took place in New Jersey, where Dempsey knocked out Carpentier in the fourth round. Some three hundred thousand fans heard the broadcast. Some audiences had to have the event read by wire report when the speakers failed, and the transmitter blew just as the fight ended.

That same year, the Newark *Sunday Call* broadcast the first World Series game from the Polo Grounds. The newspaper sent a reporter to the game to send a play-by-play over a telegraph line to the *Sunday Call* offices. The plays were handed to the sports editor, George Falzer, who read them into a telephone line to the newly established station of the Westinghouse Corporation at the corner of Plane and Orange Streets. This telephone broadcast directly over the air occurred on the second licensed station in America, WJZ.

Following farther down on the radio club report was a picture of Falzer holding a telephone of the day, keeping the earpiece to his ear while speaking into the microphone at the top of a foot-long stand. Evidently, they realized that they would have a live broadcast by just telephoning directly to the radio station rather than going through the newspaper office.

There was another claim by the Newark News Radio Club report that WJZ broadcast the first intercollegiate football by radio play-by-play in October of 1921. There was a picture of the announcer standing in what they called the "press gallery" with two other gentlemen calling the game. I always stood while broadcasting football. There was better breathing and better sighting, especially at my height.

Another first for Newark took place on May 6, 1922, when the Newark *Sunday Call* installed a radio transmitter on an automobile sent out to broadcast news from the scene. There is a picture in the Newark Radio Club report showing a man identified as Emory Lee, radio inspector, measuring the wavelength of the transmitter, which rested on the engine hood of the big four-door sedan. The antenna, four or five lines, was strung between posts mounted on the front and rear bumpers.

A hundred thousand radio receivers were produced in 1922 and five hundred thousand the following year. By 1924, all kinds of programs were broadcast around the country, and baseball was one of the major attractions in every city with a team. Listeners set the home receiver antenna just right to pick up out-of-town baseball broadcasts. Most of the earlier sports broadcasts had been sent by either code or telephone to the radio station and then rebroadcast. The first collegiate football game between Texas A&M and the University of Texas was broadcast November 25, 1920, on A&M's WTAW, then operating on an experimental license, call letters 5XB. The transmission was in code. Remote broadcast equipment that could be connected to a telephone line at a stadium was cumbersome, heavy, and difficult to maintain, but upgrades were being invented as quickly as brilliant engineers could put them together.

KDKA's first full-length live sports event was a fight between Johnny Ray and Johnny Dundee at Motor Square Garden in Pittsburgh April 11, 1921. The *Pittsburgh Post* sportswriter Florent Gibson reported live from ringside. KDKA's first live baseball game broadcast boomed out on August 5, 1921. The National League field of the Pittsburgh Corsairs was connected by wire to the radio station, and Harold W. Arlin announced an 8 to 5 win over Philadelphia. In the fall of that year, Arlin broadcast the University of Pittsburgh–West Virginia University game live on KDKA.

WRR-Radio in Dallas, on the air March 1922, was the first station in Texas but not the first to broadcast sports. Fort Worth and the *Star-Telegram*'s WBAP went on the air on May 2, 1922, and on August 30 of that year accomplished a two-man broadcast of a crucial series between the Fort Worth Panthers and the Wichita Falls Spudders. The Panthers, managed by Jake Atz, were just two games back of the leading Spudders, with a five-game series remaining.

The radio station stationed a man in the park, possibly the "press box," where he relayed each play by telephone to an announcer in the downtown studios. You wonder why they couldn't have just plugged the phone line into the transmitter, but they couldn't or didn't think of it.

Fort Worth won the first game 6 to 2, and WBAP followed the same procedure for the second game, which the Panthers won 7 to 3. The radio-listening public, probably not a sizeable majority of the population then, reacted so positively that the radio station completed a marvel of engineering. According to Bill O'Neal in his book, *The Texas League: 1888–1987, Century of Baseball*, WBAP laid eight thousand feet of telephone cable from the Panther Park to its studios in the *Star-Telegram* newspaper building for the third game in 1922.

Harold Hough was the intrepid announcer who sat on an orange crate somewhere behind home plate and broadcast a 5 to 0 Panthers shutout of Wichita Falls. There was a Saturday doubleheader scheduled where the Panthers could clinch the Texas League pennant. In a decision similar to some that modern management decrees, WBAP broadcast only the second game, a 4 to 0 Fort Worth victory. After all that energy laying more than a mile of cable to broadcast the games live, management opted to carry one game.

Seventy-two years later, it is still apparent that planning ahead for the latest technological innovations was absent in some places—particularly Johnson City, Tennessee.

Mark Nasser is the current 2005 radio announcer for the Omaha Royals of the Pacific Coast League. After telling him the story of Hough and WBAP, he gave me a colorful follow-up story. After interning with media director John Blake, formerly of the Texas Rangers at spring training, 1994, Nasser began his baseball broadcasting career at Burlington, North Carolina. It was the first step for rookie ball players in organized ball, the Appalachian League. Mark was one of two full-time broadcasters in the two-division league, and the first one to plan to broadcast live from Johnson City.

Preparing to go to a stadium where he had never been, Mark called the general manager, alerting him to the fact he wanted to broadcast the game live. There was no press box in Howard Johnson Field in Johnson City and a couple of other problems. Mark was told to bring one hundred feet of telephone cable because he would be seated on top of the first base dugout and would have to run the line to the nearest telephone outlet at the right field fence.

Bringing two hundred feet of cable to be safe, Nasser found that the only telephone connection was in the manager's office in the clubhouse outside the right-field fence! Instead of a hundred feet, as he was told, he needed an additional two hundred feet of line. The ball club management hurried to a store and brought him the two hundred feet, which he spliced into his line, then rolled out and around the right-field fence into the managers' office, and connected to his telephone. (You disconnect the actual phone from the phone box on the wall and then attach the two wires in the cable to the phone line.) The microphone amplifier that Mark used, and most of us have used, had a telephone built on, which he could use to call up his station.

Stringing the line was the first exciting problem. The second was his broadcast location: perched on top of the first base dugout with the protective screen used by the coaches pitching pregame batting practice between him and home plate—a precarious spot, no less. Mark just made it on the air with the first pitch, and had to immediately conclude his broadcast on the last out of the game so the Johnson City manager could use his telephone to call in his report to the major league team supplying the rookie ball players. Well, at least Mark has a story for his grandchildren. There have been some remarkable radio and television technical improvements, which we will pore over as we reach the twenty-first century.

In those days, the 1920s, the Texas League champion played the Southern Association champion in what was proclaimed the Dixie Series. It was a very important series until after World War II and television. So here is a dramatic conclusion to the season, first radio broadcasts and Fort Worth playing Mobile in the championship. WBAP, a pioneer broadcasting the final exciting days of the 1922 season, arranged to replace its tiny twenty-watt transmitter with a "huge" five-hundred-watt monster just in time for the Dixie Series. It was off the air and no games were broadcast. Not planning ahead started a long time back.

Let me go back a moment to that history-rendering Newark News Radio Club. They reported that twenty-five years before 1922 (the year of radio's emergence in America) "Telephone Hirmondo" in Budapest, Hungary, had created a telephone newspaper system through a party line apparatus that allowed a person with a telephone to listen to all kinds of news read between nine a.m. and ten p.m. According to the story, there was a schedule of types of news read at certain times so the listener could pick what stories he or she wanted to hear. It was also reported that live opera was fed into the telephone connections. It's no wonder radio programming developed so rapidly.

Before we move on to the startling developments in sports broadcasting, you must remember that some 1922 radio receivers were simple and easy to put together. Teenage boys and girls were frantically building crystal sets across the country to tune in one of the five hundred radio stations that went on the air in 1922, but it was difficult to hear stations if there was a storm or any interference with the signal.

In order to hear whatever programming was broadcast within range of a family's set, it was necessary for one person to wear headphones. In *Beginner's Book of Radio*, Frederick Dietrich explains that a "receiving outfit cannot be more sensitive than its 'phones.'" He wrote, "The price of a receiving set is immaterial since the phones that are purchased . . . determine its efficiency and sensitiveness."

He then explained the function of the radio. "A receiving aerial may pick up a signal and it will be carried to the tuning coil. After it passes this point, it reaches the detector where it is rectified. All of this efficiency may come to naught if the phones fail to do their part." He also suggested a particular brand: "The Brandes receivers have been developed over twelve years . . . originally designed by Reginald Fessenden . . . the radio expert."

Dietrich didn't mention that he was "Brandes," the company making the headsets. But it was true that in the early days of these little receivers, the best solution for several people to hear a broadcast was to purchase several headsets and connect them in a series. Dietrich pointed out, and it is affirmed in other articles, that purchasing "a horn attachment for the receiver so programs can be heard without headsets is extremely disappointing."

It wasn't long before more expensive sets were produced with built-in speakers. By 1923, WBAP realized that the number of radio sets was exploding, so the renowned Mr. Hough broadcast Fort Worth Panthers games "whenever he felt like it." Radio station promotion burst on the scene, with WBAP boasting that Hough was now using a "supersensitive microphone" that President Warren G. Harding had spoken into early that year!

Fort Worth returned to the Dixie Series in '23 to play the New Orleans Pelicans. This time with that five-hundred-watt transmitter humming, Hough broadcast the series emanating from a person in the out-of-town park sending play-by-play direct wire from the games to a Western Union operator in the WBAP studio. This was the first system I used in 1951 in Muskogee, Oklahoma. The operator in the studio copied Morse code description—pitch by pitch, play by play—on his typewriter. I started the broadcast thirty minutes after the announced game time, so the description was being sent in at least one-half inning ahead of my on-air time. I imagine Hough did the same thing, but since this was so early in broadcasting he might have read it off the paper as it was coming in.

It wasn't until 1926 that WRR, today the FM classical music outlet in Dallas, broadcast occasional Dallas Steers Texas League games. A couple of years later, Zack Hunt broadcast Wichita Falls games. It is really hard to believe, but the radio broadcasts became so popular the Texas League banned them for a while. Some teams broadcast out-of-town games and no home games, as some major league teams did during the 1930s. By 1940, all Texas League games were broadcast in all of the franchise cities. Again, the out-of-town games were re-created to save long distance telephone line charges and travel expenses for the announcers and a necessary engineer. One of the best-known broadcasters, Jerry Doggett, called the Dallas games in 1950 and then went on to a long career with the Brooklyn/Los Angeles Dodgers. I did not broadcast regular season road games live until I joined the Texas Rangers in 1972.

Before radio, the fans were accorded various means to keep up with their team when out-of-town and there were scores of league games posted at their home stadium. Western Union sent an "every pitch service" to press boxes where they were either announced to the crowd by some guy with a megaphone (later public address announcer) or posted on the scoreboard. Galveston's Beach Park had what they proclaimed as "Houlahan's Tally Board" with inning-by-inning reports of the other games in the Texas League.

Today's modern scoreboards follow that old path, but with one guy typing them in a computer. I have a quaint story about providing the fans in Waco, Texas, results of their team while on the road. Howard Basquette, an office boy/vender of the *Waco Herald*, worked diligently providing the fans inning-by-inning results by dragging out his ladder and climbing up to a scoreboard attached to a telephone pole at Fifth and Franklin. As many as two hundred fans would sit in chairs or on the grass watching the progress of a Sunday game, with little Howard scrambling up and down the ladder. The competitor, the *Waco Morning News*, erected an electric scoreboard in a vacant lot next to the paper's buildings in 1916. With the Waco Navigators' third consecutive pennant on the line playing in Dallas, three hundred and fifty fans watched the progress of the game through the miracle of electricity.

Entrepreneurs abounded back in those early days. In Fort Worth in 1906, nineteen-year-old Ray McKinley had a 12-by-20-foot scoreboard put up above the marquee of the city's first movie theater at 3rd and Main. McKinley paid Western Union $9 a week for the play-by-play score service he posted on his board while garnering $175 a week for advertisements!

In October 1922, the first "Chain Broadcast" was structured when WJZ and WGY transmitted a World Series game over telegraph lines from Newark to Schenectady connected to the Polo Grounds. Graham McNamee announced into a single microphone.

McNamee and another announcer, Ted Husing, burst on the scene in 1922 and '24 respectively, and became the first acclaimed stars of sports broadcasting. McNamee was trained as a concert singer before entering radio and produced vivid sports descriptions with his warm, friendly voice. He died in 1942.

Husing was probably the foremost play-by-play announcer of that era going into the 1940s. Ted had a smooth delivery and was the first announcer with the ability to capture the drama on the field. He also was very independent and lost some gigs because of his outspoken descriptions. Husing retired from sports and became one of the first disc jockeys in 1946.

Just the opposite of the two "Golden Throats," Husing and McNamee, Clem McCarthy, with a gravel-voiced, high-speed style, called the 1928 Kentucky Derby for KYW in Chicago. Clem joined NBC in 1929 and called every derby until 1947. He was a sharp boxing announcer and famed for his call of the short, dramatic 1938 fight between Joe Louis and Max Schmeling. (By the way, "Golden Throats" might be a copyrighted term coined by the southwest's most accomplished and entertaining sports reporter/columnist, Blackie Sherrod. He used that term at least once a year, usually in the fall, to describe some misguided radio broadcaster. Blackie also was my fellow broadcaster for the Dallas Cowboys in 1968 and '69. He was superb.)

The American Sportscasters Association inaugurated a Sportscasters Hall of Fame in 1980 with baseball great Walter (Red) Barber and famed fight announcer Don Dunphy heading the list. Since then, they have added Husing and McNamee, the Yankees' Mel Allen, Cubs' Jack Brickhouse, Cardinals' Jack Buck, Detroit's Ernie Harwell, and

Vin Scully, the premier announcer today and over the past forty years with the Los Angeles Dodgers. The ubiquitous Harry Caray was named in 1989. I will never join those illustrious fellows, but have been inducted into three halls here in Texas and one in Oklahoma.

While every sport was recognized as appropriate for early-day broadcasts, the one that is so essentially tied to radio is baseball. The key factor is the simple description of the pitcher, the batter, and the immediate recognition of where the ball is hit and how—a ground ball to second, a high fly to right field. For the listener, the picture is painted in his mind immediately. The announcer must always go back to the ball and strike count prior to the pitch or as it is delivered. Even if the announcer does not mention the defensive player's name, there is no loss of the "mental picture" for the listener if the announcer describes exactly where the ball is hit. Barber pointed out the use of who, what, when, where, why, and how as the six serving men of Kipling that also serve broadcasters perfectly.

Think of the difficulty in those early broadcast days of trying to call a football game when the players were not wearing numbers—or numbers large enough to be seen. Of course, football plays start with the quarterback, but in those early wing-formations, the ball could be snapped to any of the backs and then faked three times. In addition, the player runs right or left, into the line or around it, and on to other football difficulty. In football, a description of the direction of the play includes not only the progress across the yard lines, but also which team's lines—it is much more complicated than a ball hit into right field in baseball. Basketball has little to locate positions on the court, but player identification must be there instantaneously and at some place on the court.

Baseball is there every day of the season, but it wasn't on the radio every day in the 1920s and 1930s. Major League Baseball teams feared that broadcasting all of the games on radio, especially at home, would hurt attendance. Also, it was too expensive for traveling announcers and engineers to pay the long-distance telephone toll charges to broadcast road games. In his book *The Broadcasters*, Red Barber explains that when he joined the Cincinnati Reds in 1934, they only broadcast around fifteen home games and re-created the out-of-town games by Western Union wire reports in the studio. Also, many teams would not allow permission to broadcast from their parks and many did not broadcast at all on Sundays and holidays.

The New York Yankees and Giants and the Brooklyn Dodgers entered into a five-year pact in 1934 to ban broadcasting in their parks. This lasted until 1939, when Larry McPhail took over the Dodgers and told the New York teams he was broadcasting all of the games. The Yankees and Giants followed suit. McPhail understood that hearing a game on the radio was an excellent promotional tool. When the team was winning, the fans knew the best seat was in the stadium, not in the living room listening on radio.

Later, when little portable radios made their appearance, the fans brought them to the games for the double pleasure of following the announcer's description (in football, identifying the players as well) while watching the game. I remember when I first noticed this at Burnett Field in Dallas. I was looking for some note or stat and suddenly heard the crack of the bat (I should have been watching the game). Seeing the runner heading for first, I exclaimed that it was a drive to right field. I noticed folks turning around and looking up at me as the ball fell into left field! They were listening on their radios.

Through casual questions put to my sports broadcasting students at the University of North Texas, I have found that many of them in preteen years pretended to broadcast games either by using board games or watching television with the sound turned down. Several major league announcers have mentioned this early childhood desire to be a sports broadcaster. My own experience occurred when I was eleven or twelve years of age. My parents decided we should move to a little farm just about two miles from where my father worked in the Muskogee, Oklahoma, Veteran's Hospital. My father had been injured in World War I, run over while serving as an MP (military police), and had a serious leg injury that gave him problems the rest of his life. My mother decided he needed more exercise, so we headed for the farm life.

For me, an only child, farm life afforded me a lot of spare time a long way from my friends. I was a baseball fan—my father and I played catch, he pitched to me, and we listened to every baseball broadcast available. When Dad had an extra few pennies, we would go to the Muskogee Reds baseball games in the little downtown Athletic Park, sitting in the first base bleachers.

The Reds were a Class C club of the Cincinnati Reds. My favorite player was Ray Lammano, a catcher. Actually, he is the only player I remember from those years when my dad and I went to the games. Why the catcher, I don't know, except they are the guys who are on the move. Ray must have had some special personality that interested me. Maybe I met him—I hope so. He played for Cincinnati in 1941 and then 111 games in 1942, hitting .264 with twelve homers. Not bad! His biography reveals that empty space—'43 through '45—when we went to fight in the war. Ray came back to the Reds in 1946, hit .254 in 1947, played 127 games in 1948, and retired. Ray would be eighty-six as of this writing. Ray Lammano was one little kid fan's favorite in Class C baseball. That's what so great about the game.

I received a baseball board game for my eleventh birthday and played it relentlessly. When the regular season began, and I was out of school, I added my own radio play-by-play as I spun the spinner, which indicated a strike, ball, or base hit. I re-created double headers with other teams of the Western Association, the Muskogee affiliation. I must have broadcast twenty to thirty games a month, keeping my own standings of the teams I covered.

I have no idea what that must have sounded like. I can imagine I must have had some relationship to the game, at least learning to identify where the ball was hit and the players running the bases. I did this until I went to junior high school, became a better student for a while, and found an attraction for girls. The next baseball games I broadcast were the Muskogee Giants of the same Western Association in 1951. Only the major league affiliation had changed.

I had graduated from the University of Denver in December 1949 and was hired immediately as the "news director" of KCOL in Fort Collins, Colorado. That meant I was the "director" of me, the only newsman. I had a journalism/radio major and, with the help of the University of Denver radio station, I had progressed with my football and basketball play-by-play without any professorial instruction. We also read news and wrote news, and I seemed to be maturing into the business. One of our announcing instructors was a top announcer at KLZ-Radio in Denver, and he let me know he thought I was progressing very well—except when I had an audition he had arranged at

KLZ. I literally blew it! It was awful. I missed an early chance at a big city station.

A fellow Denver student was from Fort Collins and learned they were looking for a newsperson. I went up to KCOL and auditioned. They seemed to like it. It certainly was better than the one at KLZ—maybe I learned from that, and they hired me as soon as I graduated in December. It was a nice ego boost to have a job waiting for me, but in retrospect, my wife was teaching in the Denver public schools and had to give up that job. I was making $45 a week in Fort Collins, bought a car, and worked a split shift—newscasting six until nine a.m. and again four to seven p.m. I worked like I knew what I was doing! I developed contacts in town and had a great relationship with the police and fire department; everyday, the program director and I listened to my tapes to help me improve my delivery. However, the station let me go the first of March in an economic cutback. I like to think it was the end of the promotional campaign they had when I had arrived, not that I wasn't particularly good.

But the KCOL general manager hired me to work at his station KOKO in La Junta, Colorado, a big step down from Fort Collins, next to the tracks of the Southern Pacific railroad. Unfortunately, KOKO was not a profitable station. The first one to the bank on payday might have had his check cashed, or maybe not.

Next, I had a miserable sojourn in Galveston, Texas, which was a disaster from any angle, and then I went back to my hometown of Muskogee, where I hoped I would determine my future. I had a year left on the GI Bill, but was too late to enter law school at the University of Oklahoma, so my wife applied for a teaching job in Muskogee. When the superintendent asked what profession her husband was in, she mentioned that I was between jobs, looking for a sports announcing position. He let her know that KBIX-Radio needed a play-by-play announcer to broadcast the Muskogee Roughers high school football games that fall. I called KBIX and, by bluffing my way through as an experienced sports broadcaster, I was given the job. There is more detail about this in chapter 1.

After the football season, I was called by the other station in town, KMUS, and asked to meet about their sports job. Interestingly, I did not find out until about four years ago that the late Bob Murphy, famed announcer of the New York Mets, broadcast at KMUS the year before. I half-heartedly complained when the management at KMUS told me, after I accepted the job, that they also wanted me to broadcast a wrestling program once a month. I had never seen a wrestling match live, and didn't know a thing about it—but then again, I had never broadcast a live baseball game either. Of course, I had listened to hundreds of games, including the Liberty Network in Dallas where the old Scotsman, Gordon McLendon, re-created major league games with elaborate sound effects, including a flushing toilet. Of course, I also had those two years, some fourteen years before, of re-creating my own games on the farm.

Before my first baseball season with the Muskogee Giants of the Class C Western Association, there was the preseason baseball banquet, which was broadcast on KMUS, and I was introduced as the latest broadcaster. A part of that scene was my first interview of a sports figure: Mickey Mantle. Mickey had played at Joplin, Missouri, in the same association the year before and darned near knocked down the Dr Pepper distributor building in Muskogee, across the street from the left-field wall, only three hundred feet from home plate.

The stories were already out that young Mickey did not appreciate being interviewed. The preceding year, he had gone up to the Yankees and then was sent back to Kansas City for most of the season. In 1951, Mickey would go up to the Yankees, play ninety-six games, hit thirteen home runs, and steal eight bases. He was on his way—but my interview was before spring training 1951. I checked around and found that a short while before coming to Muskogee, the Mantles had their first baby, Mickey Junior. When Mickey walked up to my trembling hand-held microphone, I offered, "Congratulations on your first baby. Tell me about the boy." I hit the nerve. Like any proud father, he smiled and told me all of the details about his boy—his name, his mother, all those family things—and with both of us comfortable, I launched into baseball. It worked out very well, and I wish I had a tape of it.

When you broadcast Class C baseball, at least in those days, not one soul, including me, had any idea I should go to spring training and watch the team, the players, and practice play-by-play. All I did was meet with the owner of the Muskogee club, Joe Magota, owner of all the drugstores in town, Purity Drug. He had a monopoly. He also single-handedly kept professional baseball going in a city of thirty thousand. He was a gruff, short, rotund fellow who sat behind home plate where he controlled the new baseballs and rubbed down foul balls that the kids ran down outside the stadium. That lucky kid, who probably had to fight with several others, was given a free pass inside the game. Magota passed the balls to the home plate umpire through a hole in the stadium wall. It was a terrible moment when a foul ball escaped Mr. Magota's grasp. Waste not, want not, save a buck, was his motto.

I told him I had some experience with baseball and avowed that I was one of the oldest fans in town, going back to 1936 when my father brought me to the games. I mentioned my broadcasting of games at the University of Denver, quietly leaving any impression of baseball out of the conversation. While at Denver, I had visited the Denver Bears ballpark on occasion, keeping my hand in. You learn to kind of skirt the awful, inevitable truth. He offered that I wouldn't have a clue about the team until they came into town a couple of days before the season started. I might like to meet the bus when they arrived, which I did at two o'clock in the morning. There wasn't much to learn from grumpy, tired ball players and a manager at that time of day.

My next investigation was into the material I would use when the Giants were out of town. The station management suggested I talk with the Western Union folks who would be handling the play-by-play information from such great places as Fort Smith, Arkansas; Joplin and St. Joseph, Missouri; Salina, Topeka, and Hutchinson Kansas; and Enid, Oklahoma.

The Western Union operator who would be in the KMUS studio during the game described the procedure. There was a WU employee in the host city who sent every pitch, every play, every strike, every ball, by Morse code. My WU contact sat in the radio studio with a headset on, read the code, and typed all the information on a sheet of paper for each half inning. I recently happened to find a copy of one of those Western Union descriptions. They were the key to the broadcast, but they also sent the lineups, of course, the crowd size, the weather, temperature, wind direction, outfield distances. It was an encyclopedia of information. After that, all one had to do was pretend to be at a live game with the same pitch, pace, and enthusiasm.

For me, one tiny problem existed. When re-creating games, the Liberty Network, whether spiriting major leagues through Western Union or reporters calling in the information, had all sort of recorded general and excited crowds, reaction cheers to various-sized base hits, boos, and a fellow talking into a waste basket sounding like a public address announcer. I found out many years later that my friend at KRLD and former mayor of Dallas, Wes Wise, worked on those assignments with Liberty.

At KMUS, we had a Standard Sound Effects disc with general crowd noise that ran about five minutes. That was it. Being a neophyte in the business, it did not occur to me to try and locate other sound effects records outside the station. So there we were with a general crowd noise that became excited-crowd by turning up the volume. I was almost ready. I only had to chase down some score sheets and learn how to score a game, which I had also never done, so during the broadcast I could refer back to what the players had accomplished at the plate. (Score sheets are included later in this chapter.)

One thing I had in my favor was my relationship to Muskogee's Athletic Park, where the games were played. I attended games there in the 1930s with my father. As a kid, it doesn't make much difference which park you see first, they always are dramatic. That was a major adventure in my youth. While attending college, I had been to a larger Triple-A park in Denver, but starting my baseball broadcasting career in my hometown field was special.

Athletic Park was built in the early 1900s, a typical roofed grandstand extending from first base around to third with a small section of bleachers down the left- and right-field lines. There is a park in Gainesville, Texas, right by Interstate 35 that is a spitting image of Muskogee and most minor league parks of the era.

While Boston's Fenway Park has the left field Green Monster, Muskogee's had a left-field fence that was three hundred feet from home plate—at least, it was advertised as three hundred feet, but most players thought it much shallower. Across the street and behind the porch was the Dr Pepper Bottling plant that was an easy target for long ball hitters like Mickey Mantle who played in Joplin the year before I started. It wasn't impossible to hit one on the roof of the Dr Pepper building.

I read in a publication some years back that Muskogee was the first minor league city to have lights at their baseball park sometime around 1930. (I can't vouch for that personally since I was only four years old at the time.) The press box was on top of the roof overlooking home plate and the field. Home plate was shoehorned into the field with only about twenty-five feet back to the stands. It was a rare foul ball caught by the catcher, unless it went straight up over home plate. Anyhow, the press box, by name only, had the PA announcer, a writer for the Muskogee papers, and me. It was pretty cozy, and if someone ran across the roof, we bounced gently. However, it was a desired location to call the game, just back and over the plate, and the roof was probably fifty feet up—much better than some major league parks where the broadcast booth is a stretch for a broadcaster with less than average eyesight.

In an exhibition game in 1951 with the Enid Buffalos, manager Hal Bamberger's Muskogee Giants won 4 to 1 before 1,376 fans. With the bleachers and grandstand filled, the park would probably have a capacity of 3,000. The best attendance was recorded in 1949 when the club averaged 1,350 per game. Babe Ruth and the Yankees played the Boston Red Sox in an exhibition in Athletic Park in 1923 and drew 5,500. Like the rest of the nation, by 1957, television and air-conditioners kept folks indoors and the Muskogee baseball era ended when only three hundred or so stalwarts showed up for each and every last game.

A dramatic fact jumps up when you go back and find the rosters of those Muskogee teams of '51 to '53 and then try to find their names in the major leagues—very few made it to "the show" or had just a few games before they vanished.

Muskogee Manager Hal Bamberger was with the New York Giants in 1948 in seven games and hit .083. That's it. Jack Cooney, Muskogee first baseman, led the Western Association in 1951 with a .345 average and 176 total hits, of which 32 were doubles. Jack later played 93 games with Detroit. Muskogee outfielder Ray Johnson hit .304 in 1951, had 39 stolen bases and 18 triples, and I haven't found his name in the major leagues; Fred Sherkel won 17, lost 5, and hit .271, and he is not listed.

Part of the 1951 season was disrupted by a terrible flood in Kansas. Over ten feet of water nearly destroyed the ballparks in Salina and Topeka. A dead cow was found floating in the clubhouse in Topeka.

The schedule was delayed for a time, but the flood didn't stop Topeka. The Owls won the championship with a 74 and 44 record. Muskogee finished sixteen games out in fifth.

In the 1950s, the players were still wearing the little soft caps. The need for some protection was evident when Otis Johnson of Dothan, Alabama, in the Alabama–Florida League had his skull fractured by a pitch from Henry Clinton of Headland. Johnson died eight days later. It was the first such death since 1947, if that is any consolation. Meanwhile, a lightning bolt struck and killed twenty-three-year-old Andy Strong in the Evangeline League. The steel cleats on those black baseball shoes were the perfect lightning conductors.

Across the country, the installation of Emmett Ashford as the first black umpire in professional baseball made the news. Ashford umpired behind home plate in the game on July 17, 1951, between Yuma, Arizona, and Mexicali in the Southwest International League— almost out of sight, out of mind.

Around the Western Association in '51, a couple graduates later made it: Whitey Herzog, a famous major league manager to be, hit .295 at Joplin; Bobby Del Greco led the league in doubles and played for six different major league teams for the next thirteen years; Joplin's Butch Nieman stroked 28 homers for the leadership and later played three years with the Boston Braves.

There were so many players, so many minor leagues (coming to the end of that era), and so few major league teams that many players traversing D, C, and B ball thought making it to a "fast league" like the Texas League was quite an accomplishment. A "cup of coffee" in the Bigs was somewhat satisfying. To be exact, in 1951 there were three Triple-A leagues, two Double-As (Texas League was one), nine Bs, thirteen Cs, and nineteen D leagues with the independent Mexican league. Thirty-one minor leagues, by my count 365 teams, funneled players into eight National and American League teams. How many minor league players were there? Estimating about twenty in a club would add up to seventy-three hundred players, each harboring thoughts of one of those jewels, the sixteen major league teams. In that era, every town in Texas of any size, and many in Oklahoma, had a minor league team.

In the National League, Brooklyn had the most minor league teams—nineteen. The Dodgers' Branch Rickey developed the system, so that is understandable. The St. Louis Cardinals were next with sixteen and the Giants, a supplier of the Muskogee franchise, had fifteen. In the American League, the Yankees led with fourteen, while Cleveland was next with twelve.

Back in 1951, there were many famous major league names managing in the low minors, such as Joe Medwick (he hit .300 or more over eleven straight years) at B Carolina League. Schoolboy Rowe won twenty-four games in 1936 and managed in the A Eastern League. Vince DiMaggio, brother of Joe and Dom, never hit .300 with four major league teams and was managing Class D Florida State. Cincinnati's Billy Herman of the 1930s managed Class B, Piedmont.

Checking through the various leagues, I ran across two names familiar to Muskogee before 1951. Kelly Wingo, who played in Muskogee and some in the Texas League, was the first of five managers in 1951 in Chickasha, Oklahoma, in the Sooner State League. Kelly might have been related to Ivy and Al Wingo, who played major league ball at the turn of the century. Then there was Ray Baker, who was player-manager for Muskogee shortly after World War II. Ray played centerfield and would race in to argue balls and strikes and, ultimately, be ejected from many games. After his first year, they made a rule that player-managers couldn't come in to argue balls and strikes—it saved some time. That was the time when the players left their gloves just at the edge of the outfield grass.

My Round Rock broadcast buddy Mike Capps' famous cousin, Billy, who became a legend among scouts, managed Sherman-Denison in the Big State League in 1951. Also in 1951, one of the Muskogee players had been given a huge bonus for signing—at least for those days. I can't recall exactly the player, but I believe he was a shortstop. One day, I was sitting in the dugout with manager Hal Bamberger. As he leaned back against the wall, spitting his tobacco and talking ball, I asked if there was anything special he did for the "high" bonus player. His response snapped me to attention, "Fuck him," he said. "Let him figure it out—he has the money." I didn't know at the time how few games Hal had played in the majors, and I am sure he thought this kid would have a free pass. To Bamberger's credit, he hit .268 with 7 homers in 85 games for Muskogee as player-manager— not bad for an "old" ML reject. He was probably only in his thirties.

My first game broadcast in 1951 was in Fort Smith, Arkansas. My station thought it would be easier on me if I did the first game live. It was a nice and reasonably expensive gesture, what with transportation, hotel, and a line charge for a live game. I must admit that I was as nervous and scared about this approaching event as any. Maybe as nervous as the first time I walked on stage to play a psychopathic killer in *Night Must Fall* at Northeastern State College or awoke on deck of the LCI 439 watching the sound and fury of the Japanese air attack on our ships at Leyte in World War II. After all my worry, though, the game was rained out. That morning, I went to the hotel barbershop and had a shave! Remember, the last baseball game I "broadcast" was when I was eleven or twelve years old while playing a board game on our farm. Years later, with whiskers, I rather wished I could remember that broadcast or had a tape. I imagine I muddled through the game, then returned to Muskogee to recreate the rest of that series and all of the out-of-town games for that season and the next two years.

And so the seasons rolled by. We had little or no information about the players, the batting averages were occasionally supplied by Western Union, and the team had the Howe News Service that sent statistics. Of course, this is nothing like today, with computers and the instant availability of any player's information in the minors or majors.

I talked to the players before the games for some personal or baseball information but had no means to use a recorded interview, so we went on the air just in time to give the lineups, the standings, and drop in a few commercials.

My usual partner running the board while I was re-creating the games was Ed Dumit. Ed was a perfect announcer; I never heard him flub a word in copy, ad lib, or in news. Never. He had a rich, beautifully sculptured voice (we didn't know at the time that he was a polished singer) and was the producer and emcee of our classical music program on KMUS. We had a running "fight" about baseball replacing his beloved program in the summer.

Trying to give our re-creations of out-of-town games some extra lift, I became somewhat inventive by checking to see if a railroad ran near the out-of-town ballparks, then managed to find the various schedules so that we could use one of our few sound effects. We kept the timetable at the control board and Ed ran the train sound in Joplin, Salina, or wherever on the schedule. To create some levity, sometimes he would run it late so I could comment. If Ed could find an airplane, horns honking, or some such sound, he might surprise me with a couple of those in our nightly imagination baseball.

On one occasion, he really hit the pinnacle. We never really knew how many people listened to the games, but one of my father's co-workers at the Veteran's Hospital met me in the grocery store one afternoon at five p.m. before I was to broadcast the game being played in Joplin at seven thirty our time. My father's friend said, "How do you go to those out of town games, fly?" Yeah, sure, on our budget. I told him that we re-created the games in the studio; I did not go out of town. "I hear the crowd and all that," he said, laughing. "I was sure you were flying or driving like a madman to the game that night."

That night during the game, I brought my half inning of Western Union script into the little studio and told Ed that in the next half inning, a foul ball would hit a lady in the stands and they would take her to the hospital. I noted the possible delay and then went on with the current half inning and the next one.

So I was going through my, "Smith on the mound, checks the runner at first and delivers, called strike one," while Ed was scurrying around the control room. Then the moment: "Wilson at the plate, one ball-one strike, the pitch, lined foul into the right-field bleachers. Boy, that was a hard shot. There is a lot of commotion in the bleachers. Seems the few fans there are helping to place a lady on one of the bleacher seats. Evidently she was struck by that foul. The players are trotting over to the bleachers . . . time is called . . . a couple of fans have run down the steps. They are working around the stricken fan . . . someone has brought some water up and they are trying to revive her."

After a few minutes of speculation like this, I heard the sound of an approaching ambulance in my headset. I didn't know we had an ambulance sound effect! So I had to join in: "The officials have called an ambulance, evidently the fan is not responding well . . ." and so on The ambulance screeched to a halt, just like in those network radio mysteries. "Now the emergency team is running in with a stretcher and meanwhile the players are back on the field ready to play ball."

Which they did. So I had to call balls and strikes and, at the same time, describe an unseen image of the ambulance folks taking out the lady. As though I could see the ambulance, I described putting her in, and then Ed hit the sound effect of the ambulance siren blaring, screeching away to the hospital. We did all of this ad lib and no prior preparation—only Ed earnestly looking and finding the one sound effect that would forever make my father's friend believe I was at the game. I saw him a few days later, and he said he heard all that commotion and knew I *was* at the game! There was no way to ever convince him otherwise.

Muskogee finished second in 1952, aided by new manager Andy Gilbert. Small consolation—the Giants were fourteen games behind Joplin, that Yankees powerhouse. Gilbert was one of the strongest men I had ever met. I thought John Holibonich, my shipmate on the LCI 439 in World War II, was the strongest before I met Andy. The man had a huge chest and bulging arms and, with all that power, his home runs usually went up and out of sight.

Andy was manager of the year and first base all-star, and he led the Western Association in hitting from the first day. He finished with a .357 average. Jack Varnado, second base, and Jack Lewis, outfield, were all-stars with Norm Siebern and catcher John Blanchard, both of Joplin. The latter two played with the Yankees. Although he didn't make the All-Star team, Mel Collins of Muskogee tied Siebern with 115 runs and led the league with 156 hits. Gerald Schultz was an All-Star pitcher for the Giants.

One other important event featuring an Eastern Oklahoman was the retirement on November 4, 1951, of John Leonard "Pepper" Martin from baseball. "The Wild Horse of the Osage" had been managing in the Florida International League. Martin was one of the wildest of the all-out players on the St. Louis Cardinals' "Gashouse Gang." Pepper became a deputy sheriff in McAlester, Oklahoma, home of the state penitentiary.

The Muskogee Baseball Booster Club, probably chaired by Joe Magota, the baseball mogul, took advantage of Pepper Martin's retirement and invited him to be our special guest and speaker at the baseball banquet before the season of 1953. I recall Pepper coming to the banquet in shirt, jeans, and cowboy boots that still had barnyard evidence on them. Pepper was down to earth. Pepper is featured along with other Oklahoma greats in the Oklahoma Sports Museum in Guthrie.

Nineteen fifty-three was my last year in Muskogee, and it was just a few years later the league folded along with many others around the country. The Giants finished fifth, twenty-five games back of St. Joseph, Missouri, the St. Louis Cardinals team. Daniel Toma was the only Giants player to make the All-Star team, with a league-leading .313 average on 152 hits, also the tops. One other player had two great nights that year. Dominick Zanni, a pitcher, could also hit a little. One night, with the bases loaded for Muskogee in the ninth inning, the manager inserted Dom in as a pinch hitter. Zanni connected on a grand slam homer to the Dr Pepper plant, and the Giants won the game! The next night, Dominick hit another home run, a solo shot. Dom pitched for San Francisco in 1958 and on to 1966 with the White Sox and Cincinnati. He won 9 and lost 6 as mostly a relief pitcher for Muskogee. If he were still alive today, Dom Zanni would be seventy-five years old.

Of the three years I spent broadcasting, there were few surprises or major events, good or bad. I was learning the game and learning to broadcast. Oh, in 1953, Leroy O'Neil, a young, strong catcher with a big mouth, became a favorite. In the Muskogee Phoenix edition July 10, 2005, writer Mike Kays found that O'Neil had saved a field attendant from burning when some fireworks ignited a tarp over the infield on a July 4 celebration. The paper was doing a series on sports history in Muskogee.

O'Neil was Catholic and his parish priest and a couple of the nuns attended the game often. Unfortunately, everyone in the stands could hear what the catcher yelled, being just a few feet from the stands. O'Neil used every four-letter word in the language (I could hear him up on the roof), much to the chagrin of the Catholic folks. The priest commented one day in the paper that he was counseling O'Neil trying to tone him down. It didn't work too well.

There is a further connection in Muskogee that I must tell. Several years ago, while broadcasting in Tulsa with my Round Rock, Texas, partner Mike Capps, I was visiting with Mark Neely in the Drillers radio booth. He brought out a book on Oklahoma sports and, checking some of the history of Muskogee sports, I found that Baseball Hall of Fame announcer Bob Murphy, late of the New York Mets, had been in Muskogee at KMUS the year before me!

Quoting from the *New York Times* obituary on August 4, 2004, "Born in Oklahoma, Murphy studied petroleum engineering and called sports at Tulsa University." Ben Henneke, the college's radio director and a close friend and coauthor with my KMUS pal Ed Dumit, at the time recalled in the *Tulsa World* that Murphy was determined to succeed, although he had a "weak voice and raw techniques." He added, "He needed a lot of help." (I wonder what Ben would have thought of me.)

While in college, Murphy broadcast Minor League Hockey and Minor League Baseball—those same Muskogee Giants—and ultimately ended up calling the University of Oklahoma football when Bud Wilkinson was coach. Murphy was fortunate to work with minor league baseball announcer Curt Gowdy in Oklahoma and later, when Gowdy went to the Red Sox, Bob joined him. He was picked to be the New York Mets announcer in 1962 and became a New York legend, spending forty-two years with that remarkable team until he died in 2004.

I met Bob in the 1960s when I was with the Dallas Texans and he was with the New York Titans of the American Football League. The two teams had a game in the ancient Polo Grounds and we could not find our telephone outlet in the pigeon-stool-spattered booth hanging over the edge of the historic field where Bobby Thomson hit that famous home run. With just a few minutes before airtime and going crazy trying to find someone to help, a young man ran up and said they had me set up over at the Mets' location. I ran like a madman around the south oval of that old fading building. Lamar Hunt saw me and yelled. I yelled back that I was going to broadcast! When I reached the middle of the other side, Murphy's guys helped me and Bob Halford into the booth next to them. We were all dialed up with their equipment and were on the air in about three minutes! I was still catching my breath. Two old Muskogee announcers had found each other.

Speaking of Ben Henneke. Ed Dumit went to Tulsa University, graduated and later taught there, ran the university radio station (which is now the PBS outlet in Tulsa—they still have Ed's voice on station breaks), and coedited a textbook on radio announcing that I used at the University of North Texas for years.

If we have breakout years in this business, 1959 was mine. I had joined KRLD-Radio and Television in Dallas in 1953 to broadcast wrestling from the world famous Sportatorium. It was the biggest television draw in town. I was also a rookie staff announcer at the fifty-thousand-watt station, with a long way to go in the business. Radio stations that had lived on their network-affiliated programs suddenly were having to create new programming as the "Golden Years" of radio went dead. Television replaced radio morning, noon, and night—at least in the grand old network format. In Dallas, KRLD struggled to have guys with great voices become disc jockeys. KLIF had burst on the scene with the Top 40 format with frenetic DJs, and a new radio era was born. The announcers at KRLD were not of that format; they were talented with great voices, but they were not the type that would blow away teenagers—maybe middle-agers!

Probably the best music program on KRLD was *Music 'Til Dawn*, sponsored by American Airlines and hosted by the smooth, sophisti-cated voice of Hugh Lampman—but sophistication stopped with his voice. Hugh had the best gig in town at the time and blew it by run-ning off during his programs for "personal" appearances. The engi-neers tired of filling for him and just let the program die one night.

There was a huge hole in the programming in the evening from six to twelve on KRLD. So in late 1958–early 1959, the management de-cided to take a huge jump and broadcast Dallas Rangers baseball in its leap from Double-A Texas League to the Triple-A American Asso-ciation.

I doubt that I had ever given KRLD my brief resume of sports broadcasting at KMUS in Muskogee, Oklahoma. KRLD had called me about auditioning for the job as staff announcer and working the Tuesday night wrestling program. They knew little of my football, basketball, and baseball background, although I had been selected to broadcast Highland Park football in 1957.

I was standing in the hall at KRLD when chief announcer Wilson Shelley told me they were looking for an announcer to broadcast the baseball schedule that spring. I jumped to attention and said, "Why look, I can do it!" Wilson said, "*Really*," or something like that. So I raced up to the record library, found some crowd sound effects, general background noise, and excited base-hit crowd, and sat down and wrote up a half inning of a game: Jones flies out to right, Smith, singles to center, Anderson doubles to left-center, Smith scores, Grieve walks and Graham hits into a double play 6-4-3 (short to second to first). I then asked one of the audio engineers to run the board and turntables with the sound effects. After he got the hang of what I was doing, we recorded the half inning. I had done three years of this re-creation stuff so it was, I must say, pretty damned good! I roared downstairs, handed Wilson the tape, and said, "Here is exactly what you will have to have; a guy who knows the game and how to call it and can re-create the out-of-town games as though they were live."

Wilson played the tape for the management and the general manager, Bill Roberts, called me in, said my tape was fantastic, and I had the job. Faced with a great career moment, the rule here is don't let any time lapse. Hit it now and hard—or something like that. Years later, I would find that waiting can be fatal. Nineteen fifty-nine was another big leap for me. I began broadcasting North Texas State University football, which would continue for the next thirty-four years. You can check that out in my football chapter.

Texas had a long and generally successful experience with cities in the venerable old Texas League. As I mentioned earlier, the Texas League began in 1888 and, for the most part, was successful until national television knocked the props out of just about every entertainment venue in the country. There were early attempts to televise baseball. Red Barber was probably the first major league announcer to handle the primitive two-camera system. You cannot televise baseball with just two or three or maybe even four cameras. They kept trying, but viewer response was nil.

Right after World War II, baseball had a great rebirth of fan support. In the Texas area, the Dallas Eagles and the Fort Worth Cats played to full stadiums. WBAP-TV had gone on the air in 1948 and on April 2, 1949, telecast the first baseball game in Texas, an exhibition between the Brooklyn Dodgers and their minor league team, the Fort Worth Cats. On April 17, Channel 5 telecast the first Texas League game between the Cats and the Tulsa Oilers.

The games were telecast on Sunday, Tuesday, Wednesday, and Thursday with one camera on the third-base side (you can imagine the difficult viewing possibilities) until May 15, when La Grave Field was destroyed by fire. A new park, a beauty of steel construction, was built on the same site. It was the first stadium designed with a television booth suspended below the press box. This was a precursor of what would happen to baseball nationally. By 1951, major league games were televised across the country and minor league attendance tumbled. By the early 1960s and into the 1970s, many minor league teams didn't broadcast their games.

In 1953, major league owners had been warned by Senator Edwin Johnson of Colorado that telecasting their games nationwide had and would continue to hurt minor league leagues and attendance. The good senator was correct. Television in general, not just sports, nearly destroyed minor league baseball. None of this danger on the baseball horizon affected an East Texas oilman, Dick Burnett. He had owned minor league teams in smaller cities, but grasped the idea of buying the Dallas franchise and eventually bringing in major league baseball. In 1948, Burnett paid George Schepps $500,000 for the Dallas Steers and renamed them the Eagles. That was the highest amount ever paid for a minor league team. (For an easy history read on Burnett and the Texas League in Dallas, go on Dallasobservor.com and read the 1998 story by Robert Wilonsky.) Attendance in 1948 set an all-time season record in the Texas League with well over two million. It was later broken in the era of the Dallas–Fort Worth Spurs after 1965.

Burnett also purchased the ball park located across the river from downtown Dallas on West Jefferson for an additional $265,000 and renamed it Burnett Field. The park was originally called Steer Field for most of the 1930s and Rebel Stadium in 1939. The ballpark was built in 1919 after the original teams, the Hams, Giants, and Submarines (in Dallas!), played in a park that burned. Inhabited by the Steers, Rebels, Eagles and lastly the Rangers, the park remained until after the 1964 season, when it was demolished. Forty-one years later, the vacant lot overlooking downtown Dallas had been purchased to develop an apartment-business area.

In 1949, when Burnett presented his Eagles in a newly refurbished Burnett Field, there were 464 teams in 59 minor leagues. By the end of 1959, there were 21 minor leagues. On April 11, 1950, promoting the opening of the season, Burnett brought together a lineup of famous ball players to play the season's first game at the Cotton Bowl.

Burnett also wanted to set a new attendance record for a minor league team.

His old-timers lineup featured Frank "Home Run" Baker at third, Duff Lewis in left, Charlie Grimm (manager of the Dallas Eagles) at first, Tris Speaker in right, Charley Gehringer at second, Travis Jackson at shortstop, Ty Cobb in centerfield, Mickey Cochrane catching, and Dizzy Dean pitching. Dizzy walked the leadoff batter, and then Dallas with Tom Finger (perfect name) pitching lost to Tulsa 10 to 3 before 53,578 fans. It looked like the beginning of a big season for the Eagles, but attendance dropped 350,000 and another 300,000 in 1951. Nationally, the minor leagues lost 7 million in 1950 and another 7 million in '51.

The problem? Television, coupled with home air-conditioners and Little League Baseball, which was about the only event that took parents out of their home. If you ever lived through a Texas summer without air-conditioning, you would realize why folks sat home cool and comfortable watching the silver screen. In Dallas, no beer was sold at Burnett Field. Oak Cliff was a dry area. However, there was a "private club" in the park, so fans paid a membership fee and could drink beer there—silly, but that was the law.

Burnett soldiered on. He had made the baseball park more comfortable, added Inez Teddlie playing fan-favorite music on the organ (Inez played at baseball games for fifteen years and died at the age of ninety-one in 2002), and in 1952 introduced the first black player to the lineup. Dave Hoskins was accepted by Dallas fans with his 22 and 10 record on the mound and a .328 batting average in 62 games. Hoskins did not pitch for Dallas in Shreveport, where black players of visiting teams were not allowed.

Then, disaster. Dick Burnett died following a heart attack in 1955. Since 1948, he had been pushing major league baseball to expand into Dallas. He had architects build a model of a proposed Dallas major league stadium, which he kept in the Burnett Field office. Now this hard-driving owner, who some admired and others feared, left baseball in Dallas unresolved as attendance continued to dwindle. His family continued to operate the team until 1959.

The Brooklyn Dodgers and New York Giants moved to California in 1957, and the following year New York City attorney William A. Shea proposed establishing a new major league, the Continental

League, with a New York team, the Mets, and seven more teams located in cities without a major league franchise. The Continental was announced in 1959, but dissolved in 1960 when the major leagues established a new team in Houston and technically a new team in Washington, D.C., which relocated later to Minneapolis–St. Paul. The other teams planned for the Continental League—Atlanta, Dallas–Fort Worth, Denver, and Toronto—eventually acquired major league teams. Only Buffalo, the last member of the Continental attempt, is still minor league.

J. W. Bateson, leader of the Bateson Construction Company, and Amon Carter, Jr., of the Fort Worth Carter family empire, owner of the *Star-Telegram* newspaper, purchased the Eagles in 1959. These two powerful business leaders saw the possibility of the Continental League franchise, and if the major leagues should expand, their presence might sway them to look at Dallas–Fort Worth. Dallas moved into the American Association in 1959 with the obvious intent of showing how the city could support a higher classification team. With the possibility of a new major league, Dallas moving into the Triple-A American Association with supposedly better baseball, KRLD stepped in with its fifty-thousand watts to broadcast this adventure far and wide—and I was the little guy who was to tell that story night-by-night.

Fans who wanted to leave their cars at home could take a trolley right up to Burnett Field. There was a special incentive to ride the rails in the summer of 1959. The Dallas Transit Company had installed air-conditioners in their trolleys, and thus fans had a cooler way to the ballpark. Fans of the Texas Rangers today mutter about how it would be cool if the Dallas Area Rapid Transit and Arlington could have built lines from Dallas and Fort Worth to that beautiful major league ballpark, the Ballpark in Arlington. It would ease up the traffic problems, with up to forty thousand fans attending the games nightly.

There was a certain element of controlled excitement about the coming new season: Bill Higdon, Rangers publicist, wrote "Lone Star is one of the co-sponsors of the baseball broadcasts of the Rangers at home and abroad this summer on KRLD. Bill Mercer, a top announcer, will handle the games for KRLD." *Times Herald* columnist Louis Cox described a new Burnett Field, scrubbed, stands painted red, white, and blue, looking shining new, and tickets to the games could be purchased by phone or mail, avoiding those long lines at the ticket window. There was an exhibition game set between the Boston Red Sox and Chicago Cubs with a natural local draw, Ernie Banks of Dallas, the National League's most valuable player who became Mr. Cub.

A wonderfully talented sportswriter, Bud Shrake, was dispatched to Pompano Beach to report on the progress of the new Dallas Rangers team in spring training. The old St. Louis Cardinals' Freddie Martin, who had been expelled from professional baseball from 1946 through 1949 for jumping to a new Mexican League, was back in good graces as manager of the Rangers.

There were some carryovers from the Dallas Eagles—Joe Kotrany, who had never had a losing season (he won nineteen games in 1958), long ball hitter Keith Little, Art Dunham, and Mike Clark. A key to this ball club was Dallasite Kal Segrist who caught baseball scouts' attention when he played at Adamson High School, led the Southwest Conference in hitting while at the University of Texas, and was signed by the Yankees. Kal broke in with farm club Kansas City in 1951 with such names as Norm Seibern and Jerry Lumpe, and hit .291. The next year, he blasted out a .308 average. But three knee operations cut his major league possibility; he could still hit, but he couldn't move on the bases as well.

Rangers general manager Stan McIlvaine, operating independently of a major league team, bought twenty-five-year-old Jack Spring from Boston. The young pitcher had already spent time in San Diego, Minneapolis, and Washington. The most colorful, and successful character on the new club was Luis Marquez who was listed as thirty-four, but had been in baseball thirteen years playing three thousand games. Luis was a smiling team player who kept young players on the straight and narrow and morale high. Former New York Giants pitcher Al Corwin joined knuckleballer Marion Fricano, veteran infielder Vinicio Garcia, and veteran pitchers Jim Tugerson, Mel Wright (I have a uniform belt that Mel wore), and Kotrany. A young, tough, future major league catcher, Don Leppert, supplied the muscle behind the plate.

Practically unnoticed in this preparation for the '59 season was a little note in the *Times Herald* about a bill approved by Texas Senate State Affairs committee introduced by Dallas State Senator George Parkhouse to issue revenue bonds for a new stadium after countywide elections. The closing line of the story indicated the stadium facility was to attract a major league franchise. Five years later, Turnpike Stadium was built between Dallas and Fort Worth.

As the Continental League issue loomed large, *Times Herald* Sports Director Jere Hayes disapproved of the idea, saying the current major leagues should expand.

As the opening of the season neared, columnist Blackie Sherrod wrote that it "was not a bounded duty to go to the game except for yourself. It was not for the civic pride or the support of baseball or the potential major league—just go if you wished." As it turned out, comparatively few wished to that season.

Looking back, analyzing all the years I broadcast, those five years with those various guys on those various Rangers Triple-A teams were the most fun I ever had in baseball. There were many moments with other teams—The Spurs, Texas Rangers, and Chicago White Sox—but for everyday excitement of going to the ballyard, those years were awesome. May have been because it was my first exposure to older, mature players or the fierceness with which they approached every game—whatever, it is a beautiful memory.

I was in a huge twit before the season started. We had arranged for Western Union to send in the out-of-town play-by-play, but instead of a human being in the station taking the dictation on Morse code, they installed a machine that resembled the Associated Press wire machines. The information was sent and typed onto a continuous roll of paper with each pitch, each hit, and so on. I would start the broadcast after one-half inning was played on the road and could adjust the timing of the game to finish shortly after the actual game. *And*, there was a keyboard with instructions on how to contact the sender if the machine failed or an inning was missed. Comforting!

I wrote all the teams of the American Association—Louisville; Minneapolis; Indianapolis; St. Paul, Minnesota; Charleston, West Virginia; Omaha; Denver; and Houston—requesting their rosters, mailings, and, if possible, a picture of their stadium so I could prop it up in front of me when re-creating the out-of-town Rangers games in

# Enjoy Baseball This Summer!!

It will pay you in health and happiness to get interested in the Muskogee Giants and relax your mind from the cares of the day. We have a team of fine young men. See them play and learn their names. You can attend the home-games as often as your time and money will permit and then follow them on radio every day. First thing you know, you'll discover a whole new field of pleasure. You're missing something if you fail to cultivate an interest in baseball. Attend a few games and listen to the radio broadcasts. Try it for a month. You'll thank me for the suggestion. It's the great American Sport!

### Bill Mercer, Your KMUS Sports Announcer

#### SCHEDULE OF GAMES PLAYED IN MUSKOGEE

| MAY | JUNE | JULY |
|---|---|---|
| Joplin — 15, 16, 17*, 18 | Fort Smith — 1, 2 | St. Joseph — 1 |
| St. Joseph — 26, 27, 28 | Topeka — 3, 4, 5, 6 | Fort Smith — 4 day, 7, 8 |
| Fort Smith — 30, 31* | Hutchinson – 14*, 15, 16, 17 | Topeka — 9, 10, 11 |
| | Joplin — 18, 19, 20 | Hutchinson — 18, 19*, 20 |
| | St. Joseph — 28* 29, 30 | Joplin — 21, 22, 23, 24 |

| AUGUST | SEPTEMBER |
|---|---|
| St. Joseph — 1, 2-2*, 3 | St. Joseph — 1 |
| Topeka — 4, 5, 6, 7 | Fort Smith — 5, 6*, 7 |
| Hutchinson – 20, 21, 22, 23* | |
| Joplin — 27, 28, 29 | * - DENOTES SUNDAY GAME |
| St. Joseph — 30*, 31 | DOUBLE NUMERALS DENOTE DOUBLE HEADERS |

## Follow the Muskogee Giants at Home and Away

#### This placard contributed by a broadcast sponsor:

## SUN FINANCE COMPANY

KMUS - - - - - - - - 1 80 KC. - - - - - - - - - FM 101.5 mg.

American Printing Co.—Muskogee

My first promotion as a sports broadcaster and first baseball broadcast job, circa 1952.

"cwtsu &FLSAV?nBpOtB, oogvar"

Earth translation

"it sure doesn't taste like tomato juice.."

As "Colonel Radar" on KRLD-TV in Dallas in 1956, I introduced "Flash Gordon" on Mondays and Thursdays and "Johnny Jupiter" on Tuesdays and Fridays for the after-school crowd.

# BEAUTIFUL BURNETT FIELD

HOME OF THE

## Dallas Rangers

OFFICIAL SCORECARD • 1959                    *price* **15 ¢**

My first year broadcasting baseball in Dallas was in 1959 for the minor league Dallas Rangers.

INDPLS THIRD

MCCRAW UP-    ( HIT)
MCCRAW HIT HOMER HIGH OVER BILL BD IN RIGHT CTR PASSED
THE 365 MARK ( HIS SEVENTH)

SMITH UP,
S1C, ( PEPPER WUP RANGERS)
B1 HI INSIDE,    FOUL BACK IN STANDS S 2,    B2 HI OVER,
(  SMITH HIT A HOT ONE THRU THE MOUND, WOODS MADE A TRY FOR
IT STOPPED IT AND THATS ALL
SINGLE FOR SMITH,

KORANDA UP,
( P TO F )
B1 HI OUTSIDE,    B2 LO OUTSIDE,    KORANDA JUST SAILED ONE
OVER THE SCBD IN LEFT CENTER WAS HI BALL WENT ALL WAY ACROSS
STREET SCORED SMITH AHEAD OF HIM (PEPPER WUP DAL-FTW LITTLEFIELD
OUT TO MOUND)

PEPPER COMING IN TO PITCH FOR DAL-FTW

TAKING HIS WARMUP TOSSES

SIMPSON UP-    S1C,  S2C SLOW BREAKING CURVE GOT HARRY
ASLEEP - B1 LO OUTSIDE,    B2 LO OUTSIDE,

B3 HIT DIRT FRONT PLATE(HADNT WARMED UP TOO MUCH)

SIMPSON CAUGHT ONE THAT WENT BETWEEN CLOCK AND BILLBOARD
ATOP SCBD LEFT CENTER FOR A HOMER HIS 14TH-KORANDA HIT HIS 13TH
ON HIS HOMER

CLOUDS FORMING FAST AWFUL DARK JUST ABOVE US NOW LITES ON
CLEAR IN BACK THO SO MAY PASS OVER

MCNERTNEY UP- B1 LO OUTSIDE,  B2 LO OUTSIDE,

FOUL TIP OFF LEFT S1,  OUT-MCNERTNEY OUT ON SLOW ROLLER
WOODS TO JABLONSKI-WOODS HAD MOVE FAST ON THE THROW

JOHNSTON UP-   B1 LO INSIDE,  B2 LO OUTSIDE,  B3 HI OUTSIDE

S1C,   B4 LO OUTSIDE-JOHNSTON WALKS

VASSIE UP-   B1 LO INSIDE,  OUT-VASSIE SENT HI LAZY FLY TO
SANDY WHO TOOK UP AT SCBD GOT THERE PLENTY OF TIME

WORTHINGTON UP- S1C,   B1 LO OUTSIDE,   FOUL TIP BACK S2,

B2 LO OUTSIDE,   SIDE OUT AS WORTHINGTON SENDS HI POP FOUL
FLY JABLONSKI TAKING FRONT DAL-FTW DUGOUT
TOTALS-FOUR RUNS-FOUR HITS-NO ERRORS-NXX ONE LEFT

We re-created play-by-play of away games from 1959–1963 from
Western Union telegrams like this one.

Packing for Dallas Rangers spring training in 1959 with my sons Evan (left), Martin (lower left), and David (right).

Some wrestling figures from the 1960s: Fritz von Erich, Ed McLemore
(Sportatorium promoter), and Killer Karl Kox.

Broadcasting with Charlie Jones (right) at a Dallas–Fort Worth Spurs game in 1965.

Staff meeting at North Texas State University's station KNTU-FM with student directors, late 1960s. I had started the station and was manager.

# RICHARDSON COMMUNITY THEATRE

PRESENTS

BILL MERCER          JAMES PHILBIN

MICHAEL SORLIE

IN

## NO TIME FOR SERGEANTS

### FRI. & SAT. EVENINGS      8:15 P.M.

### THRU   FEB.   13

Broadcaster turned thespian. The slumping sergeant (far right) in *No Time for Sergeants*.

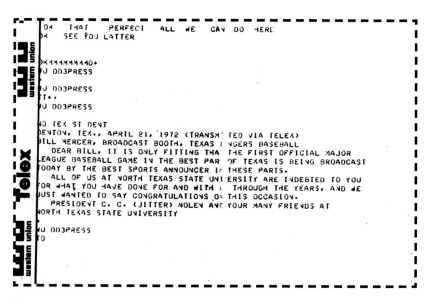

```
OK  THAT   PERFECT   ALL  WE  CAN  DO  HERE
OK  SEE YOU LATTER

western union

OK4M4M4M4M0+
U DD3PRESS

U DD3PRESS
T+.
U DD3PRESS

NO TEX ST DENT
DENTON, TEX., APRIL 21, 1972 (TRANSM' TED VIA TELEX)
BILL MERCER, BROADCAST BOOTH, TEXAS F NGERS BASEBALL
   DEAR BILL, IT IS ONLY FITTING THA  THE FIRST OFFICIAL MAJOR
LEAGUE BASEBALL GAME IN THE BEST PAR  OF TEXAS IS BEING BROADCAST
TODAY BY THE BEST SPORTS ANNOUNCER I  THESE PARTS.
   ALL OF US AT NORTH TEXAS STATE UNI ERSITY ARE INDEBTED TO YOU
FOR WHAT YOU HAVE DONE FOR AND WITH (  THROUGH THE YEARS, AND WE
JUST WANTED TO SAY CONGRATULATIONS O  THIS OCCASION.
   PRESIDENT C. C. (JITTER) NOLEN ANT YOUR MANY FRIENDS AT
NORTH TEXAS STATE UNIVERSITY

U DD3PRESS
O
```

Telex — western union

A congratulatory telegram from North Texas State University president
Jitter Nolen on my ascension to Major League Baseball broadcasting for
the Texas Rangers.

A poster done of me by Charles E. Hartman and presented at the North Texas Radio-TV Club Second Annual Awards Banquet on April 27, 1972.

**RATE CARD**
DALLAS–FT. WORTH

I am depicted at the lower left in this KVIL advertising rate card from the late 1970s.

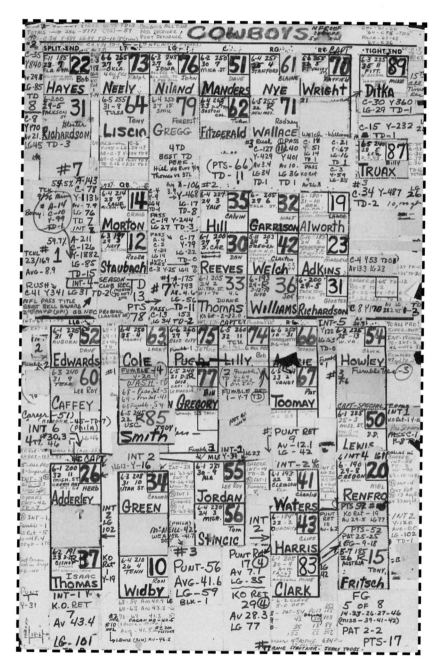

My Dallas Cowboys spotting board from the 1972 Super Bowl.

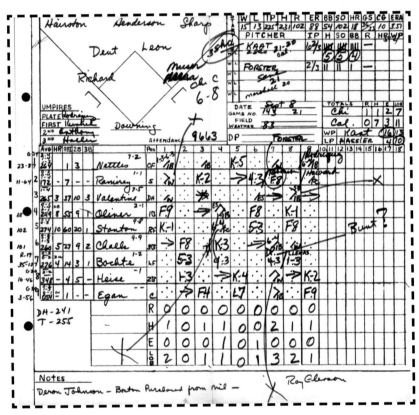

Score sheet from my stint as a Chicago White Sox broadcaster in 1974.

Teaching a class at North Texas State University (now University of North Texas).

Killer Karl Kox and Don Muroco have at it in 1978.

their parks. Now, you just bring up the website and have everything you need.

Details—details needed for a baseball broadcast. In those days we were lucky to have the daily batting averages of our team and the one we were playing. I wrote to other broadcasters and sportswriters in the league about player information. Today, when my friend Mike Capps turns on his computer while broadcasting a Round Rock, Pacific Coast League game, he can quickly find out what color eyes the player has.

I suppose, in addition to the mental view of the ballpark, the players, and each play typed on Western Union paper, a re-creation demands a vivid imagination. Plays on the road were probably more exciting than those at home because I was trying to visualize the circumstances and the difficulty of a play—and keep the listener entertained. So if there was listed "Jones grounds in a 5-4-3 double play," I would add that Jones hits a sharp grounder down the third-base line, third baseman backhands the ball, wheels and throws to second for one, relay to first . . . just in time for the double play!! Probably it was a routine hopper to third," and so on. Problem was, it was easy to become brain-tired sitting in the studio for two to three hours by yourself pretending. Sometimes, these overenthusiastic descriptions came back to haunt me.

Say the Rangers were winning by a run on the road and it was the bottom of the ninth—and I was always at least a half inning behind. I knew what happened, so when I described that inning with the home team batting, sometimes I would have a fly ball third out become a high fly to right—"Getter goes back . . . back to the track . . . he pulls it in for the third out, and the Rangers win!" Joe Kotrany's wife was listening one night when I pulled that stunt while Joe was pitching a complete game victory. He called to tell her about his great effort and she said I had described the last out as a well-hit ball to deep right. He fumed that it was actually a routine fly to mid-right field. They both let me know about that!

With the Rangers in town and ready to start the 1959 season, an introductory exhibition game with Kansas City was scheduled. Joe Kotrany, who never had a losing season, lost that night 6 to 5—a wet, cold evening with just over eight hundred fans. Wayne Terwilliger, Whitey Herzog, and a youngster named Roger Maris played for Kansas City. Maris homered in the game, just as he would do many times in the future.

Kotrany pitched the first regular Triple-A game in Dallas in April. Joe took Dallas through seven innings with just one run given up and, in what always seems like a scripted finish, Kal Segrist homered in the tenth to give the Rangers a 3 to 2 victory over Denver and their manager Stan Hack. Segrist's father was in the stands watching his son play third base, the same position the elder Segrist played for Dallas in the 1920s. Forty-seven hundred fans braved chilly, damp weather for the exciting opener.

The season was an up-and-down affair for Dallas typical of an independent team in a league with organization teams. But Dallas played hard, competitive baseball, gave no quarter going hard into bases, stole bases (Luis Marquez was always a threat to steal home), and started plenty of individual and team fights. Many resulted from pitching "inside" or close to the batter's head.

When the Rangers won a game, they charged into the clubhouse looking for Wayne Hattaway, the "clubhouse boy," and tossed him into the whirlpool, usually head first. Players nailed other players' shoes to the wall, put bananas in their shoes, gave each the hotfoot in the clubhouse and dugout, and generally acted like this was the greatest time of their lives. They also had a weekly kangaroo court to make it known to lazy (there were not any) players muffing a ground ball or making a bonehead mistake that it was not acceptable, and fined the miscreants. I was on trial there early on in the season for not coming to the clubhouse after a game to have a beer and talk ball. They fined me five bucks and later fined me for wearing a hat they didn't like. This type of camaraderie continued through the '63 season.

The key players in 1959 were pitcher Marion Fricano, first baseman Keith Little, and outfielder Luis Marquez. Thirty-five-year-old Fricano won twelve games, five by two runs or less, and won the American Association earned-run record with a 2.02. With a knuckleball sinker and an explosive grunt when he pitched, Fricano also created havoc when he decided a batter was hugging the plate. In one game, a rookie catcher was up to bat and Marion threw the first pitch in tight under his chin. The batter said something and made one step toward the mound in the batter's box; I groaned, knowing what would come next. The next pitch was aimed at his ear—the kid went down, grabbed his bat, and started to the mound. Big, tough Don Leppert, the Rangers' catcher, grabbed the batter, spun him around, and dropped him with a right to the jaw. Del Wilber, the opposing team manager and third-base coach, made a flying tackle on Fricano and, as they say, all hell broke loose. In addition to this kind of activity, Marion would teach my two oldest sons how to throw, catch, and hit before games. He was a wonderful man who died too young of cancer. His hometown of North Collins, New York, honored him for his civic duties by naming a park after him. Interestingly, after that solid season, Fricano did not have a single major league team call him up for the final two months of the season.

Luis Marquez was the kind of player every team should have. He claimed he was thirty-seven, but we guessed he was like John Franco, in his mid- to late forties. When some young player went over the line with the team or manager, Luis calmed the situation. He had a strong ethnic rapport with Hispanic players, who always respected him. And he always was smiling and laughing when wrapping miles of tape around his legs to hold everything together. Maquez was aggressive everywhere, at the plate, on the bases, in the field. Even at his advanced age, he ran like a deer.

Fort Worth's Bob Will and Marquez battled down to the last week of the season for the batting title. With four games to play, Will was hitting .341 and Luis .339. In the final game of the season, Marquez hit a home run and a single and beat Will by four points: .345 to .341. Luis contributed with 17 homers, but his presence on the field was his greatest asset.

The most popular player to the fans was big Keith Little, the first baseman who endured a severely sprained ankle, kidney infection, and other ailments, banged out 21 home runs, and received a MVP shotgun from "Good Old Dave Goldstein." In addition to those who finished with special marks, this was a team of guys I viewed as friends—Art Dunham, Venicio Garcia, Dick Getter, Kotrany, Mel Wright, we were all close. We were a team.

The 1959 All-Star game was to be played in the new Municipal Stadium in Minneapolis and all the broadcasters around the league were invited in to do at least one half inning of broadcasting. KRLD thought it too expensive to send me to the game. But when some well-heeled fans heard I wasn't going, they bought me a ticket, paid for my hotel and a few bucks to eat on, and I went. KRLD folks were a little taken aback, but didn't resist. That's where I picked up one of the funniest stories about broadcasting in a tense situation.

The announcer (who I will not reveal for fear his relatives don't know) told of a game, say, between Louisville and Indianapolis, tied for first, and Louisville down by a run in the last of the ninth. The Cardinals have a runner at second, two outs, and the announcer said: "Tying run at second, two outs and the league's leading hitter at the plate. Here's the pitch, swung on, driven to right field, base hit, the runner rounding third coming to the plate, the throw to the plate, the slide, he's out! Oh. Horseshit!" Immediately, the announcer nearly had an attack, but he weathered through to the end of the broadcast. He ran for the phone and called to tell his general manager who he felt would fire him on the spot. Maybe the GM was listening. Instead, he said to cool it, and let's see what happens tomorrow.

The announcer had a sleepless night and arrived before the switchboard opened at the radio station the next morning. He hung around waiting for religious groups to hue and cry the awful word, but nothing happened. No calls, no telegrams, until four p.m. when he received a call from a young lady, who said, "My husband and I were listening to the game last night and we have a bet. Did you say *horse* or *bull*?" Our golden voice said, "horse," and the lady laughed and said, "Great, I win," and hung up. That was all the announcer ever heard of the barnyard reaction.

This slam-bang baseball of 1959 was fun to watch, but attendance was on average less than the Texas League of 1958. Dallas averaged 2456 in '58 and six hundred less in 1959. In the next to last game of the season, only sixteen hundred fans came out to see the team finish eight and a half out.

On the last two days of the season, Walker Cooper, the manager of Indianapolis and former major league player, and his team decided to have fun. Cooper had slipped into the clubhouse before the game and nailed Marquez's shoes to the wall and tied his uniform in knots. During the last game, Cooper managed to slip into the Rangers clubhouse and steal Luis's street clothes. Luis went home in his uniform.

During that last game, Luis slipped up behind Cooper, who was coaching third base, and threw a bucket of water on him. Later, Cooper found a bucket, filled it with water and dirt, and between innings, chased Marquez, who easily escaped. But Chico (Venicio) Garcia didn't and Cooper doused him. Finally in the eighth inning, Luis singled, Cooper told J. C. Martin, the first baseman (and later my broadcast partner in Chicago), to hold the ball and Luis at first. Cooper dashed over with a bucket and drowned Luis. This was the culmination of 177 games of terrific baseball, and half of those I broadcast in the studio at KRLD.

The Continental League was still making noise at the end of the '59 season, indicating it would grant a franchise to the Dallas–Fort Worth area. J. W. Bateson talked of plans to build a new stadium in Arlington. Indianapolis general manger Ray Johnston advised the minor leagues to build new stadiums with restaurants, good restrooms, and ample parking. Already after fifty-nine years, the American Association planned expansion. And, most importantly (it seems), high school teenagers were going door to door in 1959 to encourage everyone to be inoculated for polio.

You know those "should have" situations? Well, I should have had some of most of those games recorded, but it didn't occur to me or anyone else to do that. I had not learned yet that taping and listening to your own "broadcast mistakes" was and is necessary to improve as a broadcaster. Listeners were nice, saying it was great and all those easy things they say. But doing your own critique is the best way to progress. I did receive a little postcard each day from a gentleman who was not so enamored of me. He thought I was "the worst announcer" he had ever heard. He may have had the most honest critique, but I did keep the job. I also received a letter that gave me hope. The writer said he listened to all the out-of-town games and really enjoyed being able to see every pitch and play—and I was the one re-creating. Then, he added that when the Rangers were at home in Burnett Field, he took his radio to the game and could see every play, even though he was blind. I have used that letter in my classes to indicate the necessity of being specific—give details, be colorful, and remember that all the listeners on radio (except in the park) can't see the action.

The Western Union reports of the out-of-town games were, for the most part, excellent. With every pitch recorded for me, I could really build the game for the listener to see. The sound effects we used were not what I would have liked; they were barely adequate. Also, our engineers and board operators were not keen on staying glued to my every word (that *is* a thankless job) and didn't take an active interest in what sounds were emitted. But, after the first few weeks of the season, we had no nasty letters (except the daily card from my nemeses) and journeyed through.

Nineteen sixty was a huge year for many reasons. You could purchase an Oldsmobile '88 sedan for $2,900, there was a contentious school board election in Dallas during this time of rising civil rights tension, my broadcast friend Jack Harrison was the "star" of the afternoon drive music program on KRLD, and the Dallas Texans and Dallas Cowboys landed in the city ready to play their games on different dates at the venerable old Cotton Bowl.

The Dallas Texans put their broadcasts on KRLD and Charlie Jones was the lead announcer. The Texans asked me to work with Charlie as a color commentator/announcer. When Charlie had some television gigs with NBC, I moved over to play by play. On our broadcasts together, I kept basic stats, spotted the opponent, and handled color. We were a two-man crew. It was a great three years, but these events are described in the football chapter.

The Triple-A experience never paid off in the five years Dallas and Fort Worth were in the American Association and the Pacific Coast League. Attendance continued to drop in 1960. The Rangers returned Jim Fanning as manager while adding some new names to the roster. Seven-year major leaguer Ray Jablonski, Tony Alomar, Tom Gorman, and Charlie Secrest (he physically resembled Mantle, but never his career) with the stalwarts Fricano, Mel Wright, Don Leppert, and Kal Segrist. Another big name, Lou Klimchock, joined the Rangers.

Jablonski's first two years with the St. Louis Cardinals looked like a long-term winner. Jabbo hit 35 home runs and drove in over a hundred runs in 1953 and '54. But, like Lou Klimchock, his poor fielding gave him only eight years in the majors with six different teams. Klimchock had hit .315 and 19 homers at Shreveport in 1959, but he had an up-and-down career with four major league teams and was sent down by Kansas City.

Minneapolis had won the American Association playoff the year before with Gene Mauch managing and a future manager of the Chicago White Sox, Chuck Tanner, playing. Mauch had made a name for himself in Dallas in '59 when he charged into the stands to attack a fan who had been heckling him. In 1960, Minneapolis, a Boston Red Sox farm team, hailed a $100,000 "bonus baby" named Carl Yastrzemski. It was almost a conclusion that an independent minor team couldn't compete successfully with high-priced, high-powered major league organizations.

Harry Taylor, a Fort Worth high school prospect, signed for a big bonus, but in spring training that year he refused to throw the curve ball because he planned to be a dentist and believed he couldn't hold the dental equipment if he developed muscles in his fingers! That was one promising pitcher lost.

On April 17, the Rangers opened the season at Burnett Field before 4,191 fans in a stadium that held ten thousand. Before the game, Arlington Mayor Tom Vandergriff, the Rangers' J. W. Bateson, and Fort Worth *Star-Telegram* owner Amon Carter, Jr., were introduced. Few realized these three would change the shape of baseball in the area by 1965.

The Rangers lost the opening game 11 to 2, and Carter, keeping track of foul balls hit out of the park, noted that "Steve Boros of Denver cost us $12." No amount of effort by some hard-playing ball players kept the Rangers from finishing the 1960 season in eighth place, twenty-two and one-half games out. Only Dick Tomanek with 172 strikeouts made the All-Star team.

Another sign of the times was the change in newspaper coverage. Bud Shrake, who covered the team the prior year, was replaced by young Murray Forsvall. By the latter part of the year, the out-of-town stories were sent by wire service or first-person accounts by Rangers outfielder Gale Wade, who had an eye on a future writing career. His stories weren't all that bad. Meanwhile, the local papers were finding the Dallas Texans and Cowboys front-sports-page material. The major leagues would expand in 1960 and the Continental League died before ever really taking a breath. The unkindest cut of all was Houston, awarded the first franchise in the expansion. Within this time frame, Charley Finley bought Kansas City and requested a move to Los Angeles. It is also noted that he mentioned moving the club to the Dallas–Fort Worth area. Neither occurred. He later moved to Oakland.

The 1961 Dallas–Fort Worth Rangers worked with the Los Angeles Angels, but still finished in fifth place with a 72 and 77 record. The two most exciting players on that club were nineteen-year-old Jim Fregosi and twenty-year-old Dean Chance. Fregosi was a brash youngster and probably the best shortstop I ever saw play—although not always consistently. He could go into the hole deep, backhand the ball, leap, and throw to first with amazing skill. Sometimes the ball went into the right-field bleachers, but it went in with authority! He spent part of the '62 season with the Rangers and then became a six-time Major League All-Star with the Angels. We reconnected in 1973 when Fregosi joined the Texas Rangers for five seasons. Fregosi was a major part of the trade when the Mets sent Nolan Ryan to Los Angeles and Jim to New York. He later returned in 1978 to the Angels as manager and led them to their first divisional title.

Life comes full circle too quickly. In the spring of 2007, I helped one of my students broadcast a University of Texas at Dallas baseball game against Trinity University of San Antonio. The game was played on the Dallas campus. In the Trinity lineup was a catcher named Zach Fregosi. I had a feeling he had to be related to Jim. After the game I caught up with the 6′ 2″, 184-pound catcher from Tucson, Arizona, and asked if he was related to the best shortstop I ever saw. He beamed and said Jim was his grandfather. So we exchanged pleasantries, and he promised to tell his granddad that old Bill Mercer was still alive and kicking. Boy, time has flown by.

The 6′ 3″, two-hundred-pound Chance was a flame-throwing right-hander with distinctive personality quirks. He went to the Angels to stay in '62 and won 20 games in 1964 with a ridiculously low 1.65 ERA. That brought him the greatest prize for a pitcher, the Cy Young award. In 1967, he won 20 games again with Minnesota. Dean was out of baseball in 1971. The last we heard and saw of Dean, he was a traveling carnival game host and visited the Texas State Fair many times.

Bob Rodgers, a catcher, was another youngster who went on to play nine years with the Angels and Texas Rangers 1974 and 1975. Murray Wall, a Dallas native and University of Texas player who died in 1971, had stints with the Boston Braves, Red Sox, and Washington Senators.

In all fairness to that team, they missed the playoffs by one-half game in a six-team league. They were thirteen and a half games out in fifth place. Walker Cooper, the old major leaguer and former Indianapolis manager, had them playing hard-nosed baseball.

KRLD stuck with the baseball broadcasts although the attendance was low. Maybe it was my golden throat, or possibly the ratings were okay in this transition time in radio broadcasting from the networks to local programming. In 1962, a new owner arrived on the Rangers' baseball scene, Ray Johnston. Ray had been in all of the jobs in baseball—general manager at Indianapolis, and owner of the Iowa team affiliated with the Chicago Cubs. Ray knew how to run the business on his shoestring. He wasn't stingy, just careful about business. He was a whiz in the stock market. He took this Dallas franchise because, like so many, he knew it would be a major league entity in time. His time was just three years before he was pushed aside.

Johnston's first year was a bust. He had all the old standbys of the earlier Rangers plus Cookie Rojas and Chuck Tanner. Rojas was a major league figure for sixteen years. Chuck spent seven years with a variety of clubs, but broke his ankle in 1961 and played only fourteen more games in the majors. Tanner led the league in hitting the year he played in Dallas. Tanner is better known for his managing skills. He took the White Sox to second place in '72, and in his ten years at Pittsburgh, Chuck led the Pirates to the World Series in 1979.

The '61 Rangers featured a catcher, Pat Corrales, who played with four major league clubs and then had a distinguished managing career. Pat managed the Texas Rangers to third place in their division in 1978 and then had extensive managing seasons with the Phillies and Cleveland.

Young Wayne Graham played third base for those Rangers and had a cup of coffee and a piece of pie in the majors. He played thirty games for the Phillies and the Mets. Today, he is widely acclaimed as one of the best, if not *the* best, college baseball coach having won ten straight conference championships in his fourteen-year tenure at Rice University. The Yoakum, Texas, native has taken the Owls to the College World Series on four occasions and won the College World Series in 2003.

Ray Murray managed the club that also featured Sandy Valdespino, who later played in the majors five years; Mickey Harrington, an outfielder, who played just one game with the Philadelphia Phillies in 1963; Dick Littlefield, a veteran pitcher for ten major league teams, who never won more than ten games in a year; Bob Lee, another pitcher with a short three years in the ML; Leo Burke, a hustling, light-hitting outfielder who kept the clubhouse loose, ran the kangaroo courts, and had a short major league career with four clubs; and a young right-hand pitcher, Bob Baillargeon, who remains a close friend to this day. Bob hung up his spikes in 1965 and entered the automobile retail business. His style, personality, and honesty served him well, ending with his owning Baillargeon Ford in Richardson. Bob once came into a Rangers game in the first inning as a relief pitcher when the starter developed a physical problem. He proceeded to pitch the nine innings, giving up a hit an inning and won the game.

The Rangers of '62 owned the cellar with a terrible 59 and 90 record, twenty-six games out of first place. However, had you watched them play every day, you would never have suspected they were that bad. Oh, they had no pitching to speak of, but they had that old true grit and were lambasted in an Indianapolis newspaper for being the "dirtiest" team in the league. When Indy came to Burnett Field, their dugout was festooned with pink balloons and crepe paper for the "cry babies." Every fan who brought a baby rattle, a cowbell, or something that would make noise was admitted for half price, but not many people were showing up for a team sunk in last place. The Indianapolis players thought it funny and figured they would do whatever to bring in the fans. Leo Burke and Wayne Graham made the 1962 All-Star team. Leo hit 27 homers and Wayne led with 187 hits.

While the Rangers had a terrible win-loss record that year, some important developments occurred: the Texas state poll tax was eliminated, Dick Hitt joined the *Dallas Times Herald* and became a star columnist, and Hayden Fry was named coach of the Southern Methodist University Mustangs football team.

Several new faces appeared for the 1963 Rangers, including a former catcher turned manager named Jack McKeon. We know of McKeon's record in the major leagues, at least his winning the World Series with the Florida Marlins in 2003 at age seventy-three. He managed Kansas City, Oakland, San Diego (where he was also general manager), Cincinnati and, of course, Florida, where he has just retired.

John Aloysius "Jack" McKeon signed on as a catcher in 1949 and spent ten years in the minors. At Burlington in 1951, he caught 139 or

140 games—tough rascal! Jack's first managerial job was as a player-manager in 1955 at Fayetteville, North Carolina. While pursuing his baseball career, McKeon attended College of Holy Cross, Seton Hall, and graduated in 1963 with a degree in physical education from Elon University in North Carolina. The same year he managed the Dallas–Fort Worth Rangers. The American Association disbanded and was replaced by an expanded Pacific Coast League. This actually turned out well for Dallas–Fort Worth.

Ray Johnston brought in players from various organizations, but principally from the Minnesota Twins, and gave McKeon a strong nucleus to work with. When I think of this team, I remember first twenty-three-year-old Tony Oliva, who could hit a pitch off the plate or above his head. It seemed he swung at everything and made enough contact to bat .304 with 23 home runs. Tony played his first season with Minnesota in 1964, batting .323 with 32 homers. In fact, Oliva holds the record as the only player in major league history to win the batting title his first two full years in the majors. In '65, he swatted .321 and 16 homers. He kept pounding away, with 30 and 35 homeruns his third year at Minnesota. In 1972, when the Texas Rangers visited Minnesota, I walked on the field and there was Tony. He trotted over and gave me a big bear hug—"Beel, Beel, you're in the majors!?"

Another competitive nuclei of the exciting '63 Rangers club was Cesar Tovar, who batted .297 and scored 115 runs. An infielder who unfortunately made too many errors in the majors, Cesar went to Minnesota in 1966 where he had great offensive numbers, including sizeable stolen base success. Later, he spent a couple of years with the Texas Rangers, hitting .292 in 1974.

Then there was Lee Stange who became the star pitcher, winning seven consecutive games before the Twins called him up. Ray Johnston believed the Rangers would have won the pennant if Stange had stayed, or if he could have found a pitcher of equal ability. Unfortunately, Stange's loss allowed the Rangers to finish in third place in the Southern Division of the PCL with a 79 and 79 record, the best in the five years in Triple-A. The excitement generated by this club raised attendance nearly fifty percent to 118,350 for the year, but that's averaging about 2,000 per game. That hardly paid the bills.

There were some guys who played hard for the Rangers, but had short tenures in the majors. Joe Nossek had seven years in the show; Pete Cimino later pitched four years with the Twins and California. Ted Sadowski, whose brother and uncle played in the majors, later pitched eighty-four major league games.

Even though none of the Triple-A teams won divisions or even came close, they were always fun to watch and broadcast. They played the game like each one was the last—and this '63 team had some interesting travel situations.

Hawaii was in the league and there was one trip out to the islands in 1963. The older players began telling the rookies like Tovar and Oliva that they would fly in a DC 3, the venerable twin-engine work-horse of the airlines, which would land on an aircraft carrier in the Pacific to refuel. Trying not to show terror or question guys who had been around, a couple of the young players sidled up to me and asked if that were true. I didn't want to be convicted in a Kangaroo court, so I sidestepped the issue by saying I had never heard of that—but I had also never flown to Hawaii.

The morning the Rangers took off from Love Field in their DC 3 for the West Coast, I was among those to see them off. I went on board the little plane, and there was Cesar sitting with a blanket over his head, saying over and over that he didn't want to fly. The players had at the last minute told the kids on the team that they would fly on a four-engine plane from California—no aircraft carrier. Still, you can imagine the trip to Denver, and on to California in that small plane!

There were two interesting experiences for me broadcasting that year. We were still being serviced by Western Union with the play-by-play of the games rolling in on the big news-type machine in the studio. The Rangers were scheduled for a split double header in Indianapolis on July 4. That meant at least eighteen innings with the first game starting at three p.m. eastern time (two Dallas time) and the second at six, with fireworks to follow. It was designed to have two paying games rather than back-to-back seven-inning ventures.

KRLD decided that was too much baseball, so they opted to start the first game at three p.m. our time, which would hopefully be about halfway through. The best-laid plans never cease to amaze. The Rangers were delayed by weather and did not arrive in Indianapolis until about three o'clock eastern time. By the time the Rangers made it to the stadium, dressed and ready for the game, the first game started about four our time. I had two full games to broadcast.

The engineer and I were the only folks in the studios of KRLD that afternoon and evening. With our Western Union machine humming along, the double header went twenty-nine innings! Sixteen innings one game, thirteen the other. There was no food available, so I managed to drink a gallon of coffee and eat several chocolate candy bars for the more than six hours we were on the air. Remember, this was re-creation, six hours of pretending to see baseball being played, handling the play by play by myself. I was in something of a mumbling stupor after those games ended.

The Western Union service was excellent, except of course when things failed. Talk to any broadcaster who handled re-creations and they will tell you about sudden rain delays, a lot of foul balls, and other digressions when the machine stopped for no apparent reason.

In Denver one day, the Rangers' pitcher was creamed for ten runs in the second inning. When I picked up the page off the WU machine (remember, I am an inning behind the real game), I looked for a relief pitcher or two. In Denver, with the light air to this day, pitching is a dangerous part of the profession. The curve won't break much, and contact with a fastball sends a rocket into the stands.

Well, there was no relief pitcher indicated in the long piece of paper for that half inning. Quickly, I typed a message to the operator in Denver suggesting that there must have been a relief pitcher. A few moments later, the machine barked back, "No relief pitcher for Rangers." I didn't believe any manager would leave a pitcher in to be pummeled with ten runs, but there wasn't anything I could do in Dallas with a game in Denver.

Almost before I finished with my usual, "So long everybody," the phone rang with Ray Johnston raving about firing the blankety-blank manager who didn't have enough sense to change pitchers and on and on. I finally managed to tell him not to jump to conclusions until he talked to his folks there, that I felt WU made a mistake. Sure enough, somehow the operator missed the change of pitchers in that inning. Of course, folks who were listening and read the story in the next day's paper probably thought I was crazy.

In another disaster in the making, I had a game on the road with the leading team of the Rangers' division, Louisville. I kind of picked up the pace a little in the later innings so the actual game and broadcast time was close to even. That was a mistake. I was up to the ninth inning, a three up, three down for the Rangers who lead by a run. The WU machine stopped while I was in that half inning—so the game was "over"! I pulled the bottom of the ninth paper off the machine and realized I had trouble. First, two guys are quick outs, then there is a double and the league's leading hitter at the plate—but no word on what happened. No third out? No hit to drive in the tying run? I quickly sent a message on the keyboard asking what happened to last out. Is the game still going on? There was no answer. I was back into the Louisville last of the ninth and no finish! Between pitches, I called the number of the Louisville ballpark. No answer. "Ball three." Call the number of the Louisville ballpark press box. "Foul Ball, three balls, two strikes." No answer. So I asked the engineer to call the numbers and hoped that someone picked up. "One out, and Jones up."

And so it went for two outs. Then, the last guy I have a report on hit the double and I finally thought to call the newspaper sports desk. So the engineer did the search for the number while I had a visit to the mound (can't do that but once), more foul balls. The catcher went out to the mound several times and players called time for some equipment problem. A big sack blew on the field and landed in front of second base. The home plate umpire hit by a foul ball had to have first aid—and God knows what else happened. Finally, the newspaper answered—the last guy struck out. What a climax! So you learn a lesson. Be sure the entire ninth inning is in before embarking on those pitches, and have all the necessary and backup phone numbers of the home team with you.

If ever there were a worst team in baseball, at the least the minor leagues, the 1964 Dallas Rangers would lead the list. Fort Worth dropped its affiliation with Dallas and resurrected the Cats in the Texas League. Dallas stayed on in the PCL, for the last time. Amiable John McNamara was the Dallas manager, a nice guy who looked like he was having an appendectomy every night! Charley Finley supplied the "alleged" players.

We found out in February of 1964 that Finley was furnishing the players for the '64 season and, about the same time, were told by a newspaper source he would be in Dallas for his daughter's wedding. So by hook and crook I found out when his daughter's wedding was and finagled the day and time from the airline when he was arriving at Love Field.

When Finley walked down the ramp from the plane, I was waiting for him on the tarmac. You could do that in those days. I had a cameraman with a sound camera so we could have an "enlightening" interview with Charley. The first thing he said was, "How the hell did you know I was going to be on this flight?" I told him we found out he was coming to his daughter's wedding, but wanted to talk about his baseball team and the affiliation with Dallas that year. In 1976 and again in 1977, he offered me a broadcasting job to work with Monte Moore, his number-one announcer. The pay was so small I couldn't have survived as a single person—no way with four children. Finley gave us the interview in 1964, which was not memorable.

However, the '64 team *was*. It finished forty-two and a half games out of first place, 52 wins and 104 losses. I firmly believe it was the worst team I have ever seen on a professional field. However, five years later, McNamara managed Oakland his first two years in the majors, then San Diego, and had success with Cincinnati with a first-place finish in 1979 and a second in '81. John then went to California for two seasons, and on to Boston, where he had two first-place finishes in four seasons before winding down his career in Cleveland.

The only player of quality talent on that club, who I can remember (and I shut them out long ago) was right-fielder Roger Freed. Whenever the opposition had a runner at second, and that was often, we thirsted for a ball hit to Freed's Field in right, and then we were exhilarated with a perfect no-hop throw to the plate about knee-high to the catcher, tagging the runner!

Nineteen sixty-four produced some interesting highlights in the league. First year, Arkansas won the East managed by Frank Lucchesi, who naturally was manager of the year. (He later managed the major league Texas Rangers.) Arkansas pulled in 130,000 fans and Oklahoma City drew 187,000, while Dallas managed to entice 39,391, absolutely the most loyal of fans in the world. Fort Worth was back in the Texas League and finished last, drawing just over 93,000.

Some years, there are no no-hitters thrown in a league (can't find many now with the pitch count limit), but in '64 Bill Singer of Spokane knocked out Dallas 3 to 0, and Sam McDowell (he would have a career), Dick Estelle, Jay Hook, Joel Gibson, and Lawrence Yellen all threw no-hitters. Spinning Luis Tiant won fifteen and lost one for Portland before Cleveland called him up, where he won ten more. What a year—25 and 5. You miss guys like Tiant. The Triple-A effort was ended. Long live the new AA Texas League!

As we journeyed through these past several years, remember there was a state action allowing bonds for a stadium in the area between Dallas and Fort Worth—Lamar Hunt, Tom Vandergriff, J. W. Bateson, and then Tommy Mercer working to see that accomplished. The stadium project began late 1964, and the Texas League franchise purchase by Mercer, a prominent Fort Worth businessman (no relation to me) set up the new era of baseball at Arlington in 1965. The ten-thousand-seat Turnpike Stadium became the foundation for the major league stadium expansion in 1972.

After eleven years at KRLD, the very foundation of my career in Texas, the stress and strain of being employee, union president, and negotiator finally came to a climax. In a huge fit of anger around the first of December of 1964, I raved at Eddie Barker, our news director, and told him I was quitting. I walked across the street to the main offices, wrote a letter of resignation, and gave it to vice president Ves Box's secretary. Done deal. To this day, I can't recall why I was so angry, but I did have a temper that could take off uncharted. My wife has never forgotten my decision either, as it was two weeks before Christmas when I walked out of KRLD. I missed the Christmas bonus, but I did receive two weeks' severance pay. We had a great Christmas at our house though.

Shortly after that, I worked nights at KLIF radio writing and reading news. I probably should have stayed there for a while, but a good friend, Paul Berry, invited me to come in to his advertising/public relations firm. I thought this would be a positive move, teaching me how to sell while writing and producing whatever was needed on radio and television for the company.

I produced a very solid piece of television film for one of Berry's clients and handled some radio programming but my selling ability was zero. Pay came from what Berry had me produce and what I could sell.

For some reason, I had lost contact with the baseball folks. I suppose worrying about making a living (my wife was teaching at the time) had taken my attention away from what I really wanted to do. Then, two of the best friends I have had in baseball, Joe Macko and Dick Butler, called me from the new Dallas–Fort Worth Spurs office. They asked me, "How about handling the radio for the new team?" I was over at the new ballpark in Arlington before they put the phone down. This was February 1965.

My part of the job was to locate a radio station to broadcast the games and sell advertising—that "sell" thing again. KRLD wasn't interested, but WFAA had a new young manager, Denson Walker, who was trying to build an audience. (KLIF's Top 40 format was still killing everyone!) We talked and he agreed—if I would work in Charlie Jones, his TV sports director, as my partner in the broadcast. Charlie and I had been together before, he the lead announcer with the Dallas Texans, so that seemed like a good match.

Selling was my tall mountain to climb. Macko handled a bunch of it. He knew everybody and loved to talk and sell. We had to pay WFAA a certain amount for airtime and that meant selling plenty of advertising so everybody made money including the announcers.

Somewhat frantically, I called the late Lamar Hunt and asked if he had some clues about advertisers. I suppose I sounded pathetic. Lamar called WFAA and discussed the situation with them and then contacted his father, the famed H. L. Hunt who had a kazillion businesses around. Lamar then contacted me to call his father and set up a meeting. Lamar was one of the nicest people I ever met, and he did have some connections. H. L. Hunt was then, and still is, a legendary character in American business. He probably was the first billionaire. He developed a political agenda with radio programs espousing his right-wing ideology. Hunt had companies producing personal products as well as his worldwide Hunt Oil. It was the companies making cosmetics and providing other services that served us well for years with the Spurs' broadcasts.

Macko, Butler, and I made the pilgrimage to Hunt's office. We came in just before lunch and discussed the ball club, the ballpark, and his contribution to the radio broadcast. After a rather short meeting with this icon of oil, a not-so-tall, aging person with a cherubic face and tuft of white hair, Hunt said, "It is lunchtime, and thanks for coming by. Drop by when you wish and be sure to listen to my programs [political programs] on radio." His lunch was in his office, on his desk, a little brown paper sack with whatever he brought from home. He was careful how he spent money, but he did buy a lot of our commercial time.

Butler was executive vice president and general manager and Macko was his assistant with these new Dallas–Fort Worth Spurs. The Fort Worth Cats had their last year in 1964 and wouldn't resurface again until the 2000 era when civic groups "rebuilt" LaGrave Field on its original site and today play in the independent Central League. In fact, they won the championship in 2005.

Turnpike Stadium barely was finished in time for the start of play on April 23, 1965, seven days after the Spurs opened in Austin. Opening night, the grass was still being put in squares in the outfield, some difficult mudholes developed, and there was no screen behind home plate protecting the stands. Before it was finally installed, several folks were struck by sharply hit foul balls, but it was a new era and everyone rather overlooked the problems. The player's dressing rooms were up above the hill in right field—a long walk.

The hill became synonymous with Turnpike Stadium. It was built up even with the top of the main deck of the stadium, which extended past first base down right field a short way. It was put there in hopes the major league franchise would soon locate in Arlington and expanding the stadium to major league requirements would be done quickly. So during the Spurs games, kids of any age sat on the hill, waited for foul balls, and chased same. When things were not exciting to the kids, they would roll down the long hill. Talk to anyone who was a youngster at that time and the first thing they recall is "the hill" and how much fun it was. Doug Ray, who became sports information director at the University of North Texas in 1981 and a partner on some of my UNT broadcasts, recalled the hill as the defining moment in his teenage baseball life.

The baseball management, probably with the close major league association of Butler and Joe Macko, obtained a working agreement with the Chicago Cubs. The Cubs sent Whitey Lockman to manage and a number of quality players: shortstop Don Kessinger; first base John Boccabella; nineteen-year-old outfielder Don Young out of A ball (Don hit .515 in spring training); two other outfielders, Gene Etter and "Shorty" Rodman; at third base Von McDanield; with the catcher John Felske. The Spurs' pitching staff was led by Chuck Hartenstein (whose memorable game was the highlight of the year along with the team's finish), Len Church, Bob Baillargeon for a short time, Fred Norman, Sterling Slaughter, and Hal Haydel from Houma, Louisiana.

Before we open the 1965 season at Turnpike, I need to back up to Charlie Jones, me, and radio. WFAA-Radio 570 was a powerful frequency. It was shared with WBAP 820 in Fort Worth. That is a long history going back to the early days of radio, too involved and too long ago to spend a lot of time on here. But each station alternated sharing the frequencies; when WBAP came on, they would have a cowbell ringing for Cowtown Fort Worth. It was a little bizarre, but Texans loved it.

Charlie and I had worked together on the Dallas Texans broadcast, so we were well acquainted, at least in football. But Charlie had never broadcast baseball and obviously had never re-created out-of-town games, so we begged for a trip to spring training in Arizona where we practiced. I supplied the score sheets and as much expertise as Charlie wanted and then, back in Dallas, we practiced re-creating games in the studio. But there was another severe problem. Western Union had gone out of the business of supplying game facts for the out-of-town games. The solution to that was to make arrangements with one of the reporters traveling with the Spurs to call us every other inning with basic game information. We made a deal with whichever newspaper's reporter happened to string the games, paid $10 per game, as I recall, and hoped the damned thing would work. If the game started at seven, say in Austin where the Spurs opened the season, then our stringer called in with the first half inning, and we went on the air at seven-thirty with our pregame comments. We had the teams, their records, their managers, the field and its dimensions, starting lineups, and the national anthem, which we added for "realism." When the local newspaper guys didn't travel, we arranged for one of the away "ink-stained wretches" (our colorful description of newspaper guys) to work for us.

Amazingly, I still have the notebook where I kept the schedule, player information, and my contacts for the re-creations every year. That notebook has the seal of the University of Denver still visible on the front cover. I bought that in 1948 when I was an undergrad there. The notebook has the 1971 schedule with each game marked out as played. Over on the other side are the guys who called us with the inning-by-inning game information. There was Frank Maestes at Albuquerque, New Mexico; Jim Sims and Dick Palmer in Amarillo, Texas; Mike Laughead in Memphis; Orville Henry in Little Rock, Arkansas; Ed Deforest in Shreveport, Louisiana; and Bill Merriman in San Antonio, Texas—with each name, we had the various phone numbers and addresses if we needed to check back. That was our "computer" in those re-creation days, 1965 to 1971, the year before I went to the American League with the Texas Rangers.

One great advantage we did have was the new era of cart machines in broadcasting. Gosh, young people today probably have never seen a cart machine because everything is on computer. Carts were about three or four inches long and two inches wide, plastic, and like a camera has a roll of film, carts had little rolls of audio tape inside that came in different lengths—thirty seconds, one minute, or any size needed. They slid into a cart machine (nicely named) and were activated by pushing a button on the front. With these dandies, we could have a mix of sound effects, such as the crowd reacting to a single, double, triple, or home run. We had boos and heckling, plus trains, planes, lions, and other assorted effects that might add spice to the game.

Fortunately, there was an exhibition game between two major league teams at Turnpike prior to the season opener. We took a portable tape recorder out to Turnpike and recorded the crowd, and then we came back to the studio and edited out singles, doubles, homers, and everything we needed in the carts. To have a normal baseball background, we had to take out all hits, errors, and anything that made the crowd react. We put that on two reels, so when one was finished, we could use the next one and rewind the first general crowd noise.

We had a superb engineer, who Charlie and I recall fondly except we can't remember his name, who loved the idea of doing what we wanted and then embellishing the whole thing if he saw fit. When we wanted a base hit, we would stick up one finger (whichever one we wanted) and say, "Here's the pitch to Jones, swung on, line drive to center field, base hit, Jones rounds and holds at first, and Wilson throws it back to second." A double was two fingers and on up to the four-finger homerun. The engineer had played our cart, which was real time, real sound.

The Texas League was rebuilding with six teams—three in the East and the Spurs, Tulsa, and Austin. The West had Albuquerque, Amarillo, and El Paso. My friend from the old Triple-A Rangers, Chuck Tanner, was manager of El Paso.

WFAA had wonderful facilities, as did KRLD, from the grand old days of radio. We had a spacious studio and a large desk where both of us worked the first three innings. Charlie was the lead announcer before he left to broadcast his ten o'clock television sportscast on Channel 8. Sometimes, he would run an inning or two more if the game was fast. Then I finished up the five to seven innings. Usually, our re-creations were finished just after ten p.m., unless the game was exceedingly long or tied.

The first broadcast was in Austin, April 16, 1965, at the old stadium down by City Lake Park. Charlie's first re-creation was to be memorable. Here Charlie has yet to do a live baseball game and you can imagine the problems of pacing the pitches, a base hit, and the length of time it takes for the ball to reach the outfield and the runner to advance to first. Our stringer usually just sent this kind of report: "Wilson, Struck out swinging, Jones single to right, Smith hit into double play, 6-4-3. 0-0-0 end of first half inning."

The info varied with the interest of the reporter and what happened. If there was a difficult play, the guys gave us everything to work with, although brief. Sometimes the local out-of-town reporter filed for us, like Orville Henry, a legendary figure in Little Rock at *Arkansas Gazette*. That was later, when Little Rock came in the league. But Orville gave a lot of information, like, "Wilson struck out on 3-2 pitch, Jones head first into third, line drive off the left field wall, rebound missed by the fielder, a triple for Smith."

Charlie worked through the Spurs' first inning and everything was moving along quite well. Then the Austin second inning. They scored thirteen excruciating runs in that inning. You must visualize hits all over the place, walks, and runners on base scoring in all manner of groups, two or three at a time. It was a nightmare that an experienced baseball announcer would dread. Austin won the game 17 to 1. Charlie made it through, naturally, but the next time we saw Tom Vandergriff at the opening of the season in Arlington, Tom kidded Charlie telling him that those guys hitting singles sounded like they were taking one giant step to first base. As they say, timing is everything! But Charlie was and is an outstanding sports announcer and his re-creations, as well as the live games, were professionally reported.

Charlie was selected to broadcast NBC football telecasts in 1965 and Jay Randolph, the Cowboys announcer, called me to be his color analyst on radio so both of us had to skip some Spurs games. Veteran broadcaster in football and baseball, Eddie Hill of radio station WRR, filled in for us. The next year, after the baseball season, Charlie went full time with NBC and I moved up to the play-by-play announcer for the Cowboys. I missed more games, plus I was working on my thesis for a master's degree at North Texas State University—a busy time.

Opening night was Friday, April 23, 1965, for a Spurs team that came off a seven-day road trip 3 and 4. The Spurs had opened the new park in Albuquerque and ten thousand fans came out to watch their Dodgers, an affiliate of the Los Angeles Dodgers, win 6 to 1 over DFW.

All week before the grand opening of a new baseball venue, Turnpike Stadium, the workers had been finishing up. The sod didn't have time to root and catch hold so the field was treacherous for outfielders trying to make sharp cuts. There had been a lot of rain and, for some strange reason, little frogs began invading the team dugouts. It reminded us of 1959 when one of the ground rules at Burnett Field included a rabbit nest on the infield grass on the third base side, not far from home plate. All players and managers were admonished not to step on the baby rabbits.

Arlington mayor Tom Vandergriff, Lamar Hunt, and Tommy Mercer were presented as the leading forces in bringing the area this new stadium before the 7,231 patrons/fans who attended the game. Fort Worth's Kay Bowman sang the National Anthem. Before the exciting year was over 329,294 paraded through the gates of Turnpike. Baseball was back! A new stadium location halfway between the two cities seemed to be the answer.

A lot of fringe events of great importance were occurring in 1965. Vietnam was heating up into a national problem, President Lyndon Johnson called in federal troops for the civil rights march in Montgomery, Alabama, a Ford Galaxy cost $2,200, and the *Times Herald* added more strength to their staff with Steve Perkins and Bob "Chickenfried" Galt. Frank Boggs was covering the Spurs and Blackie Sherrod styled these prescient words in a column: "TV producers, who may soon come to rule the world [of sports] swoon with rapture over the new arena in Houston." The domed football/baseball stadium, the Astrodome, opened. Blackie was on target, as we see that television does rule the world of sports today. Do you want to get your unknown team on? How about 9:15 a.m.?

The Dallas Cowboys signed the world's fastest sprinter, Bob Hayes, who had run the hundred-yard dash in 9.1 seconds. For the ladies, it was the time of big hair. It was the time of renewed interest in baseball, particularly the Texas League with the new stadium for the Spurs and another major city like Albuquerque. It was the firm, enterprising management of the game by Whitey Lockman, a group of hard-playing young men who kept the fans in the ball park with an unusually large number of comeback wins in the eighth and ninth innings. Kessinger was called up early and Roberto Pena replaced him and played so well he made the All-Star team along with his outfield partner, Don Young.

It was, as usual, the Spurs pitching staff that was my fond memory. Len Church, Sterling Slaughter, Hal Haydel, and Chuck Hartenstein were the keys. And when the staff seemed to be losing their points of release, or unable to hit the spots for strikes, roaming pitching coach Freddie Martin (the same old Martin of the Mexican League years before), came in for a few days of instruction. The staff then started mowing down the opposition again.

After that miserable '64 season at old Burnett Field, the new stadium, the new team, and brilliant Double-A baseball was drawing fans. But the main two things I remember are Hartenstein's "game" and the finish of the season. Charles Oscar Hartenstein was born in Seguin, Texas, and starred at the University of Texas. He was called Twiggy by his baseball buddies, all 5′ 11″, 165 pounds of him. We only knew him in Dallas as Chuck who had signed in 1964 with the Cubs. With a record of 4 and 4 Chuck went to the mound at Turnpike on June 17, 1965. Chuck had turned twenty-three less than a month before.

Charlie Jones, my partner, left after the third inning to do his television sports show at Channel 8. When he came back out to Turnpike Stadium, we were in the twentieth inning and he took over for me after my seventeen exciting innings. Hartenstein and Herb Hippauf of Austin battled through the first seven innings, with the Spurs leading 1 to 0. In a scoreless game in the fifth inning with Austin's Tate at the plate, Chuck buzzed a fastball at his head on the first pitch. Tate dusted himself off and with a 3-1 count bunted down the first baseline. When Hartenstein fielded the ball, Tate ran over him. It was Tate's one hit in eleven at bats in the game. Chuck righted himself and continued pitching. Hartenstein gave up a run with a triple and a single in the ninth and the game surged on at 1 and 1. Herr pitched Austin to the twelfth while Hartenstein was still mowing 'em down. Cecil Upshaw came on in the twelfth and battled Chuck in the tie game through the eighteenth. That was Chuck Hartenstein's final inning. He had pitched eighteen innings, given up one run (in the ninth) allowed only eight hits, walked four and struck out seven. The game finally wound down in the *twenty-fifth* inning when George Kopacz, the Austin first baseman, led off with a single, went to second on a wild pitch, to third on a bunt, and scored on a single.

In the bottom of the twenty-fifth, Dallas–Fort Worth left runners at first and third, finishing behind Austin 2 to 1. The Spurs' Don Young and John Felske each had eleven at bats. Felske had five hits; Roberto Pena, four. The umpires were Lloyd Childress and Bruce Froemming. Bruce has spent thirty-four years in the major leagues calling thousands of games. In 1986, he was selected by TSN (The Sporting News) as the best umpire in baseball.

"Hartenstein's Game" was the longest in Texas League history by an inning over a San Antonio–Rio Grande Valley affair in 1960. Frank Boggs of the *Dallas Times Herald* covered the game and had a note on his score sheet that John Boccabella made twenty-eight put-outs in twenty innings and his beard grew three inches. The next night at Arlington, Amarillo came in and the Spurs won 2 to 1 in thirteen innings. It was that kind of year!

Recalling that Hartenstein was very slender, I asked him this summer to give me a synopsis of his pitches: "To answer about my stuff, here goes! Two fastballs, worm-killing two-seam sinker, a four-seam absolutely straight fastball (it was turned around often), a twelve to dirt curve, a slider that endangered fans in the outfield bleachers, and a devastating change that killed a few people sitting down the lines! All these pitches could be thrown from any angle. I was basically a sinker-slider type pitcher though I always changed speeds from slow to slower."

That array of "stuff" served Chuck until 1977, his last season in the majors at Toronto and thirteen more years as a pitching coach. In relation to the 2005 World Series, Chuck pitched and coached with the Chicago White Sox when Ozzie Guillen was a rookie player.

In our discussion about the one hundred pitch count on pitchers today, Chuck explained, "the one hundredth pitch is a time to really watch your pitcher. Normally, you can hear when he's tiring from all the hard hit balls, but because these guys didn't grow up playing baseball all day, their arms are not as durable!" Chuck noted if a pitcher went over one hundred in one game, he probably was only effective for seventy-five in the next. "Another factor was how many tough situations [innings] did he really have to strain to get out of trouble."

The designated hitter—this is one of the rule changes a lot of folks don't approve of. Harftenstein says, "The DH takes managing out of the game. You let your pitcher go until the bats get loud. Then you change. It does allow a good hitter to hang around, although his defensive skills are gone. The American League is an easier league to manage in. No double switches, that makes the game interesting. I'm a National League guy. Some pitchers can actually bunt."

Hartenstein also thinks that the height of the mound today has a lot to do with arm problems. It officially was thirteen inches above home plate since the early 1900s, until it was reduced to ten inches some years back. Don Drysdale told me how he and his fellow pitchers would come back to Dodger Stadium after road trips and help the ground crew add some more height to that mound. No telling how high it finally became.

Hartenstein told me "when they lowered the mound, back whenever, it really changed pitching motions. Instead of being able to bend over to finish off a pitch and throwing downhill, you had to start pushing the ball toward the plate instead of throwing it. Guys don't finish off pitches now, because they really can't. If I could recommend one change to baseball today it would be raise the mound. Look at the many pitchers on the DL [disabled list] with elbow and shoulder problems. Raising the mound would be a very simple solution to protect your highest-paid players."

I asked Milwaukee Brewer pitching coach Mike Maddux, brother of Greg Maddux of Atlanta fame, when he was in Round Rock why his pitchers didn't finish their pitches with both feet facing the plate. Mad Dog Mike said it was the mound—it's too low to come down straight, and the pitchers' front foot hit the ground too soon.

I found an MLB website recently that said they were mulling over raising the mound to thirteen inches to help reduce injuries, but a medical group who studied the question for them thought the height of the mound made no difference. So the beat goes on and on.

Richard Hendrick, who runs the splendid Oklahoma Sports Museum in Guthrie, Oklahoma, coached high school ball all over that state before going the museum route. During a visit to the museum that features that great high-kicking left-hander, Warren Spahn, Hendrick told me that he thought the lack of a full windup also created problems for pitchers. I asked Hartenstein about the windup theory and he said he discovered that with many of his pitchers (in his pitching coach career), the full windup seemed to be too much for them and still be consistent to the plate. "I used and taught the push-off and tried to get them in a fielding position, but many of them could not do it. I used to finish facing the hitter and take a mini-hop to be ready to field the ball." There are theories galore in baseball. For the superstitious, that one run loss in the twenty-five-inning game defined the 1965 season, probably because of the way it finished. The Spurs needed to win the *one* big game.

Whitey Lockman's Spurs had to fight for every inch of baseball ground they could during the '65 season, and even though the club never had an easy stretch in the season, the fans loved this bunch of guys. One of the mercurial types was Bob (Shorty) Raudman. He was 5′ 9″ and rather like David Eckstein of the St. Louis Cardinals (but not as talented), he gave it his all. He is best remembered for an early encounter with the chain link fence that ran from the first base end of the stands down the right field to the outfield fence. It was about twenty-five feet from the foul line. Early in the season, Shorty came flying in from right field trying to catch a high-pop foul down the line and, as he grabbed the fall in his glove, he hit the chain link fence and catapulted over to the other side. Lying on his back somewhat dazed, Shorty started kicking the fence with his feet like a little boy. From then on that was "Raudman's fence."

Gene Etter, the left fielder, was adopted by the fans when he announced he was to be married at home plate. Gene was a religious young man who convinced his future wife to join him in a new religiously oriented life. The wedding was before a regular season game and filled the stadium. (By the way, if you watch the movie *Bull Durham*, the best baseball movie ever, you should understand that everything that occurred in that story happened at Turnpike Stadium.)

On September 1, the Spurs were two games back of Tulsa with five to play. Saturday September 4, the Spurs defeated Austin as Hartenstein pitched his second consecutive shutout, and ran his record to 12 and 6. Boccabella hit his twelfth homer in that game and Shorty Raudman his fifth. Then Sterling Slaughter, another slight right-hander won his fourteenth game. The Spurs were three behind with four to play. That final weekend, Tulsa was at Amarillo and the Spurs finished at home with Austin. Three down, four to play.

Tulsa and the Spurs won three straight and came down to the final game, with a one-game difference. Dallas–Fort Worth played before a final crowd of 10,907 who were there also for a night of fireworks. The Spurs won the game over Austin 3 to 2.

Tulsa was finishing the four-game series at Amarillo and there seemed no chance of an Oilers loss. Back on August second, Amarillo had ended fifty-eight scoreless innings by scoring a run against Tulsa. In that fifty-eight-inning debacle, the Sonics had absorbed six straight shutouts, so there was little hope that Amarillo could stop Vern Rapp's Oilers, probably the best in the league.

But as the Spurs finished their final game, Tulsa and Amarillo were locked in a 4 to 4 game going into the tenth inning. We had a radio in the press box that picked up the big Tulsa station, KVOO, which carried the Oilers. We put the radio up to the microphone of the public address system in Turnpike Stadium and the crowd roared as Amarillo, managed by Lou Fitzgerald, scored four runs in the bottom of the tenth on a grand slam home run to win 8 to 4.

Dick Butler was handing out beers in the press box. Charlie and I were still on the air doing an instant recap of the way the Tulsa game was going. When Tulsa finished, there was a call from the league office—a coin toss, Butler won and Tulsa would visit Turnpike Stadium the next night for the playoff to determine the champion! All of this went over our broadcast and out to the fans, who poured out of the stands to buy tickets. It was the closest to a championship I came in my years broadcasting baseball.

With 11,233 fans filling every seat and pouring over on the right-field hill, the Spurs sent out Chuck Hartenstein to pitch against twenty-one-year-old left-hander Larry Jaster of Tulsa. Chuck pitched a strong six hitter and gave up just two runs, but Jaster held the Spurs to just four hits while striking out eleven. Tulsa was the East champion with that 2 to 0 win.

Jaster was called up by the St. Louis Cardinals after the Texas League playoff and threw three complete game victories in three starts. In 1966, Jaster threw five shutouts all against the pennant-bound Dodgers, to set a major league record for most consecutive shutouts won from one club in a season. Larry finished the year with eleven wins. Jaster threw the first major league pitch in Canada for the Montreal Expos 1969 home opener. His last year was 1972, but I think of Larry as that winning pitcher against the Spurs on a September night in 1965.

Whitey Lockman was named Texas League manager of the year for manipulating an average team into a run for the championship. Hartenstein was named pitcher of the year for his 2.18 earned run average. Don Young and Roberto Pena, Spurs fielders, were named to the All-Star team. The Spurs drew 329,294 fans, leading the league in attendance.

Over the first six years, the Spurs had two winning teams. From 1966 until 1969, it was hard to watch. The Texas League became a "one-division" league in '66 with the six teams. Arkansas finished first, while the Spurs struggled to last place under three managers:

Stan Hack, Pete Reiser, and Lou Klein. The Spurs did have two fine pitchers. Lefty Fred Norman was pitcher of the year with 198 K's and Len Church sported a 6 and 4 record and was called up in August.

The zaniest part of the season rotated around a wild and crazy left-hander, Lee Meyers. He was a little boy in a man's outfit. Meyers had inherited a sizeable amount from the estate of an uncle and had made the acquaintance of actress Mamie Van Doren. Meyers was lovesick at the start of the season for Mamie and would read some of the letters he received from the delicious blonde to bachelor Dick Butler. Dick never revealed what was written, but he indicated that they had been explicit. Lee was constantly trying to have Butler let him off a few days to visit California.

Early in the season, Lee actually became ill with the flu. He was out of the rotation for several days. He didn't take his illness to California. The first night Meyers returned, there was an awesome Texas "gully washer." A huge thunder and rainstorm hit right before the game. There was no tarp to cover the infield, so the dirt part was a lake. After the rain and lightning stopped and the grounds crew was preparing to try to clear the water, Lee Meyers, possibly the most typical of southpaw theories, raced out of the dugout to first base, on toward second, where he belly flopped into the water with a long slide, then to third with the same headlong slide—and he completed the cycle into home plate. Butler, usually mild and sweet, was furious, yelling in the press box to bring the son of a bitch to his office, and he removed Meyers from the Spurs roster. Mamie and Lee married in May, and he pitched in A ball in the California League.

The exploits of Meyers made the Cubs–Sox history column of Bill Hageman and Bob Vandenberg in a 2004 edition of the *Chicago Tribune*. They wrote, "Pitcher Lee Meyers belongs in the Cubs archives, not for his mound work, but for one off-field accomplishment. The twenty-one-year-old Cubs minor leaguer married thirty-three-year-old bombshell Mamie Van Doren." This was May of 1966. But alas, there was no happily ever after. The couple divorced in early 1969. Lee never made it to the majors ("it was a great two and one-half years," he told reporters) and he died in a car crash in 1972. (And the Spurs weren't through with emotionally tested pitchers. Read on to 1970 and Greg Arnold.)

Probably unnoticed in 1966 by most was a kid named Nolan Ryan who struck out nineteen while throwing a four-hit shutout for Green-ville in the Western Carolina league. A young Reggie Jackson hit three homers in a California League game.

With Charlie Jones gone from WFAA, we were forced to scrounge around for other radio stations to broadcast the games. A couple of the station's signals barely covered both markets. Through the re-maining years, we were on at least five different stations, including KCOL and the powerful WBAP in Fort Worth. That was a plus with the professional and talented Bill Enis working as my partner. It was a long haul for me to drive to the Fort Worth studios for the out-of-town game re-creations, but the signal was strong. Unfortunately, the losing teams forced us to move stations often.

Bill Enis later worked in Houston and had a bright future with net-work television. Then he came home one day, sat down, and died at age thirty-nine. I was pallbearer at his funeral. He left two very tal-ented sons. In 2005, Bill was inducted into the Texas Radio Hall of Fame, along with current Houston Astros veteran Milo Hamilton, a spry seventy-nine.

Manager Jo Jo White managed a star-less Spurs team in 1967 to last place, sixteen games back of Arkansas. It was a thrill visiting with the former Dodger Duke Snyder, who was manager of the year at Al-buquerque. El Paso's Jim Spencer was on the All-Star team again—the same Spencer who later played for the Texas Rangers. DFW atten-dance had dropped by more than seventy thousand the past two years.

In 1968, the Dallas–Fort Worth Spurs finished last in the West divi-sion of the Texas League, but managed to achieve a goal no North Texas pro baseball team had done in twenty-one years. A pitcher tossed a no-hitter, and the Spurs didn't stop there—they had a total of three, with two back-to-back, which had never been done in Texas League history.

Bob Watkins, Luis Penalver, and Paul Doyle were the three premier pitchers. Watkins threw his 2 to 0 shutout at Memphis on May 24. Using mainly his fastball, Watkins struck out twelve, walked three, and hit one batter. It was Bob's third win, all shutouts. The previous no-hitter by a Dallas pitcher was thrown by Bobby Hogue for the Rebels in 1947.

Then to set a mark in Texas League history, Luis Penalver threw a seven inning 3 to 0 no-hitter the next night, May 25, in the first game of a double header in Memphis. Luis walked one and K'd three, while Memphis committed five errors. I didn't see those games in person; they were both re-created by me and Bill Enis at WBAP's studios. We did see the next one.

On June 29, 1968, after 26 relief appearances, left-hander Paul Doyle started his first game against El Paso, undeniably the best team in the Texas League. Doyle proceeded to pitch to only 28, threw 111 pitches, struck out 8, walked 2, and did not allow a ball to be hit out of the infield. To their credit, his fielders made some saving plays. Merle Heryford's story in the *Dallas News* included the amazing firsts: first no-hitter by Doyle in his ten years of pro ball, first no-hitter in the four years of the new Turnpike Stadium, and first no-hitter by a Dallas pitcher, or any other in the area, in a Dallas ballpark since Hogue's in 1947. Doyle finished the year leading the league with 149 strikeouts.

What happened to three pitchers of no-hit quality? Doyle played some for Atlanta, California, and San Diego, finishing in 1972. Watkins went to Houston in 1969 where he pitched just five games—15.2 innings and that was all. There is no record I could find that Penalver made it to the "show." Tough business, baseball.

There were five no-hitters in the league in 1968, and in one way or another, all had a Dallas trademark. The Spurs had been no hit by Albuquerque's Dick Armstrong on April 22. The fifth league no-hitter was thrown by a former Spurs pitcher, Dean Burke.

San Antonio and Memphis had pushed the Texas League membership to eight in 1968, and it went back to two divisions. The Spurs finished last in the West, twenty-one and one-half games back. Old friend Chuck Tanner managed El Paso to the full championship and scored manager of the year. El Paso's Jim Spencer was on the All-Star team again and one wondered if he was fated to be a Double-A player the rest of his life. The Spurs dropped another 30,000 fans to a tad over 215,000.

Meanwhile, major league baseball was expanding with franchises awarded to San Diego and Montreal. In 2005, Montreal, owned and managed by major league baseball for years, lost its team to Washington, D.C. The Nationals came back thirty-three years after the Washington Senators moved to North Texas. Ah, and then there was 1969.

Butler and Macko found the answer to local baseball woes in the Baltimore organization. The Orioles sent a cadre of outstanding players and a manager, Joe Altobelli, who became a minor league legend. These Orioles–Spurs had future major league stars: Bobby Grich, Larry Johnson, Don Baylor, and catcher Johnny Oates. Both Oates and Baylor later managed in the major leagues. Oates, the former Texas Rangers manager, died recently. The Spurs battled down to the last week of the season finishing 72 and 58, four games back of Amarillo, managed by my old buddy from the Muskogee Giants, Andy Gilbert.

Johnson and Grich were league MVPs. Larry hit .337 and Bobby .310. Grich started in Baltimore in 1972 and played fifteen years with the Orioles and Dodgers. Bobby won four gold gloves and was on six major league All-Star teams. He retired in 1986 with a lifetime .266 batting average.

Joe Altobelli, named Texas League manager of the year in 1969, attained that honor three times in his eleven years managing in the minors. Joe was a weak-hitting utility player in three ML seasons, but picked up a manager of the year in San Francisco in 1978, and in 1983, his first year as manager of Baltimore, he won the American League pennant and defeated the Philadelphia Phillies in the World Series. Altobelli won four World Series and lost one. Interesting note of the Altobelli career: Joe replaced a retired Earl Weaver in November 1982. He won the World Series in 1983 and then was fired in June 1985, replaced by a not-yet-retired Weaver.

Some interesting sidelights, terrifying and funny, occurred in 1969. The American Association came back into being. Players in the International League refused to play in Buffalo, New York, after their clubhouse was broken into by a gang and the players held at knifepoint. Most of the games were moved to Niagara.

Former 1968 Spurs manager Hub Kittle was managing Savannah and took the mound to pitch an inning and a third, giving up one run. Hub was fifty-three, the oldest pitcher in Southern league history.

Managers say you can't win without the players. The Spurs had a few good players in 1970, but not enough to avoid a third-place finish in the West Division. Actually, the Spurs had pitching, but failed in the offensive part. Dyar Miller was an All-Star pitcher, Randy Cohen again led the league in strikeouts, 151, and his Spurs teammate,

George Manx, had the lowest ERA at 1.90. Miller had a 10 to 0 no-hitter against Amarillo.

There was a young pitcher, Wayne Garland, who was one year away from a brilliant record. There was second baseman, Ron Shelton, who was a good player, but more importantly, he was taking notes that he would use to write unquestionably the best baseball movie, *Bull Durham*.

I'll come back to Ron, but first there was Greg Arnold. As they say in novels, it was a mild, pleasant night, June 13, 1970. The Dallas–Fort Worth Spurs were playing the Memphis Blues. The aforementioned Ron Shelton was playing second base (with a respectable .261 batting average). Starting his tenth game of the season was Greg Arnold, with a solid 5 and 3 record, but a high 5.31 earned run average. Greg's problem had been walks to strikeouts. He had walked forty-six and struck out forty-six. Should be two or three walks to one K.

It was the third inning, the Spurs trailing two to nothing. A run had scored in the first inning on a single and an error in right field. The leadoff batter in the third tripled off Arnold and scored on an infield out. Greg had walked another batter and was deep in the count on the next, when he suddenly stepped off the mound, walked calmly over to second base, and slammed a fist onto the chin of umpire Nick Ematerio.

Ematerio went down like a rock while Greg's teammates stood stunned for a second and then ran over to him while others aided the fallen umpire. There were only two umpires working minor league games then—the home plate ump came out and naturally tossed Arnold from the game. No one really had an answer as to why Greg hit the ump. He mentioned something about balls and strikes Ematerio had called in another game. In this game, Greg had registered five strike outs, but also four walks. It was as though he couldn't stand to walk the batter at the plate and took it out on Ematerio. Arnold was suspended the rest of the season.

The Spurs recovered from the shock of their pitcher doing a number on the umpire and scored four runs in the last two innings to win 6 to 5. In winning the game, the Spurs used all their bench players and Joe Altobelli, the manager, ended up playing first base in the ninth. Joe's Spurs finished in third place in the West Division, twenty games out and only 182,743 fans came out to Turnpike Stadium.

In addition to Miller on the Texas League All-Star team, there was Mickey Rivers of El Paso, who led the league with a .347 batting average and 69 runs. Mickey became a star player with the Angels and one of the most frustrating players to interview. He was a funny guy, but you never really knew what he might say, and sometimes the pace of his speech was so fast and slurred he was almost unintelligible. When Dick Risenhoover and I were in the second year of the Texas Rangers, Don Drysdale was with the Angels broadcasting. Before a game in L.A., Dick asked Don who would be a good pre-game interview. Big D, with his quirky sense of humor, suggested Rivers. Dick came back from the interview trying to recall exactly what had happened to him! Rivers had talked in circles, gave strange answers, and thoroughly flummoxed Dick. Don enjoyed the whole episode.

You can start an argument about the best baseball movie ever made. To those of us who have been in the total baseball experience, and who were with the Spurs, *Bull Durham* is the best. Ron Shelton had so many true composite players in the movie. LaRoosh could have been anyone of a number of pitchers, but if you put Lee Meyers and Dean Chance into one body, you had him. Of course, Chance might have qualified by himself. Susan Sarandon's part—well, there were enough "groupies" to qualify, but we also have ideas about certain people close to the ball club that we better not name. The episode in the movie of the marriage at home plate is not without precedent in other parks. But Spurs' Gene Etter was a particularly religious young man whose wedding at home plate fit the story line. At the end of the season, Shelton's year, the Spurs were to play their last games in Amarillo. Losing the first game at Potter County Stadium and out of the playoffs, the Spurs decided they had had enough. So after the park was deserted late that night, some of the players slipped in and turned on all the sprinklers. The next day, it seemed a major flood had hit only the ballpark. It was drowned out, like in *Bull Durham*. The Spurs came home early on Sunday, satisfied.

In 1969, Buffalo, New York, had moved its baseball games after the team was attacked in the clubhouse by a knife-wielding gang. In 1970, after ninety-three years in organized ball, Buffalo lost its franchise, which was moved to Winnipeg. However, it was later returned to Buffalo.

The final year of minor league baseball in Dallas–Fort Worth was a dandy. It is memorable for several reasons. The manager was the late Cal Ripken, Sr., Wayne Garland won nineteen games, and Tom Walker pitched a fifteen-inning no-hit game on August 4. Tom walked just four and faced just two over the minimum. It was the ninety-seventh and longest no-hitter in the eighty-three year history of the Texas League. Garland made the All-Star team with his wins and an ERA of 1.71. Garland pitched the next year in Baltimore. The apex of his career was 1976, when he won twenty games for the Orioles. Wayne was then traded to Cleveland and pitched five more years.

Something unusual seemed to happen each year with the Spurs. Catcher Steve Turiglianto hit his first home run of the year on August 15, stumbled while running the bases, and broke his elbow in the resulting fall. The Spurs' Enos Cabell was the Texas League All-Star first baseman, most valuable player, and led the league hitting .311 and 162 hits. Billy North of San Antonio, who later starred with Oakland, was the fastest, with 91 runs scored. Dallas–Fort Worth finished just five and one-half back of Amarillo managed by Andy Gilbert. The Spurs were 82 and 59 and drew 212,349 fans. El Paso had departed the league and the 1971 teams played an interlocking schedule with the Southern League.

Another emotional end to the minor league era was the attitude of these young Spurs ball players. They wanted to win the pennant, but when that wasn't possible they battled to at least win the last game pitched by Tom Walker. That didn't happen either and it was an unusual clubhouse because of the tears and emotions of these players who had played so well and so hard all year. Since 1882, when the Dallas Hams first played organized baseball, and sixteen different mascot names later, thus ended the minor league history of Dallas and Fort Worth.

Three weeks later, September 20, 1971, Mayor Tommy Vandergriff of Arlington and Bob Short, owner of the Washington Senators, announced a deal to move the major league team to Turnpike Stadium. Good old Charley Finley of Oakland had held up the vote trying to coerce Short into giving him the outstanding rookie Jeff Burroughs for a favorable vote. Finley was hooted down by the league owners.

Now Texas had two major league franchises, Houston in the national league and the new Texas Rangers in the American. Work enlarging old Turnpike, now Arlington Stadium, to major league proportions began almost immediately. As it turned out, forty thousand seats weren't needed until 1973 when David Clyde pitched.

Here was an interesting situation in every facet of the business of baseball. Nearly all of the management and personnel of the Senators were shipped to Arlington to run the franchise in a new territory. Some local managerial types would have been a smart move for Short, overcoming the kind of carpet-bagging atmosphere for the new group, but that didn't happen. So those East Coast marketing types were slow to gain favor in the North Texas area.

For me, it was hard to put a handle on who was managing the broadcast rights and hiring announcers and staff. There was little information coming out of the organization except on the progress of the work on the stadium. The news that would hopefully spur fan interest was the fact that Hall of Famer and the greatest hitter of all time, Ted Williams would be the manager, as he had been in Washington.

Bob Short thought marquee names like Ted brought in fans. He made another move like that in '73, but he may have never really noticed that only winning teams bring in fans—and especially so with an old and beleaguered franchise that was on its last legs in D.C.

Tracey-Locke was the advertising agency hired by the Rangers organization to conduct the search for the announcers. I sent in my resume and tape and awaited the results. Since I had been strictly a local and regional talent, I figured my presence in Dallas for the past thirteen years broadcasting baseball would suffice. Wrong all the way. In this business, especially today, you better know someone, in addition to having excellent credentials as a broadcaster.

So it was in January 1972 that I received a call from Mayor Tom Vandergriff of Arlington asking if I had been contacted by the agency conducting the search for the broadcaster. I told him I had sent in my resume and tapes but had heard nothing. Vandergriff said he was afraid of that and would be back in touch. In just a few days, I was called by the agency and asked if I was available to be the broadcaster for the Rangers. I said yes, and they arranged a meeting where I was informed that I would be the lead broadcaster with former Brooklyn/ Los Angeles Dodger Don Drysdale as my partner. My salary was to be $25,000. I now had one job earning about the same money I had received from the Cowboys and teaching at North Texas combined.

I doubt that I ever credited Tom Vandergriff enough for making it possible for me to work with the Rangers. Tom served as mayor of Arlington for twenty-six years and was instrumental in the growth of the area through the DFW International Airport, tourist attractions, and, of course, the Texas Rangers.

Tom dabbled in the broadcast business earlier and was the public address announcer at UT-Arlington football games. It was his driving force that made UTA a four-year senior institution. He was always the most accommodating, available person for interviews or information. One of the great tragedies of politics in this part of Texas was his defeat in his congressional district race in 1985. This soft-spoken gentleman worked tirelessly for the good of the people of his district. Later, Tom smiled and told me that he probably didn't campaign hard enough and then added that it probably wouldn't have mattered since it was in the midst of the great Republican tidal wave that swept over just about every office in Texas.

Tom Vandergriff had also served his public well as a member of the White House Commission on urban problems and the founding president of the North Central Texas Council of Governments. He was also rewarded by being named citizen of the year in Arlington, Dallas, and Fort Worth at different times. Vandergriff has been a county judge in Tarrant County for five terms and just announced his decision not to seek another term. Without Tom Vandergriff, Arlington, and this part of Texas, might have been just another suburb with nothing but malls and a small junior college. I will confess that I did not reward this good man after the 1973 baseball season with the respect he was always due.

A few weeks into January, the ball club flew Drysdale in for a meeting with all of us involved with the broadcast. It was explained that we were a separate entity from the ball club with our own manager and production staff. The games would be broadcast on powerful KRLD. My old station had since been sold to the J. Erik Jonsson family when the Times Mirror Company bought KRLD-TV. The new call letters were KDFW-TV. Dick Risenhoover, their sports director, would be a part of the Rangers telecasts with Don Drysdale and me alternating innings. Having Dick on board was a major acquisition. He had played baseball from his early days in Childress, Texas, through the University of Texas. Later, while coaching all sports in Childress, he began his broadcasting career, and after twelve years in the business, was hired in 1970 by then KDFW-TV. Dick's presence paid off for a long time.

Bill Knobler was television broadcast coordinator for the Rangers and recalls most games were telecast on Channel 39 as well as Channel 4. Channel 39 was an independent operation while KDFW-TV had CBS programming to work through. Hughes Sports Network handled the pickup of the games and at first worked through Tracy-Locke Advertising. Dick Blue, whose yacht we sailed on in California prior to the season opener, was the manager. But before the season started, he was replaced by Gary Rollins, who became president and general manager of the Rangers Network. The network, broken away from Tracy-Locke, came under the control of the Arlington Park Corporation, which also had the Seven Seas theme park. Their chief operating officer was Hollis Pollard, a sensible and fair executive. He proved to be a great help in maintaining the operation as the season wore on, saving the corporation money by not working through the ad agency.

Having Don as a partner was the best thing that happened to all of us. Here was a fabulously successful pitcher, obviously headed for the Hall of Fame (1983) who had a quiet, charismatic manner, was eager to be part of this new organization and, most important to me, was glad to be paired together. He told me he was still learning this business; he had been a color analyst announcer in Montreal, and wanted me to teach him everything I could. So he taught me baseball and I worked with him on the mike side.

Physically, we were quite a pair. He was 6′ 5″ and I was 5′ 7″-plus. With a nickname of "Big D," Drysdale fit perfectly for the Dallas–Fort Worth area. Dallas was Big D and here is Drysdale. However, there was very little marketing of announcers in those years and the Rangers certainly did nothing to promote the fact they had one of the great pitchers of the 1960s in their broadcast booth. The 1972 Rangers' media guide lists the broadcasts on page twenty-nine. Under the Rangers' broadcast team, in print that you almost needed a magnifying glass to read, was listed Don Drysdale, Bill Mercer, and then the stations carrying the telecasts and radio broadcasts. I thought they should have had a bit of bio on Don, who brought outstanding baseball credentials to the new team.

The media guide had a nice spread on owner Bob Short, with a picture, a well-deserved spread on Ted Williams, and pictures of all the "Rangers personnel" and "secretarial staff"—just forty pages of the basics. Actually, this compared favorably to most media guides. Atlanta's in '72 had no pictures of anyone and did not mention broadcasting at all. Milwaukee had a small box on one page mentioning radio and television and the staff who worked them.

In 1973, the Rangers' guide went way over the top with pictures of me, Risenhoover, and Terry Stembridge, who was handling TV for Channel 4. There was also a picture and two-page spread of new manager Whitey Herzog, but no pictures of the front office.

There were some grumblings by some staff members that they hoped Drysdale didn't try to coach the Rangers pitchers and upset the coaching staff. It was just the other way. Don went out of his way not to give advice. But if a pitcher came to him and asked for advice, Don would try to answer. He talked this over with Ted Williams before the season. If Don had interfered and given unsolicited advice to the pitchers, it probably would have been in vain with that staff.

Our Texas Rangers broadcast headquarters were in a small building just east of the Seven Seas theme park. The Seas, with its beautiful killer whale as the main attraction, was just east of Arlington Stadium and combined forces with the nearby Six Flags Over Texas to provide an unbelievable venue for tourists.

Don and I had an office in the space where the manager, actually a sales manager type, presided over a small staff including our TV producer Bill Knobler. One of our first discoveries was the need for theme music for our games and the Rangers. Stuck in my head from childhood was a theme from some cowboy movie like *Ride Rangers Ride*. I hummed it to our group and they thought it might work. So I called Paramount films in Hollywood and finally reached the keeper of the arrangements who sounded more like the wrestler Fritz von Erich than the woman she was. I explained what I wanted, and though she argued that we should just compose one ourselves, she finally relented and said she would search for it.

In about a week we received a package with the original composition from the 1930s—now to turn it into a piece of music. I had just left North Texas State University where I had been teaching and broadcasting, so it occurred to me to check if the famed One O'Clock Lab Band could put in the finishing touches. I took the music up to Leon Breeden, the jazz program director who said they could put it together, but that of course meant arrangements for a full orchestra and then the recording time. All that would cost a small fortune, and we had no money. I then contacted Joe Burke with the Rangers and we worked out a deal to give the band and the arranger tickets to a number of games sort of equal to the band's cost. The theme was used for several years before they decided something more hip was needed to lure in the fans. But I have always been proud of my idea for the cowboy movie background that was turned into the theme song of the major league team and our broadcast.

History demands I mention some of the key people associated with the Rangers of 1972. Joseph Burke was the vice president and general manager, one of the five managers who came in from Washington. The media's favorite among the newcomers was Burton (Burt) Hawkins, press relations director and traveling secretary. Burt had been traveling in baseball since the steam engine pulled passenger trains. He was brusque and funny and represented old-school baseball—everything and anything to protect the team. All of us in the media loved him, and I guess he tolerated us.

One local acquisition to the staff was Joe Macko, who was made business manager. It was a good public relations move having at least one person from the area with a title. Macko was greatly respected by local baseball folks for his playing skill and his front office managerial work with the Dallas–Fort Worth Spurs. In the front office, Mary Ann Bosher, who had also been in the Spurs organization, was the leader of the seven women who had as much local contact and public relations as any of the male managers.

While in my sports director duties at KRLD-TV several years before, I had encountered Ted Williams who was out of baseball, representing Sears and his line of fishing gear. Sears had called asking about setting up an interview with Ted for my TV sports show, and I gladly agreed. Then around the newsroom began all the talk about what a hard ass Ted was, impossible to be around and all that stuff. Well, it was totally the opposite. That big bear of a guy was a smiling, pleasant, cooperative sort who gave a truly interesting interview. We talked about bone fishing, his favorite, and all the other activities relevant to handling a rod and reel—plus a little baseball.

Nearly a decade later, here I was working with the ball club that "Teddy Ball Game" is managing. Being a manager of a good ball club is not an easy task—being the manager of the worst team in baseball was a mind-crunching chore. Terrible for a former player who dedicated endless hours working on his game, taking extra batting practice until his hands bled, Ted could not comprehend, and said so, why every one of his players was not as dedicated.

Ted Williams's batting average of .406 in 1941 was the last foray into .400 hitting since 1922, when George Sisler hit .420. Ted's lifetime batting average was .344. Between 1939 and 1960, he was an All-Star fourteen times and player of the year five times. He also served in World War II and the Korean War, which I will try to give due credit for later. On Ted's coaching staff was one of baseball's most revered second baseman, Nellie Fox. Nellie, with his bottle bat, played for the Chicago White Sox for fourteen years, hitting over .300 six of those seasons while striking out only 216 times in his entire career. Little Nel and his shortstop partner Luis Aparisio were the dominant middle infield duo those years. Nellie finished his final two seasons with Houston and died in 1975. Nellie was as loveable as a cocker spaniel.

Sid Hudson was the pitching coach and could claim that in one season in his ten-year career with the old Washington Senators, he won more games than he lost. That was a 17 and 16 record in 1940, his first year. Sid was a dignified, hard-working gentleman who tried as hard as humanly possible to build a decent pitching staff.

The Rangers' third base coach, Willard Wayne Terwilliger, was eighty-one on June 25, 2006, and in 2005 managed the independent central league Fort Worth Cats to the league championship. He was the oldest active manager in baseball before announcing his retirement. The Twig, 5' 11" and maybe 170, played with five major league teams and nearly every other minor league team from coast to coast! Twig has been in uniform for seven thousand professional games.

If ever a cartoonist searched for the ideal subject for an old, gnarled, beat-up catcher, George Cyril Methodius Susce Sr. was the one. George turned sixty-three in August of 1972, still handling the Texas Rangers pitchers in the bullpen. Every finger on his right hand had been broken over those more than fifty years of catching. Each digit pointed in a different direction. The "Good Kid," as he was called in his playing days, was in charge of the physical training and continued conditioning of the players. Ted Williams, dramatically gesturing, claimed Susce could do more push-ups and knee bends and run farther for endurance than any of his players. The players called Susce a tyrant in response to his workout regimen and laughed behind his back for his work in the bullpen. George, who waddled rather than walked, started playing major league baseball in 1929 with the Philadelphia Phillies. He played seventeen games that year and did not play in the majors again until 1939 with Pittsburgh. Susce coached for five major league clubs, including the Washington Senators, before coming with Ted to Texas. At one point in 1936, he caught for the Fort Worth Cats of the Texas league. Oh, if he could have been in *Bull Durham*! Susce died in 1986.

It didn't take long for us to realize that the new Texas Rangers were a major league team in name only. The spring training headquarters were less than sumptuous—Surf Rider Club motel on South Ocean Boulevard in Pompano Beach, Florida. It did have a swimming pool and a decent bar across the street. The spring training ballpark, Municipal Field, resembled old Burnett Field in Dallas. The home radio booth was so small, Don and I were barely able to shoehorn into the area, which had heavy screen wire over the small opening in front to protect us from villainous foul balls. For the fans who ventured to the park, it was only a $2 ticket for general admission.

KRLD had obtained the rights to the Rangers while still broadcasting the Dallas Cowboys, becoming the King of the Hill in sports in North Texas. That football/baseball combo was to cause some serious conflicts at various times. The two Johns, Barger and Butler, managed the station in its news and sports format. Verne Lundquist, my former partner with the Cowboys, had moved in to their play-by-play position.

Having been around the area longer than most of the folks in broadcasting, John Butler asked who I would like to have as our broadcast engineer. No question, the one and only, one-eyed Jim Birdsong. He had been at KRLD for just about forever and was one of the most competent engineers on the staff. Jim had a glass eye, which he would remove on humorous occasions. He quickly became a favorite of the ball players and management. Jim had gray hair and a beard and looked older than anyone except Susce. The ball players vied to carry his broadcast equipment when we traveled.

The spring training broadcast schedule listed one game per week on KRLD. I imagine selling the new major league franchise to savvy advertising agencies was considered difficult, thus only one game per week. But Don and I were roaming around in the car provided us by the station trying out the best restaurants and bars while waiting for the week's lonely game. We attended the home games and commiserated with the players and Ted Williams, but felt like a pilot without an engine in its plane.

I am sure I never learned diplomacy, ever, and this spring training episode was one that had me in some warm water with the two Johns at KRLD. I called them and the ball club and suggested we were wasting our time and their money just broadcasting one game per week. Also, we needed to educate the North Texas sports public to the teams and players of the American League who the Rangers would play that season. I recall a rather nasty retort that I should worry about broadcasting baseball and let everyone else manage radio. My answer to that was that Don and I learned more doing actual games than just sitting and watching. In a week or so, we began broadcasting two and three games a week.

John Barger and John Butler were a couple of wild and crazy guys who had fun managing KRLD. We survived that little spring training crisis and became lifelong friends. Barger, a salesman who could find clients where none had existed, brought me in years later to work the San Antonio Gunslingers of the spring football league and Butler gave me a lot of great games later, mostly Texas A&M, when Mutual Radio had the Southwest Conference rights. I still hear from Barger on email, but Butler died about five years ago from cancer.

My total time at spring training prior to 1972 had been about six days—three in 1959 when the Triple-A team came into being and with Charlie Jones and the Spurs in 1959 out in Arizona where we heard Leo Durocher cuss for thirty minutes. But now this was the real thing! We had a month of hanging out daily at the ballyard, broadcasting the odd games, and roaming around Florida checking out its beaches, sun, and bars. The majority of baseball fans at the games reflected the massive white-haired, retirement population of the Sunshine State. Like going to some of the cafeterias for dinner at five. For half prices, the older population flocked to the ball games to see their stars for just a couple of bucks. At two bucks a general admission ticket, the Rangers, with Ted Williams the main attraction, drew an average of nearly eighty-five hundred people per game in the thirteen home games.

Let me touch briefly, with representative stories, on the major attention to detail we spent on things other than baseball—the nightly investment in dinner and bars. The *Dallas Times Herald*, *Morning News*, and Fort Worth *Star-Telegram* had semipermanent reporters like a young Randy Galloway, veteran Harry Gage, the late Harold McKinney, and a couple of others. The featured columnists put in short appearances as well. An occasional TV sports type came in for a whirlwind tour of videotaping to show the fans back home how great major league ball could be. Someday. And there were also the quick visits by members of the Rangers' management and broadcast "executives."

Don and I had journeyed about, scoping out various fashionable bars and accompanying dance facilities for ourselves but mainly for our visitors. I recall one day Big D and I checked out a place that Don said was really special. We dropped in for the usual grapefruit juice and vodka. Don's theory was that the grapefruit juice cut the calories in the vodka, and thus we wouldn't gain weight. Don was recognized the moment he went into a Florida establishment, so we had numerous long baseball conversations with the locals while sipping on the local grapefruit juice. This particular day, I went to the restroom and when I returned, there was no Don. As I went to the front door, he was driving off. I caught a cab back to the glorious Surf Rider. When I walked into the nice bar across the street, Don looked up smiling and said, "Where have you been?" We had days like that.

When our short-term guests arrived in Pompano, the "Mutt and Jeff" combo, as Don and I were called, took them on a whirlwind dinner and barhopping evening. One particular occasion an exec enjoyed himself so much and for so long that Don and I gave up, went home, and left our friend dancing the night away. As he told it later, a day or two after recovering, he finally ran out of gas (grapefruit juice) and called a cab. When he told the driver to take him to the Surf Rider, the cab pulled away from the bar, crossed the street, and deposited him at our sumptuous digs. That was one of the highlights of the intense away-from-home living it up that makes spring training such a fond memory.

But now on to the tedious business of broadcasting those spring training games. I had made up books of score sheets that I had used during the Spurs episode. Don and I had one practice game to be sure the broadcast lines at grand Municipal Field were functioning and that our basic four-microphone input amplifier also was functioning. As we worked through the game, I mispronounced a player whose name was spelled Salmon and called it like the fish. Drysdale went into spasms of laughter—"Sa-mone, Bill, Sa-mone." After that, we never held back on questioning each other and having a great time doing it. He was never malicious or insulting, as Harry Caray was, who I would spend time with on Devil's Island for two years, but Don did had a devilish sense of humor.

I got him back early on though. He always mentioned this when being interviewed or in his book, *Once a Bum, Always a Dodger*. We were preparing for our first regular broadcast and Don was to record the pregame interview. He walked up to pick up the portable tape recorder and showed me the list of questions he prepared to ask the player. I took the paper, looked at it, wadded it up, and threw it in the wastebasket. I asked him if he knew a lot about baseball. He scowled and said of course. "So why in the hell do you have to write down the questions?" I asked. You ask the guy what you know he is going through in spring training. In the postgame interviews, you use all the journalistic W's: who, what, when, where, why, and how things happened in the game based on your observation and expert knowledge. Don said in a bio that it was hard doing an interview when he knew the answers! That was the point of this little incident.

Right in the middle of this reverie of spring training loomed a players' strike. I recall sitting around with the "ink-stained wretches of the printed word" (reporters) talking with Frank Howard, who was holding out on the Rangers' spring training demanding more money, and Don about the various issues. They agreed that the owners were never going to figure out how to stop the onslaught of player's demands because they were too selfish, concerned only for their own teams obtaining the best players at the expense of owner solidarity.

Sure enough, as the new Texas Rangers won five of their last eight spring training games, including the last three straight, the player's (all of them) for the first time ever went on strike April first, an April Fool's gift to the owners. Spring training ended with the Rangers owning an 11 and 14 record.

In a later edition of the *Times Herald*, Blackie Sherrod disputed the claim that it was the first strike. His example was May 15, 1912. Ty Cobb, who fought with everyone including his teammates, went into the stands that day to beat the bejesus out of a fan who heckled him. The commissioner of the time threatened Cobb with a season suspension. His Detroit teammates, not so happy with Cobb but feeling the episode an injustice to any ball player in the same circumstance, said they would strike the game of May 18 unless Cobb was reinstated. After all, they did possibly need him to win the pennant. So that day, Detroit came out in their uniforms, asked the umpire if the suspension had been lifted, and, when it wasn't, walked off the field. Philadelphia A's teammates rounded up a bunch of volunteers and played a game, won by the pros 24 to 2. The commissioner relented, fined the players a hundred bucks for not playing, and cut Cobb's suspension to ten days and a $50 fine.

The Major League Baseball Player's Association had been trying to find their footing for several years when they suddenly discovered and hired Marvin Miller in 1966. Curt Flood had sued baseball for the right for free agency, which had not been resolved. Miller organized the players into a cohesive unit and began his campaign to improve the financial lot of professional baseball players. One of his first successes was having the owners agree to an increase in the minimum wage from $7,000 to $10,000.

Miller had presented the owners with a new demand in the winter of 1972 to increase the contribution to the players' pension fund. This was promptly refused by a vote of 24 to 0. Miller then began his tour of the spring training camps, explaining his plan and laying out the way it would be accomplished. When the owners continued to refuse negotiating on the pension fund, the players voted 663 to 10 to strike.

Meanwhile, back at the ranch in Texas, we prepared for a short strike or a long strike. The first home game was scheduled for April 6 with Kansas City at newly refurbished Turnpike Stadium, now called Arlington Stadium with a total of 35,165 seats. In a way, the strike was a blessing to the stadium folks finishing up details of the enlargement from its original ten-thousand-seat capacity. A huge new scoreboard was erected above the left field stands. The seating now stretched all the way around from left and right field to center. It was 330 feet from home plate to the left field stands, 380 to left center, 400 to center, 380 and 350 to the right field side. The press box had been newly built and expanded to major league dimensions. Our radio booth was large, with an upper level behind us for "visiting dignitaries." We never had any.

The players had workouts at the stadium during the strike, which gave the media an opportunity to become closely acquainted with the newcomers. This was one of the true "April showers" with rain just about every day. In fact, the Tuesday before the strike ended, a reporter from the *Washington Post*, Russ White, who happened to be a severe critic of Williams and his Senators, was locked in the press box following a rain-shortened workout. Absorbed in his writing, White finished and noticed there was no one in the box. The door was locked. White finally called the Arlington police to extricate him from his working cell. White probably thought Ted had engineered the scheme.

April 10 arrived with rumors beginning to surface that the strike could be settled any day. It was determined—after missing the four-game openers and a long road session beginning April 11 in Oakland followed by California, winding down with Chicago—that Don and I should go to Los Angeles to be within striking distance of one of those West Coast parks if all was settled. The next home stand, actually now the first, was April 21 with California. There were three open dates in the long road venture after California.

We had a pleasant time in California playing tennis, sailing with some broadcast friends, and preparing for our official debut. Suddenly, the strike ended April 13 and our best-laid plan was perfect. At Arlington Stadium, traveling secretary Burt Hawkins, who stayed by

the phone waiting for the conclusion of the strike, called Ozark Airlines to bring its charter in for the Friday flight to L.A. Most of the
players remained in the Dallas–Fort Worth area, but the half-dozen
who went home (one to Puerto Rico) were instructed to make the Friday flight or pay their own way. All made it. Our first official game
was Saturday, April 15, in Anaheim with Gene Autry's Los Angeles
Angels.

The Rangers were ready to play the season opener in Anaheim
April 15—at least everyone except Jeff Burroughs, the number one
draft pick who had missed half of spring training with a tender back.
He had injured it while swinging a heavyweight bat prior to batting
in an early game. Jeff still managed to hit three home runs in the
spring, but his aching back was so tender the week the strike ended
that he was flown to Minneapolis to be checked out by a prominent
orthopedist. There was no timetable for his return to the lineup.

Though this club is still maligned as one of the worst ever, there
were some pretty decent ball players: left-hander Larry Bittner, first
base and outfield, briefly with Washington in '71 in just his fourth
year in pro ball; Dick Billings, a former first baseman and outfielder
who converted to catching in '70; and six-year Washington veteran
pitcher Dick Bosman, who had winning records twice in those season.
Dick was the opening day pitcher. Dartmouth University, movie-star
handsome, twenty-two-year-old Pete Broberg came right from the
college campus to Washington in 1971 and finished with an impressive 3.46 ERA. Jeff Burroughs was in his third year in professional
baseball and showed power with twenty-nine home runs in two seasons at Denver. In fifty-nine games with the Senators in '71, Jeff hit
five homers. Another veteran Senators pitcher for the past four years,
Casey Cox had established himself as the key player out of the bullpen. The pitcher or player with the longest name, Bill Gogolewski,
naturally called Gogo, won six and lost five with a 2.76 ERA for the
Senators the year before. Twenty-four-year-old Tom Grieve, the same
one who works the Rangers telecasts today and once was Texas's general manager, was a hard-working, considerate young man. Right-
hander Rich Hand came over in a trade with Cleveland, which included Mike Paul and future catching star Ken Suarez. Hand would
win ten games and finish with an ERA of 3.32. Another star of the
future, shortstop Toby Harrah, called us Mr. Drysdale and Mr. Mer-

cer and became a standout for Texas. There was the huge Frank Howard, all 6′ 7″, 285 pounds, nearing the end of his career after hitting double-digit homers for 11 years with the Dodgers and the Senators (48 in 1969). Left-handed hitting catcher Hal King played for the Dallas–Fort Worth Spurs in 1965. Last, but not least, lefty Paul Lindblad led the Senators with 8 saves in '71 and was counted on as the anchor of the bullpen.

In his rookie major league season, twenty-one-year-old Joe Lovitto had a great arm and speed to handle centerfield, while swift Elliot Maddox, also in the outfield, could go get 'em but was light at the plate. The other shortstop, twenty-one-year-old Jim Mason, was also in his rookie year with the Bigs. Texas was veteran Don Mincher's sixth major league club where he would share duties at first base with Howard. Base-stealing third baseman, Dave Nelson (whom my twelve-year-old daughter, at the time, adored and still does to this day) was a question at that position. Mike Paul, a lefty and Horacio Pena, a right-hander, both had been in the Cleveland organization and were being counted on to strengthen the pitching staff. Finally, a number-one draft choice in 1970, Lenny Randle, had been in baseball just three years, one in Washington, and was the second baseman for the Rangers.

These players were the foundation for the team that had some forty-five players in the lineups during 1972. The Rangers lost 100 games while managing to win 54, the fewest in the American League. The team batting average, figuring pitchers and pinch hitters, was an anemic .217. Toby Harrah and Larry Bittner led with .259 each. Pinch hitters had only 26 hits in 181 at bats for a miserable .144 average. No pitcher had a winning record in 1972, although Mike Paul came close with an 8 and 9 record. Ten wins by Rich Hand led in total victories.

The misery of this club was reflected in an individual like Pete Broberg, expected to be a future star. He won five games through June 13 and didn't win another game for the rest of the season. Pete finished 5 and 12.

The Rangers started the 1972 season in California April 15, after the strike, and lost a tough one 0 to 1 as the Angels' Andy Messersmith had a no-hitter through seven. The next game, Sunday afternoon in Anaheim, was reported in the paper as the first telecast of the season. Pete Broberg pitched a gem, 5 to 1 over the Angels. The expectations for this flamethrower rose dramatically.

But no one saw the game in Texas. Ten days before, Channel 39, the originating station in Dallas, cancelled the future telecast because of the strike. Unfortunately, no one notified the media about the change. Bill Knobler, the television coordinator for Tracy-Locke Advertising, said they couldn't clear enough stations on the Rangers network for a Sunday telecast, after the strike was settled on Friday. So Texas fans missed a chance to see some early Rangers success.

The next game in Chicago was a White Sox 14 to 0 pasting of the new Texas bunch. For the Rangers' final game in Chicago, Don Stanhouse gave up one hit, struck out nine in six and two-thirds. The Rangers lost to the White Sox 2 to 1 in the last of the ninth and were coming home 1 and 3.

It was one of those wet Aprils in the Dallas area, and Mayor Tom Vandergriff later said he had not been able to sleep the night before the opener. When he watched the morning arrive, he saw sunshine and it became the best day of his life!

That evening the Arlington High School band performed a pre-game concert, and everyone who was anyone of public stature was on the field and Vandergriff, rightfully so, threw out the first pitch before 20,105 fans. There would not be a sell-out until 1973. The players were presented with white ten-gallon cowboy hats, which none of them probably ever wore again.

I received a telegram in the broadcast booth just before the game. It read, "Dear Bill, it is only fitting that the first official major league baseball game in the best part of Texas is being broadcast by the best sports announcer in these parts. All of us at North Texas State University are indebted to you for what you have done for and with North Texas through the years, and we just wanted to say congratulations on this occasion. President C. C. (Jitter) Nolen and your many friends at North Texas State University." I was so flattered by their support.

Dick Bosman was the starting pitcher against California. The Rangers won the game 7 to 6. No one can remember the score, but they can remember Frank Howard. Nine minutes into the game, big Frank hit a high slider off Clyde Wright that looked like a low-flying rocket clearing the four-hundred-foot sign in centerfield. Third baseman Dave Nelson crunched a 385-foot shot over left-center field in the fifth while Lenny Randle had two singles and a double, driving in four runs. Bosman picked up the win with solid ninth-inning relief by Paul Lindblad. Williams claimed this left-hander was the best relief pitcher in baseball. Lindblad finished the season 5 and 8 in sixty-six games (the most by any Rangers pitcher) with a 2.61 ERA and nine saves. Then he was traded to Oakland. On to Chicago and a 14 to 0 pasting by the Sox followed by a close 2 to 1 losing effort by Texas. Don Drysdale walked into the booth in September of '72 and reflected on the fact that Texas was thirty-six games out of first. Laughing, he said, "So what the hell do we do now?" Without Don's sense of humor and knowledge of the game, it would have been a miserable year.

Once in the old ballpark in Kansas City, the one with all those girders and steel, Don had gone down for the postgame interview, which he handled. He usually left in the middle of the ninth, depending on the score. This day, the game was tied in the last half of the ninth and went on to the tenth and eleventh. Suddenly, a telephone started ringing, its tone punctuated by the girders surrounding our booth. Jim Birdsong and I couldn't locate it until I was back on the air. It had been tucked under a girder directly below our broadcast table. I pulled it out and answered it on the air. Don said, "Listen, when the game is over, give me a call across the street here in the bar and I'll come over for the postgame." Laughing hysterically in his quiet way, he hung up.

We had a televised game scheduled in Milwaukee on a June weekend, so that meant a pregame interview on camera. The first time I met Bob Uecker, the Milwaukee broadcaster, was in the 1960s when he played for Denver in the Pacific Coast League. Even as a catcher, he had a comedic personality. In a game in Dallas, he baited the fans with his antics behind the plate, relishing the boos and reactions. Then he hit a solo home run and, as he ran the bases, clapped his hands over his head. The fans enjoyed it.

So in 1972, I called on Bob to be on the afternoon pregame before the Brewers–Rangers game. We had the usual introductions, and then I asked him what he was doing other than the Brewers. He proceeded to tell me about his "Passed Ball School," which he claimed he ran in the off-season coaching youngsters how to make the passed ball a key part of the catcher's job. In his famous style, he described how a catcher should react, creating a thing of beauty while chasing a ball

he should have caught. And, of course, he asked that youngsters interested in improving their passed ball play contact him for the off-
season camp. My friend Frank Gleiber, a network sportscaster and
Dallas sports guru, told me it was the funniest performance he had
ever seen while rolling on the floor laughing at Bob's serious de-
meanor.

Heavy on the minds of everyone in 1972 was the Vietnam War.
For journalists, broadcasters, and others interested in politics, it was
constantly on our minds. After every road game, I mean *every* one,
four or five members of the newspaper group—we three broadcasters
(when Dick Risenhoover was along), Burt Hawkins, the traveling secretary of the club, and an occasional outsider—would congregate in
the hotel bar, or one nearby, and proceed to thrash out the pros and
cons of the war and all related to it—principally Richard Nixon and
his team. Under Don's direction, each of us threw in $25 and pro-
ceeded to drink it up and argue like hell. It usually broke into three
against three or four and four, with Don opposed to my opinion. Naturally, these wild debates broke into battles over the quality of the
leadership of Nixon. As Watergate unfolded that summer, the accusa-
tions and arguments became more intense.

When the U.S. went into Cambodia, the postgame powwow took
us to about three in the morning. The rest of the bar had closed, but
the bartender stayed on. I apologized to him for keeping him, and he
laughed, saying, "Hey, I really enjoy this!" When I finally made it out
of bed, dressed, and headed for some breakfast later that morning, I
was on the elevator with a nice-looking older couple when we
stopped. The door opened and in strode Ted Williams. He immediately launched a missile attack on me—how could you be against the
president, our country, this war, everything holy and unholy? In his
thundering voice, he had the little couple cringing in the corner and
me holding my aching head. I tried to tell him my position, but he
just kept on proclaiming his unwillingness to believe anyone could be
against our president and our country.

These were wonderful times with Ted and Don. When we went
into Boston the first time that season, Don and I were sitting in the
dugout with Ted. He looked up and, with a descriptive series of expletives, followed with, "Here come those goddamn Boston writers!" A
passel of guys was descending on the dugout, and even Ted was laugh-

ing as he was introduced to all. In Boston on a hot summer day, August 25, the Red Sox celebrated the beloved Jimmy Fund, a particular favorite of Ted's. When the Rangers played on the road, they normally didn't draw large crowds. But with the Jimmy Fund and Ted Williams with Texas, nearly thirty-four thousand people crammed into Fenway. Ted Williams was one of the original supporters of the fund to help children and adults suffering from cancer. The fund began in 1948, and in 1953 became the official charity of the Red Sox. Ted was a lifelong member of the foundation that is today the Dana-Farber Cancer Institute. Each year on Jimmy Fund day, a large contingent of old Red Sox players hit in a mini-game before the regular game. Various ex-players came up to bat and finally, they called out Ted Williams. The fans erupted in a frenzy of shouting: "We want Ted."

There had been bets on whether he would show. Then, after a couple of minutes with the clamor rising, Ted strode out of the dugout with a heavy jacket over his obvious middle-age bulge, grabbed a bat, and walked to the plate. First pitch, he slammed a drive to right field and we thought Fenway would collapse. Ted didn't like the spotlight, but for the Jimmy Fund, he would even show off his increased girth.

I have kicked myself over these thirty-three years for not having the intelligence to turn on my portable tape recorder one day on a charter flight. Ted and Don were sitting across from each other on the plane and, for some unremembered reason, began a full-blown, full-blast discussion of who was dumber—pitchers or hitters. I can't recall all of the derogatory statements made about those opposites of baseball, but it was a crowd pleaser for all of us in the first class section.

Don made the point that Ted never changed his stance even when they put the Williams-defense against him; everyone on the defensive unit congregated on the right side of the infield and outfield. Ted made a point of saying he wasn't going to give in to the (expletive) idiots who played unfairly. And he did say he was never stopped from getting his base hits. Don also chided him about not moving closer to the plate when Ted couldn't reach the outside breaking pitch, particularly the slider, which he hated with a passion. Again, Ted said the pitchers were afraid to pitch to him and he wouldn't adjust for anyone.

Ted's attack on pitchers was about how dumb they were when they were ahead of a hitter 0 and 2 and thought they could sneak a fastball by for the third strike. As I faintly recall, Ted also declared that pitchers who used a foreign substance on the ball (known as a spitball) were some pretty (expletive) bad guys. Don couldn't defend that much since he had been accused most of his career of loading up the ball (with K-Y Jelly, as I heard later). It has been too long ago to remember the details, except the key words were: "dumb f-ing hitter, dumb f-ing pitcher." It was probably a draw but may have surpassed in entertainment our nightly discussions of world affairs. And when the plane landed and we started off, Ted asked me to let him carry my big baseball information bag and I politely told him I could handle it, but thanks. Why didn't I let Ted carry my bag? It would have been a small talk item to use defending Ted and his personality. I still kick myself for not allowing him that nice gesture.

Ted let go on pitchers if anyone just hinted at what a hard time they had, and we decided he didn't particularly care for his own pitchers. Ted began to pay attention to the "one hundred pitch" unwritten rule. Pitching coach Sid Hudson may have been involved in that. As the season progressed, Williams yanked pitchers right and left on the one hundred count. Then we were in Baltimore late in the season and Rich Hand was handling the tough Orioles leading 1 to 0 going into the last of the ninth inning. We were conjecturing that Rich was at or near the pitch count as he worked in that final frame. Suddenly, Ted Williams lumbers out of the dugout, calls time, and heads to the mound. There was activity in the Rangers' bullpen. Rich looked over, saw him, and stalked off the mound toward Ted. Laughing that we might see the first manager-pitcher fight in the new franchise, we watched these two verbally go nose to nose. There was no way in Baltimore that Rich would leave, except by physical force. After considerable jawing, Ted turned and returned to the dugout, and Rich finished the game successfully.

Rich Hand worked 30 games, won 10, lost 14, and finished with a 3.32 ERA, best of all the starting pitchers. Rich was an outgoing, delightful man who everyone liked. So it became my fate one day to step into an "I know something about baseball" page. We were in Arlington Stadium working into the late innings when Rich came out to the bullpen and started throwing. He only failed to start two of his thirty games, so it was possible he was just "throwing on the side." Anyhow, I glanced at Rich and then stared as he wound and delivered and stepped in the bucket. Instead of finishing his delivery toward the plate, he was falling off to his left.

On a break between innings, I told Don to watch Rich throw and wondered why he was falling off the mound. Don said that something was a little wrong there, and we left it at that. I didn't say anything on the air about my observation.

After the game, we took our Ozark Airlines charter to Kansas City for the start of a long road trip. The next afternoon, Don and I visited the Rangers clubhouse in the old KC stadium, and when we reached Rich Hand's locker, Don stopped and told Rich, "Bill has something to tell you about your pitching." Man alive, I would never suggest to any of the players something I thought I saw. Rich looked up from his stool and, with a serious expression, asked what it was. With Don grinning like the proverbial cat, I explained what I observed in the pen the day before. Rich actually seemed surprised, asking me if he really was doing that. So I thought maybe I contributed something to Rich Hand's success. Sadly, he developed arm trouble and the next year was 2 and 3 with the Rangers. He was traded to California, where he struggled to a 4 and 3 record. Hand was traded to St. Louis in 1974 but did not play, and he ended his career.

The Texas Rangers Baseball Network was a division of the Arlington Park Corporation. Gary Rollins was the executive vice president and general manager of our broadcast unit while Hollis Pollard headed the total operation. Bill Knobler had joined our group, coming over from the ad agency as television coordinator.

All was not well with morale in our unit, principally due to everyone being new to the operation and trying to make the thing work. Rollins led the day-to-day operation and was considered the lead sales person. Rollins dressed well, was a very social person, and played a lot of golf with prospective clients. It started to become a joke around the office that Rollins spent more time golfing than acquiring the advertisers he allegedly played with.

In August of 1972, we flew into New York on an off day for a midweek three-game stand with the Yankees. Gary took the charter with us, confiding that he was to work on some major advertisers about the next season. After arriving in New York, we didn't see Gary again until the charter left. Drysdale picked up the information that Gary had been playing golf with various sports personalities including

Phil Rizzuto, partying in the evening, and making no contact with ad people. Don told me he had been checking up on Rollins and was sure he had not been working the agencies. Don said we were going to call Mayor Tom Vandergriff and discuss what he knew. I called the mayor and scheduled a meeting that I dreaded. I had been involved in one of these meetings, revealing the shortcomings of a manager, in another organization, and it did not go well. I had negotiated enough union contracts in my life, too.

Tom Vandergriff was very patient, listening to Don explain how he had talked with his sources about the lack of sales activities through the year. He laid out the past trip to New York as an example of a good time for our general manager, but there was no business activity. The mayor was courteous but felt that advertising had been about as good as we could expect in the first year, and he had no other complaints about Rollins. Thanks for your concern and for coming by. Nothing really was resolved. However, knowing Vandergriff, I felt he would do some investigating, having run a very clean city operation for years.

Ted Williams quit the managing business forever when the season ended and set sail for the Florida Keys, his home, and his beloved fishing. I still marvel at that season with Hall of Famer Ted Williams and Don Drysdale. It was one of the premier moments in my sports broadcasting career.

Owner Bob Short and general manager Joe Burke interviewed thirty applicants for the Rangers' managerial position. Out of that search came the man that we thought would be the Rangers manager for a long haul, Whitey Herzog. Short said Whitey "was the best possible man for the job" with his eight years of experience as a major league player, his five years as director of player development for the New York Mets, and his reputation for handling young players. The Rangers had one of the youngest teams in baseball in 1973. Whitey had witnessed the fourteen teams in the Florida Instructional League a year before and said then the Rangers had the best crop of youngsters. Whitey hit the Texas dirt running, making fifty appearances around the state—luncheons, dinners, radio, TV broadcasts, and countless other public appearances. Other baseball people all predicted that Whitey Herzog (affectionately named The White Rat) would be just the guy for the job. It sure looked like that to us. After that first season, I dropped into my routine of North Texas basketball broadcasts, missing my first full year of football since 1959.

Don went back to California, and we came in and out of the office checking on any chores we might do. We suggested to Gary that we would be glad to make personal appearances or help on sales, but he never indicated it was necessary. Then in December, the news came that Don Drysdale had been signed by the California Angels to work with Dick Enberg. It was a personal loss to me, but it made sense because Don lived in Southern California. The discussion started about a replacement, and the consensus was Dick Risenhoover. Dick had a softer voice than mine and our different personalities would make us a good team.

In December, Gary Rollins presented me with a new contract for 1973, and in a way, I had a raise. The contract called for a pay scale of $22,500 for broadcast services and $5,000 for personal services in the off-season. It was stipulated from the end of the baseball season to spring training that I would participate in network activities such as broadcast and sales coordination, sponsor sales, and promotion. I also had a sort-of title, director of radio broadcasts. I was still able to continue my broadcasts with UNT.

One day in January, as I recall, Hollis Pollard came in the office and said that Gary Rollins was no longer with the broadcast group. The story went something like there was a special meeting with a major advertiser, but Rollins had a golf trip or some personal commitment and wouldn't be there. Evidently, combined with other information, that was the proverbial straw, and Rollins was gone.

Hollis asked who I thought might be a strong replacement for the job. It was no contest. I suggested Roy Parks, the key sales guy at WRR-Radio. I had worked with Roy on various sports projects at his station, including a sports talk show, before I was the Cowboys' announcer. Roy could sell. He knew how to sell, who to contact—he was relentless in making sales happen. But he also was a good judge of talent and understood radio and television production. They interviewed three different people. Roy was selected.

Nineteen seventy-three gave us hope. Roy Parks was working like a golden retriever flushing advertisers; Herzog was the hit of spring training, candidly talking about his plans for trades, players, and building the team. Whitey brought in three young coaches: Chuck Estrada, Chuck Hilling, and Jackie Moore. Jackie and I are still going strong together over thirty years later.

The Rangers were basically the same team with some additions that helped and some that didn't. Long ball hitter Rico Carty (Big Boy) was picked up in a trade with Atlanta, where he hit 25 homers in 1970. Carty had a .317 lifetime batting average. Carty didn't pan out. Bill Madlock was brought up from Denver in just his fourth year in pro ball. The assessment was that he could hit. Correct. He played 22 games for the Rangers, hit .351, and was traded with Vic Harris to the Chicago Cubs for Fergie Jenkins—a trade that helped both clubs. Madlock hit over .300 nine of the next twelve years! It would have been ten years, but he missed by two percentage points, hitting .300 one year. Jenkins had won twenty-plus games in six years with the Cubs. He racked up 25 wins for Texas in 1974 and was traded to Boston in 1976.

We were desperately looking for ways to promote the ball club and, of course, our broadcast network. The ball club had an ongoing "Panty Hose Night" to attract women customers. There was an occasional fireworks display. I had been the emcee of the Dallas Cowboys' luncheons during my tenure there, and they had turned into huge success stories. So I suggested we have a Rangers luncheon during every home stand, inviting some player from the visiting team and a couple of the Rangers' players. It wasn't exactly greeted with thunderous ovations, but we did work out the details and set up the first one when the Yankees came to town. I called the Yankees media office, explained our promotional device, and asked if they would let us have one of the Yankees players at our first luncheon. They agreed.

As the day approached, we realized we had little publicity available, with only our broadcast and a tiny mention in the newspapers. So the Arlington city folks, led by Hollis Pollard, encouraged city employees to take extra time to come to the inaugural luncheon so we would be sure of a crowd.

Then the Yankees told us Thurman Munson, their catcher, would be available. Honestly, Thurmon had had some bad press, and we were concerned if he would cooperate. We had the crowd, buffet lunch, and head table, and Thurmon was perfect! He was funny, gracious, signed autographs, and couldn't have been better. We had invited the newspaper reporters and other media as our guests and received a lot of publicity. The luncheons became a big event and were only dropped years later when they became impossible to manage.

One strange event happened to me in Boston in 1973. Like so many fans and broadcasters, my favorite stadium is Boston's Fenway Park. If someone offered to pay my way to any ballpark in America, I would pick Fenway. I admire Yankee Stadium, but for pure affection, it is the old Green Monster field. My family has some very close friends in the Boston area who formerly lived in Dallas, so I looked forward to visiting that town for reasons other than baseball.

In 1973, we had just checked into the ballpark two hours prior to the game when a gentleman approached me in the radio booth and asked if he could speak with me in private. He was a member of the security detail at Fenway.

He said not to be alarmed, but they had received a report of a death threat for me. I wasn't exactly elated over such an announcement. He said that it was probably a hoax, but he asked if I had a girlfriend in Boston. No, and my wife was happy about that. Was there anyone in the area who I had an altercation with? No, I avoid altercations. He explained that they had received a phone call from a person who said he was in a bar with a few friends, and one of them said he hated the Texas Rangers' announcer Bill Mercer (guess he found my name in the media guide) and was going to go to Fenway to kill him. The man on the phone said he would be happy to come out to the park and talk to security about it. Security figured he wanted in the ball game. The man was to show up before game time. It was then about 4:30 p.m. I was told to go on about my routine, and they would keep track of me. So with Dick Risenhoover, my partner, I sauntered down on the field and met up with newspaper guys. Dick told them that I was possibly in great danger and explained the story. So all of a sudden the guys decided they would walk somewhere else—anywhere other than where I was going!

I truthfully thought it was a big, well, with me, a *little* hoax, and we continued our usual pregame routine.

The man never showed up to visit with Fenway's security, but they maintained a plainclothes man outside our booth. After my third inning broadcasting, I turned it over to Dick and walked out to go across to the pressroom for some coffee. Just as I stepped out in the walkway, which was covered by plastic sheeting, a foul ball landed right above my head with a great bang. I must admit I jumped about three feet and then laughed my way to a much-needed cup of coffee.

But that's not the end of the story. Randy Galloway put a note in his story about the death threat, and I was besieged with phone calls. I had said nothing about it on the air, and I hadn't called Ilene to tell her. No use bothering folks. Randy is still a good friend. I still love Boston and Fenway.

Texas again lost over a hundred games, 57 and 105. But four events defined the 1973 Texas Rangers' season: David Clyde, Jeff Burroughs, Jim Bibby, and Billy Martin.

Finishing last does have its advantages and, in this case, it was a first-round free agent draft pick for Texas in June '73. David Clyde, 6′ 1″ and 185, was the best pitcher in Texas high school baseball. As a sophomore at Houston's Westchester High School, he pitched a perfect game. In his senior year, 1973, Clyde's record was 18 and 0—he struck out 328 and walked just 18 in 148 and a third innings. He also pitched five no-hitters with several one-hitters thrown in.

In an article on ESPN.com Jeff Merron reported on the deal the Rangers made with David and his father. They wanted a major league contract that put the player on the forty-man roster and the option guaranteed that after three years another team could pick him up on waivers. According to Merron's story, "His total package broke down to a $65,000 signing bonus, a $22,500 salary [same as I was making!], and a standard $7,500 incentive clause. The Clyde show worked—in 1973, the Rangers averaged 18,187 when the phenom pitched, and just 7,546 when he didn't." David also mentioned to Merron that he was comfortable with Whitey Herzog who he and his family felt would watch out for him. Not so with Billy Martin.

After the Rangers signed David following his graduation from Westchester High, they brought him up to Minnesota to see how he looked against major league hitters, his new teammates. I was standing behind the batting cage that afternoon and the mere sound of that missile heading for home plate was frightening. The Rangers players were awed, hopping back from the movement of the fastball out of David's left hand. Twenty days out of high school, the Rangers scheduled David to pitch against the Minnesota Twins. The first media blitz about the new Rangers phenom stirred the sports community like nothing since the first Dallas Cowboys Super Bowl appearance. By the time we came back from the road trip, there were no tickets to the game to be had. The Rangers managed to save a special enclosed box for family members who were unable to find stadium seats. And those in the box had to listen to Dick and me broadcast the game; there were no open windows.

David drew the first sell-out in Rangers brief history, 35,698. That was exactly why Bob Short brought him in and kept him in the majors, to sell tickets. There was no thought about David's need to learn to pitch (sounds odd, but it's true) in the minors, developing a curve ball, change-up, control, and personal maturity. Herzog and his coaches knew what was best for David and that clashed with Short's plan. And that probably had a lot to do with Whitey's departure. Herzog wanted to pitch David in two Rangers games and send him to the minors. He went to the minors in '76 and '77, but then it was too late.

David was a splendid young man. He had no great ego, but believed in himself and was probably the least excited player on the team the night he pitched. He had let it be known that his idol was Sandy Koufax, that Hall of Fame lefty who pitched with my pal Don Drysdale. Several times prior to the June 27 game, David mentioned his admiration of and desire to be like Koufax.

Sandy was living the life of a recluse up in the Northeast. I called Drysdale in California and told him about the upcoming event and asked if he would give me Sandy's phone number so I could tell him about David. I knew Don had to check with Sandy, and in a few hours he called me back and gave me the number. I placed the call, left a message about the reason for the call, and asked Sandy to please call me. He called a couple days before the game and I suggested it would be the greatest part of David's debut if he had a telegram from his idol. Koufax listened and said he would see what he could do.

Late afternoon of game day, the telegram arrived and David was ecstatic. "Good luck, No. 32" was the message—and that was all needed. He couldn't believe that Sandy knew about him. David said he was more excited about the telegram than pitching that night. I never told anyone about that bit of my involvement and if David reads this, I trust it won't detract from the honesty of the message. Don said Sandy wouldn't have sent it if he wasn't sincere.

David went to the mound accompanied by an earth-shaking roar from the sellout crowd; he walked the first two batters, then struck out the side. He gave up a solo homer to Mike Adams, a Twins rookie, and won the game 4 to 3. He struck out eight and walked seven in five innings.

In an article on the thirtieth anniversary of David Clyde's debut, Dave Buscema of the *Times Herald-Record* wrote in "Record On-line" that baseball owed David for twenty-seven days. There were only twenty-seven days until he was eligible for his major league pension. The Texas Rangers should have signed him for no other reason than the debt they owed him. Quoting Busceme, "David wasn't ready for the success or failure that followed. He wasn't ready for Billy Martin, notorious for his overworking pitchers and for his temper (and his moral turpitude). David wasn't ready for the teammates who took him partying, which led to rumors of alcohol abuse, which David has denied."

In that same article, former Orioles manager Mike Hargrove, who was a player with the Rangers and Clyde, was quoted: "And they took him to the big leagues and he wasn't ready." The pitcher for Minnesota that day, Jim Kaat, commented, "That's the worst that's gonna happen to that kid." I worked with Kaat when he pitched for the White Sox and he is now a broadcaster for the New York Yankees. David's Rangers years were 4 and 8 in 1973, 3 and 9, and 0 and 1 in 1976. He went to the minors and was traded to Cleveland, where in the '78 season he was 8 and 11 and then 3 and 4. He retired in 1981. David has attempted to return to baseball as a pitching coach, which he knows something about now. Also those twenty-seven days are certainly owed him.

Jeff Burroughs and Jim Bibby became the success stories of 1973. Jeff clubbed out 30 homers and drove in 118 runs while hitting .279. Beginning July 26, he crashed three grand-slam home runs in ten days. The other was the no-hitter that Bibby threw against Oakland on July 30, striking out 13 in the 6 to 0 victory over Vida Blue. It was the first no-hitter for the young Rangers franchise. But the thrill of that call, my first no-hitter in the majors, was diminished when we found that KRLD had put our broadcast on the almost unknown FM station. They had dumped the regular season Rangers for a preseason Cowboys exhibition game—and there was no pregame promotion that the game would be on the FM dial! This so infuriated everyone at the Rangers network that they moved to WBAP in Fort Worth when the KRLD contract ended. WBAP had even a stronger signal than KRLD.

Bibby had come to the Rangers in a trade from St. Louis in June. He finished the year 9 and 10 and was traded to Cleveland in 1975. Burroughs was traded to Atlanta in 1977 where he hit 41 home runs. Over an eleven-year span from '73, he hit homers in double figures, highlighted by the Braves year. Jim Bibby was awarded the player of the year award at the last of our frequent luncheons and was presented a brass-embossed jockey strap! I wonder if he still has it. And finally, Bob Short decided on another way to sell tickets: fire Whitey and hire Billy Martin. Media folks were shocked. Whitey had a master plan to build the team, and Short had a master plan to sell the team, which he did in '74 to businessman Brad Corbett.

But first Billy Martin. I'll give him the fact that in 1974, the Rangers won eighty-four games behind Fergie Jenkins' twenty-five victories, and for the first time drew a million fans. But September 6, 1973, when he came into the pressroom at the stadium just before a road trip to Minnesota, the pleasure of baseball coverage went to tatters.

Martin joined the media crew at the bar talking about various baseball subjects and then pronounced that he expected discipline on the club (with him an oxymoron), and the players would wear shirts, ties, and coats on charters. He said, "I would expect the media to do the same." My red flag jumped up my throat. He was manager of the team, not us. No one from the network or the ball club had informed us that we must adhere to what Martin told us.

The next morning, I arrived for the charter, the only member of the media (or anyone else associated with the team), without a tie, but in a sport coat and appropriate attire. Funny Ted Williams and Martin would probably have come to blows over such an edict. Ted never wore a tie. I know, I know, it would have been simpler to accede to his demand and follow his dress order. His threat, as it turned out, certainly caught the attention of the media guys, even Dallas news writer Randy Galloway found a tie to wear. After that, Billy made remarks about me not being a member of the team. On the flight,

Martin sat behind me, leaned over, and made some comment about some thing he wished the media would do. Then he adding something to the effect that "Mercer isn't a team player, so I doubt he will agree."

I must say I didn't really care, since I had no respect for the oily demagogue and figured it was going to be a long, rough ride into next baseball season. Mike Shropshire, Fort Worth *Star-Telegram* writer who covered the Rangers, has a delightful book, *Seasons in Hell*, which gives you the depth of the mess with Martin and his failed reign as a manager (for just over a year) and human being. "Most of the pitchers on that team would candidly, and off the record, tell me that Billy didn't know anything about pitching," said Shropshire in an interview with Jeff Merron on ESPN. "At least when Clyde came up he had Whitey and Chuck Estrada who were very sympathetic to pitchers. Short looking for another gate attraction, it was a boost for the Rangers but the beginning of the end for David." Martin's pitching coach in 1974 was Art Fowler, whom I will describe later.

Texas finished in 1973 with the worst record in baseball, 57 and 105, and drew just 686,085 fans, even with David Clyde. Oakland won the West Division, beating (former DFW Rangers manager) Jack McKeon's Kansas City Royals. Rod Carew led the league in hitting with a .350 average, Chicago's Wilbur Wood, the pudgy knuckleballer, won 24 games, and Nolan Ryan struck out .383 and pitched two no-hitters. The Dallas–Fort Worth Spurs first manager, Whitey Lockman, led the Chicago Cubs to fourth place five and one-half games out.

In the final home stand of the season in late September, Hollis Pollard came into our radio booth to talk to me, Dick Risenhoover, and Jim Birdsong in private. Hollis said they were losing too much money with the ball club and the radio/TV corporation and were looking to sell the broadcast rights to some other entity in the off-season. Pollard was a rare gem, a compassionate manager, and suggested he could not guarantee we would be rehired if someone did buy the rights; therefore, if we were offered another job or wished to seek one, we had his permission. Hollis was obviously upset over having to give us this announcement, telling us we had been a good team for the Rangers.

I found some solace broadcasting North Texas basketball games that fall. I even filled in on a couple of the late season football games. But much of the time was spent with Dick discussing what we might plan to do: look for a job or wait out this mess.

Dick, with his initial radio year with the Rangers, said he would wait and see. I called around to a few friends about possible jobs, just in case, but there had not been much movement. Then one day in December the White Sox called!

Leo Breen, business manager of the Chicago club, called to ask me if I might be interested in a White Sox radio job. I assured him I would be happy to talk with him and he suggested that he would stop off on his way to Houston for the winter baseball meetings. He explained that they had been monitoring various other major league announcers that summer and liked my work. I was stunned. But also I knew that Harry Caray was the broadcaster of record, the major one, for the Sox. That was a concern as I awaited Leo's trip to town.

We met early one morning so I would have time to hear their proposition and discuss the offer with anyone I needed to. He laughed and said that he expected to sign me by that evening! The deal was $45,000 to work radio only. Caray would do the pregame program and also the middle three innings. I worked six innings alone. That was great—Vin Scully broadcasts his innings by himself (not to say I am in his league), but most announcers would like that arrangement. The club had a medical plan, insurance, and would pay my AFTRA (American Federation of Television and Radio Artists) dues.

Also, I would not be required to move to Chicago immediately because it would be a burden financially. For the two years of that contract, I could remain in Dallas and just spend the summers in Chicago.

The White Sox had weathered the caustic, downright bilious, comments about players, coaches, and management by Harry Caray during his contract. All of us in broadcasting knew his reputation. We also knew his reputation as an egotist who would attack his broadcast partners to appear superior. His mantra was "I tell it like it is," but I found he didn't need facts, know baseball, or have any concern for the privacy of the lives of the players. He sold Harry.

Their plan was to allow Caray to finish his contract, which would be up in two years, and if I worked out during that time, I would take over his position. I was satisfied with just the radio portion of the broadcast while Caray and another announcer, Bob Waller, shared the televised games, nearly every game the Sox played.

Leo said, "Go talk to everyone you know and make up your mind. I want you sign the contract this evening!" So I raced home to talk to my wife, Ilene, and the two children at home. The money angle was important with two sons in college and another starting in two years. Compared to Dallas at the time, Chicago was a huge city, and the thought of living there in the summer intrigued everyone. My two college boys thought it was "neat."

I talked to my old friend Fred Graham at the North Texas State University and his quick reaction was, "Take it!" I called Jack Buck in St. Louis and he echoed what Fred said. I asked Jack about working with Harry and he laughed and said he thought Harry had mellowed since their time together with the St. Louis Cardinals. That was comforting.

Back when I was at KRLD having the opportunity to work on the CBS-Radio broadcasts of the annual Cotton Bowl postseason games (for seven years, in fact), one year I worked with Harry. He did the play-by-play and I was his color announcer. Color announcers didn't really do much then, so it was an enjoyable event. I have a picture with Harry on which he inscribed the message "to my friend."

Later, when I was broadcasting North Texas basketball games, Harry and I visited when he came to Denton with the St. Louis University Bilikens. All was quite jovial and friendly, so I imagined with this background he and I might hit it off. Oh, such wishful thoughts!

I have had moments of great attacks of conscience about the manner in which I left the Rangers. For some reason, I did not talk to Roy Parks and I don't recall why. I went by to see Mayor Tom Vandergriff that afternoon, but he was in meetings and could not be disturbed. I may have talked to Hollis Pollard in response to having told us in September that we were free to make other deals. I did not tell Dick Risenhoover before I signed. Mainly, I feel I let Vandergriff down after he had gone to bat for me for the job initially. And to cap off that lack of respect, Leo Breen saw Vandergriff in Houston and told him he had hired away his announcer before Tom knew.

My manner of leaving was not polite or professional. Roy Parks resented me for the rest of his time with the Rangers and refused to recommend me in later years with other clubs. He once referred to me as a "traitor" when Ron Chapman discussed broadcasting the Rangers games on KVIL in the late 1970s. In the 1980s when there was an opening on the Rangers' broadcasts, Eric Nadel, the current main announcer, called and asked me to come out and talk about the job. I made an appointment and went in to see Parks. He said he appreciated my coming out, but they were looking for a particular type of voice and I wasn't it. He also mentioned that he found that I had actually been offered the broadcast job with Oakland (which he had disputed to someone and it came back to me at the time) and he would now be happy to recommend me. I told him he need not bother; I was no longer looking for baseball jobs.

The salary the Rangers network was paying was not of major league proportions, but I loved the work and had little right to complain because I had agreed to the terms. It was the ultimate job: Major League Baseball.

In January of 1974, the White Sox management invited me and my wife and daughter to visit Chicago. This was tied in to an annual promotional bus trip to various cities for a week with Caray, a couple of Sox players, and management. This year, I was going along to be introduced as the newest announcer. The day we left Chicago, a blizzard blew in. Our travel was not particularly dangerous, but Ilene and Laura had a wild time trying to combat the elements in the Windy City. Not having to live in Chicago in the winter pleased them greatly after that week.

Laura had never been on a train, and we decided to take the Santa Fe back to Dallas. The club provided us a suite in the Pullman car. It was a pleasant change from flying until the train slowed coming into Ardmore, Oklahoma, just before lunch. We were sitting in our room playing cards when the sound of the train on the rails changed to flying rocks under the car. The Pullman car tipped to the left and I yelled, "We are going in," and lunged in between the two women, holding them against the seat. Our car ground to a halt, lying at an angle on its left side. We weren't hurt, just stunned by the accident.

There was a great commotion in the car and outside as people emerged. We climbed up and out and found that three cars, including the dining car, had left the tracks and were on their side. Ambulances, fire trucks, and police roared to the scene. I ran up to a building nearby and called Dick Wheeler at KRLD to give him an on-the-scene scoop of the train wreck in Oklahoma. Several passengers were injured and our porter had sustained burns and other injuries. We were lucky.

I called my old friend and North Texas sports information director Fred Graham seeking his assistance. I was to broadcast the North Texas basketball game in Denton that night and we needed a ride. Fred drove the sixty miles to Ardmore and we departed our train disaster. I guess it was an omen, as the Chicago broadcasting experience became something of a train wreck as well.

Spring training in Sarasota was nicer than Pompano Beach. With an established major league club, the facilities were better, as might be expected. The only person I knew on the Sox was Chuck Tanner, the manager. He and I had been together, or bumping into each other, since the 1960s. Chuck took me around, introducing me to his players, making me feel like one of the team. I didn't wear a tie—so there, Billy Martin! The Sox general manager was Roland Hemond, an energetic, brilliant baseball man who was especially helpful to me then and through the two years in Chicago. I ran into Caray that evening at, of all places, a bar. He said hello, we had few seconds of small talk, and he went on paying attention the rest of the time to other folks.

The two years with the Sox were volatile and pleasant. The first game in April in Chicago, it snowed and the game was cancelled. I mean it was cold. I was bundled up in heavy clothes, an overcoat, and a hat in the first home stand. Nolan Ryan pitched for the Angels in one night game. I screwed up that one royally. I recall Red Barber talking about concentration and not feeling sorry for yourself in his book *The Broadcasters*. How he had made a major mistake because of that. This night in Chicago I was cold and really miserable. The next day, reading about the game in one of the papers, I found that Ryan had been relieved in the eighth inning and I had pitched him through the ninth. I checked with the visiting clubhouse man who said Nolan was listening to the game in the clubhouse and wondered what game the announcer was seeing. Correct, Nolan.

I stayed in the Executive House just off the Loop until my wife, one of my sons, and my daughter came up after school was out in May. The first year, we had an apartment way out in Palos Hills, and the second year a comfortable suite in the Executive House. That first year, I would drive to the ballpark in midafternoon, my family would take the train, and we would drive back after the game. The second year, I usually took the elevated train (the "L") to Comiskey Park from downtown. WMAQ was our radio station, which was a strong union organization. Our local broadcasts always had the engineer on hand to maintain the proper levels—same as Birdsong with the Rangers. I rode the train to the ballpark and our engineer drove me to the Executive House after the game.

Three things happened that were interesting in my broadcast relationship with Caray. One game, Stan Bahnsen, the Sox pitcher who had a reputation as a slow starter, had two outs in the first inning when he kind of fell apart and two runs scored. The next two innings he was okay. Caray came in to do his middle three, and first thing he said on the air was, "What did you say about Bahnsen?" I repeated what I have just written above, and he railed, "You never say anything bad about anybody, do you?" In a broadcast with Harry as his "sidekick," I mentioned the batting stance of the hitter, and he sneered, "Where else do you think he would put his feet?" As the season moved along, and I realized Harry would rather be the sole descriptor of the action, I began staying away during his three innings.

In an old fable about the scorpion riding on the back of the frog to cross the river, finally, in the middle of the river, the scorpion stung the frog to death and drowned himself. As he was dying, the frog asked the scorpion why he killed them: "It's in my nature." Similarly, it was in Caray's nature to find a convenient player on his own team to sting. This was exemplified in the early travails of Jim Kaat in 1974. Kaat was the Minnesota pitcher when David Clyde started his brief career in 1973. Later that year, he was traded from the Twins, where he had pitched for twelve years (winning twenty-five games in 1966), to Chicago. Kaat won four games in his short Sox season in 1973.

Now he was struggling. The big left-hander lost all of his starts, was 0 and 5, and couldn't fool any hitter. Harry was having a field day when Jim pitched: "Get him out of there, he can't pitch!" He lambasted Kaat for being over the hill, having no fastball, being a waste of money to the Sox, and on and on as Jim suffered his early losses.

Then pitching coach Johnny Sain and Kaat devised a new pitching scheme. Kaat took no windup. As soon as the ball came back from the catcher, Jim stepped on the rubber and fired. Some called it a quick pitch, but it gave Kaat renewed confidence and he won ten straight games. I never heard Caray commend Kaat for his turnaround with Sain. Kaat won 21 and lost 13 with a 2.92 ERA in '74.

One of our major sponsors was Old Chicago beer. I can't say it was the best beer in town, but it was our sponsor. One day, the ad agency rep asked me to go with him and Harry to a production meeting for a new commercial. It was just a courtesy to me since Harry was the focus of the advertising.

When we reached the agency headquarters, we were introduced to a young lady who had flown in from California to supervise production of the commercial. After a few minutes of small talk, she began to tell Harry what they wanted in the spot. Harry began a brazen, insulting attack on her asking why the agency had to fly a woman in to do this job. What did she think she could add to the effort? What did she think she possibly could tell Harry on doing the talent? And on and on. I felt like a fool listening to this mephitic attack of this woman. The ad guys were pale as Harry continued his vicious speech. Thankfully, one of them suggested we leave. This was what I found in Harry in many occasions—an egomaniacal guy who evidently was paranoid about anyone around him. I finally decided that underneath all that brusque nature was an insecure person. And yet he was great for Chicago fans in his own personality-driven work. The fans adored him on the south side and later with the Cubs.

Every radio station has some young men and women who intern or are willing to act as "gofers"—running errands, answering phones for talent on the air, and any number of activities with very little pay. There was a young guy who worked with one of the sports reporters on WMAQ and hung around the press box adoring Harry and the whole media scene. Well into the season, WMAQ let it be known that they may not renew their contract with the Sox. For whatever business reason, it caught a great deal of attention. A day or two after this information came to light, the young WMAQ gofer was at the park. Harry grabbed his tape recorder and interviewed the kid for the pre-game broadcast. Harry asked him damning questions about WMAQ, nosing around about whether they were wrong in making this decision, and other questions that even a person in management might take a pass on. But not this kid—he answered the questions to the satisfaction of Harry.

WMAQ fired the gofer and told the Sox that Harry was no longer welcome to broadcast on their station—baseball or anything. Leo Breen called me in and told me what had happened. He then asked if it would be possible for me to handle the games on radio by myself. Rather than leap around the room with joy, I quietly said I had broadcast games by myself for my first fifteen years in the business, and had also re-created games in the studio by myself. I was happy to help. I was happy, period. I hadn't been sitting in with Harry in his three innings anyway.

Ed Herrmann, one of the Sox catchers, sustained an injury about this time of the WMAQ episode, and it was suggested Ed could sit in with me, if I was willing. Ed was a gregarious guy. He also did not talk too much on the broadcasts. And he added some interesting color, such as during our visit to Baltimore. I had visited some friends in Washington who introduced me to Senator Birch Bayh. It was the time of the Nixon Watergate scandal. That night on the broadcast, I mentioned the D.C. visit and how beautiful the city was. Ed chimed in, "Yeah, the lights are burning brightly, and the government is still functioning even with Tricky Dick Nixon as president." I went right on calling balls and strikes and no one ever complained about the statement, as far as I know.

My memorable game of that year was on August 7 in Comiskey Park, an almost no-hitter by Nolan Ryan. Nolan and the L.A. Angels were leading 1 to 0 on the strength of his no-hitter going into the last half of the ninth inning. There was one out with Ryan facing Dick Allen. With no one on base, the infield played back. Dick, in his swan song year, was hitting over .300 and 30 homers. On a 1 and 1 count, Allen swung and topped the ball, sending a slow roller on the infield artificial turf toward third. The third baseman charged in, fielded, and made his throw. Allen beat it by an eyelash. Manager Jimmy Williams complained he was out, but the decision stood. Nolan had lost his no-hitter. The adrenaline seemed to leave Ryan and the Sox went on to win a thriller 2 to 1. I have the audiotape of that game.

Harry made peace with WMAQ before a long road trip to California where he enjoyed many great social events, so he was back with us for the latter part of the season. The management of WMAQ told me they received not one letter complaining about Harry being off the air. Harry announced in the newspapers that the fans had besieged the station with demands for his return. I think both may have stretched the truth.

Your reaction here may be that I am writing about Harry Caray. Working with him pretty much overshadowed many things pleasant around the club. My work was okay. I don't think it was up to my expectations, though. We broadcasters strive for perfection, which is nearly impossible to attain. I was working to fit into a new location while maintaining my style of describing the intimate details of the game. Harry's style was the opposite, reading phone messages from people in Chicago bars, swigging beer and other high-calorie beverages during the game, and ridiculing anyone he felt deserved such treatment. I thought his singing of "Take Me Out to the Ball Game" while waving a bottle of beer was a questionable gesture, but it certainly caught on with the fans. It is a national seventh inning must-have, a guest sing the song. So I was wrong.

The fans of Chicago and Caray fit like a glove. They were very rambunctious folks. It was a wild time with naked streakers, some of them big-busted women prancing around the ball park nearly unclothed, and some fights in Comiskey Park's upper and lower decks that stopped the action on the field. Players would come out of the dugout to watch a brawl running across an area of the stadium like an ocean wave. My third son, Martin, facing his senior year of high school, spent the summer in Chicago and worked at various jobs in the concession area. On bat night, with regulation size bats given to fans, he came back to his concession area to reload his depleted soft drink case and found the attendant lying unconscious on the floor. He had been clobbered by someone with a regulation bat. (By the way, Martin loved that city and still lives and works in the Evanston area.)

The White Sox franchise had been struggling for years. Though there were some fine individual efforts on the Sox in 1974, it was still pretty much a mediocre club finishing 80 and 80, fourth in the division nine games out. There was no depth to make it a contender, but well over a million fans trooped to the south side for Sox baseball that year.

Wilbur Wood and Jim Kaat won twenty and twenty-one games respectively, but after that there was little to show for the other fifteen pitchers—except for Terry Forster, a tenacious reliever who saved twenty-four games. A young pitcher name Rich (Goose) Gossage would step out next year.

The leading hitter on the club was Jorge Orta. George, as he wanted to be called, slammed out a .316 average in 139 games. The young Mexican had joined the club in 1972, had an average year in 1973, and then was tearing up the league in '74. I inquired about interviewing Orta. His friend and interpreter came back to tell me George was studying English and when he could speak well enough, I would be the first one for an interview. Midway into the summer, he stopped me in the clubhouse and said he was ready. He and Wilbur Wood were my best friends on the club.

The famous and ubiquitous Dick Allen clubbed thirty-two home runs while hitting .301. Only eighty-eight runs were produced by Allen's bat. He and I discussed his racehorses, Texas as a horse-raising center, and other pithy subjects. A slower Bill Melton had twenty-one homers, while switch-hitting Ken Henderson stroked twenty and drove in ninety-five.

My family loved Chicago. Friends in Dallas thought it weird that we liked that windblown, gutsy place, but Chicago had a special feel about it, and I was looking forward to many years there. My wife, Ilene, and our young teen daughter, Laura, took trips to all the historical places Chicago had to offer. Every time you turn a corner, some new or old scene of that great old city attracts you. As my time with the Sox moved into the second year, I became more of a recognizable part of the White Sox broadcasting team. Laura tells this episode, if she doesn't laugh so hard she can't finish, about leaving old Comiskey Park one evening. Ilene and Laura had driven over in our lovely second-hand brown Cadillac to pick me up after the game. Ilene moved over to the passenger front seat. I walked up to car with some fans who were asking for my autograph. When I could, I opened the door and stepped into the back seat, but then to my chagrin, I had to come out and step into the driver's side. Laura thought it hilarious.

Her great experience there was when the Texas Rangers came to town. We were still Rangers fans after my two years with them. Her favorite player was the handsome Dave Nelson, who played the infield and stole bases. She had met him when we were in Dallas. We were standing outside the visitors' clubhouse at Comiskey when Dave Nelson strode out, came over, and picked up Laura in a big bear hug and kissed her on the cheek. She didn't wash that spot for days and says she can still smell Nelson's cologne.

But as it turns out, 1975 was a pivotal year—and my last in major league baseball. Following in the footsteps of his television partner Caray, Bob Waller let go with an attack on the White Sox management, players, Tanner, and the coaching staff on the final Sox telecast in 1974. It was his final appearance. He was sacked. Bob went to Oakland later.

Harry Caray had been extolling the great managerial efforts of Billy Martin, who he called the best in the game, especially when Texas was finishing just five games behind the West leader Oakland. The Rangers' Jeff Burroughs led the league in RBIs with thirty-two and Fergie Jenkins won twenty-five games. But most important to Bob Short was the fact that Texas drew over a million for the first time: 1,193,000. Texas outdrew all the teams in the American League except the Yankees, Red Sox, and Detroit. What Harry and everyone else didn't know about was the disintegration of the Billy Martin year.

The Sox were in need of a new color commentator in 1975. Bob Waller had been Harry's color announcer for six innings and then handled the play-by-play on TV when Caray came over to radio. I was in the middle of the North Texas basketball season when I received a call from Leo. He asked me, as a speech/radio teacher, if I thought I could help a person improve his speech, diction, whatever, during spring training. I told him I wasn't sure unless I could meet that person and talk with him. Leo asked if I could come to Chicago, and then I noticed on the schedule that North Texas was playing in Peoria, which was not too far south of the city. So on a wintry day in December, I met J. C. Martin. Martin had been in major league baseball nearly fifteen years, starting with the White Sox in 1959 as a catcher/first baseman (.261 was his best BA in 1965)—he was traded to the New York Mets in 1968 and played on the World Champion Mets in '69. He finished with the Cubs in 1972.

His hometown was Axton, Virginia. At first, I thought he was from West Virginia, as he had such a flat, regional twang in his accent. We had dinner and talked about the possibility of handling television with Caray. We agreed that would be a difficult assignment in the best of circumstances, even if he smoothed out his speech. I interviewed him on our radio broadcast at halftime and thought it was going to be an enormous undertaking to improve this speech, sound, and quality.

I checked in with Breen. I gave him my report, a cautious appraisal having heard Martin on the air and discussing the teaching situation with him. I told Leo I would bring some of my speech books to spring training and would expect him to tell J. C. that this was to be a daily classroom experience. We planned to spend six weeks in Sarasota prior to the season. He said J. C. was all for this reinvention of his speech.

To give you a rural term, Caray had a wall-eyed fit when he heard what was to transpire with Martin. He was red in the face and bellowing like a castrated steer that this was crazy; there were people around who could do this better than Martin, even if he had a decent voice! I told Harry this was management's idea and they asked me to help out. Harry said I should have refused. (I was thinking "yeah, but I might be number one next year.") I told him to go talk to Breen and Hemond. I was going to do the best I could in this project.

As that year progressed, Harry became more virulent about my teaching college students to be broadcasters. He stormed at me that it was better for them to go out and find jobs on small stations and work up. And besides, he said, if you teach too many kids, they will give us more competition. Was it paranoia?

When we were in California playing the Angels, Dick Enberg and I had an early dinner in the press dining room when Caray walked in and yelled, "There they are—two college professors planning on teaching all these kids how to be broadcasters."

Enberg had been a professor before coming into broadcasting. At one point, I told Harry that I understood how he felt, but he had to remember that not everyone was born with the God-given talent he had. Preparing students in college still left them with the prospect of going into small stations for experience. Just a few had the ability to step into a major market or team broadcast.

Well, the Sarasota Spring Training Speech School met every day. I gave J. C. assignments to practice. I showed him how to use his mouth and lips correctly, breathing from his diaphragm, projecting his voice, recording and listening to his exercises, and so on. It was really frustrating for a guy who had never faced such daily terror. But I must say that we made progress and by the time we went to Chicago, I believe he had smoothed out some of that flat Virginia rural sound. It made no difference to Harry, as he refused to acknowledge he was in the booth with J. C.

This also changed my job a bit. I moved over to television for the middle three innings and worked play-by-play with J. C. He really enjoyed having an opportunity to share his baseball expertise with me. We had a very good time and often did some extra things that weren't related to the game. One night, J. C. noted that the night-hawks were flying thick around the Comiskey Park lights chasing bugs, and recalled how he watched them back when he was a kid in Virginia. Later in the season, this anecdote was brought up in a column that one of the writers fired off.

Harry was becoming more and more antagonistic toward the White Sox management and the organization. I had no knowledge of what was transpiring about the final year on his contract. Possibly, they were unwilling to discuss it, with him leaving the impression that there would be difficulties, or he may have already discovered that they were not having him back.

The Minnesota Twins had the best pressroom in the majors, or at least the best bartender. We eagerly looked forward to our visits to old Metropolitan Stadium. On one series, Harry really fell into the spirit of the alcoholic beverages. He particularly liked the martinis that the great drink master made. When he came in to do the three middle innings on radio that day, he had a martini and was slobbering and slurred his speech. He said he wanted to show how cheap the Sox were, comparing their players' salaries to the Twins. He went on and on, rarely paying attention to the action on the field, but he made his point that Minnesota paid more for player's salaries than Chicago.

As the season stumbled on, the tempers of the players and management were fraying. On a pleasant summer afternoon, the Sox had

family day with the players and their children on the field playing a
pregame game of ball. Harry made comments on the air that it was
great to see the guys with their kids. These were a good-looking
bunch of guys, like Bucky Dent, who always had a lot of girls waiting
outside the visiting clubhouse on the road. Of course, when the team
was flying back to Chicago, someone always reminded them to put
their wedding rings back on.

Bucky Dent's wife was named Stormy. The name was appropriate
at the time, as she and the players were ready to revolt or do bodily
harm to someone. Wilbur Wood and I were standing on the field one
evening when Harry came sauntering out of the runway to the field.
Wilbur said, "Bill, you see that son-of-a-bitch. Well, if he should have
a heart attack and fall across the foul line into fair territory, we'll call
you to come down to drag him off the field. None of us would touch
him!"

We had only Jorge Orta hitting well, Kaat pitching well, and the
young Goose Gossage, who saved twenty-six games, won nine, and
had an ERA of 1.84. Dick Allen had retired after the '74 season. The
Sox were struggling all year long, and then came *the* game in Milwaukee.

Yes, it is another Caray story, but an important part of the finish
of the year. The Sox were trailing 2 to 0 in early innings, but had
Deron Johnson at second and Bill Melton at first with no outs. Both
runners were slow, very slow. Bill Sharp, a newcomer to the club,
smacked a single to left, Johnson rumbled around third heading for
the plate, Melton rounded second, and third baseman Don Money
cut off the throw from left field, faked Melton back to second, and
threw to first, putting Sharp in a run down and an out. The Sox failed
to tie the game. Caray was on television with J. C. and heading for
the radio booth in a red-faced rage. He was screaming that Melton
screwed up the play and probably cost the Sox the game. It was the
pinnacle of Caray's outbursts in my short time with him.

When I came in on television, J. C. and I recapped the play, and it
was his opinion that Money made the right play to hold Melton at
second. A play at the plate might not have caught Johnson, but a bad
throw might have gotten Melton to third and Sharp to second. But
hey, Martin was only a fifteen-year major league veteran catcher.

Money was interviewed and also said it was the proper play—Melton would have been thrown out if he tried for third.

Caray milked that dispute for every inch of newspaper coverage he could find. One paper ran a story that Caray told it like it was, and Tanner was covering up for the inept play of Melton and the Sox. So the thing went on and on.

Ken Henderson, who had been hitting .300 for most of the season, injured his hand sliding into home plate and as the season slipped away, so did his average, down to .251. Harry complained about his inability to hit, and then a big story appeared in a Chicago paper headlining Henderson as a white elephant for the team. Orta was the only player hitting .300, and the next best were around the .270s, so there wasn't anyone who could have done a lot better.

On TV that night, J. C. asked me if I had seen the story about Ken. I replied that I had read the story, but had never seen the columnist around the ballpark. Of course, the inference was that it was an unreliable feature based on hearsay. The players thought Harry had been the source of the information. A few days after that, the writer wrote a column with withering comments about the awful work of Mercer and Martin, saying we were clowns, unknowledgeable, talked about unimportant things, and were generally putrid.

The timing was not good. The Sox were going on the road right after a game two nights later. When we were all on board and headed for the airport, an obviously nearly drunk Wilbur Wood yelled some expletives at Harry about helping the newspaper guy attack his partner. When Harry made some reply, Wilbur charged down the aisle of the bus threatening to do unwelcome things to Harry. Players pulled Wilbur away and yelled at Harry, and the situation quieted down for a second. Then Harry made a caustic comment, and Chuck Tanner leaped out of his front seat, grabbed Caray by the throat, and told him that if he said any more bad things about his players on the air or fed crap to the newspapers, he would regret it.

It is great fun to broadcast baseball and other sports, but it is constant, daily work: researching information, interviewing, concentrating, and trying to be 100 percent accurate. I have worked with some of the best announcers in the business, and never before had I gladly reached the end of a season—especially a baseball season.

I had signed a contract for 1975, but Leo Breen warned that John

Allyn was having financial problems—there was a recession and he would probably sell the club. If so, the contract would be nullified. That last week, the Sox announced that Harry was not asked back for 1976.

Reading some of the history of the poor old Sox, before 2005, it's clear they were a team just hanging on for a long time. In the 1970s, there was speculation the team would be bought and moved. When John Allyn, who we were told had lost a sizeable amount of money in the recession, agreed to sell, it was to a group headed by Bill Veeck. Speculation was that Veeck coming back to the Sox was based on the fears of the team leaving the south side, and Chicago business and baseball people did not want that to happen. But some baseball people also were not happy with Veeck in charge of the operation.

All this had to do with me was that my contract was null and void when Veeck took over. Harry Caray was hired back and I was in Texas thinking about my next job. The course of my career had been one major move after another, thanks to the intercession of the right people at the right time. I owed so many so much in providing me all of the great opportunities I had. The only thing I thought I didn't know how to do was find a job in the network of broadcasting and baseball. Then it happened again.

When you are between jobs or wanting to change jobs, sometimes you must choose between two of equal pay but from totally different areas of your profession. I was sitting around feeling sorry for myself when I received a call from my former ace student Gary Brobst. Gary had been working at KVIL in Dallas since he graduated from North Texas and was one of KVIL's top salespersons. He had talked to Ron Chapman, the morning guru of the station, about me being between jobs. Chapman told him that my friend and colleague from KRLD, Wes Wise, the morning sports personality on the station, was thinking about running for mayor of Dallas again. He had been mayor in the 1970s. If he did, then Wes would have to leave the station and there would be an opening. We would know in a few days.

Within days of that conversation with Gary, I received a phone call from Monte Moore, the longtime lead announcer of the Oakland A's. He heard good things about me and wondered if I would come to Oakland as his broadcast partner. I almost shouted that I would be there tomorrow. He told me Charley Finley would call me and we could discuss the particulars.

Charley, who I had met in Dallas back in 1964, called and said it would be great to have me come out. He laughed that it should make Caray upset, my taking a job he once had. I didn't see much humor in that, but grinned along. Charley then said I would be Monte's partner and be paid $25,000. I almost choked. It was that awful number again. I told Charley that I doubted that would be possible since I had four children, three of them in college, and just the moving and living expenses would be impossible. I couldn't imagine trying to live on that amount in California. He said to think it over, as that was all he would pay.

Ron Chapman called me in a day or two to set up an interview as Wes had decided to try for mayor again and couldn't work in broadcasting while running for public office. I had known Ron from his days at KLIF, the originating station for the Dallas Cowboys in the 1960s, and we had a solid discussion about the job. I would offer a couple of minutes of sports every half hour in the morning, working from six to nine a.m., and the rest of the time was free. The pay was, hold your turban, $25,000—and I didn't have to move.

I talked to Dick Butler, who was supervisor of American League umpires and my friend of forty years, about the Oakland situation. Rumors were that Finley was debasing the franchise and preparing to sell it. He was not signing his expensive players, and the whole operation was degraded. Dick warned that once out of baseball, it was almost impossible to come back in. I called Monte and told him the financial problem. He was sympathetic, but assured me he couldn't ask Charley to do anything. He also assured me that he would like to have me on board.

My wife, Ilene, and I wrestled with a perplexing problem: my desire to broadcast baseball while trying to make a family operate on that amount of money. Finally, it was obvious financially that I couldn't make the move. Finley was not as cooperative as the White Sox organization had been—and obviously didn't pay enough! So I turned down the nebulous offer and went to work at KVIL. It was a great station and I had a great seven years there with Ron and that wonderful group of talented performers.

The next year, Monte Moore called me back. He had been fired in the off-season by Finley for going on a charter cruise with the players. Monte said there was never any particular logic to what Charley would do, but I should call him about taking the job. That was on a weekend, so the next week I called Finley and he said Monte was back and that job he offered me was still open—at the same salary. I told him I still hadn't found a way to live on that in Oakland with four children and my wife. Thanks a lot. That was as close as I came to another major league baseball job.

I did have a couple of auditions in the next couple years, but as Dick Butler advised, they hired guys in the majors at the time. One was in Pittsburgh, where Chuck Tanner was managing. Milo Hamilton, the longtime veteran announcer there, had agreed to move to Chicago with, of all people, Harry Caray. I was not hired in Pittsburgh, and if you mention Harry today to Milo, he turns apoplectic! Milo has a book out about his long career: *Making Airwaves: Sixty Years at Milo's Microphone.*

Here I am in the minor leagues again! Twenty years to my last gig in the majors, I was back in baseball with my old and dear friend, more like a son, Mike Capps. I first met Mike and his wonderful family when he was eight years old. Mike's father, Ben Capps, was an undertaker in Fairfield, Texas, southeast of Dallas. When a Braniff Airways plane crashed near there, our KRLD reporters met Mr. Capps at the ghastly scene. From that day on, we visited the Capps ranch for fun and hunting, and the Capps were welcome guests in the KRLD newsroom. Mike came to Dallas to visit his grandparents and was a frequent visitor at Burnett Field, watching baseball and listening to my games on KRLD.

On the day of the Dallas Cowboys' "Ice Bowl" game with Green Bay, Mike's father had a massive heart attack and died. Mike was a teenager and, since then, he and I have corresponded almost daily about our twisted strange broadcast lives. I followed Mike as he attended Sam Houston State University in Huntsville (it's the better of the two institutions in that city), where he studied journalism and broadcast baseball. Mike had been an accomplished participant in every sport in his high school and was once offered a chance to go to a minor league baseball camp. He has superior knowledge about the game.

The common piece of equipment to broadcast college games live at home in the 1960s and 1970s was the reliable old Marti unit—a little FM transmitter with an antenna aimed at the receiver back at the studio. It was reliable for those Sam Houston home games. We used the Marti at North Texas for our remotes when KNTU went on the air in 1968. I met the inventor of that unit, George Marti, a few years ago in Cleburne, Texas, south of Fort Worth, where he always lived and built those famous units.

Mike's postcollege news career carried him through Texas, St. Louis, and Dallas, and with various organizations and the world while he was with ABC and CNN. His work at the Branch Davidian disaster outside Waco was a journalistic masterpiece. He earned many journalistic awards over those more than twenty years. Always on his mind, though, was baseball. He helped scout players with the famed scout Red Murff. Red was the one who found Nolan Ryan. Mike and I would talk about baseball when we visited and said that it would sure be fun if we could ever work together. We did in 1976, and have nearly every year since. Mike left CNN in a state of burnout and called me, asking if I thought he could become a baseball announcer. With his reporting skills and his work with Murff (Mike wrote the book *The Scout: Searching for the Best in Baseball* with old Red), there was no doubt in my mind that he could. All it would take was practice on actual games. Before we ever hit the practice field, Mike had a job with Tyler, Texas, in the independent Texas–Louisiana League.

With a far-flung league to the Texas valley and out to Abilene, that year in Tyler tested the players' and broadcasters' resolve. I would drive to Tyler and sit in with Mike on some of those early broadcasts. The primitive equipment was a microphone amplifier with a telephone coupler, which was supposed to improve the sound. The mixer had portals for two headset mikes and a crowd mike. The minor leagues had turned to broadcasting road games live, and those recreation days were over.

Mike moved on to Nashville in 1997 in a big jump to Triple-A using basically the same type of equipment. All the mixer did was give more amplification to a tinny sound on the telephone line. I didn't work with Mike that year, but in '98 he moved to Sioux Falls, South Dakota, to work for a team owned by Mike Veeck, son of the immortal Bill. I spent six weeks with him in that far-flung northern league.

New technology was available that improved the sound of our broadcasts. Nearly everyone in the minors was broadcasting live. The main feature of the equipment was a tie-line, which is a computer-aided, more sophisticated device for cleaning up a telephone line's thin sound, making it sound more like good radio.

Broadcasting for the Canaries with Mike was a blast. Mike had to leave for several days for family business and I carried the games alone. Can you say, amen? Ah, that was a rejuvenation of my whole being! I was back broadcasting by myself like I had from 1951 through 1963. Most announcers like the solo experience. Mike next slipped off to broadcast the independent Atlantic City franchise. I was wallowing in no-baseball despair. Then the great move!

Capps became the first and only broadcaster of the new Nolan Ryan, Ryan-family, Round Rock Express baseball franchise just north of Austin in Texas. Maybe Mike will write another book about the birth of that organization and the textbook manner in which the Ryans and their personnel have built a baseball institution in Round Rock. Round Rock is the prime example on how a minor league team, actually any baseball organization, should be operated.

I rode with Mike in the Express during inaugural year 2000, broadcasting road games around the historic old Texas League. There's nothing like swinging around the old Double-A to Wichita, Kansas, Midland and San Antonio, Texas, and that wonderful over-seventy-year-old monster park in Little Rock, Arkansas, Ray Winder Field. It was a good trip back in time to the old-fashioned facilities with the benevolent old ex-umpire, that sly curmudgeon of a general manager, Bill Valentine.

Our equipment was that tie-line computer configuration, which was not foolproof. Some nights, particularly in Wichita, we had to use a regular hand-held telephone to do our duty for baseball and the listeners. Technology is great, but failure occasionally causes many blue words and smoke emanating from frustrated broadcasters—but not on air!

Baseball gods have smiled—no, guffawed—around the Round Rock Express. How can you explain a Stephen-King ending to the first season? The Express youngsters won the championship! The championship game brought in more than eleven thousand Express fans and overflowed the Dell Diamond. Round Rock had established the attendance leadership in Double-A that first year, and the attendance has climbed ever since. In 2007, Round Rock entered its third year in the Triple-A Pacific Coast League. Now the club has what every organization broadcasting regularly from leagues, conferences, or districts should have for radio quality. The Pacific Coast League requires ISDN—Integrated Services Digital Network. Essentially, the ISDN system integrates several phone lines and turns the signal into studio-quality sound.

That line costs each club about sixty bucks per month, but it is money well spent. I sit with Mike watching the various contraptions sending out our quality signal, and I'm amazed as he checks the Internet for stats, scores, standings, player bios, and answers e-mail, all while broadcasting! We had nothing, absolutely nothing like that when I started fifty-five years ago.

It is great to know that the players' families spread from California to the East Coast can bring in the Express games on the Internet—and keep us informed when we misstate something! Back when I was broadcasting, the players called home after the game to tell their wives or families how well they'd played.

In 2003, I missed some of the season thanks to a triple bypass on Valentine's Day, but in the 2006 season, not only working weekend home games at Round Rock, I also took a trip to Tacoma/Portland. Astoria, Oregon, a couple hours up the road from Portland, has a renovated landing craft infantry type of boat I served on in World War II. It is probably the last one left after more than sixty years. My LCI (G) 439 didn't carry troops, but nearly four hundred five-inch rockets and three forty-millimeter and four twenty-millimeter cannons. We led the first wave of troops in to safe landings in Leyte, Luzon, Guam, and Okinawa. Although only 153 feet long and 23 feet wide, when those rockets went off with all our "big" guns, old 439 had the firepower of a cruiser for about thirty seconds!

With the expansion to Triple-A for Round Rock, the Ryans built a new stadium in Corpus Christi, Texas, down by the Gulf of Mexico, and they have been successful with their new Double-A Texas League franchise.

Every year, there are rumors in the bowels of baseball that the

Ryans will buy a major league team, but so far their main concern has been the continuing success of these two teams. Mike Capps is more than ready for the major league scene. If the Ryans obtain an MLB team, they have part of their broadcast crew built in with Mike.

Five years ago, the Mandalay Company, with far-flung business interests in Las Vegas and other cities, brought their Shreveport Texas League franchise to Frisco, Texas, just thirty minutes north of downtown Dallas. In a cooperative effort with the Texas Rangers, that franchise has flourished in a beautiful retro-type stadium in Frisco, a little farming community of about five thousand people ten years ago that is now a major suburban entity of more than eighty thousand!

The young broadcaster for the Frisco Rough Riders, Scott Garner, and I became friends through my professional critiquing of his baseball broadcasting. I sat in with him on a few broadcasts his second and third years, and then last season, 2006, we worked in more than thirty-five home games. I had cut back my trips to Round Rock with Mike because of the ghastly travel problems up and down I-35. At my age, I need to stay closer to home or at least not drive on horribly congested highways.

It turned out that Scott sent in a tape recording of one of our 2006 games, and lo and behold, we won a Katie Award from the Dallas Press Club as the best play-by-play of the year out of more than forty entries! That is only the second of two individual awards I have ever received. The first was the Best Actor award at Northeastern State College in 1947. So the two "award winners," Garner and Mercer, are enlarging our partnership to forty-five games this season.

I owe this "life-after-baseball-death" to Mike Capps for bringing me back in his baseball career in 1997. I truly believe that Mike's decision to use me as his sometime partner has made all the difference in my longevity. So to this boy, who is like a son to me, I say, "Thank you, and I will probably be good 'til at least ninety!" I turned eighty-one on February 13, 2007!

# 3

# Body Slams

---

The first professional wrestling match was broadcast on a radio station in Wichita, Kansas, in 1922. That wrestling debut followed KDKA in Pittsburgh, Pennsylvania, the first station to broadcast regularly after it was licensed in November 1920. Before KDKA was licensed, its founder was playing music on a little transmitter in his garage. The Westinghouse Corporation discovered as many as a thousand people were listening daily to his music on their simple crystal receivers. In 1920, Westinghouse signed on KDKA, and the first regular broadcast was the reporting of the presidential election returns. Radio excitement was growing all over the country, and in 1922, several hundred stations had been licensed across the country. All of the stations shared the same and only frequency, 833 kHz. In Wichita, The Lander Corporation put WEAH on the air in March 1921, principally to broadcast market reports. In May of the same year, WAAP was founded by Otto W. Taylor.

WAAP then made local history by broadcasting a church service. Doesn't it follow that this same station would step forward to broadcast the first-ever professional wrestling match? This story appeared in a Wichita paper.

Wichita KS: March 3, 1922 (Forum, att. 4,928, #17,000 . . . (World Title) Ed (Strangler) Lewis beat Stanislaus Zbyszko (2-1) . . . Dick Daviscourt drew Cliff Binckley (30:00) . . . Promoter Tom Law . . . NOTE: Zbyszko, with a body scissors and arm lock, took the first fall in 41:30. . . . Lewis answered with headlocks at 18 minutes and three minutes. . . . Jack Herman, manager of the defeated champion, screams foul. . . . Zbyszko received $7,000 for the bout; Lewis $5,000 . . . THIS WAS SAID TO BE THE FIRST MATCH EVER BROADCAST ON

RADIO. . . . Tickets priced at $10.00 up. . . . The following morning it
is reported, Zbyszko ate scrambled eggs, milk, toast and not much
more for breakfast. That's how sore his jaw was where Lewis popped
him in the heat of battle.


J. Michael Kenyon, the noted broadcast historian, provided the
Wichita clipping. Orin Friesen of the Journal Broadcast Group con-
curs that it was probably WAAP that made the historic "grunt and
groan" broadcast. This was professional wrestling on the cusp of the
cutting edge of radio broadcasting as it was to become when television made its appearance—a point in history. The famous, or infamous, goat gland doctor, John R. Brinkley, bought WAAP and moved
it to another location in Kansas long before he got in trouble with the
medical profession and moved his popular operation to Mexico.

WEAH, on the other hand, was purchased shortly afterward and
licensed by a Wichita hotel. The call letters changed to KFH and it
remains on the air today. Sports events, church services, and live
music programs were tried by the various new stations popping up
around the country after 1920. The WAAP radio sports pioneering of
wrestling was certainly feasible.

By the time I noticed radio in Muskogee, Oklahoma, in 1930, it
was becoming sophisticated. A month before I was born in 1926, the
first Rose Bowl game was broadcast live to a country with few radio
receivers. It was a historic game pitting a Southern team, Alabama,
against the powerful Washington Huskies. Alabama won 20 to 19.
Radio was off and running.

There were networks with programs of all kinds and sports broadcasts. However, it was still difficult to pick up stations unless a family
was blessed with a lot of money to spend on the best radio receiver
around. My family had a little Crosley that demanded a lot of antenna adjusting to hear WLW in Cincinnati, a powerful station. When
there was lightning, rain, or any kind of bad weather, it took even
more patience and adjustment to bring in programs.

Entertainment, after the Depression settled in in the 1930s, demanded some creative work. Movies for children were ten cents.
Some weeks, we couldn't afford that dime for my Saturday cowboy
movie fix. Adults paid a quarter and everyone tried to squeeze into a
movie house when they had Bank Night or Grocery-Give-Away night

to lure the patrons in, hoping for something they couldn't afford to buy every day, like groceries. High school football and an occasional Minor League Baseball game were about the extent of our entertainment.

There were magazines and newspapers, and all were relatively cheap. A paper was a nickel. For free, there were picnics, fishing, and parking downtown to walk around, people watch, or window-shop the department stores. My family was addicted to radio, and that was probably true of more than 90 percent of the people in the country. It was free.

I came home from school to listen to the *Air Adventures of Jimmy Allen*, the *Lone Ranger*, and all those kids' shows where we could get free decoder pins for eating the right cereal. But my main interest was sitting with my father and listening to every sports event broadcast. Late at night, after my folks went to bed, I tuned in to Don Dunphy and the fights from St. Nicholas Arena in New York or Madison Square Garden. Dunphy broadcast more than two thousand fights and was indeed the greatest of boxing announcers. Clem McCarthy, with his gravelly voice, handled many top events, including the second Joe Louis–Max Schmeling fight.

My first foray into broadcasting was the re-creation of Minor League Baseball games in my room in the farmhouse in Muskogee when I was just twelve years old. I discussed that in the baseball chapter, but for some oddball reason, I had it in my young mind that I could broadcast sports. I recall telling my dad that I could do as well as some guys I heard—pretty fresh for an uneducated kid. I was very shy and tried to play sports, but I wasn't that successful, and I wasn't as good a student as I should have been, especially in high school. I guess the start of World War II put all of us guys into a bit of frenzy figuring we were going to fight—and just about everybody did starting in 1941 and continuing through 1945. My time came in 1943.

I learned early on that a person didn't have much say about occupations. I didn't plan on being a signalman in the Navy; they made the decision. I didn't plan on being a teacher; it just evolved. In 1951, I also didn't plan on being a wrestling announcer, but the radio station management at KMUS in Muskogee said it came with the sports broadcasting package of baseball, football, boxing, and basketball. This was my first "big" job as a sportscaster, so why not?

Well, for one thing, I had never attended a live professional wrestling match, and I had only seen one briefly on television while in Chicago during a cross-country college debate trip in 1948. I had never broadcast a real baseball game or boxing match either, but only the wrestling assignment worried me. KMUS broadcast one event a month, so I had to quickly learn on the job.

Jimmy Barry, our general manager, suggested I visit with the local promoters and with some of the wrestlers who arrived early. They would give me Wrestling Holds 101! The promoters were pleasant fellows, local businessmen who dabbled in the promotions for a few bucks. This was fifty-five years ago and their names escape me, but not the wrestlers who went over the basics for me: Danny McShain, Wild Red Berry, and the Fabulous Moolah, the woman wrestler champion. They demonstrated the hammerlock, full and half Nelsons, head locks, and others, plus a few of their own inventions. They used me as a guinea pig, laughingly putting enough pressure on me that I understood the significance of each hold. They didn't tell me any "secrets" of the business and I had no idea about the preplanning of the evening's various matches. I wasn't aware that the winner and loser were preplanned, and I certainly didn't hear the term "Kayfabe" until I was in Dallas.

Kayfabe is a term that evolved out of the carnivals. "Always keep up the illusion, and never allow a moment of candor to reveal it's all an act." In pro wrestling, that includes the victors, the cage matches, the "loser leaves town" (they were signed for another promotion), and the grudges. There are wrestlers who still refuse to reveal the obvious secrets of the business. However, there are guys who didn't like each other, showing some pretty damned messy bouts, and the great ones endured a lot of pain and aggravation (some broken bones, torn cartilage, and gaping wounds) to give the crowds a great show. It is not fair, I believe, to use the word "fake" because I have seen a tremendous amount of reality, both in their athletic ability and lack of concern for personal injury.

Some announcers, news reporters, and maybe a sportscaster might have had the nerve to ask a wrestler if the business was fake, but it could be dangerous to life and limb. In the 1980s, a reporter named John Stossel asked pro wrestler David "Dr. D." Schultz in a studio interview if the business was fake. Dr. D. hurled Stossel across the studio with some degree of physical damage. The wrestler asked him if that felt fake. Stossel later sued and won.

Somewhat earlier than that, in the early 1970s, my friend of nearly fifty years, Mike Capps, was a young TV reporter in Beaumont, Texas, and assigned to an interview with a black wrestler named Tiger Conway, Jr. They were to discuss the wrestling card at the local auditorium for that evening, and after listening to Tiger talk on and on (as some wrestlers do if you don't control them) Mike asked what his duties were as a referee. Tiger responded that he looked for foreign objects (hidden in the trunks of the grapplers) and Mike, new to the business, responded, "I think the whole thing is foreign rather than real." Tiger grabbed Capps's belt, slung him up on his shoulder, and gave him the old airplane spin before dumping Mike on the floor. "How foreign is that?" demanded Conway. Capps replied, "Thanks so much for the physical display, Tiger."

Mike still enjoyed wrestling and would bring the Dallas WFAA, Channel 8 sports/news guys to the Sportatorium in the 1980s. He also is friends with Killer Karl Kox now, but he never asks the question about whether or not wresting is fake.

This moves way ahead, but when Chris Adams banged Kevin von Erich on the head with a metal chair at the Dallas Cotton Bowl in World Class Championship Wrestling (WCCW) in the 1980s, a rivulet of blood poured down the side of the ring by my broadcast location. These effects, in some bouts and with some individual wrestlers, caused fans to attack them with chains, fists, and knives. They attacked personalities like Rita Romero and Buddy (Nature Boy) Rogers, who suffered stab wounds in Texas.

So I approached the new experience, the wrestling bout, like any other sports broadcast—which wasn't too difficult since my experience was so far limited to football and basketball. I recall writing down the names and descriptions of the various holds in a notebook. I began by describing the antics of very talented athletes and actors. It all went okay, I suppose, since I stayed in that job the rest of my tenure in Muskogee—three years learning the ropes of sportscasting, reporting, and disc jockeying.

I mention the notebook that I used for reference until I became familiar with the various wrestling features because identification of the athletes in all sports is absolutely necessary. In my first Golden Gloves boxing event, I was not paying close attention to the details, and when a bout started, realized I was not at all sure which boxer had been in the blue corner and which was in the red. Thus, at the end of the first round, I identified the wrong boxer with the bloody nose. That sort of mistake can happen when you are careless in this business. Red Barber talks about a ball player he mistakenly identified as playing an entire major league game in his book *The Broadcasters*. It can happen easily.

There may have been a wrestling match broadcast in 1922, but we know for sure that there were many radio stations broadcasting the business in the 1930s. The broadcast historian Kenyon identified several stations and announcers broadcasting wrestling: WHBQ in Memphis in 1931 with Bob Alburty announcing; WCBM in Baltimore in 1932 with Lee Davis at the mike; and WHK radio in Cleveland.

It will surprise Texas wrestling fans that Paul Boesch in 1938 was broadcasting a weekly wrestling show over KXA in Seattle, Washington. The Seattle promoter George Adams broadcast his bouts on KOL in 1929. My colleagues in Texas, who ribbed me about associating with wrestling, should know that Pacific Coast League baseball announcer Ken Stuart was the announcer for KOL. In 1950, just up the road from Muskogee at Joplin, Missouri, an old stomping ground of Mickey Mantle, there was a weekly wrestling card on WMBH-FM. A prominent bout featured Angelo Savoldi, Sonny Myers, Dutch Schultz, Billy Raeburn, Angelo Martinelli, and Jimmy Lott. All were major national stars at the time.

Keep in mind that great wrestling stars wrestled in small towns, medium-size cities like Muskogee, and metropolitan areas. There was money to be made in those out-of-the-way places. Broadcasting wrestling on radio requires the same careful skills of description as any other sport. In a Wichita seminar titled, "Radio Recollections: Reflecting on the Pioneers of Kansas Radio Broadcasting," produced by Bill Shafer in Wichita and Tony Duesing of that first radio station in Wichita, KFH, they commented that "in the early days of radio they had studios with live programming, creating a theatrical kind of event, doing theater of the mind. And that's still a lot of the challenge in radio—to paint a picture for the listener's mind."

I enjoy radio description of any sport more than television. You can build the excitement and drama, as in wrestling for example, without including some of the obvious imperfections of the matches. You have seen them, guys missing a blow and the opponent falls flat in a moment of bad choreography. That was especially true of the less experienced wrestlers. Don Dunphy always broadcast exciting bouts from St. Nicks Arena or Madison Square Garden in New York. Not every bout was a stem-winder, but Dunphy's brilliant description made them exciting.

As a broadcast journalist, I always approached wrestling the same as any other sport. I have talked with former announcers who said they made fun of the contests and ridiculed the guys. I am not sure how long they broadcast in that manner, but I could imagine it would not have gone over well with the promoters. There were those announcers who became strange personalities in their own right, screaming, carrying on what had to be planned verbal attacks on wrestlers in interviews. I found many wrestlers to be talented actors who were also very tough athletes succeeding by demonstrating true, tough competition in the ring.

In Muskogee, our broadcast was very simple, with a small Western Electric amplifier and one microphone connected to KMUS radio by telephone lines. I sat at a table ringside and we could do an interview only if the wrestler came to the table. My friend and studio engineer, Ed Dumit, who also ran the board when I re-created baseball games, introduced me: "And now from the Muskogee City Auditorium, KMUS presents professional wrestling with your announcer, Garbo Plodnik." I corrected him early on, but after that we just carried it on. I am not sure where he came up with that name, but I have never forgotten it and have sometimes used it in humorous situations outside of wrestling.

As a once-a-month promotion, there was never any real continuity from one broadcast to the next. None of the personal conflicts carried over to the next month's bouts because it was usually a different group of wrestlers.

A highlight of my Muskogee wrestling days was with the former world heavyweight champion Joe Louis. Louis was a tremendously popular champion in the 1930s. Because he was black, he was reviled by a great many during a time when segregation was the norm. Louis solidified his fan base with his second fight and quick victory over the German Max Schmeling. Louis was a beauty in the ring—moving, sticking, jabbing, and hitting with power. He joined the army in World War II and entertained troops with boxing matches. After the war, his talent faded, and the government took most of his money for back taxes. Joe's fate was left to the generosity of people who had him appear in clubs and events and as a wrestling referee. When he came to Muskogee, I asked if he would come to the KMUS studios for an interview. It was a night we were not broadcasting. He was a quiet, humble man. Following the interview introduction, I played a recording of his second fight with Schmeling from the Ed Murrow recording of *I Can Hear It Now* with the voice of Clem McCarthy describing the fight: "A right to the body, a left up to the jaw, and Schmeling is down. The fight is over!" Joe sat quietly listening, with no expression. I imagined he relived that fight often.

Joe talked about training for that fight. Because of all the Nazi propaganda in Germany, he had added more desire to defeat Schmeling in addition to making up for the loss in the first fight. I had listened to that fight broadcast live in 1938, and here had this great fighter sitting across from me in that little studio. It was the most memorable moment in my young career.

At that time, the new medium, television, had barely made it to Muskogee. Few people had one of the six-inch, black-and-white screen TV sets. I was too busy with radio to pay attention to it even though wrestling and boxing were ideal for this new medium. Most of the country could still not see it in 1951, even though television programming came on shortly after World War II ended. Some even came on before the war ended. And wrestling played a big role.

Some of you who grew up with television in the late 1940s and 1950s will remember the sparkling personality of Dennis James, who celebrated some twenty-five "firsts" on the squared screen. James was a young radio actor/announcer in 1938 when his brother, who was working with the originator of the Dumont Television system, asked him to do some programs on the experimental television station. James emceed a sports show where he brought on guests—he wrestled with wrestlers and fenced with fencers. There were three hundred television sets in New York, so it was not a huge audience.

The Museum of Television and Radio in New York supplied programming notes of other television programs in that early experimental era. In 1939, NBC had local programs that included movies, interview programs, live drama, and every sport imaginable, including pro wrestling. The museum, at 25 West 52nd street in the Paley Building, is a great viewing experience as well as a research instrument for work like this.

After World War II, in 1946, Dennis James came back to New York and, while playing in a TV dramatic program, was asked by the Dumont Network to announce professional wrestling. James claims to be the first announcer for wrestling on network TV. I feel vindicated here! Like me, Dennis had never seen a wrestling match. He asked a sports friend to help him on the basics of the business, and during a bout he thumbed through a book on wrestling holds and described the action. James geared his remarks to his mother, "Mother, that is a hammerlock" and the style became so popular, the network started what may have been the first audience participation show, *Okay Mother!* around 1947.

A spin-off of that network wrestling program may have been the emergence in every wrestling venue of an older woman sticking wrestlers with hatpins, canes, or whatever was handy. Dennis James recounted a woman in the Jamaica Arena in New York who was always on camera (those fans knew exactly where to be seen on TV) and would run up and stick a hatpin in the derriere of a hated wrestler. Watching this over many shows, James suggested a contest to give the woman a nickname and "Hat Pin Mary" won. In Dallas, there was an elderly woman who stuck her cane into the bad guys in every bout at the Sportatorium.

Announcers knew better than to irritate wrestlers who were several times larger, stronger, and prone to violence. James recounted how he used spontaneous poetry in his description of wrestlers and bouts. One line he used was, "look at the suet on Hewitt" describing the overly large belly of Tarzan Hewitt. James said Hewitt, who was an undercard nobody, became a star performer through the TV show. But one day, when James went into the dressing room, Hewitt grabbed him in a hammerlock and made him promise not to use the term "suet" or "fat" again.

Two weeks later in 1948, Milton Berle asked James to bring a wrestler on the show for Berle to playfully wrestle. James took Hewitt, who made $1,500 for the event, but Dennis forget and introduced him with the same line, "look at suet on Hewitt," whereupon the grappler leaped out of the ring and put James on the floor. James claimed Hewitt never gave the announcer credit for making him a star. James stopped announcing wrestling in 1951 and continued his career as an emcee of network programs and became a premier commercial announcer.

One of the first wrestlers to appear on the Dumont Television Network with James, Sandor Kovacs, died in 2004. He was a famed international wrestler and promoter as well as an ardent supporter of ballet and drama in British Columbia, his home. Wrestlers have come in all types and sizes.

J. Michael Kenyon, the historian, says the first regular commercial telecast of a wrestling match that he knew about occurred in Los Angeles on KTLA with announcer Dick ("Whoa Nellie"—his trademark term) Lane in March 1945 before the end of World War II. In an interview written for the Associated Press in 1976, Lane described covering wrestling in 1945 in the TV studios "because promoters were afraid TV cameras would cause empty stadium seats. Even though at that time there were very few television sets owned by the public. But after seven months [in the studio] they changed their minds."

According to Kenyon, famed talent Steve Allen was a wrestling announcer in 1950 on KECA-TV in Los Angeles. The critics wrote that Allen was "too clever, too polished, and that his subtlety [was] too intellectual for that type of program." He then went on to grander things.

By the time I "entered the ring" in Muskogee in 1951, wrestling was a regular on the Dumont and ABC networks. One of the big-name wrestling announcers on the short-lived Dumont Network, Jack Brickhouse, went on to a wonderful broadcasting career with the Chicago Cubs. Brickhouse worked the old Marigold Garden in Chicago every week for about six years.

Radio history buffs will recall the great Ted Husing. Husing started Dumont's longest running television boxing program in 1952 and handed the job to young Chris Schenkel a year later. After Dumont went under in 1954, Schenkel joined ABC, where he branched into other sports.

KRLD-Radio went on the air in 1926 and was purchased less than a year later by the *Dallas Times Herald*. KRLD was a latecomer to the area following WRR in 1921, and three others in 1922. WBAP claims to be the first radio station in Fort Worth, coming on the air in May 1922. It was owned by the famous Amon Carter, publisher of the Fort Worth *Star-Telegram*. However, history records that the *Fort Worth Record* on March 16, 1922, put WPA on the air (long before President Roosevelt's WPA program). WFAA followed the parade in June of 1922. WBAP's call letters stood for "Bringing a Program." WRR was "Where Radio Radiates," and KRLD was "Radio Laboratories of Dallas." KRLD had three other frequencies before becoming 1080, which it still is today.

KRLD broadcast wrestling on Tuesdays from 10:15 to 11:15 p.m. in 1941. It had been active with the Sportatorium since its inception in 1936. KRLD was an early affiliate of the CBS network, which supplied much, if not all, of its programming at night, thus the late time slot for wrestling.

When I joined KRLD-Radio and TV (Channel 4) in 1953, I did not realize that it was actually a very young television station. It was established in December 1949. Channel 4 telecast wrestling on Tuesday nights from eight to ten because programming from CBS was not yet fed live to the entire country. Before 1952, programming in New York was kinescoped and sent by plane, train, or mail to affiliates across the country. Those old TV network shows of the 1940s and 1950s were black and white and a little blurry because they were photographed with a movie camera off a television monitor. In the case of East Coast news programs, they were filmed, placed on a plane where they were processed during the journey across the country, and then aired many hours later on the West Coast.

In 1952, AT&T began to electronically link the East and West Coasts. Some coaxial cable transmitting live programming had been in place to some areas of the Midwest since 1949, but it wasn't until the late 1950s that the entire country was connected. So on Tuesday nights before the network cable, wrestling was telecast live in Dallas while programs like Red Skelton, Red Buttons, and Suspense were being seen live in other parts of the country.

As the coaxial cable snaked closer to Dallas, the future of telecasting live wrestling at the Sportatorium was doomed. Live network programs would preempt it, and wrestling would be moved to the studios of KRLD. The first videotape recorder, an invention in 1951 by the Ampex Company, would revolutionize the industry and make such studio programs possible; in 1956, Ampex sold its first videotape recorder to a television station for $50,000. When KRLD-TV brought in its first videotape recorder in the early 1960s, wrestling moved to a ring in the largest KRLD studio.

Wrestling in its many forms is not a modern phenomenon. Wrestling was a major event in the first-ever Olympics, and the winners received more than medals. We are reminded by picture and myth that Abe Lincoln wrestled in his youth. What might have passed for professional wrestling in the nineteenth century featured large athletes in the circus, carnivals, and traveling groups appearing in small towns challenging local toughs who thought they could whip anyone in the world.

Robert Friedrich, born in 1891, started wrestling when he was fourteen and is credited with turning this traveling show into a legitimate, fan-supported business in the mid 1900s. Compared to the behemoths of today, Friedrich was small at 5' 10", but he carried a solid two-hundred-plus pounds. You will find Friedrich in wrestling history under his ring name, Ed "Strangler" Lewis, probably the greatest wrestler in the history of the business—the same one from the bout in Wichita on radio in 1922. According to Steve Slagle in a Hall of Fame piece for *The Ring Chronicle*, Lewis won "no less than five undisputed World Heavyweight Championships between 1920 and 1931, holding the title five of the eleven years, making him the World Champion with the most World titles for 30 years, until Lou Thesz broke his record."

The actual legitimate matches or "shoots" in the mid 1920s were mostly two-out-of-three falls. Today there are no bouts in that category. Lewis was involved in probably the longest match in wrestling history: it lasted five and a half hours. This certainly wouldn't fit in a television program schedule today. There were no costumes or masks in those days. In fact, The Strangler was opposed to what he called "slam-bang" wrestling matches. Lewis was known for his submission holds and his dangerous "hooks," which could be crippling. Lewis retired in 1947. He trained and managed the future champion Lou Thesz. Lewis died in 1966 at the age of seventy-six.

If you check the Internet today, you will find reams of names of professional and amateur women wrestlers. As best can be determined, the first overall women's champion was Cora Livingstone back in the 1930s, succeeded by Mildred Burke in 1936 and June Byers of Houston in 1954, who was beaten by Lillian Ellison, better known as "The Fabulous Moolah," in 1957. Moolah held the title for the next twenty-seven years. Windi Richter became world champ in 1984, eliminating The Fabulous Moolah, who then became Harley Race's valet and ran her own wrestling school.

There were guys wrestling for regional championships all over the country. Texas had its wide variety of impressive belts and titles: National Wrestling Alliance World Tag Team, Texas Heavyweight Champion, Texas Brass Knuckles, and Texas Tag Team Title. Going back to the 1930s, Martino Angelo is listed as the first Texas heavyweight champ, followed by Leo Savage, Chief Little Beaver in the late '30s, Lou Thesz in 1944, and handsome Buddy Rogers in 1945. My first wrestling favorites, Danny McShain and Wild Red Berry, were champs in 1948 and 1949, respectively.

But I am pushing ahead of my progress in broadcasting pro wrestling. I have to admit that wrestling was not my major priority in Muskogee. My lifelong dream was football and baseball broadcasting. I worked an eight-hour board shift—I guess you could call it deejaying—and produced a daily kid's show called *Uncle Merky's Story Time*. This was my training ground for sports broadcasting—eight hours on the air and a nightly baseball game, weekly football game, or monthly wrestling show, plus an occasional Northeastern State College or local Bacone College football game.

So how did I make it to Dallas in 1953? With wrestling! Who would have guessed? When I was inducted into the Texas Radio Hall of Fame, the thrust of my grateful acceptance speech was the credit I needed to give to those who helped me through my career. I can't think of any opportunity I have had that wasn't brought to me by my reputation or through a referral.

So here is the way Dallas happened. Hugh Neeld worked at KMUS as a broadcaster for about a year. We were close friends. We didn't make much money. Minimum wage was $1 an hour. Hugh was more interested in sales and management and left KMUS for a small radio station in Seymour, Texas, where he was general manager. On a trip to Dallas in late September 1953, Hugh stopped by KRLD to visit with a friend who introduced him to Wilson Shelley, the chief announcer of KRLD. Mr. Shelley said he needed a sports announcer who could broadcast wrestling, and Hugh replied that he knew the "best" sportscaster in the country.

The next week, I received a phone call from Shelley asking if I would be interested in auditioning for a staff position and announcing wrestling at KRLD AM, FM, and Channel 4 Television. A day or two later, I rode the MKT Katy passenger train to Dallas. I took a cab for the first time since the war and walked into this huge studio complex of KRLD across the street from the equally awesome *Dallas Times Herald* building. I brought my little resume of my broadcasting background plus a tape of my sports events, including wrestling, commercial and public service copy, a newscast, and several interviews. Hopefully, my three years reading live commercials, newscasts, and sportscasts and broadcasting the myriad sports had improved my ability. I had a chance to move up from one-thousand-watt KMUS to fifty-thousand-watt KRLD.

A few days after I returned from Dallas, Wilson called and offered me the job that paid a starting salary of $75 per five-day week, with annual guaranteed raises. Plus, working on off days meant I would get overtime, something missing in the smaller market of Muskogee's radio. I had already talked it over with my wife, Ilene (she was pregnant at the time and we had one son), and said I would be honored to join them. There was one major problem. I had no clue about being a performer on television. I was very confident by then about my radio work, but I had only one tiny experience with television. A business friend who ran commercials on KMUS in Muskogee and Tulsa had arranged an audition for me at a Tulsa television station where he had talked up my talent.

I went over to the station in Tulsa, was handed the copy, practiced for awhile, and then delivered it in studio with the floor man holding cue cards containing the copy under the camera, the same way they would do them in Dallas. The director and other folks complimented my work and said they would call me. They called few days later and suggested I come over and do it again for the general manager or some such station mogul. As we went into the studio, I asked for the cue cards and they told me they didn't have them; I should just ad lib the commercial from memory. I protested that I hadn't memorized the spot, but I gave it a try. Obviously, I was not hired. That was the only television I had been exposed to. I was to find that TV was a mountain to climb in Dallas.

In their schools and meetings, the Quakers have a settling in time. We had sort of the same at KRLD. It was sixty days of settling in, learning the system, and practicing television spots in studio when possible. For the major part of our time, we split our eight-hour shifts broadcasting commercials and announcements in the television and radio booths. If we made progress, we were hired permanently after that break-in period. I spent Tuesday nights at the Sportatorium observing the process of telecasting a live wrestling program from eight to ten p.m. Charley Boland had been the television announcer, but was preparing to leave for another broadcast position in Texas. Charley was an experienced announcer and performer. He had been at it for a year or so and one incident in which he became involved was legend by then. Because of the location of the cameras, those huge turret studio types, it was necessary to have interviews originate in the ring. There were no hand-held cameras back then. Charley had become part of the wrestling scene, which means he praised some wrestlers, questioned others, and berated the bad guys. This particular incident involved a heated exchange between Charley and a heel, as a bad guy wrestler is called. What the fans and TV audience didn't know was that it had been arranged in advance for the wrestler to deck Charley. Charley, of course, knew it was coming, took the "pulled blow," and fell to the mat. Well, all hell broke loose. The referee tried to revive him, seconds (who assisted the wrestlers) came in to help out, and the wrestlers had one big brawl while Charley was lying on the mat, faking unconsciousness and injury. Finally, it was all sorted out. Charley "recovered" and went back to his microphone, but Clyde Rembert, president of KRLD, did a flameout. He threatened to pull the program and fire everybody, and he had Charley on the carpet. Even when it was explained that it was all a part of the show, Mr. Rembert said, in his Texas-Southern drawl: "It will never happen again. No announcer of mine is going to be hit for real or otherwise." He passed this on to Ed McLemore, the Sportatorium promoter. It never happened again. And when I came along, with my five-foot, seven-and-a-half-inch frame, no 275-pound behemoth was going to stomp around on me! Even if the station said they could.

Although I had three years of experience describing wrestling on radio, TV was proving to be a move in which I was not comfortable. I had trouble relaxing and talking to the camera. My lack of experience on television was one factor, but I also knew nothing about the Dallas wrestlers or the various competitive situations that continued week after week. While there were a few hundred people at the events in Muskogee, in Dallas I performed before a jam-packed Sportatorium of forty-five hundred avid fans. There were three cameras and a floor man, with me in the area above the floor where I observed the action. Directly across and to the right from the announcer's location was a camera that you looked at and spoke to on breaks. There was a strict format of timing matches, commercial breaks, and interviews in those two hours, so timing was important. But much more important was the ability of the announcer to connect with the matches and the viewing audience. I had yet to reach that level.

After the sixty-day break-in period, I was assigned to read the news headlines at a break in the daily television schedule. The reading was no problem, but working the camera was. I was as stiff as a corpse, I didn't use much facial movement, and I was not convincing. My announcer friend, the late Jerry Houghton, took me aside and said I needed to relax and talk to the camera—that was the "person" I needed to talk to. Don't think about the people watching, he said, just tell the camera the news. In addition to Jerry's advice, my aunt and family I was staying with in Waxahachie, thirty miles south of Dallas, told me the same. "You look scared!" I was. When I was ready to come to Dallas. my wife's doctor advised her not to travel because of her pregnancy. Ilene had an Rh-negative blood type and I was positive, so it could pose a serious problem. It hadn't been an issue with the birth of our first son, David, but this warning forced me to come down alone to Texas. To this day, I can't see why she didn't ride down on the train, which would have been easy—except that we might have had to deal with the Rh thing. On the other hand, there were some outstanding doctors in Dallas who could have handled the problem.

I stayed with my aunt and uncle, Madrienne and Clarence Feaster, in Waxahachie. My aunt was slowly dying of cancer, which put more pressure on the situation. Before World War II, my aunt had suggested that I come down to Texas, stay in their big home, and go to college at Trinity University in Waxahachie where my cousin, Clarienne, had graduated. It would have been a great arrangement. But Trinity University moved to San Antonio during the war. My aunt didn't tell me until after I came home, afraid I would be depressed out there in the Pacific during those battles. That was a wonderful family. Madrienne was as dear to me as my mother.

Some days you just feel tired when going to work; so it was when I came in to work well into my short tenure at Channel 4. I took the news copy into the studio, relaxed, and calmly looked up at the camera as I was cued; I smiled slightly and delivered my first decent newscast. I guess if you don't have one of those breakthrough days, you go into some other business. It happened to a young fellow, Terry May, who had come to work from a radio station in Texas and wanted to be a TV announcer. He was everything a person needed for television. He was tall, handsome, had a solid voice, and great desire to be a television personality. After his sixty-day initiation, he was given his first opportunity to broadcast a commercial live in studio during the six o'clock news block. Terry practiced that commercial until he knew it cold. He was sitting at a nice desk and was cued by newsman Eddie Barker. Terry said about five or six words and fell face down on the desk, passed out. A startled news team went back to their business and Terry left the studio mortified. Wilson Shelley and the experienced announcers assured Terry he would be okay, that he just hyperventilated.

Next week, he was back and ready for a second chance. In order to allow him to breathe easier, they put a tiny microphone on his jacket and he stood to "do the spot." Barker again introduced Terry and as he started to speak, he blacked out and fell face down on the concrete floor. Everyone was gasping except the audio engineer, who went over and took the mike off Terry to see if it was broken. Terry woke with a bad bump on his forehead, picked up his coat, and walked out of the station never to be seen again! He did go back into radio, successfully, but never ventured into television again.

The National Wrestling Alliance (NWA) controlled the national business while I was breaking in at Channel 4. The NWA came into being around 1949, and according to "NWA Official Wrestling," in March 1952, the alliance accomplished the seemingly impossible: "a close association of promoters, impresarios, bookers, et al, who now pull together for the betterment of wrestling instead of operating in a catch-as-catch-can fashion to the satisfaction of none." It was kind of unionized management to control the flow of wrestlers around the country. The NWA claimed thirty-six active members in five hundred wrestling clubs in the U.S. and Canada.

When someone mentioned the NWA back then, they almost reverently spoke of Sam Muschnick, who was president. The greatest accomplishment of Muschnick and his "board" was the recognition of one and only one world champion in the heavyweight class; that was Lou Thesz. My old professor from Muskogee wrestling, Danny McShain, also became the world junior heavyweight champion. The NWA article, "They Make Wrestling Tick," listed several of the key promotions around the country, including Tulsa, Oklahoma, and Houston, Texas. No Dallas promotion was listed. Of Tulsa, they hailed Leroy McGuirk and Sam Avey. McGuirk had been a great wrestler and champion, but he lost his sight in an automobile accident and turned to promotion. Under the Houston headline, the NWA said of Texas, "the largest and most solid wrestling territory in the country, Morris Sigel [Houston] head of this vast enterprise." The article went on to report that the wrestlers "get the highest pay but earn it both inside and outside the ring. They cover thousands of miles weekly and a six hundred mile jump is just average." This is probably why so many had auto accidents.

Famed wrestler, announcer, and promoter Paul Boesch joined Sigel and took over the Houston promotion after Sigel's death in the 1960s. Lou Thesz united the championship in 1948 after winning the title in Indianapolis. He actually won it the first time in 1939. Then in 1949, Thesz was awarded the new NWA world title in St. Louis when Orville Brown couldn't appear due to one of those many auto accidents that befell wrestlers. Thesz took another step for unification by knocking off the colorful "Gorgeous George" Wagner, then world champion in Boston, in 1950 and finished it in '52, taking a regional "world" title in Los Angeles from Baron Michele Leone. Other champions in the 1940s, '50s, and '60s included Bronco Nagurski, Bill Longson, Bobby Managoff, Pat O'Connor, Killer Kowalski, Gene Kiniski, and Dory Funk, Jr.

After the consolidation of the NWA, champion Lou Thesz appeared in as many as fifty title bouts a year in various promotions around the country, including Dallas. Other high-profile wrestlers also traveled the circuits, adding to the glamour and excitement of local promotions. Local promotions had special matches to determine a winner who would then wrestle the world champion. The world champion of the NWA, whoever it may have been, could also wrestle for regional or state championships without putting his world title on the line. Texas has a long, storied history of great name wrestlers and champions. One of the earliest Texas heavyweight champions was Martino Angelo in the 1930s as well as Chief Little Beaver in 1938. Thesz won the Texas crown in 1944, twice.

The list is too long to relate all of them, but I will give you some highlights of events that happened while I was working the Sportatorium 1953 to 1958. The live wrestling telecasts ended when CBS could transmit their programs live to the station by coaxial cable. The true definition of a coaxial cable, as per Wikipedia, is "a high-frequency transmission cable in which a solid or stranded central conductor is surrounded by an insulating medium, which in turn is surrounded by a solid or braided outside conductor in the form of a cylindrical shell and used to send television impulses." When the cable and network programming arrived live during the week at KRLD, wrestling moved into the studios. The ring was set up in one of the two large TV studios and folding chairs were placed around the ring. The program was videotaped around nine to ten in the morning once a week. Announcements inviting the fans to a free studio wrestling taping were made at the Sportatorium, still happening on Tuesdays. This was a rather strange but interesting weekly group of die-hard, esoteric folks who never missed wrestling wherever it may be. That they lived and bled for the business was evident by one female fan who gripped her hands to her elbows so fiercely that blood ran down her arms during the matches.

The matches lasted an hour. We had fewer wrestlers, but even in that setting, at that time of day, they gave it their absolute best. The individual competitiveness of the business brought out all the usual bumps and bruises. One morning, I walked to the back of the station where the wrestlers dressed in a little upstairs room off the back indoor parking area and suddenly was confronted by a body lying on the concrete and another on the stairs. The guys had turned the place into a backroom brawl. They were still duking it out upstairs. After all that, they still came out and performed.

Professional broadcasters and newspaper types always kidded me about the wrestling gig. "How can you do that stuff? It is so fake," and all the other verbal abuses they could conjure up. I always plotted to show them up, but never had the opportunity—at least until Frank Boggs came to work at the *Times Herald* sports department. Frank is a brilliant writer and a humorous individual, always finding some different slant in a story. He and I covered some of the same events and became friends. We also had sons about the same age who were starting to find out about baseball and football competition. We also have a great love of baseball. Frank gave me a hard time about wrestling. So one day I invited him to bring his cowriter Bob Gault, a loose-jointed, fun guy, over to watch studio wrestling. It was just across the street from the newspaper. So here they were one morning, in front-row seats I had saved for them. They were enjoying the drama and then it was time for the interview segment, which was conducted on the floor right in front of them. Fritz von Erich was my usual adversary, and after we had used up about three-quarters of the time, I suggested to Fritz that "there are some folks who think you may be well past your prime. Newspaper guys like Frank Boggs observed that you may be slowing down, over the hill." Fritz raged in his loud voice that he was far from over the hill and he would destroy anyone who suggested such a thing. Frank and Bob kind of slunk back in their metal chairs, figuring my next jab would be to point them out. But I let it go there.

The bouts continued and the two newspapermen scurried out of the studio. After the bouts, I told Fritz why I had brought Frank's name up and suggested we go across the street and visit them. So here we were, huge Fritz and I, crashing into the sports department, Fritz calling out he wanted to find Frank Boggs and throw him out the window. Fritz was laughing while yelling this, and the newsroom was in pandemonium. We located Frank and Gault and had a great time. Fritz did not throw Frank out the window. I talked to Frank recently and he is still laughing about the episode nearly fifty years later. Frank left the *Times Herald* in 1965 and later became the sports editor of the *Daily Oklahoman* in Oklahoma City. He is the type of friend that you cherish. When I was in Muskogee in 2004 with a hometown book signing of *When the News Went Live: Dallas 1963*, written by four of us who covered the Kennedy assassination era, Frank and his wife Luann drove from Edmond, about a hundred miles, to buy a book and have it signed. That is friendship.

But before the wrestlers, there was the Sportatorium. It wasn't a pretty building, just tin siding with a dump of a parking lot around it. That was the second building. From what we see in the only picture available, the original looked rather classy, and it did have a history. Percy Pringle, a sometime wrestler and manager, wrote a piece about Sportatorium history for the wrestling program more than sixteen years ago. He hit all the key historical moments with the help of venerable Bill Hines, who was in charge of the building for nearly forty years. The original building was constructed by Bill Cox's fence company for Burt Willoughby, the entrepreneur and promoter, in time for the celebration of the one hundredth anniversary of Texas independence: the 1936 Texas Centennial in Dallas.

Its first location was at the corner of Cadiz and Industrial streets on the southwest corner of downtown Dallas. The original Sportatorium was an eight-sided edifice with a flat roof. It was an attractive looking building, especially compared to its less-than-attractive replacement. Holding forty-five hundred folks on its wooden benches in an octagon configuration, it provided excellent views for any event—wrestling, boxing, and later the Big D. Jamboree, the Saturday night country-western show. Willoughby hired a young entrepreneur-type, Ed McLemore, as his concession director for all the wrestling and boxing events. Ed McLemore owned the entire business by 1940. McLemore was a sharp promoter and marketer. Wrestling boomed under his control and the country-western live program, Big D. Jamboree, became a headline event at the Sportatorium. But McLemore and the fledgling NWA had a falling out in 1952, and a competing wrestling promotion was established in Oak Cliff just across the Trinity River from Dallas. The ensuing competition resulted in various violent attacks at both venues until finally on May Day, 1953, someone torched the Sportatorium.

Rumors have persisted through the years that the competing promoter was backed by Sigel in Houston. No one was ever accused of arson or arrested for setting the fire. I have been assured that the wrestlers of the time knew the individual who set the fire. I have heard his name, but since there was no official indictment, it seems prudent to avoid mentioning him. After it was rebuilt, there were no more incidents. The Dallas promotion rejoined the NWA.

If the fire was intended to drive McLemore out of business, that failed. McLemore moved the operation to a livestock arena at Fair Park, where the famed State Fair of Texas is held annually, while rebuilding the Sportatorium. It opened in just four months on September 22, 1953, a grand event covered by KRLD-TV with every celebrity in Dallas attending. Evidently, few noticed that the walls were corrugated steel and there was no air-conditioning, only large fans to bring in the hot Texas air when the upper sides of the building were opened in the summer. There were several large electric heating units, but it could be cold enough to wear a topcoat and gloves in the winter.

Jack Pyland, noted for Jack's Fries at the State Fair of Texas and the dirt track Devil's Bowl Raceway, controlled the concession area for twenty-five years. Jack dished out those great greasy hamburgers and French fries, raising the cholesterol level to unbelievable heights for all who partook. A fan told me recently that those burgers were what he missed most. After his death, Pyland's son assumed the concession business.

The split dressing rooms, for the "heals" and the "baby faces" (bad guys/good guys) were on the north side of the building, but all the wrestlers essentially dressed and showered together in a very cramped space. I often wondered why there was a split dressing room, but it was probably for talent that came in for other shows. The booker or "director of operations" office was east of the dressing rooms below the ticket area. The offices of the promoter and his assistant plus a wired-in viewing area for the wives and friends of the wrestlers were upstairs to isolate and protect them from the crowds. It wouldn't do to see the good and bad guys' wives and girlfriends sitting together.

The television announcer was located on the northeast corner of the building in a raised balcony-type area with a catwalk leading directly across to the television camera location. The other camera was on the south side of the building. By the time World Class Championship Wrestling came along in 1980, the television crews refused to use the restrooms, which were, well, unpleasant. So the crews journeyed back to the station. No one ate there, either, although the fans loved the fatty hamburgers and fries. The crew ordered in meals from some reputable restaurant.

The building had never been upgraded or improved in any way. It had just gotten downright seedy, smelly, and disgusting. It was demolished in 2003. I can't say I was sorry to see it go. However, when it was in its prime, it was *the* place in Dallas. Pictures of the crowd in the 1950s dressed in suits and dresses included all of the top people in town—the mayor, police chief, everyone came to the matches. When I arrived in the fall of 1953, everyone spoke glowingly of the Sportatorium. I thought of it as the Madison Square Garden of Dallas.

The internationally famous old building also was a music venue, equally famous among country-western music folks as it was for wrestling fans. The Big D. Jamboree originated in the late 1940s and roared on until the early 1960s.

Some still dispute the fact that KRLD-Radio was the first to broadcast a live music show from there, but the music show was on live every Saturday night from eight to ten p.m. The first broadcast was October, 1948, emceed by the immensely popular DJ Johnny Hicks. In the early 1950s, CBS picked up some of the programs for its *Saturday Night Country Style*. Legends of music appeared there: Hank Williams, Ray Price, Lefty Frizzell, and even young Elvis Presley. Willie Nelson performed there often and, in later years, produced a show each year in the old Sportatorium just to relive old times. Naturally, he filled the building to the rafters.

John Hicks, a coproducer the Big D. Jamboree, once said he and Ed McLemore never got along, so that may have been one of the reasons Hicks left for California and was replaced by another KRLD announcer Johnny Harper.

Such was the sixty-year history of that corner of Cadiz and Industrial just southwest of downtown Dallas.

The Texas heavyweight champion in 1953, my rookie season, was Ray Gunkel, who had a fabulous history in the Atlanta promotions. Ray, born Frederick Herman Gunkel in 1910 in Altoga, Texas, did not win another individual championship in Texas, but did win the Texas Tag Team Championship several times through 1959. Gunkel was articulate and an accomplished wrestler. Gunkel won that championship the first time in 1951 in Dallas, then in '52 in Houston and in '53 in Austin.

After Gunkel's win in Dallas in 1951, there was not another Texas champion crowned in Dallas until Johnny Valentine in 1958. But wrestlers who were famous in Dallas won the belt in other cities, mostly in Houston, and carried it back to the Sportatorium: Duke Keomuka; Cyclone Ayala; Wild Bull Curry; The Sheik; Pepper Gomez, who was an immensely popular figure in the ring; the handsome Buddy Rogers; Danny McShain, who seemed to go on forever; Nick Kozak, of the famed Kozak brothers; Mark Lewin; Fritz von Erich; the former pro football great Ernie Ladd, whose main defense seemed to be sticking his foot into some opponent's face; the former University of Oklahoma football and professional standout, Wahoo McDaniel, who wore an Indian headdress into the ring and was tougher than most; Jose Lothario; Red Bastien; Al Madril; and many others won, until 1978 when Fritz von Erich's sons came on the scene.

The first von Erich son to win the Texas crown was David in '78 in Dallas and he reclaimed it many times over the next five years before his death. The other champions who made World Class Championship Wrestling famous in the 1980s included Bruiser Brody; Gino Hernandez; Mark Lewin; Killer Tim Brooks from Waxahachie, Texas; Gorgeous Jimmy Garvin; and Brian Adias. After World Class Championship Wrestling withdrew from the NWA in 1986, Kevin von Erich won the Texas title in '88, then Kerry von Erich won it four times, the last one in 1990. Kevin won his last Texas title in 1990. But WCCW was no longer the enterprise it had been, and it faded away.

Fritz von Erich (Jack Adkisson) was born and raised in Jewett, Texas, but attended high school in Dallas to have a better opportunity in athletics. An uncle, Rosie Adkisson was a coach at old Dallas High School and Jack became an athlete of legendary proportions, earned a scholarship at Southern Methodist University, and played briefly with the Dallas Texans of the new American Football League. Injury finished his football career, but he evolved easily into professional wrestling, where he devised his nom de guerre, von Erich. Fritz was a family name and Erich was his mother's maiden name. Put that together with his physique, a face that would frighten a charging bull, and the postwar hatred of anything German, and this slab of a man became one of the most despised heels in the business.

Before coming back to Dallas to wrestle for McLemore, von Erich's extreme personality filled arenas around the country; he held the attendance record in Detroit for years. It was in Detroit that the first devastating tragedy occurred for the young Adkisson family. Their oldest son, Jack, Jr., not quite seven, was accidentally electrocuted. The younger Kevin was then followed by David, Kerry, Mike, and Chris. The family was alive and well again. Holder of the NWA American heavyweight title thirteen times, Fritz was feared in the ring because of his "heavy hands" and his famous "Iron Claw." When Fritz attached his huge hand, the Iron Claw, on an opponent's head or abdomen, it literally squeezed out any desire a wrestler might have to continue the bout. Fritz relished physically demolishing his opponents.

And along came Johnny Valentine. Valentine and von Erich were both born in 1929, almost identical physically, except Valentine could be described as handsome. Ironically, they died just a couple years apart. Valentine quickly became a huge star in the 1950s and 1960s, when he and von Erich had some notorious battles: exhausting matches of blood, broken bones, and frenzied fans. I asked Johnny a couple of years before his death in 2002 about the intense physical effort he and Fritz exhibited in their matches. "I don't want some guy just slapping me; I would rather let it go in the ring. That's what Fritz and I did. I enjoyed being hit hard and then I would hit him harder."

Johnny Valentine's fabulous career ended in 1975 when he, the then relatively unknown Ric Flair, and three others were injured in a private plane crash. Compensating for the increased weight in his plane, the pilot reduced his fuel load and ran out of gas just before reaching the airport in Wilmington, North Carolina. The pilot was killed and Valentine's back broken. He later could only walk with the aid of arm crutches and never wrestled again. Flair and Valentine had changed seats before the flight, Johnny moving to the front right seat,

Flair to the rear. Flair's epochal career might never have happened without that fateful exchange of seats.

With no health insurance available to wrestlers, Valentine paid all his hospital and rehabilitation costs and became nearly destitute, living in a small house in Fort Worth, Texas. But he stayed active, appearing at events while training his protégé and son, Greg, who became "The Hammer" and has pursued a successful career for nearly thirty years.

One of my favorites in the early Sportatorium era was Duke Keomuka. Fans still talk about when the Duke was arrested by the Dallas police after a roaring bout with Fritz von Erich. While Fritz was the "hated" German World-War-II type, the Duke was noted as the dreaded Japanese enemy. But the truth is Duke was born of a Japanese American family in California and was interned during World War II with the other members of his race. After the war, Duke enlisted into pro wrestling and utilized his expertise in the Asian martial arts. Because of his Japanese ancestry, it wasn't difficult for Keomuka to enrage the fans in the fifties. Duke was a gentleman out of the ring, one of my favorite individuals at the Sportatorium and in studio wrestling.

Once, in Channel 4 studio wrestling, Fritz and the Duke were to battle in a revenge match, but prior to the conflict each was to have a couple of minutes to express their hatred of the other. Fritz went first and as always delivered a sinister tirade. Then it was Duke's turn, but Fritz kept interrupting until I (without prior planning) turned to Fritz and yelled at him, "Shut up, Fritz! Just shut up, you have had your turn!" I think inside he was laughing, but he did stop interrupting, giving me the sinister von Erich glare. My hysterical mother called me after viewing the televised event, warning me not to tell Fritz to shut up, that he and those other dangerous people could really hurt me.

After his career in the Texas area, Duke became a promoter in Florida. Hisao Tanaka, a huge star as a heel but a gentleman out of the ring, died of heart failure in 1991.

There were some wrestling characters I was never completely comfortable with around the ring, even though I knew what was planned. Brute Bernard was one, the other Wild Bull Curry, he of the enormous eyebrows. The guy would do anything to anyone, and it is legend that they created the Brass Knucks (or knuckles) title just for Wild Bull.

The Bull, whose real name was Fred Koury, grew up in a tough immigrant area in Hartford, Connecticut. Fighting came naturally to Fred, who joined a circus as a teenager and offered to fight all comers. After his circus days, he earned his nickname while he was a Hartford policeman. Legend is that one day, a bull broke loose from a stock-yard and rampaged down the main street. Fred Koury stopped it by leaping on it and wrestling it down. The newspaper proclaimed that Wild Bull tamed a runaway steer. He got his first wrestling break in Detroit, Michigan, from promoter Alan Weissmuller who happened to be Johnny "Tarzan" Weissmuller's uncle. Wild Bull Curry lived up to his name in the ring with a chaotic style that left his fellow wrestlers unsure what injury he might inflict on them. The Bull's reputation created a great fan base. He blasted through Texas wrestling for twenty years, winning a variety of championships, much to the dismay of the wrestling fans, who filled arenas to watch and hate his fury.

*Wrestling from the Sportatorium* was a great draw locally and on television in the 1950s. Texas wrestling film was seen all over the country and was popular in many states. So, as KRLD-Radio began the transition from dying network programming to local productions, it was decided that wrestling on radio might work. KRLD's nighttime fifty-thousand-watt signal was heard in far-away places as well as over Texas. A simulcast (radio/TV together) was never considered, thank goodness. Even though it happens today, I have never liked the simulcasts. Radio usually suffers since it isn't necessary to describe all the details on TV. And fans don't like a radio style while watching television; there's too much talking. Except today, these "analysts" talk all of the time without giving the play-by-play guy much chance. Rarely do we know what is happening during a game, as the analyst and announcer evidently like to hear themselves talk, whether it is about the unfolding game or not.

When KRLD started the idea of separate radio and television broadcasts of the wrestling program, the original announcer of wrestling on KRLD-TV, Ves Box, was called back to handle the television while I would describe the play-by-play on radio located next to the ring apron. This system worked well and we received mail from as far away as Saskatchewan, Canada.

Then Bull Curry came to town. We were broadcasting our split radio and TV—Ves upstairs, and I was at ringside with my engineer handling the audio levels on the large remote unit. Curry had one of his raging battles and was disqualified. He was furious—slamming, gesturing, and yelling about the ring. Then he jumped over the ropes and marched up and down on the apron of the ring. When he came to the side where I was broadcasting, he yelled and screamed and then when he saw me talking and looking at him, he kicked at me and struck me under the eye. I was momentarily stunned, and my first thought was, "Did I say an off-color word?" Then I noticed that my engineer, who was handling the remote radio gear, had jumped up and run up the aisle to safety. The crowd went berserk and Curry had to be escorted from the arena by security. Unlike Charley Boland, who cooperated in taking the fall in the ring, this was spontaneous on Curry's part. I filed a complaint through our union at KRLD, claiming that I should be compensated for the injury I sustained in the dangerous assignment. At the same time, I proudly showed the slight bruise under my eye.

Gary Hart's nickname was "Playboy," but I gave him my own: Simon Legree. He never said he didn't like mine. I thought he looked the part of the sinister character in those early nineteenth-century books. You know, smarmy, mustached, with slick hair and a devious smirk on his face while he lurked around the ring helping his wrestler while doing dirty tricks to the opponent. Our association went way back to his wrestling days at the Sportatorium. The funniest interview we ever performed was an interview that never aired, unfortunately. I will tell you about that one after this one.

One session of a Hart–Wahoo McDaniel interview centered on a strap match between the two. That is a match in which each man has this long leather strap about two inches wide that the wrestler can hammer on the bare back or legs of his opponent. This interview was being taped in our KRLD-TV studio to edit into the next program. Hart went first and described how he was smarter and craftier than McDaniel, and just as we were concluding the session, in storms Wahoo with a strap and proceeds to pelt the devil out of Gary. I am sure there were some welts raised on his back. When I asked Wahoo after the interview why he slammed Gary so hard, he replied: "I don't like the son-of-a-bitch." There were no cameras rolling, so I guess he was sincere.

Gary and I always tried to show up each other. I asked difficult questions, and he insulted me or ridiculed the choice of interrogation. Off the set, Gary and I worked on the idea that I was a journalist and Gary the combatant, and it made for an unusual interview if one could outsmart the other. So that is what we did with all the wrestlers he managed. He had some doozies. The one I did not trust was "The Brute" Bernard. I mean, he put Bull Curry in the shade as a strange person. Gary told me that The Brute one time used a knife to extract his own abscessed bad tooth. I believe it. Then there was the Great Kabuki, whose real name was Akihisa Mera, a very gentlemanly Japanese man away from the ring. He was feared in the ring for the "dangerous" green mist he spit on opponents. The mist was allegedly a disabling factor, but I never had the contents explained to me. One time, Kabuki accidentally sprayed me and my favorite tweed sport coat. Kabuki apologized every time I saw him after that. The jacket still has green stains.

Gary's wrestling career was severely curtailed following a near-fatal plane crash in Tampa Bay. He and several other wrestlers were flying in a private plane when the pilot got lost in the fog and flew the plane into the bay. Hart was thrown through the top of the craft into the bay with a severely broken leg and other injuries. Hart dove back in and rescued a couple of the men, but he had to float to the shore some distance away. He was more fortunate than Johnny Valentine. He was able to continue in the profession as the manager.

Gary and I remain friends today, having worked together in other wrestling venues after the WCCW collapse. He, Mickey Grant, and I even tried but failed to keep the Sportatorium programs going a couple of years before it was demolished. But now, on to my all-time favorite interview.

Gary was to wrestle Fritz von Erich in a match that sundered the fans trying to determine which of the two bad guys they hated more. When Gary came up to the booth at the Sportatorium to tape the interview that would be inserted in the program, I told him I was genuinely concerned about the possibility of his being injured by Fritz in the match. He naturally took umbrage to this tack.

"So you think I am not good enough to go in the ring and wrestle von Erich," he snarled. I told him he was good enough, but not in the physical condition needed to face Fritz. Hart's retort, "You think you are smart because you teach at that college and are a professor and all that." And I replied I was not trying to indicate I was smarter than he, that I was just concerned for his health, and his life.

"Yeah, well I have been to school, too," Hart growled in my face.

I said, "Oh, you've been to school. When did you matriculate?"

His answer, after a pregnant pause, "Oh, two or three times a week."

I tried to keep a straight face and so did Gary, but the crew was falling down laughing and finally we both broke up, ruining the taping. Gary said, "What the fuck is matriculating?"

I didn't know Killer Karl Kox's real name, Herb Gerwig, until I began writing this book, even though I have been closely acquainted with Karl for about forty years. When I was announcing, I didn't want to know the real names of the guys, fearing I would forget and use them while describing their bouts. One fellow changed his name after being away from Dallas quite awhile, and I would mix up his names all the time.

Killer was a massive fellow with facial expressions that could incite a crowd to fury in just moments. Killer would walk into the arena glowering at people, the place in turmoil. When he reached the ring, he would face me, point his finger, and yell my name and other things I couldn't hear because of the screaming fans. I am five years older than Karl, who was born in Baltimore and didn't finish high school because he knocked down a teacher umpiring a baseball game after the teacher had hit him. Karl spent nearly four years in the Marine Corps. His experiences when the Marines retreated from the Chosin Reservoir in Korea are private, horrible secrets he won't reveal. During an interview Mickey Grant was taping for a documentary, Karl did briefly mention the experience of stacking frozen American bodies on a Jeep before he teared up and stopped the story. After the Marines, Karl played semipro baseball and football and worked in construction. He was a well-conditioned athlete. He and a friend worked out in a gym with some wrestlers, and one night while attending a pro wrestling match, one of the wrestlers didn't show for a bout. His friend urged Karl to volunteer for the bout. The old guy wrestler (as they described his opponent) proceeded to wipe up the mat with him.

The old guy was Ruffy Silverstein, the wrestling coach at the University of Illinois. Karl realized there was more to this wrestling than just being an in-shape athlete. That match convinced him to study and practice the art of pro wrestling—then he jumped into it.

Karl struggled in his early days of pro wrestling. The name Herb Gerwig wasn't drawing much reaction from fans. But when Joe Dusek in Omaha put him on a card and gave him the name Killer Karl Kox, it made all the difference. Karl had "KKK" emblazoned on his trunks and jacket. That was enough. These names and labels caused some fans, after several beers, to believe they should show this wrestling dude that real Americans could beat some sense into Karl. A couple of idiots tried that one night at the Sportatorium after a bout, and Karl dispensed them quickly, leaving them bloody and unconscious. He was tough. He still is tough!

Don Drysdale and I were broadcasting a Texas Rangers–Orioles game in Baltimore when a wide-eyed young attendant slipped into our booth to tell me there was a big tough guy named Killer Karl Kox wanting to see me. Karl brought his father to the game and came by to visit. Karl was tough in the ring but had a great sense of humor and has always been a dear friend. There is that old cliché "this is the guy you would want in a foxhole with you"—and boy, is it true with Karl.

Another wrestler I admired was Dick "The Destroyer" Beyer, a former college football player from Buffalo, New York, who began his wrestling career in 1954. He later put on the Destroyer mask and became famous with it. He was merely introduced as The Destroyer, and he became that title. After several bouts in this area, he liked the way I described the business and gave me one of his masks. I still have it. Dick was a huge international star, particularly in Japan, and retired in 1993 in a tag team match with his son Kurt. Dick had earned a master's degree in education and returned to coach high school football, wrestling, and swimming.

During the years I was broadcasting major league football and baseball, I would occasionally meet some of my wrestling friends in airports around the country. It always impressed the pro athletes when I introduced them to Baron von Raschke, Dusty Rhodes, or whoever it may have been. I must digress briefly with the Baron. Raschke assumed a "Nazi style" accent, shouting in the ring and ringside interviews. He also goose-stepped around the ring to annoy the fans. One day in Dallas, I had one of those interviews in the studio for editing into the next program. It was with the Baron, and I brought my young teenage son, Evan, down to watch. We met the Baron in the hall and he told Evan (in his normal Midwestern speech) he had been the state high school wrestling champion in Nebraska and played football for the Huskers. Evan posed the question, "Did you study acting in college?" Baron laughed and said no, but he had a degree in biology.

When I returned to Dallas in 1976 after my stint broadcasting the Chicago White Sox with the famous and irrepressible Harry Caray, I took the morning sportscaster job at KVIL, the top FM station in Dallas. Also working there was a high velocity young man named Mickey Grant. Mickey was Ron Chapman's right-hand man in the morning drive time. I also was hired by Fritz von Erich to handle Saturday night wrestling on Channel 11 in Fort Worth.

I had returned to teaching and public relations work at the University of North Texas, and broadcast football and basketball for UNT and later for the Southwest Conference, as well. Chapman told me one day that I was on every station in Dallas! This was a slight exaggeration, but it was a heady time for me, who had forsaken Dallas for Chicago.

While at North Texas, I had been examining the new chip video cameras that were replacing film for recording our athletic events. They were becoming smaller and lighter and provided amazing picture quality. Mickey and I would sit around in our brief spare time planning how the wrestling program, which was still using the same old studio cameras, could be improved with this new technology. As for Mickey, he went into film producing, tried Hollywood, and returned to Dallas in 1979. Mickey and I planned a production company with the latest television equipment to produce a new type of wrestling program. We took the idea to Fritz von Erich, suggesting he join us in the enterprise, an independent television venture. He turned us down.

Fortunately, a short time later, Mickey was hired as program manager by Channel 39, a local TV station owned by televangelist Pat Robertson. All that discussion about producing a better wrestling program came to fruition; when Channel 39 was desperately looking for a new program, Mickey pitched *World Class Championship Wrestling*.

Fritz von Erich wasn't too keen about this new wrestling program, concerned what it would do to his Fort Worth Channel 11 program. But once he had met Pat Robertson, he decided it was a great idea and has been given credit for it in many of his biographies. Fritz agreed to allow Channel 39 to begin videotaping Friday night wrestling at the Sportatorium. *World Class Championship Wrestling* was born!

My Saturday night wrestling on Channel 11 in Fort Worth was tremendously popular, but I quickly decided to go with Channel 39 for the new style program *and* more money.

Fritz was not known as a generous person. Mark Lowrance, who had been the Fort Worth ring announcer, a talented young man, took over Channel 11's program and was successful. He is now a Methodist minister.

With two cameramen on the apron on opposite sides of the ring holding the newest video chip color cameras for "never-before" tight close-ups of the action, two other stationary color cameras for wide and medium shots, and a bevy of microphones, this new production took a few weeks before it roared to the top in ratings and exploded all over the world in syndication.

Mickey Grant had set up Continental Productions through Channel 39 and was the general manager in charge of the wrestling program. There were several producers and directors throughout the life of the program: Earl Goodrich, Keith Mitchell, Gil Gilliam, and Dan Bynum. Through their creative guidance, the show set the new standards for televising wrestling programs, but there are three cameramen who made the program: Will Tyler, Vic Sosa, and Oz Coleman. These young men carried Sony chip video cameras on their shoulders working the entrance of the wrestlers and moving up and down the apron of the ring (on either side) to present the close-up of muscles, pain, and blood. When the action went to the floor of the arena, they leaped down to keep the action tight and hot, and most of the time they stayed out of the range of the other three cameras.

Interestingly, when they were approached about the plan to take the cameras to the ring, something that wasn't thought of before, the three cameramen were hesitant. Would the crowd throw beer bottles at them? Would the wrestlers intentionally knock them down? Were their very lives and well-being in danger? They learned quickly that wrestlers are disciplined, for the most part, appreciated what the camera guys were presenting, and would do no intentional harm. As for the fans, their beer came in cups! They sometimes threw their drinks in the face of wrestlers and then were escorted from the arena. The three cameramen became heroes to the crowds at the Sportatorium. On a miserably hot summer night in the Sportatorium with no air conditioning and little breeze, Oz, Vic, and Will would sweat down five pounds racing around that arena to make the show perfect. It also helped that the cast of wrestling characters happened to be the perfect fit: the von Erichs (David, Kevin, Kerry, and later Mike); Gentleman Chris Adams from England; Bruiser Brody; and the bad guys— Gorgeous Jimmy Garvin with his startlingly attractive girl sidekick Sunshine (later his real wife, Precious, filled this role); Gino Hernandez; the Freebirds; and a score of others. Bringing this cast together was an accident of timing. No casting director could have done better in a Hollywood movie!

The von Erichs were the all-American boys, adored by young teenage girls, smothered with kisses and hugs as they struggled to the ring. David had the charisma and the leadership of the group. Here was youth, beauty, and amazing athletic ability in the ring. Fritz told us when the program started that he wanted to emphasize the athletic part more than the various scenarios of heels and baby faces, disputed matches, and referee mistakes, but all that would also play a part.

Another production technique that had not been tried before was recorded features about the wrestlers away from the ring. We went on location every week to give the program a more personal look at the wrestlers. Here are just a couple of examples. Before Sunshine, the girl with the amazingly expressive face (her nickname was "Face") left the promotion and Jimmy Garvin's wife took over the role of ringside manager, it was sort of understood that Jimmy and Sunshine were an item. So with our camera crew, I went out to Jimmy's condo one day to interview him about Sunshine.

When the front door opened, there was Precious in a skimpy lacey "teddy." None of the fans knew she was Jimmy' real wife. It was a sensational little vignette for the program.

My favorite piece was with David von Erich at the ranch near Lake Dallas, north of Dallas. The focus was on the great life of the rancher, who also was a wrestler. David and I mounted horses and rode out into the sunset talking about ranch life and, in the final editing, there was Willie Nelson singing "Mamas, Don't Let Your Babies Grow Up To Be Cowboys." Beautiful.

Another feature we did with Kamala turned out to our advantage again thanks to my size and clumsiness. "The Ugandan Giant," who actually hailed from Birmingham, Alabama, was supposed to be roaming around the "bush country" and I was out to track him and his manager for an on-location interview. When I caught up with them in the bush (on the banks of the Trinity River), we had a spirited discussion with his manager, and when I went up to Kamala, he made a move at me and I reacted by falling on my back in the bushes, accidentally. The poor man looked like he would die thinking he had injured me. He hadn't even touched me; it was just my clumsiness. We had a lot of fan feedback on that one.

One of the most complicated feature productions we accomplished centered on the aqua philosophy of one Bugsy McGraw. Bugsy was not one of the great stars who came into and out of *World Class*, but he had a shtick that was funny and off the wall. In interviews, Bugsy kept spouting off about the value of water as our basis of being, or some such philosophy. To prove his point, one night in an earlier production, he wrapped a garden hose around me and tied me up rather tightly. The idea was that I should respect the water that flowed through the hose. The promotion suggested he refrain from tying up the announcer again.

In one concocted feature, Bugsy was scheduled to make a speech at one of the new water slides in the Dallas midcities area about the essence of water as the source of life. He mentioned this during the taping of *World Class* and wanted me there to record it. I put on my summer-weight sport coat, pants, shirt, and tie and proceeded to this three-story contraption that circled around and around and finally deposited the sliders in the pool at the bottom. Bugsy was sitting in the pool at the top of the slide and went into his spiel for me and the camera.

I was sitting on the edge of the pool when he suddenly grabbed me, pushing me into the pool and down the slide. I was the first, if not the only, person ever to go down that slide fully clothed. This was not planned, and the production crew then realized the story was only partially completed. Would I mind going down two or three more times so they could place the cameras in the various locations to shoot me sliding by? We did three more slides, Bugsy and I, and on the last one, I jumped on him in the pool at the bottom and tried to drown him—or so it looked. It was a riot. Funny thing, Fritz couldn't believe we would feature an "under-card" wrestler in a special feature.

Those "under-card" wrestlers who opened the programs couldn't hold the television audience's attention; the ratings would dip while they went through paces. To hold the audience, *World Class* would do a clever feature on someone like Bugsy, a journeyman but a pleasant one, around the time of the opening bout. We would talk that up at the start of the program, and it held the viewers. Another key with Fritz—if it didn't highlight his boys or himself, it didn't make sense . . . to him. This was part of the underlying problem in the Dallas promotion. All the wrestlers were to make the von Erichs look good. It was their show.

Fritz, however, was greatly admired in small Texas communities for a charitable part of his wrestling promotion. The late Ed Watt, a dour business type and long-time member of the Sportatorium scene, arranged what were called "Spot Shows" with four to six wrestlers presenting a card in some small community like Gainesville, Texas, where a charitable organization was the sponsor and received a substantial percentage of the gate. To the wrestling organization's credit, a lot of charities arranged these Spot Shows yearly to aid in their philanthropic endeavors. Looking at old tapes of the *World Class Championship* productions, I am impressed with the basic intent to entertain the fans with the most realistic athletic outcomes that can be expected in a Kayfabe business. The decisions were determined in advance. Wrestlers knew when it was time to conclude a match, but there was no exploitation of the women, Precious and Sunshine, in a sexual way. Nor did the producers overtly display blood; if anything, we avoided it. We did not allow the abusive, insulting language or grotesque relationships that occur today on television networks. If egregious violence affects children, then content in wrestling programs today must have a negative impact on children and teens.

"Wrestling, at its best, is sports soap opera. Yet, the mat as most of us knew it in its most entertaining days always preserved the sanctity of good conquering evil." This was an apt description of why the business flourished by Steve Beverly, a professor of communication arts at Union University in Jackson, Tennessee, and noted television columnist and critic. Beverly expanded on this theme: "Even if a villain won, eventually a fan favorite would bring him down to earth. A distinct line was drawn between good and evil. You could take your son to a card and while the violent side was always there, you knew he had specific heroes whom he revered." Beverly is disturbed by wrestling's format today:

> Wrestling is vulgar, profane, celebratory of the antihero and exploitative of [women] children and teens. Vince McMahon was desperate for ratings in the late 1990s and turned his product into one of coarse language, gratuitous sex, unrepentant violence and a glorification of insolence and alcohol. Yet, look who his commercial advertising targets: children and teens. The character of Stone Cold Steve Austin not only thumbs his nose at authority, the role was groomed to make the audience celebrate and honor his arrogance. Wrestling's evolution has gone far over the edge of making bad behavior become preferred behavior. Much as in today's television reality shows, wrestling now taps into the worst of our emotions and behavior, rather than reflects and glorifies the best in us. Wrestling is the total antithesis today of anything I would want my children or grandchildren to watch.

Steve Beverly is a television and academic veteran. Beverly spent eleven of his twenty years in television in the management of a newsroom. He won fifteen Associated Press and United Press International awards, is a professor of broadcasting at Union University, and has been an active monitor, writer, and researcher of television programming. Beverly is the author of *Professional Wrestling as Television Programming Form: 1944–1988*. He is also webmaster of TVgameshows.net.

*World Class Championship Wrestling* quickly became popular all over the world. I was the fourth most popular TV personality in Israel, preceded by the von Erichs: Kevin, David, and Kerry. When the program came on in Israel, whole towns like Nazareth shut down their business to watch it. Iseed Khoury, originally from Nazareth, who attended North Texas State University (now the University of North Texas) and was an outstanding soccer player and kicker on the football team, called me one day to describe the scene in his old hometown. His mother and brothers still lived there and could not believe that Iseed had played football with Kevin von Erich and knew David. And to their further surprise, Iseed said I was a good friend of his. To prove Iseed knew me, we called Nazareth and talked to his family. They told me the house would have twenty people stuffed in watching *World Class* when it came on the telly.

The promoter in Lebanon who handled the *World Class* program in that country came by the Sportatorium and seriously told us that when *World Class* was on, the shooting in the civil war stopped. When I walked across the North Texas campus, Middle Eastern male students would run over to shake my hand, having seen the program back home. My daughter complained that wherever we went, we had to put up with wrestling fans seeking my autograph. That happened in a lounge in Las Vegas and on a football field in Florida as well. It was a sensation for about four years. And then it died.

David von Erich had an important engagement in Japan, and even though he was suffering with the flu and looking pale and drawn, he flew off to fulfill the commitment. The official report was that David died alone in his room in Tokyo on February 2, 1984, from an acute inflammation of the intestine. The rumors still persist today in some quarters that he died from an overdose. I never knew of a drug problem with David. There were eight thousand people at his funeral in Denton, Texas, thirty-five miles north of Dallas. Fritz had embraced the born-again Christian life the years after I returned to Dallas in the late 1970s. And as Fritz went, so went the boys. The family made reference to their religious belief whenever there was an opportunity. Fritz suggested to Channel 39 that we have his minister sit in with me as the color announcer! I firmly objected, though we did have the Reverend on once for a brief interview. Fritz cornered me one night in Fort Worth, before *World Class* went on the air, and wanted to know if I was a Christian. I told him that was a personal matter and none of his or anyone else's business.

After David died, Fritz suggested we videotape a family gathering in memory of the star performer. It turned into a religious memorial with the well-known statements that God had wanted David, but the family would go on, strong in their belief—and also Kerry would win the World Championship in David's honor. God and the right kind of promotion would make it occur.

Sure enough, on May 5, 1984, Kerry defeated the veteran World Champion Ric Flair before over forty thousand fans at Texas Stadium, home of the Dallas Cowboys. Interestingly, Flair regained the title eighteen days later in Japan! Kevin and Kerry were joined by a "cousin," a handsome young man who hung around awhile until younger brother Mike was able to join his brothers. Kevin was a dashing type, wrestling barefoot. I referred to him as the All American boy with cheeks of tan. Kerry had an amazing physique and wrestling ability. He was a decent young man, but he required great concentration to make it through a brief interview. Mike's physique resembled David and he tried unsuccessfully to fill those shoes.

Several months after David died, our production crew, essentially the producers and director, discussed what we perceived as a drop in the general intensity, interest, and enthusiasm for *World Class*. There were some great crowds, such as Texas Stadium and the Cotton Bowl, but the week-to-week interest was beginning to wane. As we watched this over the months, it became obvious to us that David von Erich had been the spark that ignited the fire in the belly of *World Class*.

Mike von Erich, following an operation to correct an injured shoulder in 1987, developed toxic shock syndrome, had a fever of 108 degrees for several days, and just barely survived. It is a highly unusual infection in men, and medical reports indicated that he would have some damage to his nervous system because of the high fever.

A year later, with scars from all of the medical invasions still visible on his lean body, Mike wrestled and won before a huge crowd in the Cotton Bowl on the grounds of the State Fair of Texas. Mike did not look fully able to endure much in the ring, even a year after his illness, but Fritz, ever the promoter, knew this would be a great fan draw.

Once again, the von Erichs come back! In reading some articles about this sad situation (we in WCCW thought it way too early for Mike to return), I came across an exclusive article by Steve Slagle in the "Professional Hall of Fame presented by the Ring Chronicle," in which on page 4 he was describing Mike's return to the ring: "Once again the WCCW cameras were there to capture the drama of another real-life von Erich tragedy . . . something that many later pointed to as the *true* cause of the von Erich's troubles." As happens so often today with right-wing politicians blaming the media for all our troubles, this hit a nerve. Possibly Slagle didn't know that Fritz was the promoter as well as wrestler and father of the boys, and called the shots of who wrestled, when, where, for how much pay, and for whom.

Mike could have come back in Fort Worth on WBAP-TV's Channel 11 Saturday night wrestling, but to gain the coverage and the crowd, Fritz picked the Cotton Bowl. If Slagle blames television for the von Erich boys' problems, then he is not living in the real world. Basically, it was the father who called all the shots.

Prior to that Cotton Bowl match, I interviewed Mike for our program. His incoherent answers were laced with religious expressions, such as his doctor was Jewish "but he was a nice guy." There were other strange stories that he and his little brother Chris regaled us with that were out of character and shocking in regard to the family's religious beliefs. Mike, who rather amazingly had never lost a wrestling bout, disappeared shortly after this return to the ring, took an overdose of tranquilizers, and left a note that said he was sorry he couldn't live up to the von Erich wrestling code. He would see his family in heaven. His body was found resting on the bank of Lake Dallas.

Kerry had a near-fatal motorcycle accident in Argyle, a small town west of Denton, a short time after David died. Kerry's foot was nearly severed in the crash and the claim was made that it had been repaired. Actually, it had to be amputated and to his great athletic credit, Kerry learned to continue his wrestling career with a prosthetic foot. The fake foot came off in a couple of matches but that wasn't widely known until shortly before his death. But Kerry had a history of drug use. On his return from his honeymoon in Mexico, he was stopped in the Dallas–Fort Worth airport for possession of illegal drugs. In the early 1990s, long after *World Class* had faded away, Kerry was wrestling in New York. He had been arrested for trying to buy drugs on a fake prescription. Following another arrest and the possibility of prison, Kerry shot himself with a forty-five-caliber pistol in a field on his family ranch in February 1993.

The youngest brother, Chris, who had been hampered by severe asthma through his young life, tried to pursue a wrestling career, though he wasn't physically built for it. In frustration, Chris shot himself on the family farm in 1991.

After Mike's death, Fritz understandably seemed to lose interest in the business. He and his wife Doris had built a palatial home on some beautiful acreage in East Texas, but the pressure of these deaths overcame them and they separated and divorced. Doris blamed Jack for running his sons into the grave. Competing promoters, with offers of guaranteed contracts, attracted the attention of all the super talent that *World Class* and Fritz collected. Wrestling promotions in Atlanta and New York were gobbling up the best talent in the country and without guaranteed contracts, smaller city promotions folded. Fritz refused guaranteed contracts and other operations signed his most exciting talent.

In 1985, one of the most popular wrestlers in *World Class*, Bruiser Brody, was stabbed to death in Puerto Rico following a match by a disgruntled fellow wrestler. The 6′ 8″, 320-pound Brody (his real name was Frank Goodish) was not a stylistic wrestler, more of a pounder and a slammer, and sometimes, seemingly out of control, he would throw chairs and other dangerous items around the arena.

Gino Hernandez followed the ghastly parade of wrestlers in dying tragically in 1986 with what officially was described as an overdose of cocaine. Gino was just twenty-nine and handsome, with a personality that could beguile as well was inflame fans and opponents. Some of his fellow wrestlers believe he was murdered. He lived hard outside the ring, with a penthouse apartment in Dallas and a bevy of female admirers.

"Gentleman" Chris Adams was another crowd favorite during the *World Class* heyday. Chris came to this country from England, where he had been a martial arts champion, and he became an instant star with his handsome features, that English accent, and great athletic ability. When he arrived, we produced one of our features in Dallas at a Quadrangle restaurant, having tea with the Brit. Chris had a beguiling smile and personality, but like so much of wrestling then, became a dangerous alcoholic. Coming back from a trip to the Caribbean area, Chris became drunk and knocked down the copilot. Chris went to federal prison, and by the time he returned, *World Class* was gone. Chris had other professional opportunities, but alcohol and drugs ruined his career and life. He was shot dead by a friend during an altercation a few years back. In 1986, *World Class* withdrew from the National Wrestling Alliance and Channel 39 ended its production. Attendance at the matches in the Sportatorium once again reverted back to the public perception of the wrestling fan—less than affluent folks who couldn't afford more expensive entertainment venues. Gone were the college kids, folks dressed in suits, and coverage by local media. Kevin and Kerry continued to wrestle in the waning days of the promotion. Kevin won the Texas Heavyweight title on November 23, 1990, and the place shut down in January 1991.

Others came along trying to rebuild what once had been the excitement of the Sportatorium, but the same unknown wrestlers kept circulating while the famous names appeared on the national television shows out of New York and Atlanta.

If there ever was a person who would have been a poster boy for avoiding smoking, Fritz was the one. Over the forty years that I knew him, he smoked constantly, and in the mid 1990s was diagnosed with lung cancer. He was living by himself in a small house near Lake Dallas, near the family ranch where this family settled. On September 9, with Kevin by his bedside, Fritz died.

Kevin von Erich still lives out near Lake Dallas on the old family ranch with his lovely wife Pam and their children. Kevin enjoys communing with his cattle and taking care of all those ranch duties. He also dabbles with various ventures promoting and selling videos, having sole possession of all those *World Class* videotapes and hundreds of canisters of film from the early Sportatorium. A couple of years ago Kevin, Mickey Grant, and I spent a week in Costa Rica trying to establish a wrestling program of *World Class* matches for television there, which unfortunately was unsuccessful. Kevin thought while we were in Costa Rica we might run over and try putting the program on television in Cuba. I wished them a nice trip, but none went.

I was very fond of the Adkissons (their real name), having known the boys since they were little kids hanging around the Sportatorium while their father Jack built his wrestling empire. I attended their weddings, their funerals, and delivered the high school commencement address at Lake Dallas High when Kerry graduated. Their mother, Doris, was a sincere, warm lady who doted on her sons. How she managed to survive all that tragedy is amazing.

After *World Class* faded away in the mid 1990s, I was approached by a friend who had connections with businessmen in the Mideast. A promoter in that region wanted to obtain the services of several wrestlers, mine as a television announcer, and Kevin von Erich to star in a series of televised matches in that part of the world. He was willing to pay us well. I called Gary Hart, who had his finger on the pulse of a number of better-than-average wrestlers, and it looked like we had the deal sealed. But when my friend asked Kevin, he was told that under his personal contract, Fritz had to have $10,000 for doing nothing. Naturally, that killed the deal.

A biography about Fritz on the Internet claims he syndicated *World Class*. That is not true. He had nothing to do with the production. The sales staff at Channel 39 handled all the sales and promotions. In fact, he resisted, enlarging the scope of the program when it became apparent that it was a sensation. He refused to take us, Channel 39, to videotape the bouts he had arranged in Israel where the von Erichs and I were huge TV stars. He failed to take advantage of the opportunity to make *World Class* into what Jim McMahon has done with the promotion in New York.

It has been about twenty years since I last described a wrestling bout on television. Today, I was shopping in the Central Market in Plano when one of the employees looked at me and asked the usual question, "Don't I know you from . . . someplace?" Wrestling was the someplace. Though as is usual in business operations, Fritz von Erich and I had some giant blowups, we respected each other's talents. And I have always had a genuine appreciation of the role wrestling played in my career. When I first broadcast wrestling on radio in 1951, I didn't realize it would bring me to the market that made my career. My thanks go to the late Jimmy Barry, the manager of KMUS in Muskogee, Oklahoma, who brought me on to be the sportscaster and wrestling announcer, and to all the other people who believed in my broadcasting ability. It has been and continues to be a marvel.

# Afterword

Now that you have slammed through sixty years of broadcasting, I can again remind you that this was not a play-by-play textbook. I can give you some information on that subject.

First, find a copy of the famous broadcaster Red Barber's book, *The Broadcasters*, through old book dealers or some book sites on the Internet. Red has two chapters near the conclusion of his stories that I use for my text in the sports classes I teach.

Our sports play-by-play program at the University of North Texas emphasizes Barber's various edicts, such as Preparation, Concentration, Impartiality, and then my own requirement, Practice. We demand that the play-by-play students turn in eleven recorded football games, one per week, high school or college. These are critiqued each week to help the students improve. Sitting in the stands with a portable recorder broadcasting a game in all weather conditions is the most difficult assignment a person will ever endure in this business—but it works.

The same requirements are in effect for basketball and baseball. If you are an earnest, dedicated person wanting to try your hand at this business, you may contact me through the Radio, TV, and Film department at the University of North Texas, Denton, Texas 76201.

# Index

ABC, 234
Adams, Chris, 243, 279–80
Adams, George, 244
Adams, Mike, 214
Adkisson family, 263, 278–80, 280
advertising, 169, 208
AFC-NFC rivalry, 55
AFL (American Football League),
    30–32, 35, 39. *See also* NFL-AFL
    merger
African-American, 29, 89, 246
AFTRA (American Federation of
    Television and Radio Artists), 44,
    64, 217
*Air Adventures of Jimmy Allen*, 241
air-conditioners, 149
airplane: crash, 122, 233, 263–64,
    267; technical failure of, 94
Akihisa Mera "The Great Kabuki,"
    267
Ali, Muhammad, 26–27
Allen, Dick, 223, 225, 229
Allen, Ermal, 60, 73
Allen, Steve, 248
All-Missouri Valley Conference, 90,
    95, 96
All-Star game, 155–56
Allyn, John, 230–31
Altobelli, Joe, 184, 185
Alworth, Lance, 85
American Association, 163, 184
American Federation of Television

and Radio Artists (AFTRA), 44,
    64, 217
American Football League. *See* AFL
American Sportscasters Association,
    130
Ampex Company, 250
amplifier, 87, 245
Andrie, George, 70
announcers: ability to connect with
    audience, 254; play-by-play v.
    color, 49, 82
antiwar student movement, 103
Aparisio, Luis, 193
Arbanas, Fred, 40
*Arkansas Gazette*, 173
Arlin, Harold W., 125
Armstrong, Dick, 183
Arnold, Greg, 185
Ashford, Emmett, 139
athletes: death of, 139, 148–49, 279;
    long hair on, 60
attitude, 79
Atz, Jake, 125
audience, 247
audition, 252, 253
Austin, Steve "Stone Cold," 275
Avey, Sam, 256

Bacone College, 14, 70
Bahnsen, Stan, 221
Baillargeon, Bob, 162
Baker, Frank "Home Run," 149
Baker, Ray, 140

Baltimore Orioles, 184, 187
Bamberger, Hal, 138, 140
Banks, Ernie, 151
Barber, Red, 2, 53, 69, 113, 131, 147, 220, 244
Barbour, Bernie, 91, 95
Barger, John, 112, 195
Barker, Eddie, 42, 43, 168, 255
Barry, Jimmy, 14, 17–18, 242, 281
baseball, 197, 203–4; American League of, 85, 139, 177; broadcasting for, 16, 191–92, 216–17, 245; cameras needed for, 147; class C, 133, 134; Double-A, Texas League of, 168, 173; field, lights for, 138; game, best location for calling, 138; Major League of, 23, 49, 148, 183–84, 198; Minor League of, 139, 145, 148, 149, 158; National League of, 139, 177; pitching, 165, 175, 177–78, 178, 181, 206; radio and, 123, 131; Triple-A, 29, 146, 168. *See also* Major League Baseball; Minor League Baseball; *specific teams*
Baseball Hall of Fame, 145
basketball, 9, 10, 15, 26, 84
Basquette, Howard, 129
Bateson, J. W., 150, 157, 168
Bayh, Birch, 223
Baylor University, 108
Baynham, Craig, 67
Bean, Duane, 90
Beatty, Charles "Hatchet," 90
*Beginner's Book of Radio* (Dietrich), 128
Berle, Milton, 248
Bernard, Brute "The Brute," 267
Berry, Paul, 44, 92, 168
Beverly, Steve, 275

Beyer, Dick "The Destroyer," 269
Bibby, Jim, 212, 214, 215
Big D. Jamboree, 259, 261
Big Seven Conference, 26
Billings, Dick, 200
Bill Teegins Award, 122
binoculars, 33, 113
Birdsong, Jim, 195, 203, 216
Bishop, Sonny, 40
Bittner, Larry, 200, 201
Blair, Sam, 57, 79, 84
Blake, John, 126
Blanchard, John, 143
Blanda, George, 36, 40
Blue, Dick, 190
Blue, Vida, 214
Bluebonnet Bowl, SMU v. Oklahoma at, 97
Boesch, Paul, 244, 256
Boggs, Frank, 122, 175, 176–77, 258–59
Boland, Charley, 253–54
Boryla, Vince, 9
Bosher, Mary Ann, 192
Bosman, Dick, 200, 202–3
Boston Braves, 36, 139, 160
Boston Patriots, 36
Boston Red Sox, 36, 160, 205
Box, Ves, 265–66
Boydston, Max, 13, 39; joining Dallas, 19
Branch, Mel, 39
Brantley, Ed, 90
Brawner, Hoyt, 9
Brawner Memorial Youth Basketball Tournament, 10
Breeden, Leon, 192
Breen, Leo, 218, 226–27, 230
*Brian's Song*, 72
Brickhouse, Jack, 248
Briscoe, Brian, 120

*The Broadcasters* (Barber), 53, 131, 220, 244, 283
broadcasting, 33, 122, 247, 266; ad-libs in, 28, 34; art of, 99–100; attendance v., 131–32; booth, 76, 84–85, 199; chain, 130; identification of players for, 244; Internet and, 236; player identification in, 7, 244; power failure during, 28; preparation for, 28, 32, 53–54, 141; problems with business of, 107, 216; re-creations of games for, 136, 141, 142, 147, 152–53, 165, 171–73; six important areas of, 53, 69, 283; specificity in, 157; students of, 110; teaching, 132, 227, 270; technique of, 89; technological aspect of, 87–88; television v. radio, 48–50, 146, 245, 252, 265; unbiased, 16; at University of Denver, 6–9; weather v., 18, 19–20, 69; wrestling, 21, 30, 134, 146, 239, 245, 247, 266. *See also* announcers; baseball; football; radio
Broberg, Pete, 200, 202
Brobst, Gary, 113, 231
Brooker, Tommy, 41
Brooklyn Dodgers, 132, 147, 149
Brookshier, Tom, 86
Brown, Jim, 46, 83
Brown, Orville, 256
Brown, Tom, 56
"Brown Bomber." *See* Louis, Joe
"Bruiser Brody" (Frank Goodish), 279
"The Brute" (Brute Bernard), 267
Bryant, Paul "Bear," 26, 60
Buck, Jack, 49, 55, 86, 90, 218
Buffalo Bills, 77, 89

*Bull Durham*, 179, 185, 186, 194
Burford, Chris, 39, 40
Burk, Leo, 162
Burke, Dean, 183
Burke, Joe, 208
Burke, Mildred, 251
Burnett, Dick, 148–49
Burnett Field, 148, 174
Burris brothers, 13
Burroughs, Jeff, 200, 212, 214, 215, 226
Buscema, Dave, 214
Butkus, Dick, 71
Butler, Dick, 44, 51, 169, 170, 171, 180, 181, 195, 232, 233
Butler, John, 105, 195
Byers, June, 251

California Angels, 107
cameras, 272; for baseball, 147; Dumont, 22; necessity of tripod for, 110; television, 73–74, 84; video, 110, 250, 270–71
Campbell, Earl, 101, 108
Cannon, Billy, 40
Capps, Ben, 233
Capps, Mike, 70, 140, 144, 153, 233–34, 235, 236, 237, 243
Caray, Harry, 27, 49, 131, 197, 217–22, 226, 233, 270; outbursts of, 229–30; peace made with WMAQ, 224; professors of broadcasting v., 227; White Sox management and, 223, 228–29, 231
Carew, Rod, 216
Carlin, Vidal, 90
Carpentier, Georges, 123–24
Carter, Amon, 249
Carter, Amon, Jr., 150
Carter, John, 103
cart machines, 172–73

Cartwright, Alexander J., 123
Cartwright, Gary, 84
Carty, Rico, 210
Case, Jordan, 102
cassette recorder, 26
catcher, job of, 203–4
CBS, 24, 25, 28, 50, 117, 190, 249, 261; telecasts of Dallas Cowboys, 86–87
CBS-Radio, 49, 218
CBS-Television, 30, 49, 55, 77, 87, 122
censorship, 73–74
chain broadcast, 130
Chamberlain, Howard, 22
Chamberlain, Wilt, 26
Chance, Dean, 160
Chandler, Don, 70
Channel 4, 22, 92, 109, 255, 264
Channel 8, 74, 86, 173
Channel 39, 270–71, 276, 280
Chapman, Ron, 23, 81, 219, 231, 232, 270
Chapman, Walter, 99
Chicago Bears, 71
Chicago Cubs, 161, 171, 216, 248
Chicago Tribune, 181
Chicago White Sox, 100, 152, 161, 177, 193, 214, 226, 270; broadcasting for, 217, 225; fans of, 224–25; Harry Caray and, 223, 228–29, 231; history of, 231; Los Angeles Angels v., 223–24; management, 219; spring training of, 220; struggle of franchise of, 224–25; Texas Rangers v., 202–3
Chief Little Beaver, 251, 257
Chiles, Eddie, 103
Cimino, Pete, 164
Cincinnati Reds, 131, 133
Clark, Phil, 70
Clarke, Frank, 56
Clarke, Mike, 151
Cleveland Browns, 45–47, 56, 60, 67, 72, 78, 81
Cleveland Indians, 140, 161
Clinton, Henry, 139
Clyde, David, 188, 212–13, 214, 216, 221
CNN, 70, 234
coaching, 91
coaxial cable, 257
Cobb, Ty, 149, 198
Cochrane, Mickey, 149
Cole, Larry, 73
Cole, Vernon, 29–30
Collier, Blanton, 60, 79
Collins, Mel, 143
color commentator, 27–28, 32, 38, 67, 82, 90, 99, 106, 117, 120; definition of, 48–49; for Harry Caray, 218; for Jay Randolph, 174; money as incentive for being, 112; play-by-play v., 49, 82; for San Antonio Gunslingers, 112; student as, 110, 115; White Sox in need of new, 226
Comiskey Park, 221, 224
Como, Perry, 24
Conference USA: Missouri Valley Conference turning into, 97–98
confidence, 5
Continental League, 149–50, 152, 157, 159
Continental Productions, 271
Conway, Tiger, Jr., 243
Cooney, Jack, 138
Cooper, Walker, 156–57, 161
Cornelison, Jerry, 40
Corrales, Pat, 161
Corwin, Al, 151

Cotton Bowl, 22, 25, 27, 28, 31, 36, 66, 78, 148, 218
Cowboy Club, 57–58
Cowboys. *See* Dallas Cowboys
Cox, Bill, 259
Cox, Casey, 200
Cox, Louis, 150
critique, 16, 106, 157
Cronkite, Walter, 24
cursing, 88–89, 156
Cy Young Award, 160

*Daily Oklahoman*, 259
Dallas, 93
Dallas Cowboys, 8, 60, 66–67, 86–87, 159, 175; broadcasting quality of, 16–17; Buffalo v., 77; business of, 31, 63; champions of Capitol Division, 67, 72, 78; Chicago Bears v., 71; Cleveland Browns v., 45–46, 56, 67, 72, 78, 81; club, 58–58; Detroit Lions v., 81; doomsday defense of, 55, 85; draft picks, 55, 82; duties with, 50; Eastern Conference Championship of, 56, 72, 78; fans of, 46, 48, 56, 67, 84; first offensive play of, 66; Green Bay Packers v., 52, 56–57, 63, 67–71, 81; Los Angeles Raiders v., 79; Los Angeles Rams v., 79, 106; luncheon, 53, 57–58, 64, 73, 210; Miami Dolphins v., 85; Minnesota Vikings v., 72, 81; New England Patriots v., 84; newsletter, 77; new stadium for, 78; New York Giants v., 45–47; NFC championship games of, 75, 81, 85; 1960 record of, 35; of 1965, 45; 1966 record of, 55; 1966 statistics of, 52; 1967 year of, 62; 1968 record of, 71; 1969 record

of, 78; Philadelphia Eagles v., 46; play-by-play position for, 49, 174; practice of, 47; San Francisco 49ers v., 52, 75, 81; St. Louis Cardinals v., 46, 81; Super Bowl VI victory, 85; Texans v., 31, 34–35, 41; Washington Redskins v., 45–46, 55–56, 81; World Championship of, 85
Dallas Eagles, 150; Fort Worth Cats v., 147
Dallas–Fort Worth Spurs, 44, 51, 169, 170, 187, 216; Austin v., 176, 179; Memphis Blues v., 185; 1968 record of, 182; pitching staff of, 175, 181; Tulsa v., 179–80
Dallas Mavericks, 94
*Dallas Morning News*, 57, 64, 118, 196
*Dallas News*, 58, 183
Dallas Press Club, 237
Dallas Rangers, 146, 166
Dallas Steers, 129, 148
Dallas Texans, 32, 40, 78, 158–59; Cowboys v., 31, 34–35; dispute between Cowboys and, 41; 1960 record of, 35; 1961 losing streak of, 38; Oilers v., 40–41; Patriots v., 37; Raiders v., 39; statistics of, 35
*Dallas Times Herald*, 58, 59, 64, 68, 77, 122, 150, 152, 162, 167, 175, 176, 196, 198, 249, 258–59
Dallas Transit System, 150
Dana-Farber Cancer Institute, 205
Davidson, Cotton, 35, 39
Davis, Scott, 114, 115
Davis, Ted, 51, 93–94
Dawson, Len, 40
Dean, Dizzy, 149

death threat, 139, 211
Dempsey, Jack, 123–24
Dempsey v. Carpentier, 123–24
Dent, Bucky, 229
Denton Broncos, 23
Denver American Basketball Association, 9
Denver Nuggets, 9
depth chart, 12
designated hitter, 177
"The Destroyer" (Dick Beyer), 269
Devil's Bowl, 24
Dial, Buddy, 58
Dickey, Darrell, 114
Dickey, Imogene, 88
diction, improvement of, 226–28
Dietrich, Fredrick, 128
DiMaggio, Vince, 140
Ditka, Mike, 85
Dixie Series, 127–28
Dobyns, Dorothy, 6
Doggett, Jerry, 129
Dolan, Jimmy, 27
Dowler, Boyd, 70
Doyle, Paul, 182–83
Draper, Paul, 90
drugs, 61, 71
Drysdale, Don, 85, 107, 177, 186, 189–90, 197, 203, 205–6, 213, 269; signed by California Angels, 209
Dubberly, Jack, 23, 33
Duesing, Tony, 244
Dumit, Ed, 21, 141, 145, 245
Dumont Network, 246–49
Dundee, Johnny: Johnny Ray v., 125
Dunham, Art, 151, 155
Dunham, George, 117, 120
Dunlap, Leonard, 91
Dunphy, Don, 241, 245
Dusek, Joe, 269

Eastern Conference Championship, 56; Cowboys v. Browns at, 72, 78
editing, 25
Edwards, Douglas, 24
Elkins Institute, 45
Ellison, Lillian "The Fabulous Moolah," 21, 242, 251
El Paso Police, 33
Elston, Gene, 79
Ematerio, Nick, 185
emotions, 96
Enberg, Dick, 209, 227
engineers, 74–75, 173, 195
Engler, Duncan, 109
Enid, Oklahoma, 11–12
Enis, Bill, 65, 79, 182, 183
equipment, 245; to broadcast college games, 233–34; primitive, 234; updated broadcast, 93
Erich, Chris von, 278–79
Erich, David von, 262, 272–73, 277; death of, 276
Erich, Fritz von, 258–59, 262–63, 270, 271, 274, 278, 279, 281; as born-again Christian, 276; death of, 280; Duke Keomuka v., 264; Gary Hart v., 267–68
Erich, Kerry von: motorcycle accident of, 278; suicide of, 278; wins Texas Heavyweight title, 280; wins World Championship, 277
Erich, Kevin von, 243, 262, 280, 281
Erich, Mike von, 277; suicide of, 278
ESPN, 216
Estrada, Chuck, 209–10, 216
Etter, Gene, 179, 186
exhibition game: Boston Red Sox v. Chicago Cubs, 151; New York Yankees v. Boston Red Sox in, 138
Ex-Pros Baseball Hall of Fame, 122

"The Fabulous Moolah" (Lillian El-
lison), 21, 242, 251
Fallon, Frank, 105
Fallon, Steve, 38, 105, 106
Falzer, George, 124
fans, 35, 81, 129, 168, 180, 183,
186, 196, 226, 257–58
Farragut Naval Base, 3
FCC (Federal Communications
Commission), 105, 117, 121
Fechtman, Don, 99
Federal Communications Commis-
sion (FCC), 105, 117, 121
Fenway Park, 137, 211
Fessenden, R. A., 123, 128
fifteen-minute essays, 28
Fighting Irish, 9
Finger, Tom, 149
Finley, Charley, 43, 166–67, 187,
231–32, 232–33
fire: of Dallas courthouse, 43–44; of
Sportatorium, 260
Flair, Ric, 263–64, 277
Fleeman, Donnie, 151
Flood, Curt, 198
flood, of Kansas, 138
Flores, Tom, 35
Florida Instructional League, 208
Florida International League, 143
"The Flying Worm" (athletic em-
blem), 98
Foldberg, Hank, 92
football: army teams of, 60; broad-
casting, 12–13, 16–17, 131;
championships, 40–41; childhood memories of, 1; college,
79–80; defense, 94, 101; draft
picks for, 55, 82, 95–96; field, dirt
v. grass, 17–18; salaries of stars
of, 31; World Championship

game of, 47. *See also* AFL; NFL;
*specific teams*
Forster, Terry, 225
Fort Collins, Colorado, 10
Fort Worth Cats, 147, 193
Fort Worth Panthers, 128; New Or-
leans Pelicans v., 128; Wichita
Falls Spudders v., 125–26
*Fort Worth Record*, 249
four-division alignment, 67
Fouts Field, 110
Fowler, Art, 216
Fox, Nellie, 193
Franco, John, 155
Freed, Roger, 167
Fregosi, Jim, 160
Fregosi, Zach, 160
frequency, of 833 kHz, 239
Fricano, Marion, 38, 151, 154–55,
158
Friesen, Orin, 240
frostbite, 69
Fry, Hayden, 92, 97, 98, 99, 100,
101, 103, 162; show, 101, 102

Galloway, Randy, 212, 215
Galveston, 11
Garcia, Vinicio, 151, 155, 157
Garland, Wayne, 187
Garner, Scott, 237
Garrison, Walt, 72–73, 85
Garvin, Jimmy, 272
Gault, Bob, 258–59
Gehringer, Charley, 149
Gent, Pete, 57, 58, 82; NFL purists
v., 61; TV show, 58–60, 73
Gerwig, Herb "Killer Karl Kox,"
268–69
Getter, Dick, 155
Gibson, Florent, 125
Gilbert, Andy, 143
Gilliam, Joe, 40

Gleiber, Frank, 61, 77, 79, 122, 204
Goad, Richard, 1
Gogolewski, Bill, 200
Golden Gloves Boxing, 14
Golden Throats, 62, 130
golf, 27
good, v. evil, 274
Goodall, Alva, 109
Goodish, Frank "Bruiser Brody," 279
"Gorgeous George" (George Wagner), 257
Gossage, Rich "Goose," 225, 229
Gowdy, Curt, 145
Graham, Fred, 25, 34, 87, 92, 93, 94, 100, 101, 104, 109, 218, 220
Graham, Sidney Sue, 94
Graham, Wayne, 161, 162
Grambling Band, 78
Grant, Mickey, 267, 268, 270, 271, 280
Great Depression, 3, 240–41
"The Great Kabuki" (Akihisa Mera), 267
Greco, Bobby Del, 139
Green Bay Packers, 47, 52, 56–57, 63, 67–71, 81
Greene, Joe, 90, 94, 95, 109; of North Texas State, 79; Pittsburgh Steelers, drafted by, 95–96
Green Monster, 211
Grich, Bobby, 184
Grieve, Tom, 200
Grimm, Charlie, 149
groupies, 186
Gunkel, Frederick Herman, 262
Gunkel, Ray, 262

Hack, Stan, 154
Haight-Ashbury Park, 82
Haley, Arthur, 57
Halford, Bob, 32, 37, 145

Hamilton, Milo, 182, 233
"The Hammer" (Greg Valentine), 264
Hand, Rich, 200, 201, 206–7
Hardman, Cedric, 90
Hargrove, Mike, 214
Harkless, Burkley, 90
Harper, Johnny, 261
Harrah, Toby, 200, 201
Harris, Vic, 210
Harrison, Jack, 158
Hart, Gary, 267, 281; Fritz von Erich v., 267–68; Wahoo McDaniel v., 266
Hartenstein, Charles Oscar, 176, 177, 180
Harvard, 108
Harvey, Paul, 31
Harwell, Ernie, 121
Haskell County Tribune, 6
Hatchett, David, 115
Hattaway, Wayne, 154
Hawaii, 164
Hawkins, Burton, 192, 199–200, 204
Hayes, Bob, 56, 58, 59, 67, 69, 82, 175
Hayes, Doc, 22, 26, 92
Hayes, Jere, 152
Haynes, Abner, 29, 35, 38–41, 88–89, 100
Headrick, Sherrill "Psycho," 39
health insurance, 264
Heinrich, Don, 35
Heisman Trophy, 85, 108
Helwig, Craig, 120
Hemond, Roland, 220
Henderson, Ken, 225, 230
Hendricks, Richard, 122
Henneke, Ben, 145
Henningan, Charlie, 40

Henry, Orville, 173
Herman, Billy, 140
Hernandez, Gino, 279
Herrmann, Ed, 223
Herzog, Whitey, 139, 153, 191, 208, 209, 212, 213, 216
Hewitt, Tarzan, 247–48
Hicks, John, 105, 261
Higdon, Bill, 150
Highland Park High, 17, 23
highlights, 92
Hill, Calvin, 82, 85, 89
Hill, Eddie, 51, 174
Hilling, Chuck, 210
Hines, Bill, 259
hippie movement, 60, 82
Hitt, Dick, 162
Hitzges, Norm, 97
Holibonich, John, 143
Holland, Henry, 90, 96
Holland, Reg, 45, 66
Holloway, Glen, 90
Holub, E. J., 39
"Home Run" Baker (Frank Baker), 149
homosexuality, 4
Hopp, Julius, 123
Hoskins, Dave, 149
Hough, Harold, 126, 128
Houghton, Jerry, 254
Houlahan's Tally Board, 129
Houston Astros, 182, 188
Houston Oilers, 36, 40
Howard, Frank, 197, 201, 202
Howard, Jay, 112
Howe News Service, 141
Howley, Chuck, 82
Hudson, Sid, 193, 206
Hughes Sports Network, 190
Hunt, Bobby, 39
Hunt, H. L., 169–70

Hunt, Lamar, 30, 37, 41, 42, 54–55, 145, 168, 169
Hunt, Zack, 129
Hunt Oil, 169
Hurley, Al, 108, 111, 112, 118, 119, 120, 121
Husing, Ted, 2, 130, 248–49
hyperventilation, 255–56

Ice Bowl, 96, 233; Cowboys v. Packers at, 67–71
Indianapolis Colts, 55
injuries, 58, 72, 85, 89, 96, 178, 200, 223, 230, 266; drug use to fake, 61; lack of concern for, 242; missing games due to, 67
Integrated Services Digital Network (ISDN), 236
integration, 29, 149
International League, 184
Internet, 236
interviews, 197
"Iron Claw," 263
ISDN (Integrated Services Digital Network), 236

Jablonski, Ray, 158
Jackson, Frank, 39
Jackson, Reggie, 182
Jackson, Travis, 149
Jacobs, Jack, 2–3, 29
James, Dennis, 246–47, 248
Jenkins, Fergie, 210, 215, 226
Jennings, Waylon, 4
Jimmy Fund, 205
*Joe Palooka* (comic strip), 73
Johnson, Deron, 229
Johnson, Edwin, 148
Johnson, Larry, 184
Johnson, Lyndon, 175
Johnson, Otis, 139

Johnston, Ray, 43, 138, 157, 161, 163, 165
Jones, Charlie, 32, 44, 51, 63, 158, 169, 171, 173, 174, 176, 182, 196
Jones, Jerry, 84, 85
Jones, Michael, 100–101
Jonsson, J. Erik, 189
Jordan, LeRoy, 59
Journal Broadcast Group, 240

Kaat, Jim, 214, 221–22, 225, 229
Kamala (wrestler, "The Ugandan Giant"), 273
Kamerick, John, 103
Kansas City Chiefs, 31, 40–42
Katie Award, 237
Kayfabe, 242, 274
Kays, Mike, 144
KBIX, 11, 13–14, 15, 21, 134
KCOL, 10, 11, 133, 134, 182
KDFW-TV, 190
KDKA, 123, 125, 239
KDNT, 23, 87, 88, 90, 93, 100, 104, 105, 112, 117, 118
KECA-TV, 248
Keillor, Garrison, 3
Kelly, Chuck, 121
Kemp, Jack, 35
Kennedy, John F., 42–43, 47, 259
Kentucky Derby, 130
Kenyon, Michael, 239–40, 244, 248
Keomuka, Duke, 262, 264
KFH, 240, 245
Khoury, Iseed, 99, 275–76
"Killer Karl Kox" (Herb Gerwig), 243, 268–69
Kiner, Steve, 82, 83
King, Hal, 201
Kittle, Hub, 184
KJZY, 105

KLIF, 23, 44, 52, 70, 75, 146, 168, 169
KLUV, 75
KLZ, 10, 133–34
KMOX-Radio, 49
KMUS, 14–15, 16, 17, 19, 37, 134, 135, 136, 141, 145, 241, 245, 252, 281; audition for, 253; banned from McAlester, 18; budget problems of, 17; gratitude to, 21; Joe Louis interview at, 246; KRLD watts v., 22; Standard Sound Effects disc at, 137
Knobler, Bill, 190, 202, 207
KNTU-FM, 104, 110, 117, 120, 121, 234; coaches' show on, 111; commercial time for, 112
KOKO, 11, 134
KOL, 244
Korean War, 193
Kotrany, Joe, 151, 153–55
Koufax, Sandy, 213–14
Koury, Fred "Wild Bull Curry," 264–66
Kovacs, Sandor, 248
Krebs, Jim, 23
KRLD, 17, 25, 27, 28, 29, 42, 43, 52, 105, 112, 116, 117, 137, 150, 155, 157, 161, 164, 169, 194, 214, 215, 218, 265; announcing for AFL on, 32; audition for, 252; call letters of, 249; Columbia Broadcasting System of, 23; leap from Double-A to Triple-A baseball, 146; scheduling at, 33; spring training on, 195
KRLD-Radio, 63, 146; interview show with Hayden Fry, 92; purchased by *Dallas Times Herald*, 249
KRLD-TV, 22, 30, 58, 59, 146, 192,

266; sold to J. Erik Jonsson family, 189
KTLA, 248
KVIL, 42, 81, 94, 100, 107, 110, 219, 231, 232, 270
KVOO, 180
KXA, 244
KYW, 130

Lambeau Field, 68
Lammano, Ray, 133
Lampman, Hugh, 146
Lander Corporation, 239
*Landry* (St. John), 84
Landry, Alicia, 80
Landry, Tom, 31, 45, 79, 86; Duane Thomas v., 83; press conferences of, 62
Lane, Dick, 248
Laughter, Victor H., 123
LeBaron, Eddie, 35, 55
Lee, Emory, 124
Leone, Baron Michele, 257
Leppert, Don, 151, 155, 158
Levias, Joe, 79
Lewis, Duff, 149
Lewis, Ed "The Strangler," 250–51
Lewis, Jack, 143
Liberty Broadcasting Network, 23, 135, 137
Lindblad, Paul, 201, 203
Little, Keith, 151, 154, 155
Little, Ret, 91
Livingstone, Cora, 251
Lockhart, Carl, 90
Lockman, Whitey, 175, 178, 180, 216
Lombardi, Vince, 67
Los Angeles Angels, 159–60; Chicago White Sox v., 223–24; Texas Rangers v., 200–202
Los Angeles Chargers, 36

Los Angeles Dodgers, 85, 131, 174
Los Angeles Rams, 36, 106–7
Los Cruces, 102
Louis, Joe "Brown Bomber," 21–22, 241, 245–46; Max Schmeling v., 22, 130, 241, 246
Louisville, v. Indianapolis, 156
Love, John, 91, 93
Lovitto, Joe, 201
Lowrance, Mark, 271
Lucchesi, Frank, 167
Luksa, Frank, 68
Lumpe, Jerry, 151
Lundquist, Verne, 67, 74–77, 82, 83, 85–87, 194
Lyerly, Nevin, 58, 64

Macko, Joe, 44, 51, 169, 170, 171, 192
Maddox, Elliot, 201
Maddux, Mike, 178
Madlock, Bill, 210
Magnolia High School, 27–28
Magota, Joe, 135–36, 143
Major League Baseball: demand for jobs in, 49; expanding franchises of, 183–84; Player's Association, 198; on television, 148
*Making Airwaves* (Hamilton), 233
management, 79, 86, 126
Mandalay Company, 237
Mangus, Clinton, 112
Mantle, Mickey, 57, 134, 244
Maris, Roger, 153–54
Marquez, Luis, 151, 154, 155, 156–57
Marshall High School, 116
Martha, Paul, 61
Marti, George, 234
martial arts, 264, 279

Martin, Billy, 212, 214, 216, 219, 226

Martin, Dean, 57

Martin, Freddie, 151

Martin, J. C., 157, 226–28, 229, 230

Martin, John Leonard "Pepper," 143–44

Martino, Angelo, 251

Marti unit, 234

Mason, Jim, 201

Matthews, J. C., 103

Mavericks, 84

May, Terry, 255–56

Mays, Jerry, 40

McAlester High School, 17–18

McCarthy, Clem, 21–22, 130, 241, 246

McClinton, Curtis, 40

McCully, W. C., 121

McDaniel, Wahoo, 266

McGraw, Bugsy, 273–74

McGuirk, Leroy, 256

McIlvaine, Stan, 151

McKeon, John Aloysius "Jack," 162, 216

McKinley, Ray, 130

McLemore, Ed, 254, 259–60, 261, 263

McLendon, Gordon, 23, 134

McMahon, Jim, 281

McMahon, Vince, 275

McMillan, George, 66

McNamara, John, 166

McNamee, Graham, 2, 130

McPhail, Larry, 132

McShain, Danny, 21, 242, 251, 256, 262

media, 74

Medwick, Joe, 140

Melton, Bill, 225, 229–30

memorization, 32–33

Memphis State, 94, 96, 98–99, 101, 102

Memphis Turtles, 123

Mercer, Tommy, 168

Meredith, Don, 39, 45, 56, 66, 70–71; missing games due to injuries, 67; popularity of, 79; retirement of, 77–78

Merron, Jeff, 212, 216

Messersmith, Andy, 201

Metro Sports News, 79

Mexican League, 151, 175

Meyers, Lee, 181

microphones, 128

Miller, Marvin, 198

Mincher, Don, 201

minimum wage, 11, 198, 252

Minnesota Twins, 163, 212, 228

Minor League Baseball, 145; attendance of, 149, 158; television v. attendance of, 148

Minor League Hockey, 145

Mississippi State University, 104

mistakes, 27, 157

Mitchell, Odus, 88, 90, 91, 94, 116

Molina, Benny, 59

money, 112

Money, Don, 229–30

Montreal Expos, 180

Moody Coliseum, 26

Moore, Barry, 91, 93

Moore, Jackie, 210

Moore, Jerry, 103

Moore, Monte, 167, 231–32, 232–33

Morris, Pete, 99

Morse code, 128, 136, 152

Morton, Craig, 58, 65–66, 67, 78, 85

Munson, Thurman, 210

Murchison, Clint, 30

Murff, Red, 234
Murphy, Bob, 14, 134, 145
Murray, Ray, 161
Murrow, Ed, 246
Muschnick, Sam, 256
Museum of Television, 247
music, legends of, 261
*Music 'Til Dawn*, 146
Muskogee, Athletic Park of, 137
Muskogee Baseball Booster Club, 143
Muskogee Giants, 14, 134, 145; attendance of games of, 138; Enid Buffalos v., 138; 1953 record of, 144
Muskogee Radio Station, 11
Muskogee Reds, 133
Muskogee Roughers, 12–13, 15, 16, 134; defeating McAlester, 18; fiftieth reunion of, 117
Mutual Broadcasting Company, 105
Mutual Radio Network, 38

Nadel, Eric, 219
Namath, Joe, 55
Nash, Laura, 108
Nasser, Mark, 126–27
National Amateur Wireless Association, 123
National Broadcasting Company, 30
National Collegiate Athletic Association (NCAA), 26, 105, 119
National Football Conference Championship, 85
National Football League. *See* NFL
National Hockey League (NHL), 84
National Sportscasters and Sportswriters Association, 79
National Wrestling Alliance (NWA), 256, 280

National Wrestling Alliance World Tag Team, 251
Navy, 2, 3, 4, 5, 22, 34, 68, 78, 241
Nazi propaganda, 246
NBC, 32, 63, 174, 247
NCAA (National Collegiate Athletic Association), 26, 105, 119
Neeld, Hugh, 23, 252
Neely, Mark, 144
Neely, Ralph, 55
Nelson, Corky, 108, 114, 115; coaches' show with, 111
Nelson, Dave, 201, 202, 226
Nelson, Willie, 84, 273
Neuheisel, Rick, 112
Newark News Radio Club, 124, 127
New York Giants, 36, 45–47, 90, 91, 123, 132, 138, 140, 149
New York Jets, 55
New York Knicks, 9
New York Mets, 14, 134, 145, 160, 161, 208
*New York Times*, 108, 145
New York Yankees, 132, 140; Boston Red Sox v., 138; Texas Rangers v., 207
NFL (National Football League), 30, 35, 43, 55, 61, 82; Championship game, 75, 81; hippie movement v., 82; Kennedy assassination v., 43
NFL-AFL merger, 42, 54–55
NHL (National Hockey League), 84
Nieman, Butch, 139
Nixon, Richard, 204, 223
no-hitters, 168, 182–83, 201, 214
Nolen, C. C., 103, 202
Norman, Pettis, 87
*North Dallas Forty* (Gent), 61
Northeastern Redmen, 19
Northeastern State College, 5, 14, 19

North Texas Athletic Hall of Fame, 122

North Texas Eagles, 28–29, 88, 91, 98; Baylor v., 115; Chattanooga v., 91; Cincinnati v., 95, 96; Colorado State v., 94; Corky Nelson, new coach for, 109; Florida State v., 101; Golden Hurricane v., 29; history of, 97; Houston v., 98, 99; Kansas State v., 115; Louisiana Tech v., 101; Louisville v., 94; Marshall v., 114; Memphis State v., 94, 96, 98–99, 101, 102; missing games of, 51; Mississippi State v., 99, 101; New Mexico State v., 101, 102; 1965 record of, 90; 1967 record of, 94; 1977 record of, 101; 1989 record of, 115; Northeast Louisiana v., 109; Oklahoma State v., 98, 101, 102; presidents, succession of, 103; Razorbacks v., 80, 95; Rice v., 114; San Diego State v., 96, 98; search for coach of, 116; SMU v., 101, 115; Southern Illinois v., 34; Southern Mississippi v., 102; statistics after Rod Rust was fired, 96; Tennessee v., 98, 99; Texas Tech v., 114; Tulsa v., 94; University of Nevada–Reno v., 110; University of Texas v., 101, 102, 114; UTEP v., 95; Wichita v., 94; win Southland Conference championship, 109

North Texas Hall of Fame banquet, 89

North Texas University, 24, 87, 88, 147, 192; Division 1-AA v. Division 1-A at, 118–20; duties at, 104; end of career at, 120–22; fighting of staff at, 118; integration of, 29; sportscasting class at, 53; teaching broadcasting at, 132, 270. *See also* North Texas Eagles

Nossek, Joe, 164

Notre Dame, 9, 22

NTTV, 111

NWA (National Wrestling Alliance), 256, 280

officials, 95, 139

*Okay Mother!*, 247

Oklahoma Sooners, 13, 16

*Oklahoma Split T Football* (Wilkinson), 15

Oklahoma Sports Museum, 122, 144, 178

Oklahoma State, airplane crash of, 122

Old Chicago Beer, 222

Oliva, Tony, 163

Olympics, 250

Omaha Royals, 126

*Once a Bum, Always a Dodger* (Drysdale), 197

O'Neal, Bill, 125

O'Neil, Leroy, 144

One O'Clock Lab Band, 192

Orta, Jorge, 225, 229, 230

Outstanding Reporting Award, 44

Pacific Coast League, 163, 203, 236, 244

Pacific Coast League Round Rock Express, 70

Panella, Bob, 25–26

"Panty Hose Night," 210

Parilli, Vito "Babe," 35

Parker, Dennis, 116, 117

Parkhouse, George, 152

Parks, Roy, 209, 218–19

Paterno, Joe, 105–6

patriotism, 29, 34

Paul, Mike, 200, 201
Pena, Horacio, 201
Penalver, Luis, 182–83
Penn State University, 105
"Pepper" (John Leonard Martin), 143–44
Perkins, Arthur, 89
Perkins, Don, 56, 66, 78
Perkins, Steve, 58, 59, 60, 77, 84
Peschel, Randy, 80
Philadelphia Phillies, 161, 184, 193
phone line problem, 37
photography, 25
physicals, 4, 5
Piccolo, Brian, 71–72
"Pick up the Tempo," 4
pitcher, 165, 175, 177–78, 181, 206
Pittsburgh Corsairs, 125
*Pittsburgh Post*, 125
Pittsburgh Steelers, 89, 95–96, 109
play-by-play announcer, 48
player-managers, 140
players' strike, 197–200, 202
Playoff Bowl, 47; Dallas Cowboys v. Los Angeles Raiders at, 79; Dallas Cowboys v. Minnesota at, 72
Pollard, Hollis, 190, 207, 209, 210, 216, 218
postgame show, 74–76
power failure, 28
pranks, 154, 156–57
pregame show, 52, 67, 74
prejudice, 22
press box, 126
Pringle, Percy, 259
production technique, 272
"Professional Hall of Fame presented by the Ring Chronicle," 277
professional responsibilities, 51
*Professional Wrestling as Television*

*Programming Form* (Beverly), 275
pronunciation, 197
prosthetics, 278
public relations, 48
Pyland, Jack, 260

racism, 22, 29, 89, 149, 246
radio: baseball marriage with, 123; broadcasting, 7, 131; broadcasting, ban of, 129, 132; cursing on, 156; excitement for, 239; portable, 132; receivers, 124, 127–28, 240; station gofers, 222–23; story production, 25–26; television v., 23, 48–50, 146, 245, 252, 265; transmission, 125; transmitter, 124; wrestling on, 265. *See also specific radio stations*
"Radio Recollections" (seminar), 244
Ramsey, Steve, 90, 91, 93, 94, 95, 96, 114
Randle, Lenny, 203
Randolph, Jay, 45–47, 49, 61, 174
Raschke, Baron von, 269–70
Raudman, Bob "Shorty," 179
Ray, Doug, 104, 170
Ray, Johnny, 125
rebroadcasting, 50–51
recognition, 54
re-creation, of games for broadcasting, 136, 141, 142, 147, 152–53, 165, 171–73
Reeves, Danny, 56, 67, 71, 72–73
Rembert, Clyde, 253–54
remote amplifier, 20
Renfro, Mel, 56
Rentzel, Lance, 58, 66, 69, 71
Rhodes, Dusty, 269
Rhome, Jerry, 65–66, 67

Richter, Windi, 251
*Ride Rangers Ride*, 191–92
*The Ring Chronicle*, 250
riots, 74
Ripken, Cal, Sr., 187
Risenhoover, Dick, 186, 190, 191, 204, 209, 211, 216, 217, 218
Rivers, Mickey, 186
Rizzuto, Phil, 208
Roberts, Bill, 147
Robertson, Pat, 271
Robinson, Dave, 56
Robinson, James, 5
Rochester, Paul, 39–40
*Rod Rust North Texas Show*, 92
Rogers, Buddy, 251, 262
Rogers, James, 24, 103
Rogers, Susan, 118–19, 120
Rojas, Cookie, 161
Rollins, Gary, 190, 207–8, 209
Rose Bowl: Washington Huskies v. Alabama, 240
Round Rock Express, 235–36, 236, 243
Royal, Darrell, 79, 80, 114
Rust, Rod, 91, 93, 95–97, 101
Ruth, Babe, 138
Ryan, Billy, 89
Ryan, Nolan, 181–82, 216, 220–21, 223–24, 234–35

Sain, Johnny, 222
salary, 31, 134, 189, 209, 212, 219, 232, 252
San Antonio Gunslingers, 114, 195
Sand Springs, 18
San Francisco 49ers, 52, 75, 81
Santa Claus, 81
Sarasota Spring Training Speech School, 228
*Saturday Night Country Style*, 261

Savage, Leo, 251
Sayers, Gail, 72
schedule, 33, 34, 51, 92, 111
Schenkel, Chris, 249
Schepps, George, 148
Schmeling, Max, 22, 130, 241, 246
Schramm, Marty, 80
Schramm, Tex, 31, 54–55, 60, 64, 83, 86, 87, 122
Schultz, David, 242–43
Schultz, Gerald, 143
*The Scout* (Capps and Murff), 234
Scully, Vin, 217
Sears, 192–93
*Seasons in Hell* (Shropshire), 216
segregation, 29
Segrist, Kal, 151, 154, 158
Shafer, Bill, 244
Sham, Brad, 97, 107, 122
Shanklin, Ron, 91, 93, 94–95, 96, 104
Sharp, Bill, 229
Shea, William, 149
Shelley, Wilson, 146, 252, 255
Shelton, Ron, 185, 186
Shepherd, Harwell, 87, 104, 105
Sherrod, Blackie, 52, 62–63, 66–67, 68, 74, 75, 79, 80–81, 84, 130, 152, 175, 198
Short, Bob, 187–88, 191, 208, 213, 226
Shrake, Bud, 151
Shropshire, Mike, 216
Siebern, Norm, 143, 151
Sigel, Morris, 256, 260
signing players, 31
Silverstein, Ruffy, 269
Sisler, George, 193
Slagle, Steve, 250, 277–78
Sloan, Steve, 118, 119
Smith, Bobby, 89
Smith, J. T., 99

smoking, 39, 280
sound effects, 137, 141, 142–43, 147, 157, 172
Southern Illinois, 88
Southern Methodist University (SMU), 22, 24, 92, 97–98, 101, 115, 162
Southland Conference: North Texas Eagles join, 109
Southwest Conference, 97, 104; broadcasting rights of, 105; disappearance of, 116
Southwestern State, 19
Speaker, Tris, 149
speech, improvement of, 226–28
Spencer, Jim, 183
Spikes, Jack, 39
spitball, 206
Split T formation, 16
Sportatorium, 146, 253, 254, 257, 259, 271, 280; cameramen of, 272; condition of, 261; fire of, 260
Sportscasters Hall of Fame, 130
*Sports Illustrated*, 55
Spot Shows, 274
spotter, 7, 11
spotting board, 7–8, 32, 53, 54, 80
spotting sheets, 13
Spring, Jack, 151
spring training, 197
stadium facilities, 36
Stanhouse, Don, 202
Starr, Bart, 56, 70, 71
Stars, 84
*Star-Telegram* (Fort Worth), 125, 150, 159, 196, 216, 249
Staubach, Roger, 78, 85, 86
Steadman, Jack, 31
Stembridge, Terry, 191
Stern, Bill, 2, 11

St. John, Bob, 84
St. Louis Cardinals, 27, 46, 81, 140, 158, 179, 180, 218
"Stone Cold" Steve Austin, 275
Stossel, John, 242–43
Stram, Hank, 31, 40
Strange, Lee, 163
"The Strangler" (Ed Lewis), 250–51
Street, James, 80
Strong, Andy, 139
Suarez, Ken, 200
suicide, 278–79
Sullivan, Ed, 113
Sun Bowl, 29, 33, 88, 94
*Sunday Call*, 124
Sunshine (Jimmy Garvin's sidekick), 272
Super Bowl, 55, 65, 74, 81, 83, 85, 86, 96
Susce, George Cyril Methodius, Sr., 194

Tanner, Chuck, 161, 183, 220, 230, 233
Taylor, Harry, 159
Taylor, Leo, 90
Taylor, Otto W., 239
technology, 87–88, 126; disasters of, 74–76, 90, 103, 124, 165–66; improvement of, 93, 127, 153, 270; new, 235
Teddlie, Inez, 149
telephone lines, 90, 104, 126–27; cleaning up, 235; no outlet for, 145
television, 22; attendance of live games v., 148–49; cable, 249–50, 257; museum of, 247; new medium of, 246; radio v., 23, 48–50, 146, 245, 252, 265. *See also specific channels/stations*

Terrell, Marvin, 40

Terwilliger, Wayne, 153, 193

Texas, University of, 125, 160

Texas A&M football, 26, 92, 105–6, 125

Texas Association of Broadcasters, 107

*Texas Books in Review*, 119

Texas Brass Knuckles, 251

Texas Christian University, 24, 103

Texas Heavyweight Champion, 251

Texas League, 44, 127, 235; pennant, 126; San Antonio v. Rio Grande Valley of, 176; Tulsa v. Amarillo, 179–80

*The Texas League* (O'Neal), 125

Texas Radio Hall of Fame, 122, 182, 251–52

Texas Rangers, 85, 97, 100, 103, 150, 152, 188; Baltimore Orioles v., 206; Baseball Network, 207; Brewers v., 203; Chicago White Sox v., 202–3; Denver v., 154; fans of, 226; Kansas City v., 199; Los Angeles Angels v., 200–202; losing money broadcasting, 216; luncheon, 210–11; media guide of, 191; Minnesota Twins v., 212; New York Yankees v., 207–8; 1960 record of, 159; 1962 record of, 162; "Panty Hose Night," 210; pitcher v. relief pitcher of, 165; sellout crowd of, 213; spring training of, 194, 198; statistics of 1972, 201; theme music for broadcast of, 191–92

Texas Senate State Affairs, 152

Texas Stadium, 78, 84

Texas State Sports network, 111

Texas Tag Team Title, 251

Texas Tech University, 103–4

*Tex Schramm Show*, 63

theme music, 191–92

Thesz, Lou, 250–51, 256, 257

"They Make Wrestling Tick," 256

Thomas, Duane, 82–84, 83, 84, 85, 86, 89, 97

Thomson, Bobby, 36, 145

The Ticket (radio station), 117, 120, 121

*Times Herald-Record*, 214

timing, 254

Tipps, Kern, 122

Titans (New York football team), 37

Tolar, Charlie, 40

Toma, Daniel, 144

Tomanek, Dick, 159

*Tom Harmon Sports Show*, 25–27

*Tom Landry Show*, 61–62

Topeka Owls, 139

Tovar, Cesar, 163, 164

Townes, Willie, 70

Tracy, Sterling, 25

Tracey-Locke (advertising agency), 188, 202

train accident, 219–20

travel, 33–34

Trinity University, 160, 255

Tripucka, Frank, 35

Tubbs, Jerry, 52

Tugerson, Jim, 151

Tulane Stadium, 85

Tulsa University, 145, 179–80

*Tulsa World*, 145

Turnpike Stadium, 168, 170, 172, 174–75; *Bull Durham* and, 179; first no-hitter in, 183

Tyler, Bob, 104

typing, 3

Uecker, Bob, 203

"The Ugandan Giant" (Kamala), 273

**Index**

**303**

Ulys Knight Spirit Award, 122
umpire, 139
Underwood, Jim, 25, 52
uniforms, 98
University of Denver, 6–9, 133, 136
University of Iowa, 103
University of Kentucky, 60
University of Oklahoma, 103, 145
University of Pittsburgh, 125
University of Tennessee Hall of
    Fame, 83

Valentine, Bill, 235
Valentine, Greg "The Hammer,"
    264
Valentine, Johnny, 262, 263–64, 267
Vandergriff, Tom, 85, 159, 168, 174,
    187, 188–89, 202, 208, 218
Vandiver, Frank, 103
Van Doren, Mamie, 181
Varnado, Jack, 143
Veeck, Bill, 231
Veeck, Mike, 234
video cameras, 110, 270; color, 271;
    invention of, 250
Vietnam, 27, 175, 204
Villanueva, Danny, 56, 70
voice: care of, 113; loss of, 15–16,
    34, 113–14

WAAP, 239–40
*Waco Herald*, 129
*Waco Morning News*, 129
Waco Navigators, 129
Wade, Gale, 167
Wagner, George "Gorgeous
    George," 257
Walker, Denson, 169
Walker, Tom, 187
Waller, Bob, 218, 226
Ward, Al, 63–64

Warren Spahn Award, 122
Washington, Ken, 100
*Washington Post*, 199
Washington Redskins, 45–46, 55–
    56, 81
Washington Senators, 85, 160
Watergate, 204, 223
Watkins, Bob, 182
Watt, Ed, 274
Way, Craig, 116, 121
Wayne, John, 57
WBAP, 23, 115, 125–28, 147, 171,
    182–83, 215, 249, 278
WCBM, 244
WCCW. *See* World Class Champi-
    onship Wrestling
WEAH, 239, 240
weather, 68, 95, 127, 138
Weatherford, Oklahoma, 19
web pages, 73, 148, 212, 275
Webster, Dave, 39
Weissmuller, Alan, 265
Western Union, 136, 141, 142, 152,
    153, 157, 164, 165–66, 171
Westinghouse Corporation, 123,
    124, 239
Westlake High School, 121
WFAA-Radio, 23, 44, 100, 169,
    171, 182, 243, 249
WFAA-TV, 32, 63, 109
WGY, 130
WHBQ, 244
Wheeler, Dick, 220
*When the News Went Live* (Mercer
    et al.), 43, 259
White, J. Andrew, 123
White, Russ, 199
White House Commission, 189
Whitfield, A. D., 89
WHK, 244
Wikipedia, 257

Wilber, Del, 155

"Wild Bull Curry" (Fred Koury), 264–66

Wild Red Berry, 21, 242, 251

Wilkinson, Bud, 13, 15, 16, 145

Will, Bob, 155

Williams, Jimmy, 223–24

Williams, Ted, 188, 191–96, 199, 204–6, 208, 215

Williams, Vic, 90, 96

Willis, Dontrelle, 122

Willoughby, Burt, 259

Wilonsky, Robert, 148

Wilson, Larry, 72

Wilson, Susan, 110–11, 118

Wingo, Kelly, 140

wire machines, 152

wire recording, 9

Wise, Wes, 137, 231, 232

Wismer, Harry, 37

WJY, 123

WJZ, 124, 130

WLW, 240

WMAQ, 221, 222–23, 224

WMBH-FM, 244

WOAI, 112, 113

Wood, Wilbur, 216, 225, 229, 230

Woods, Billy, 91

Woods, Sears, 99

WOR, 123

World Championship: of Dallas Cowboys, 85

*World Class Championship Wrestling* show, 113

World Class Championship Wrestling, 243, 262, 271, 275, 277, 280

World Heavyweight Championships, 250

World Series, 130, 184; 2005, 177; College, 161; first, 124; Florida Marlins win, 162

World War I, 132

World War II, 2, 34, 127, 140, 141, 143, 193, 236, 241, 246, 248, 255; fan support after, 147; Germany and, 264; Japan and, 264

WPA, 249

wrestlers: broadcasting, 21, 30, 134, 146, 239, 245, 247, 266; health insurance for, 264; history of Texas, 257; offstage fighting of, 258; pay of, 256; women, 251; under-card, 274

wrestling, 146; acting and, 245; champions, 257; holds, 242, 243, 247, 251; illusion v. reality of, 242–43; matches, length of, 258; Olympics, 250; organization, charity of, 274; preplanning of professional, 242; present-day, 275; on radio, 265; stars of, 244

*Wrestling from the Sportatorium*, 265

Wright, Clyde, 202

Wright, Mel, 151, 155, 158

Wright, Rayfield, 66

Wrigley Field, 71, 72

WRR, 119, 129, 249

WRR-Radio, 51, 125, 209

WTAW, 125

WWJ, 123

Yankee Stadium, 211

Yastrzemski, Carl, 159

yelling, 9, 15–16

Young, George, 117, 120

Young, Paul, 12–13, 16

Zanni, Dominick, 144